Intrinsic Motivation and Self-Determination in Human Behavior

PERSPECTIVES IN SOCIAL PSYCHOLOGY

A Series of Texts and Monographs • Edited by Elliot Aronson

A Continuation Order Plan is available for this series A continuation order will bring delivery of each new volume immediately upon publication Volumes are billed only upon actual shipment. For further information please contact the publisher

Intrinsic Motivation and Self-Determination in Human Behavior

Edward L. Deci

and

Richard M. Ryan
University of Rochester
Rochester, New York

PLENUM PRESS • NEW YORK AND LONDON

Library of Congress Cataloging in Publication Data

Deci, Edward L.
  Intrinsic motivation and self-determination in human behavior.

  (Perspectives in social psychology)
  Bibliography: p.
  Includes index.
    1. Intrinsic motivation. 2. Psychology—Philosophy. 3. Personality. I. Ryan,
Richard M. II. Title. III. Title: Self-determination in human behavior. IV. Series.
BF503.D43   1985   153.8   85-12413
ISBN 0-306-42022-8

10 9 8 7 6 5

©1985 Plenum Press, New York
A Division of Plenum Publishing Corporation
233 Spring Street, New York, N.Y. 10013

Printed in the United States of America

To Our Parents:
Janice M. and Charles H. Deci
Jean M. and C. James Ryan

Preface

Early in this century, most empirically oriented psychologists believed that all motivation was based in the physiology of a set of non-nervous-system tissue needs. The theories of that era reflected this belief and used it in an attempt to explain an increasing number of phenomena.

It was not until the 1950s that it became irrefutably clear that much of human motivation is based not in these drives, but rather in a set of innate *psychological* needs. Their physiological basis is less understood; and as concepts, these needs lend themselves more easily to psychological than to physiological theorizing. The convergence of evidence from a variety of scholarly efforts suggests that there are three such needs: self-determination, competence, and interpersonal relatedness.

This book is primarily about self-determination and competence (with particular emphasis on the former), and about the processes and structures that relate to these needs. The need for interpersonal relatedness, while no less important, remains to be explored, and the findings from those explorations will need to be integrated with the present theory to develop a broad, organismic theory of human motivation.

Thus far, we have articulated *self-determination theory*, which is offered as a working theory—a theory in the making. To stimulate the research that will allow it to evolve further, we have stated self-determination theory in the form of minitheories that relate to more circumscribed domains, and we have developed paradigms for testing predictions from the various minitheories.

In working toward a broad motivation theory, we hope to contribute to the accelerating movement toward a motivational analysis of human functioning. For the past several years, theorists have been increasingly turning to motivational variables as central explanatory concepts in order to explain phenomena that were not well handled by previous theories that focused exclusively on behavioral or cognitive variables.

Our goal is to develop a truly organismic theory within empirical psychology. By assuming human agency (i.e., an active organism), by exploring the needs, processes, and structures that relate to it, and by exploring both the possibilities for and the limitations to human agency, we are attempting to explicate the dialectic of the organism's acting on and being acted upon by the social and physical environments. Since metatheories can be judged in part by the coherence and empirical utility of the theories that are built upon their foundation, we have tried to develop a theoretical framework that would give credence to this philosophical perspective.

Finally, our overriding, sociopolitical interest is examining the possibilities and obstacles for human freedom. In our thinking, this pertains not only to social, political, and economic structures, but also to internal psychological structures that reflect and anchor the external ones. It is our hope that, by engaging in a serious investigation of motivational issues, we can make some small contribution toward the larger goal of human freedom.

Preparation of this book, along with some of the research described in it, was supported by a grant from the National Science Foundation (BNS 8018628) and by the Xerox Corporation, through the efforts of John W. Robinson. The Department of Psychology at the University of Rochester has also supported our efforts. We are deeply indebted to all three organizations for helping to make this project possible.

For the past few years, we have been working to create the Human Motivation Program at the University of Rochester. Through the juxtaposition of scholars interested in motivation from the divergent viewpoints of social, developmental, personality, and clinical psychology, we have been able to stimulate dialogue, to facilitate research and scholarship, and to provide doctoral training in motivation as it relates to those basic areas and to their applied ramifications. Much of the work presented in this book has been done in collaboration with other people affiliated with the Human Motivation Program. In particular, James P. Connell has worked closely with us in developing the theory of internalization that appears in Chapters 5 and 9. We are indebted to Jim as well as to other faculty members in the Department of Psychology with whom we have collaborated, and we are grateful to all of the graduate students who have contributed to the research effort. We would especially like to acknowledge the significant empirical contributions of Wendy Grolnick, Richard Koestner, and Robert Plant. In addition, we express our appreciation for the efforts of our colleagues at other universities who have contributed greatly toward an explication of the issues raised in this book. Robert J. Vallerand made comments on several chapters of the book, and Elliot Aronson has been an important source of moral support. We thank both of them.

Betsy Whitehead did a heroic job of typing and editing the manuscript. Not only did she continually retype to keep up with our rewriting and with new word processing systems, but she continually spotted errors and inconsistencies in construction and content. We thank Betsy, and we also thank Cathy Ward and Shirley Tracey for their clerical assistance.

EDWARD L. DECI
RICHARD M. RYAN

Contents

PART II: SELF-DETERMINATION THEORY

PART IV: APPLICATIONS AND IMPLICATIONS

I

BACKGROUND

1

An Introduction

The study of motivation is the exploration of the energization and direction of behavior. Psychological theories are *motivational* theories only insofar as they address these two aspects of behavior.

Energy in motivation theory is fundamentally a matter of needs. An adequate theory of motivation must therefore take into account both the needs that are innate to the organism (i.e., those that must be satisfied for the organism to remain healthy) and those that are acquired through interactions with the environment. *Direction* in motivation theory concerns the processes and structures of the organism that give meaning to internal and external stimuli, thereby directing action toward the satisfaction of needs. Simply stated, then, the field of motivation explores all aspects of an organism's needs and the processes and structures that relate those needs to behavior; motivational theories organize the findings of those explorations.

It has often been said that the study of motivation is an inquiry into the *why* of behavior. Indeed, the field of motivation is concerned with answering *why* questions, although there are theories that have offered nonmotivational answers by focusing only on direction, to the exclusion of energization. These theories, therefore, are not motivation theories.

MOTIVATION THEORIES

Motivation theories are built on a set of assumptions about the nature of people and about the factors that give impetus to action. These assumptions, and the theories that follow from them, can be viewed as falling along a descriptive continuum ranging from the mechanistic to the organismic. *Mechanistic* theories tend to view the human organism as passive, that is, as being pushed around by the interaction of physiological drives and environmental stimuli, whereas *organismic* theories tend to view the organism as active, that is, as being volitional and initiating behaviors. According to the latter perspective, organisms have intrinsic needs and physiological drives, and these intrinsic needs provide energy for the organisms to act on (rather than simply to be reactive to) the environment and to manage aspects of their drives and emotions. The active organism view treats stimuli not as causes of behavior, but as affordances or opportunities that the organism can utilize in satisfying its needs. When theories are based on the assumption of an active organism, they give primacy to the structure of people's experience, and are concerned more with the psychological meaning of stimuli than with the objective characteristics of those stimuli.

Drive Theories

When we survey the historical development of the field of motivation, it strikes us how, despite the diversity of interests and methods, there have been parallel and convergent discoveries. For decades, theories of motivation, whether based on data from clinical interviews with people or on laboratory experiments with rats, were focused on drives and their vicissitudes. In the psychoanalytic and the empirical traditions, for example, theories began with the postulate that behavior can, ultimately, be reduced to a small number of physiological drives. All behaviors were said to be motivated either directly by a drive or by some derivative thereof. Within psychoanalytic psychology, motivation theory began with Freud's (1914, 1915) drive theory (often called instinct theory), whereas within empirical psychology it can be said to have begun with Hull's (1943) drive theory (although motivation had previously been discussed by a number of important empirical psychologists). Freud (1917) asserted that there are two important drives—sex and aggression—whereas Hull (1943) asserted that there are four—hunger, thirst, sex, and the avoidance of pain.

For several decades theorists and researchers worked to develop systems for the explanation of behavior that were based in drive theories. Psychoanalytic scholars organized their investigations around the role of drives, particularly the sexual drive, in the development of pathology, whereas empirically oriented researchers studied the role of drives in animal learning. With continued work, it became increasingly clear that drive theories were not adequate for dealing with many of the observed complexities of behavior. In psychoanalytic psychology, the main impetus for change from a strict drive theory of motivation came from its difficulty in explaining normal developmental patterns, what Hartmann (1958) refered to as development within the "conflict-free sphere." In empirical psychology, which had concentrated on learning through reinforcement, the main impetus for change came from the theory's inability to explain various phenomena related to animals' avid exploration and manipulation (e.g., Berlyne, 1950; Harlow, 1950).

Intrinsic Motivation

White (1959), in a now classic paper, argued for a different kind of motivational concept, one that would complement drives and could be the basis of a motivational theory with greater explanatory power. This new motivational propensity could account for play, exploration, and a variety of other behaviors that do not require reinforcements for their maintenance. As well, it could explain various psychological processes that are involved in normal maturation and in volitional behavior. White refered to this propensity as *effectance motivation*, because, he argued, organisms are innately motivated to be effective in dealing with their environment. According to White, the feeling of effectance that follows from competent interactions with the environment is the reward for this class of behaviors and can sustain behaviors independent of any drive-based reinforcements.

In psychoanalytic theory this motivational force is generally referred to as independent ego energy. The term refers to the fact that the energy of the ego, which is the portion of the personality structure responsible for volitional responding, rational processes, exploration, and play, had originally been hypothesized to be derivative from, rather than inde-pendent of, the basic drives of the id. Although many psychoanalytic theories (e.g., Rapaport, 1960) continue to hold the derivative view, some psychoanalytic theorists ascribe to the ego its own, innate energy source and view much of the development of the ego in terms of the unfolding of inherent potentials rather than merely the outcome of con-flicts between the id and the social environment (e.g., Shapiro, 1981; White, 1963; Wolstein, 1982).

In the empirical tradition, psychologists are most apt to refer to the non-drive-based motivation as *intrinsic motivation*, suggesting that the energy is intrinsic to the nature of the organism. Although there has been considerable debate over the best way to conceptualize this moti-vation source, we will see in Chapter 2 that there seems to be a con-vergence toward the view that intrinsic motivation is based in the organismic needs to be competent and self-determining.

Self-Determination

Concomitant with the recognition of the need for a concept such as intrinsic motivation, psychologists have been grappling with the utility of concepts such as volition, autonomy, and choice. Although it is true that very early in the history of formal psychology James (1890) emphasized the significance of concepts such as will, most psychologists who wrote during the subsequent decades underplayed or ignored the importance of such concepts. Instead, the organization or direction of behavior was attributed to associative bonds between stimuli (whether internal or external) and responses. In the psychoanalytic theory of motivation, emphasis was on unconscious urges and their relationship to cathected objects, although the volitional ego was given a secondary role in the regulation of behavior. In the behavioral theory of motivation, emphasis was on stimulus–response associations that developed through reinforcement (i.e., drive-reduction) processes. In both theoretical domains, the motivation of behavior tended to be viewed as mechanistic, because choices and intentions were given either a secondary role (psychoanalytic) or no role at all (behavioral) in the determination of behavior. Behavior was said to occur because a drive was operative and an association had developed between the drive stimulation and an object or a response.

In psychodynamic psychology, the study of volition and self-direction developed slowly but has become increasingly integral. Freud's (1923) hypothesized ego functions set the stage for later theorists such as Nunberg (1931), Hartmann (1939), and White (1963) to study self-regulation while preserving the fundamental drive aspect of Freud's theory. As Shapiro (1981) explained it, drives or impulses account for tendencies to act, but they do not provide an adequate theory of action. There needs to be, he suggested, a concept of self-direction, entailing conscious processes such as imagining future outcomes, to account for the wide range of volitional activity that we observe. The key issue for self-direction, he added, is flexibility in psychological structures—flexibility that allows one's attitudes to direct action toward the effective achievement of one's aims.

In empirical psychology, the growing interest in cognitive processes, stimulated by the pioneering work of Tolman (1932) and Lewin (1936), brought unobservable intervening variables to the foreground. Increasingly, choice and decision making replaced stimulus–response associations to explain the direction of behavior. Most cognitive theorists have treated all behaviors as if they were chosen and based on expectations about future outcomes (e.g., Vroom, 1964) or future reinforcements (e.g., Bandura, 1977a). Many of these theories are, technically speaking, not motivational theories because they do not address the aspect of energization, although the theories of Tolman (1932), Lewin (1936), and Atkinson (1964) did. Nonetheless, all these cognitive theories have had an important influence on the field of motivation by directing attention to the concept of choice.

Heider (1958), having been strongly influenced by the early cognitive theorists and by phenomenology, introduced the construct of "perceived locus of causality," distinguishing between personal causality, where intentionality mediates one's outcomes, and impersonal causality, where the outcomes one receives are not intentional. Subsequently, deCharms (1968) suggested that personally caused actions can have either an internal perceived locus of causality—one's interests and desires are experienced as initiating action—or an external perceived locus of causality—some external event is experienced as initiating action.

Our own work on self-determination has been heavily influenced by each of these prior developments. Our theory is, however, motivational rather than cognitive because it addresses the energization and the direction of behavior and it uses motivational constructs to organize cognitive, affective, and behavioral variables. Because it has been influenced by the perceived-locus-of-causality construct, our theory also differs from the cognitive theories in its assertion that only some, rather than all, intentional behaviors (those with an internal perceived locus of causality) are truly chosen. As such, it allows for an exploration of the interplay between self-determined and non-self-determined behaviors and processes.

It is our contention that intrinsic motivation and self-determination are necessary concepts for an organismic theory. As the importance of these concepts has been increasingly recognized by psychologists, psychological theories have become less mechanistic and more organismic. Theories that recognize these concepts while giving attention to the energization and to the direction of behavior are organismic motivation theories.

Alternative (Nonmotivational) Approaches

Within empirical psychology there have been nonmotivational theories that have been applied to many of the same problems and phenomena that have been addressed in the psychology of motivation. Operant psychology, which is perhaps the most noteworthy of these, has explored the direction and persistence of behavior but has steadfastly refused to postulate about the nature of organisms' needs. Operant theory, like Hullian drive theory, is called a reinforcement theory because the direction of behavior is said to be caused by past reinforcements. It differs from drive theory, however, because it defines reinforcements in terms of the observable behavior change they effect rather than in terms of the drives they reduce. Although the operant tradition can be traced directly to the work of Thorndike (1913), Skinner (1938, 1953, 1971) has served as its primary spokesperson for several decades.

An extension of the nonmotivational approach of operant psychology can be seen in the strands of cognitive psychology often referred to as cognitive-behaviorism. Most clearly represented by social learning theory (e.g., Rotter, 1954; Bandura, 1977b), this approach asserts that behavior is a function of one's expectations about future reinforcements. As in operant theory, reinforcements are functionally defined in terms of the behavior change they produce rather than the needs they satisfy.

The prominence of these nonmotivational psychologies through the 1950s and 1960s was largely due to their success in controlling behavior and to their relatively easy application to a variety of settings. The problems they precipitated, however, were that they precluded the study of needs and of a wide range of spontaneous, intrinsically motivated processes and behaviors (Schwartz, Schuldenfrei, & Lacey, 1978), and that they left unrecognized the detrimental effects of surplus controls. In this book, we will address those very problems.

THE ORGANISMIC APPROACH

An organismic theory begins with the assumption of an active organism; it assumes that human beings act on their internal and external environments to be effective and to satisfy the full range of their needs. In the process, behavior is influenced by internal structures that are being continually elaborated and refined to reflect ongoing experiences. The life force or energy for the activity and for the development of the internal structure is what we refer to as *intrinsic motivation*. The assumptions of activity, or the proactive engagement with one's environment, and of an internal structure with inherent principles of coherence or unity are the defining characteristics of an organismic approach in psychology (Blasi, 1976).

Deci (1980) pointed out, however, that although the human organism is innately active and is inclined toward the development of an internal, unified structure of self, it is also vulnerable to being passive and to developing fractionated structures. These vulnerabilities are the means through which the organism becomes conditioned and through which its psychological functioning becomes rigid.

The general motivational theory presented in this book begins with the organismic assumptions of activity and structure, recognizing that human beings attempt actively to master the forces in the environment and the forces of drives and emotions in themselves. In mastering these forces, human beings integrate them into the internal, unified structure called self. The theory also, however, begins with the recognition of the previously mentioned vulnerabilities. It is this dialectic, the organism's acting on the internal and external forces and being vulnerable to those forces, that is the focus of the research and theory herein discussed.

Self-Determination Theory: An Overview

Our work is within the tradition of empirical psychology. It began with the experimental study of the effects of environmental events on intrinsic motivation, and from there has moved, both inductively and deductively, toward a broad motivational theory of personality.

The core of this book presents our organismic theory of human motivation as it has been thus far formulated, and it reviews research that has been the basis for that formulation. It begins with a discussion of the meaning of intrinsic motivation and the evolution of its current conceptualization. In Chapter 2 we also introduce the concept of self-determination and discuss its emergence as a centrally important concept for psychology.

Chapters 3 through 6 present the three mini-theories that together comprise self-determination theory as it currently stands. Chapters 3 and 4 present cognitive evaluation theory, which is the best articulated of the three mini-theories. It has a great deal of empirical validation, which is presented in those chapters and in the applied chapters, 9 through 12. The theory, which was developed to deal with the effects of external events on intrinsic motivation and motivationally relevant processes, has recently been extended to include the effects of intra-personal, as well as interpersonal, events (Ryan, 1982). The theory analyzes the effects of events relevant to the initiation and regulation of behavior in terms of their meaning for a person's self-determination and competence.

Chapter 5 presents the initial formulation of organismic integration theory, which is an account of the development of intrinsic and extrinsic motivation. The theory is based on the proposition that the needs for competence and self-determination motivate the ongoing process of elaborating the internal, unified structure of self through the continual integration of internal and external stimuli. With regard to the development of intrinsic motivation, it explains how one's undifferentiated interest and curiosity become channeled and elaborated as one's innate capacities interact with the environment. With regard to the development of extrinsic motivation, it suggests that one is inclined to internalize and eventually to integrate extrinsic regulations that are useful for effective, self-determined functioning. Here, our interest is in the processes through which, under optimal circumstances, one comes to value and self-regulate behaviors that are not initially interesting or spontaneous.

Finally, in Chapter 6, we present the third mini-theory, causality orientations theory, which is a description of individual differences in the initiation and regulation of behavior. We argue that it is heuristically useful to assess people's generalized tendencies to be autonomous, controlled, and impersonal, respectively, with regard to the determination of their behavior. These assessments have been shown to be predictive of a wide array of constructs, affects, attitudes, and behaviors.

The lines of research presented in Chapters 3 through 6 are the empirical bases through which self-determination theory is evolving. They are our most up-to-date attempts to address empirically the issue of the interaction between human freedom and its limitations. Working within empirical psychology, we have attempted to address many of the same issues that are being addressed by the newer theorists (e.g., Schafer, 1968, 1976; Shapiro, 1981) working in the psychoanalytic tradition. As such, the parallels in the way motivational issues have been addressed in the two traditions appear to be continuing.

Chapters 7 and 8 review alternative accounts of some of the conceptual and research issues explained by self-determination theory. Chapter 7 discusses the operant and attributional perspectives and shows how the so-called failures to replicate results predicted by our organismic approach were, in fact, not failures to replicate. In Chapter 8, we outline several information-processing, expectancy theories leading up to Deci's (1980) representation of some aspects of self-determination theory in information-processing terms.

Perhaps the most exciting aspect of the current work is its direct applicability to practice in many fields of human endeavor, as all too often the connection between theory and practice is vague and thin. In the last four chapters we discuss the relevance of the theory to education, psychotherapy, work, and sports. Education and sports have been extensively studied from our perspective, and that research is reviewed, as is the first of our large organizational studies. These applied chapters demonstrate the relevance of self-determination theory to various domains of life, and they represent research agendas for the future.

Conceptualizations of Intrinsic Motivation and Self-Determination

The human organism is inherently active, and there is perhaps no place where this is more evident than in little children. They pick things up, shake them, smell them, taste them, throw them across the room, and keep asking, "What's this?" They are unendingly curious, and they want to see the effects of their actions. Children are intrinsically motivated to learn, to undertake challenges, and to solve problems. Adults are also intrinsically motivated to do a variety of things. They spend large amounts of time painting pictures, building furniture, playing sports, whittling wood, climbing mountains, and doing countless other things for which there are no obvious or appreciable external rewards. The rewards are inherent in the activity, and even though there may be secondary gains, the primary motivators are the spontaneous, internal experiences that accompany the behavior.

Intrinsic motivation is the energy source that is central to the active nature of the organism. Its recognition highlighted the important points that not all behaviors are drive-based, nor are they a function of external controls. These points have raised the important problems of how to conceptualize this new energy source and how to integrate it into psychological theory. In this book we describe various attempts to clarify the issues and resolve the problems, beginning with a historical discussion of the emergence of the concept of intrinsic motivation in the empirical and psychodynamic traditions of psychology.

HISTORICAL BACKGROUND

As early as 1890, William James, one of the important forerunners of empirical psychology, had discussed aspects of motivation. His assertion that interest plays an important role in directing attention, and thus

behavior, is similar to the current belief that, when intrinsically motivated, one follows one's interests. Woodworth (1918) was the first psychologist to outline a theory that directly addressed the issue of
intrinsically motivated behavior. Woodworth proposed that an activity
can be initiated by an extrinsic motive but that "only when it is running
by its own drive . . . can [it] run freely and effectively" (1918, p. 70).
This notion, that an activity, regardless of its initiating motive, can become
intrinsically motivated, was given the name *functional autonomy* by Allport (1937). Clearly, in Woodworth's work we see an active organism.
"It may at least be said to be part of the native equipment to be active
in a motor way, as well, indeed, as in the way of exploration" (1918,
p. 50).

Because Woodworth's theory appeared at about the same time that
the nonmotivational viewpoints of Thorndike (1913) and Watson (1913)
were having a dramatic impact on the nature of empirical theorizing,
Woodworth's motivational hypotheses received relatively little sustained
attention. The small amount of motivational research that was done in
the following decades focused on the nature of drives and laid the
groundwork for the 1943 publication of Hull's drive theory.

Empirical Drive Theory

According to Hull all behaviors are based in four primary drives:
hunger, thirst, sex, and the avoidance of pain. These drives, which are
non-nervous-system tissue deficits, activate consummatory behaviors
that have previously been successful in reducing drives. Any behavior
that results in the reduction of a drive is strengthened by virtue of its
becoming more firmly bonded to a drive stimulus. According to this
view, drives provide the energy for behavior, whereas the associative
bonds that develop between drive stimuli and behaviors through the
process of drive reduction provide the direction for behavior.

Of course not all behaviors were said to be motivated directly by
primary drive stimuli; some were said to be motivated by derivative
sources. Secondary reinforcement was the process through which the
derivation was said to occur. This process involves the pairing of a
neutral stimulus with a primary reinforcer such that the neutral stimulus
acquires the reinforcing potential of the primary reinforcer. For example,
if an animal were continually fed out of the same dish, the dish could
gradually become a reinforcer in its own right and could strengthen
various responses that led the animal to be in the presence of the dish.
To maintain its reinforcing potential, however, the dish would need,
from time to time, to be re-paired with a primary reinforcer, namely the
food.

There was a tremendous amount of research stimulated by Hull's drive theory that served to confirm and elaborate various aspects of it. Gradually, however, anomolies kept appearing in the animal experiments that could not easily be reconciled with the basic tenets of the theory. In fact, the earliest evidence that a strict drive theory was inadequate had appeared even before Hull's formal statement of the theory, although the import of that earlier work did not become clear until the 1950s when a wide range of these anomolies appeared. In 1925, Dashiell had related anecdotal evidence that even hungry rats will, under certain conditions, forego food for the opportunity to explore novel spaces, and in 1930, Nissen had reported preliminary data indicating that rats would cross electrified grids for the opportunity to explore novel spaces. Because drive theory leads to the prediction that rats would eat when hungry and would avoid pain by not crossing the electrified grid, these preliminary findings were not easily reconciled with drive theory. Then, when numerous studies showing the reinforcing value of exploration and manipulation appeared in the 1950s, these phenomena began to receive serious consideration. What follows are some of the important pieces of evidence that demonstrated the limitation of drive theory and eventually led to the concept of intrinsic motivation.

Berlyne (1950, 1955) demonstrated that rats were quick to explore novel spaces and objects and that they persisted at this exploration as long as novel stimulation was available. Welker (1956a,b) found similar results for chimpanzees. When the experimenter placed a novel object in the chimpanzees' presence, they readily explored it, and once they had explored and manipulated it, they appeared to lose interest. Montgomery (1952, 1953, 1954, 1955; Montgomery & Segall, 1955) also discovered that rats spontaneously explored novel places and that the opportunity to explore could itself be used to reinforce other responses. Harlow, Harlow, and Meyer (1950) demonstrated that monkeys learned to solve a puzzle apparatus for no other reward than the enjoyment of doing it, and that they persisted at it for long periods. In fact, Harlow (1950) reported finding a formidable resistance to the extinction of manipulation behavior in monkeys, and Premack (1959, 1962, 1963) demonstrated the reinforcing potential of manipulatory responses in both children and monkeys. Parenthetically, the Harlow (1950) report contains the first use of the term *intrinsic motivation* of which we are aware. Finally, Harlow (1953a) reviewed studies from his laboratory that demonstrated that monkeys performed certain problem-solving activities better when they were intrinsically motivated than when they were extrinsically rewarded.

These findings, of course, represented anomalies for the then dominant theory of motivation, which was based on drive reduction principles. However, as is generally the case when anomalies emerge (Kuhn,

1963), the initial response of the scientific community was to use the existing theory to try to account for these findings, and then, when it was found inadequate, to extend and modify the theory. Thus, drive theorists first attempted to explain the phenomena of exploration and manipulation with the existing principles of anxiety reduction and secondary reinforcement, and, finding those explanations inadequate, they extended the theory by naming new drives.

Anxiety Reduction. Because anxiety is an unpleasant or painful state, any behavior that is associated with the reduction of anxiety would, according to drive theory, be reinforced, because the avoidance of pain is one of the primary drives. If one assumes that novel stimuli arouse anxiety, one could say that the exploration of those stimuli is motivated by the drive to reduce that anxiety.

There are, however, two major problems with the anxiety reduction account of exploration and curiosity-related behaviors. First, observational data suggest that exploration is typically accompanied by interest and excitement rather than fear and anxiety (Harlow, 1953a). Exploratory behaviors simply do not appear to be motivated by pain avoidance. Further, as White (1959) pointed out, if novelty does induce anxiety, flight or avoidance would be a more logical response than exploration. Exploration would induce greater anxiety, at least in the short run, if novelty were anxiety-eliciting. Thus, even if novelty did stimulate anxiety, which it probably does in some cases, exploration would not be the drive theory predicted response to it. Why would Nissen's rats endure the pain of crossing an electrified grid to encounter the anxiety of a novel space? In short, anxiety reduction does not provide a very plausible explanation for the phenomena related to exploration.

Secondary Reinforcement. The secondary reinforcement explanation holds that, through the pairing of exploratory and manipulatory behaviors with primary drive reduction, those behaviors acquire reinforcing properties. Because, for example, infants engage in exploration at the same time they are being nursed, this explanation holds that the exploration by itself eventually becomes a reinforcer—a secondary reinforcer. To retain its reinforcing value, of course, the behavior would need to be periodically re-paired with the primary reinforcer.

Both White (1959) and Berlyne (1966) argued that the acceptance of a secondary reinforcement explanation would require the assumption that exploration had often been paired with the reduction of primary needs such as hunger. This assumption is quite implausible, however, since avid exploration occurs in neonates soon after birth. It seems unreasonable to believe that this could have developed so quickly and strongly through the process of secondary reinforcement. Furthermore, evidence indicates that the reinforcing value of exploration does not require its re-pairing with a primary reinforcer. In an experiment by Butler (1953), monkeys learned discriminations by being reinforced with the opportunity to engage in visual exploration. Butler reported that these responses showed remarkable resistance to extinction; in other words, they persisted even without the re-pairing of exploration with any primary reinforcer. It appears, then, that the opportunity for exploration functions more like a primary reinforcer than a secondary reinforcer.

In short, neither anxiety reduction nor secondary reinforcement, both of which are aspects of orthodox drive theory, provided a full or reasonable explanation of most exploratory behaviors.

Drive Naming. Because none of the four primary drives specified by the Hullians—hunger, thirst, sex, or pain avoidance—appeared to be invariantly or necessarily implicated in the explanation of the seemingly spontaneous curiosity, exploratory, or manipulatory behaviors displayed by a variety of species, elaborations of classical drive theory developed. The first involved the specification of additional drives that might underlie these anomalous behaviors. When the house cannot shelter all of its children, it is time to add on new rooms, and a number of such additions were proposed.

The work by Montgomery (e.g., 1954, 1955) showing that rats spontaneously explore novel spaces led him to suggest that there is an exploratory drive, though he also suggested that novel stimuli can elicit a fear drive that can block the exploratory drive if the fear drive is of sufficient magnitude. Glanzer (1953, 1958) took a similar position. Butler (1953, 1957, 1958) and Butler and Harlow (1957) reported that visual exploration of novel stimuli is rewarding for monkeys and that the probability of such a response increases as the interval between successive opportunities to explore increases. The opportunity to explore was even shown to work as a reward that could strengthen other responses. Butler accounted for his findings by positing a "drive for visual exploration" of the environment.

Myers and Miller (1954) and Zimbardo and Miller (1958) reported results supporting those of Montgomery and Butler, although these investigators suggested that animals explore novel stimuli in order to relieve a "boredom drive" that results from unchanging stimuli. This drive explanation focused on the boredom that results from insufficient stimulation (i.e., the absence of a stimulus), whereas Montgomery's drive explanation focused on the elicitation of an exploratory drive by a novel stimulus (i.e., the presence of a stimulus). Isaac (1962) took a position similar to the boredom-drive position, although he used the term *sensory drive*, suggesting that organisms have a cross-modality need for stimulation that is activated when there is insufficient stimulation.

The drive-naming approach to explaining intrinsically motivated behavior was also used by Harlow in the realm of manipulative behaviors. Harlow and his associates (Davis, Settlage, & Harlow, 1950; Gately,

1950; Harlow, 1950, 1953a,b; Harlow *et al.*, 1950) showed repeatedly that manipulating a complex mechanical puzzle made up of hasps, hooks, and hinges was intrinsically rewarding for monkeys and could be used to strengthen other responses. He posited a manipulation drive to account for these findings.

In sum, a plethora of data supported the notion that manipulation and exploration are not derivatives of the primary drives. From the time of birth, organisms seem to need a certain amount of novel stimulation to function effectively, and the opportunity for novel stimulation (e.g., manipulating an object or exploring a new area) has frequently been used to strengthen other responses. The drive-naming explanations of these phenomena during the 1950s was one, perhaps not so parsimonious, attempt to explain the behaviors while maintaining the larger, preexisting motivation theory. Many writers, however, recognized its shortcomings and criticized it accordingly. For example, Hunt (1965, 1971a) charged that drive naming was essentially a return to the instinct naming of McDougall (1908) and could hinder the chances of a real understanding of these phenomena. Naming is not the same as explaining.

White (1959) made a more detailed criticism of the drive-naming approach. He began by saying that if exploration is to be considered a drive, it must have the same functional properties as the established drives such as hunger, thirst, and sex. According to the traditional view, drives involve a deficit or need in body tissues outside the nervous system and energize behaviors that result in a consummatory response that reduces the deficit and produces learning. White demonstrated that the exploratory "drive" does not fit this definition. First, it does not seem to be correlated with any non-nervous-system tissue deficit, so no tissue need can provide the impetus for behavior. Second, even if one were to broaden the definition of drive to include a general drive in the reticular activating system that is responsive to sensory stimulation, it would not satisfy the condition of being a strong and persistent stimulus toward a consummatory response. It is true, of course, that the exploration of a particular area can become satiated (Berlyne, 1950; Welker, 1956a); however, that does not make exploration a consummatory response, because it is not the tendency to explore, but merely the exploration of that area, that becomes sated. Third, there is not the same climactic termination that accompanies drive reduction from consummatory responses.

Finally, and perhaps most detrimental to drive theory, there is the fact that animals often behave to increase rather than to decrease what would be called the exploratory drive. White (1959) used the work of Montgomery (1954) to support this point. If the exploratory drive is instigated by a novel stimulus, as Montgomery and others suggested, animals should avoid novel stimuli, because the novel stimuli would be expected to increase the drive rather than reduce it. Yet, just the opposite is true: animals seek out stimuli that would, by the drive account, increase the exploratory drive. Therefore, the use of this drive explanation necessitates that one consider animals to be drive-inducers as well as drive-reducers. But that would be unacceptable given drive theory's central premise that animals seek only to reduce drives.

The one new-drive explanation that would not necessitate the drive-inducer assumption would involve the boredom drive (Isaac, 1962; Myers & Miller, 1954). That explanation, however, has its own problems. For example, if boredom is said to cause exploration, then the consequence of exploratory behavior would be the return of the animal to a state of boredom. With eating, the end state is a full stomach and the reduction of hunger, whereas with exploration, the end state would be a return to inactivity and boredom. This of course is not logical. As White stated, "It is distinctly implausible to connect reinforcement with the waning of an agreeable interest in the environment or with a general progress from zestful alertness to boredom" (1959, p. 302).

It is clear from the above analysis that drive naming was inadequate as an approach to explaining intrinsically motivated behaviors. The newly named "drives" did not possess the traditional properties of drives, and if one were to redefine the concept of drive to accommodate intrinsic motivation, it would necessitate a radically different theory, one that was not based in drive reduction. That indeed was the suggestion made in 1956 by Koch who, in a provocative essay, asserted that motivation theory needed to be wholly revamped to give full consideration to non-drive-based sources of motivation.

Attempting to use the drive theory approach to explain intrinsically motivated behaviors such as exploration and manipulation did prove useful, however, in that it clearly isolated this motivation source as being different from drives. What we call intrinsic motivation was identified as a primary central nervous system need that does not have an appreciable effect on non-nervous-system tissues. This definition allowed for a clear distinction between intrinsic motivation and drive-based motivation, for drives were said to be based in non-nervous-system tissue deficits. The distinction is an important one since it points to the innateness of intrinsic motivation and describes the difference in the bases of the two types of motivation at the time of birth. However, the definition is basically a physiological rather than a psychological one and turns out not to be particularly useful for a psychological (as opposed to physiological) theory. Because learning, socialization, and maturation affect intrinsic motivation and drives in a complex way, the distinction between whether or not a need is based in a non-nervous-system tissue deficit does not provide an adequate and useful way of defining and describing the increasingly complex, motivated behavior.

One final approach to explaining intrinsically motivated behaviors within the drive theory framework was advocated by people such as Fowler (1965, 1967), who suggested that the theory could be maintained if it were modified to include the concept of optimal arousal. This approach will be addressed later in this chapter, where we will see that organisms do seem to seek some level of optimal arousal. However, even if drive theory were modified to allow for the notion of optimal arousal, it would not serve as a very satisfactory account of intrinsic motivation because it would still be primarily physiological and would not be useful in explaining a complex range of human phenomena that have now been observed.

Psychodynamic Drive Theory

As we mentioned in Chapter 1, Freud proposed the other major drive theory three decades prior to Hull's. Freud's pioneering work with the clinical method allowed him to uncover the importance of the sexual and aggressive drives—drives that are so often frustrated by sociocultural inhibitions—and to comprehend their psychodynamic activity. Focusing particularly on the sexual drive, Freud outlined a theory of personality development in which he proposed that the core of one's personality develops from a series of conflicts between the sexual drive and the socializing environment. Adequate resolution of these conflicts was implicated in the development of a healthy personality, whereas inadequate resolution was the basis for neuroses.

As in Hullian theory all behavior was said to be either a direct or derivative function of drive energies. Freud (1923) introduced the concept of neutralization to explain the transformation of drive energies into energies that are available to motivate a range of activities that appeared to be either distantly related or wholly unrelated to the sexual drive. Freud used the concept of neutralization, much like Hull used the concept of secondary reinforcement, to account for those behaviors that appear to be free of the drives but are theoretically derivative of them.

The structural aspect of psychoanalytic theory suggested that the id, which is present from birth, is the locus or origin of the drives. Through continual conflict between the id and the environment, the ego develops to play a mediating role, with capabilities to redirect and eventually to neutralize energy. The idea of neutralized energy at the disposal of the ego still left both the ego and its energy as derivatives of the id and its drives, but it represented the foundation of an ego psychology that would later be elaborated by other psychodynamic theorists. Hartmann (1939), for example, gave the ego new importance by stressing its role in adaptation. He suggested that the ego derives "conflict-free" pleasure through the exercise of its functions and apparatuses, although he, like Freud, held to the position that the energies underlying this activity were neutralized rather than innate.

Increasingly the conception that ego energy—what we call intrinsic motivation—was derivative became inadequate for dealing with human behavior in ways that are parallel to those that led empirical psychologists to be dissatisfied with their drive model. As a result, Hendrick (1942) proposed adding an "instinct to master" to the psychoanalytic conception, much like the behaviorists had begun to name new drives. And, as was the case with the behaviorists, Hendrick's attempt proved inadequate, for it too would have required a dramatic change in the meaning of drives. Fenichel (1945) proposed to explain exploratory and mastery behaviors within a psychoanalytic framework by using anxiety reduction, but this explanation fared no better in the psychoanalytic framework than it did in the drive-theory framework.

White's Proposal

By the 1950s it was clear within the empirical and psychoanalytic traditions that much activity is motivated by independent, non-drive-based energies. Consequently, White (1959), in discussing these theoretical traditions, proposed the concept of *effectance motivation,* which is an innate, intrinsic energy source that motivates a wide variety of behaviors and is central to much of a child's development.

Within empirical psychology, White's proposition required a dramatic reformulation of motivation theory, because a full explication of his hypothesis necessitates an active-organism, teleological perspective rather than a passive-organism, mechanistic perspective. It is just such a formulation that we have attempted to outline in this book.

Within psychoanalytic psychology, White (1960, 1963) used the concept of an independent ego energy to reinterpret Freud's theory of psychosexual development, highlighting the joint contributions of the sexual drive and effectance motivation. He demonstrated that the inclusion of effectance motivation would provide a more satisfactory account of the child's striving to master each of the critical conflicts in its early life.

In presenting this brief historical discussion we have attempted to show how the concept of intrinsic motivation emerged logically from the drive theories that dominated the field of motivation during the first half of this century. Since that time intrinsic motivation has been conceptualized in a variety of ways. We now turn our attention to a review of those conceptualizations, noting that they fall into two broad classes. As will be reflected in the review of the conceptualizations, the bulk of the discussion of intrinsic motivation has been within empirical psychology. However, the new psychoanalytic ego psychology and other current psychodynamic perspectives (e.g., Greenspan, 1979; Loevinger, 1976a; Shapiro, 1981) are congruent with the assumption of an independent ego energy (or an intrinsic motivation) for certain types of behavior.

OPTIMAL STIMULATION

Much of the work related to intrinsic motivation is based on the premise that organisms approach, and function most effectively in, situations that provide a moderate level of stimulation. This premise is indirectly supported by much of the animal research reported earlier and has received more direct support from studies with humans. Jones (1961) and Jones, Wilkinson, and Braden (1961) found for example that subjects, when deprived of information, engaged in instrumental behaviors to obtain more information. Similarly, Bexton, Heron, and Scott (1954) and Heron, Doane, and Scott (1956) found that subjects became very uncomfortable during prolonged periods of stimulus deprivation even though their drives were well satisfied. In spite of being offered substantial monetary payment to remain in the deprivation situation, subjects chose to forego the rewards to get stimulation. Humans, as well as other animals, seem to need some optimal amount of stimulation.

Some of the optimal-stimulation theories have posited a need for an optimum of physiological arousal in the central nervous system, whereas others have posited that organisms approach stimuli that provide an optimum of psychological incongruity vis-à-vis one's cognitive structures. We now consider the two types of theories along with related research.

Optimal Arousal

Hebb (1955) postulated the need for an optimal level of physiological arousal and suggested that functioning is most efficient when there is this optimal arousal. Because organisms have a need for optimal arousal, responses that lead the organism toward that optimum will be strengthened. If arousal is too high, a response that decreases it will be strengthened, whereas if arousal is too low, a response that increases it will be strengthened. For example, if a man walking in the woods were confronted with an angry bear, his arousal would probably be above the optimum for effective functioning. If it were not so high that he froze, he would flee. The response of flight would lower his level of arousal and thereby be reinforced. On the other hand, if he were bored and the bear was safely behind a glass wall at the zoo, seeing the bear might raise his arousal toward the optimum, so the response of going to the bear cage would be reinforced.

Although Hebb's theory focused on physiological arousal, he did briefly address the psychological level, suggesting that "this taste for excitement must not be forgotten when we are dealing with human motivation. It appears that, up to a certain point, threat and puzzle have positive motivating value, beyond that point negative value" (Hebb,1955, p. 250). Stated differently, optimal (physiological) arousal may be achieved through optimal experiences with threat and puzzle.

Fiske and Maddi (1961) took a position similar to Hebb's. They suggested that there is a characteristic (i.e., optimal) level of arousal that organisms seek to maintain. That optimal level, however, is not stationary; it varies with the stage of a person's sleep–wakefulness cycle. In other words, organisms do seek an optimal level of arousal; however, this optimum is a continuous variable and is a function of the organism's degree of wakefulness.

Discrepancies from the optimal level at any given time motivate the organism to engage in behavior that will restore the optimal stimulation. This stimulation can come from activity associated with internal tissue needs, as well as from external stimuli. When a person is hungry, the hunger and the process of getting and ingesting food provide stimulation. Accordingly, when primary tissue needs such as food and sex are satisfied, the organism will be more likely to seek out stimuli (either external, such as a puzzle, or internal, such as daydreaming) to increase arousal. This suggests that people are most likely to engage in intrinsically motivated behaviors, such as exploration and manipulation, to increase their level of stimulation (up to the optimum for that stage of wakefulness) at times when their primary tissue needs are well satisfied. Of course when people are in a state near sleep, their optimal level of arousal would be quite low, so they would not be likely to seek out much stimulation. A soft pillow would probably suffice.

Fiske and Maddi's notion that the optimal level varies with the sleep–wakefulness cycle seems to be an important addition to the theories. Whether one is considering physiological arousal or psychological incongruity, the organism's optimal level is undoubtedly variable, and the variation is surely related to sleep and wakefulness, though there may also be other factors that affect the optimum.

Optimal Incongruity

Several writers, working primarily in the cognitive tradition, have attempted to explain intrinsically motivated behavior with the psychological construct of incongruity. The central question in this work is, To what extent do people approach versus avoid incongruous (i.e., dissonant or discrepant) inputs or cognitions? We will now review the thrust of the work related to this issue.

Some writers have maintained that people are motivated to reduce all incongruity or dissonance between stimuli. Festinger's (1957) cognitive-dissonance theory, for example, asserted that two dissonant cognitions produce an aversive state that motivates people to behave in such a way as to reduce the dissonance and avoid situations that would produce further dissonance. For Festinger, all dissonant cognitions produce discomfort and energize behavior to reduce the dissonance. This proposition, however, is difficult to reconcile with a variety of studies, many of them mentioned previously, which indicate that novel or incongruous stimulation is rewarding and produces approach behaviors. It seems that although people often behave to reduce and avoid dissonance or incongruity, they sometimes behave to induce and approach dissonance or incongruity.

Kagan (1972) presented an argument somewhat similar to Festinger's. He proposed that many behaviors are motivated by the human need to reduce uncertainty. Uncertainty, he suggested, can be characterized as incongruity between cognitive structures or between a cognitive structure and some incoming stimulus. Although there is considerable evidence that organisms do behave to reduce uncertainty (e.g., Lanzetta, 1963, 1971), just as there is much evidence to indicate that organisms behave to reduce dissonance (Wicklund & Brehm, 1976), there is also considerable evidence that organisms behave to induce uncertainty and dissonance, for example through exploration.

Kagan (1972) did include in his formulation a type of uncertainty related to future expectations, suggesting that people gather information to avoid unpleasant or painful events in the future. By including this type of uncertainty his theory can explain some exploratory behaviors that might induce (as well as reduce) incongruity. However, as Berlyne (1971a) explained it, there are two types of exploration. Specific exploration refers to behaviors that are responses to a person's experience of uncertainty, but it does not include exploration that is aimed at providing stimulation or that derives from a person's desire to know. Those behaviors are examples of diversive exploration. When people experience too little stimulation they seek out novelty; they explore and manipulate.

Exploratory behavior that deals with the avoidance of future, anxiety-producing events would be considered specific exploration, so the uncertainty-reduction perspective fails to provide an account of diversive exploration. Furthermore, the notion of reducing uncertainty and gathering information to avoid unpleasant events does not capture the essence of intrinsic motivation. People are active, development-oriented organisms who behave to encounter challenges, to toy with danger, to experience more facets of their being, including, at times, pain and displeasure. True, they often behave to reduce uncertainty, but their intrinsically motivated behavior goes far beyond the reduction of uncertainty.

In an attempt to account for the seemingly discrepant findings that people sometimes behave to reduce incongruity or uncertainty and other times behave to induce incongruity or uncertainty, several writers have proposed that people are attracted to stimuli that provide an optimal level of psychological incongruity. This notion, or a similar one, has appeared in the work of McClelland, Atkinson, Clark, and Lowell (1953), Dember and Earl (1957), Walker (1964), Berlyne (1967, 1969), and Hunt (1965).

McClelland *et al.* (1953) were concerned with an optimal incongruity between some aspect of a person's perceptions and the corresponding adaptation level (see Helson, 1964). A person at any given time will have developed an adaptation level in relation to perceptual inputs, and that amount of the stimulus will cause a neutral response. Modest deviations from that amount, either above or below, are said to be desired and to cause an affectively positive response. Large discrepancies, however, cause negative affect. Hence, people approach moderately discrepant situations but avoid highly discrepant ones. Haber (1958) supported this position with a study using human subjects who immersed their hands in water of varying temperatures above and below their adaptation level. Slightly discrepant temperatures were chosen, and highly discrepant ones were avoided.

The McClelland *et al.* theory is an affective-arousal theory. An optimal discrepancy between a perception and an adaptation level is said to cause a primary emotional response, and cues that have been paired with that affective state become capable of redintegrating that state. Thus, cues that were associated with optimal discrepancies would redintegrate positive affect and motivate approach behaviors, whereas cues associated with large discrepancies would redintegrate negative affect and motivate avoidance behaviors. In this theory, although optimal incongruity is a central notion, the optimal incongruity does not have to be present at the time an activity is being motivated. Rather, a cue need only redintegrate the affective state that was initially aroused by the discrepancy.

Dember and Earl (1957) posited that the important incongruity or discrepancy in intrinsically motivated behavior is between a person's expectations and the properties of the present stimulus. A person encounters a stimulus with certain expectations about the relevant dimension of the stimulus—loudness of a noise or brightness of a light, for example. The discrepancy between the expected level and the actual level of the stimulus value is referred to as complexity, and the total complexity value of the stimulus for a person is based on the complexity value of each dimension. The theory asserts that the person will approach stimuli that have optimal complexity, and these stimuli are called pacer stimuli. Walker (1964) also postulated that organisms prefer optimal levels of psychological complexity, and that they behave so as to move toward optimally complex stimuli.

Hunt (1963, 1965, 1971a,b) incorporated these notions of optimal discrepancy into a theory of intrinsically motivated behavior. He regarded the human as an information-processing system and asserted that people approach optimally incongruous stimuli as an integral part of information processing and action. As is typical of cognitive theories, Hunt's theory made no postulate about human needs. Instead of suggesting that organisms have a need for optimal incongruity, he merely asserted that behaviors called intrinsically motivated are inherent to the information-processing mechanism and are directed toward stimuli that are optimally incongruous.

Hunt analyzed behavior in terms of the relationship between internal cognitive structures and stimulus inputs. When some stimulus input is discrepant from an internal standard, such as an expectation or an adaptation level, organisms act with respect to the stimulus to reduce the incongruity. When the stimulus is different from one's expectations, one may either change the stimulus (i.e., assimilate it) or change the expectation (i.e., accommodate it), but in either case the person will be operating to achieve congruence.

Hunt's theory asserts that organisms tend to approach stimuli that represent some optimal level of incongruity, and this assertion is the central hypothesis of his theory of intrinsically motivated behavior. Organisms, he implies, seem to approach optimal levels of incongruity at the same time that they work to reduce incongruity. Although he did not do so, the process would need to be conceptualized as an ongoing one in which people approach an incongruous stimulus, operate to reduce the incongruity, and then move on to another incongruous stimulus.

Hunt's (1965) postulate that behavior is initiated by incongruity between a stimulus and an internal structure raises what we consider to be a metatheoretical problem. It portrays intrinsically motivated behavior as being initiated by stimuli that impinge on the organism, rather than by organismic needs or other internal states. In a later discussion, however, Hunt (1972) recognized that the concept of incongruity does not work very well as the central concept for intrinsic motivation, and suggested that a concept such as optimal complexity or optimal challenge might work better. This newer position is more compatible with the notion of an active organism and with the emergent conception of intrinsic motivation that will be presented later in this chapter.

A final theorist who made important contributions to the intrinsic motivation literature, working with concepts such as incongruity and stimulation, was Berlyne. Intrinsically motivated behaviors, he suggested (1971a), are ones that are aimed at establishing certain internal conditions that are rewarding for the organism. These conditions are bound up with the needs of the brain and may be sought in order to avoid or reduce threats to the functioning of the brain. These threats to functioning, Berlyne pointed out, may be real-time needs, such as a frightening stimulus, but if there is no need for immediate attention to a stimulus, the organism will be involved in normal maintenance. This means maintaining the optimal level of stimulation that is necessary for effective functioning.

Berlyne (1963, 1966), like Hunt, viewed the human organism as an information-processing system that uses information from the environment and its memory to make choices. In the course of normal information processing, the organism must compare and contrast various stimuli from the environment or memory in order to note differences and similarities. It must also categorize these elements into a meaningful system for operating and storing. Berlyne referred to these processes as collation, and pointed out that things like novelty and incongruity all involve collation of stimuli from the environment and memory. Thus, he suggested, collation is central to intrinsic motivation, and "collative stimulus properties" are intrinsically motivating as long as they are not greater than what is needed for an optimal level of stimulation.

Collative stimulus properties hold what Berlyne (1960) called *arousal potential*. He suggested that people approach stimuli that offer an optimum of arousal potential, and he then related arousal potential (properties of stimuli) to the functioning of two brain mechanisms (Berlyne, 1971b, 1973). He referred to them as the *arousal reduction mechanism* and the *arousal boost mechanism*, and described a physiological basis for intrinsically motivated as well as drive-motivated behaviors by building on Olds and Olds' (1965) work on the pleasure center in the brain.

Berlyne's theory is the most comprehensive of the optimal stimulation theories. It addresses the nature of stimuli that organisms approach and the relationship of the stimuli to the information processing system. As such, it is similar to the cognitive, incongruity theories. Berlyne's theory, however, went beyond the others in that it explained the physiological processes implicated in the hedonic consequences of intrinsically motivated action. In so doing, Berlyne, unlike other cognitive theorists, employed the concept of organismic needs, although he focused on physiological needs (i.e., needs of the brain) rather than psychological needs.

To summarize, the central premise of optimal incongruity theories is that organisms approach stimuli that are optimally discrepant from some existing cognitive structure. Several lines of empirical evidence have provided descriptive support for this assertion, and theories of intrinsic motivation will need to take account of the fact that the structure of intrinsically motivated behavior involves approaching incongruous stimuli and then working to reduce that incongruity.

The major problem with these theories is that they, like most cognitive theories, fail to postulate about human needs. As such they are able to explain the direction of behavior but not the energization of behavior. This point will be made clearer in Chapter 8 when we discuss Hunt's theory in greater detail. As we mentioned previously, Berlyne's theory did consider needs though it did so in physiological rather than psychological terms, so it failed to provide the basis for a psychological explication of the energization and direction of intrinsically motivated behaviors and processes.

NEEDS AND AFFECTS

Other theorists have conceptualized intrinsic motivation in terms of generalized needs and affects that are psychological rather than physiological in nature. This approach, which was evident in the early writings of McDougall (1908), Engle (1904), and Woodworth (1918), has gained widespread acceptance in the last decade. Currently, it is being used in the formulation and interpretation of a great deal of empirical research and in the theoretical integration of findings and perspectives from many areas of psychology. In essence, the central concerns being dealt with relate to the human needs for free and effective interactions with the environment and to the feelings of interest and enjoyment that are integrally involved with these needs.

The Need for Competence

Woodworth (1918, 1958), in his behavior–primacy theory, proposed that behavior is generally aimed at producing an effect on the environment. This behavior is ongoing and primary, so drives such as hunger must break into its flow of activity in order to achieve satisfaction. In motivational terms, this implies a need for having an effect, for being effective in one's interactions with the environment. Prior to Wood-worth, McDougall (1908) had proposed a curiosity instinct that is closely related to an effectance need, yet the idea of effectance is able to encom-pass a greater array of phenomena than a curiosity instinct. Curiosity is implicit in effectance.

White (1959), in the landmark paper mentioned earlier in this chap-ter, formally proposed a need for effectance as a basic motivational propensity that energizes a wide range of non-drive-based behaviors. There is, he suggested, inherent satisfaction in exercising and extending one's capabilities. White referred to the energy behind this activity as *effectance motivation* and to the corresponding affect as the feeling of *efficacy*. He used the term *competence* to connote the structures through which effectance motivation operates. Competence is the accumulated result of one's interactions with the environment, of one's exploration, learning, and adaptation. In the broad, biological sense, competence refers to the capacity for effective interactions with the environment that ensure the organism's maintenance. Because the capacity is called com-petence, the motivational counterpart is often called competence moti-vation as well as effectance motivation. Some writers, such as Kagan (1972), use the term mastery motivation.

The development of competencies—walking, talking, manipulating abstract symbols, or formulating a story—are in part maturational, according to White, yet they are in large measure learned, and the learning is motivated. The need for competence provides the energy for this learning. Effectance motivation is broader in its scope than learning, however. Whereas the biological aim of competence motivation is sur-vival of the organism, the experiential aim is the feeling of competence that results from effective action. Thus, for example, children seem to exercise their newly acquired competencies simply to experience the sense of satisfaction that they provide. In time, of course, the children move on to new undertakings, for the old ones become repetitious, and thus less interesting. Stated differently, the reward for competency-motivated behavior is the inherent feeling of competence that results from effective functioning, yet the motivation is such that the feelings seem to result only when there is some continual stretching of one's capacities. With each new acquisition of a skill there is some room for playful exercising of that skill, but boredom soon sets in when one merely exercises the same skill over and over.

Whereas drives tend to operate cyclically in that once satisfied they do not reemerge for some number of hours or days, effectance moti-vation is persistent and is always available to occupy "the spare waking time between episodes of homeostatic crisis" (White, 1959, p. 321). In other words, effectance motivation is not intense and immediate like

thirst or fear, but rather is an ongoing process that is periodically interrupted by tissue needs, though of course there are times when a hungry,
cold, or pained person will stick to an intrinsically motivated activity in
spite of the tissue needs. Like Berlyne, White located the source of this
non-drive-based energy in the central nervous system of the organism.

Deci (1975) suggested that the need for competence leads people to
seek and conquer challenges that are optimal for their capacities, and
that competence acquisition results from interacting with stimuli that
are challenging. A study by Danner and Lonky (1981) provided support
for this contention by showing that when children were free to select
the activities they would work on, they selected ones that were just
beyond their current level of competence.

Harter (1978a) took the position that White's generalized need for
effectance was too broad and should be broken into components. She
suggested three components—preference for challenge, curiosity, and
independent mastery—and then used these three components to develop
three subscales in her intrinsic versus extrinsic motivation scale for children (Harter, 1981b). Although it may be useful to conceptualize components of intrinsic motivation for purposes of measuring individual
differences, we assert that it is necessary to maintain the generalized
conception for purposes of greater theoretical integration.

Interest-Excitement and Flow

Another important strand of the current perspective on intrinsic
motivation is represented by theories that focus on affects and emotions
as either initiators or concomitants of intrinsically motivated behavior.
As previously noted these relatively invariant qualities associated with
intrinsic motivation include interest, enjoyment, and direct involvement
with one's environment. Affective theories place these features at the
core of their explanation of intrinsic motivation.

Izard (1977) proposed that there are 10 different human emotions;
that each is involved in the motivation of behavior; and that each has a
unique experiential component. Among these emotions, interest-
excitement is said to be the basis of intrinsically motivated behavior, and
joy is said to play a relevant though secondary role. Interest is involved
whenever one orients toward an object, and it plays an important role
in the amplification and direction of attention. Interest-excitement can
therefore activate many types of investigatory or manipulative behaviors, particularly under conditions of novelty and freedom from other
pressing demands of drives or emotions. Because interest can amplify
other emotions it also plays a regulatory role with regard to a variety of
experiences and behaviors. Izard (1977) thus recognized the centrality

of interest-excitement in the adaptation, development, and coordination of human behavior, and even labeled interest the fundamental motivator.

Csikszentmihalyi (1975) placed greater emphasis on enjoyment. For him, intrinsically motivated activities are ones characterized by enjoyment, those for which the reward is the ongoing experience of enjoying the activity. He uses the term *autotelic* to refer to the fact that the goal of intrinsically motivated behaviors is indeed their inherent experiential aspects. Csikszentmihalyi proposed that true enjoyment accompanies the experience of *flow*, that peculiar, dynamic, wholistic sensation of total involvement with the activity itself. In the state of flow, action and experience seem to move smoothly from one moment to the next, and there seems to be no clear distinction between the person and the activity. Flow involves a "loss of ego" and an experienced unity with one's surroundings.

Csikszentmihalyi's research suggests that flow states emerge under some specifiable conditions. Most important among these is optimal challenge. When one engages an optimally challenging activity with respect to one's capacities there is maximal possibility for task-involved enjoyment or flow. Activities that are below one's optimal challenge (i.e., activities that are too easy) lead to boredom, and activities that greatly exceed one's current capacities generate anxiety and disrupt flow. Thus the perspective offered by Csikszentmihalyi also implicates the competence theories previously discussed, indicating that people will be intrinsically motivated under conditions of optimal challenge.

In sum, interest and excitement are central emotions that accompany intrinsic motivation, and the concept of flow represents a descriptive dimension that may signify some of the purer instances of intrinsic motivation. When highly intrinsically motivated, organisms will be extremely interested in what they are doing and experience a sense of flow.

The Need for Self-Determination

The previous approaches have highlighted the significance of competence and interest in intrinsically motivated behavior. However, many non-intrinsically motivated behaviors may be competence-oriented, and some may even be characterized by interest. To be truly intrinsically motivated, a person must also feel free from pressures, such as rewards or contingencies. Thus, we suggest, intrinsic motivation will be operative when action is experienced as autonomous, and it is unlikely to function under conditions where controls or reinforcements are the experienced cause of action.

Because self-determination or freedom from control is necessary for intrinsic motivation to be operative, several theorists have posited that intrinsically motivated activity is based in the need for self-determination. DeCharms (1968) for example, proposed that intrinsically motivated behaviors result from a desire to experience personal causation.

> Man's primary motivational propensity is to be effective in producing changes in his environment. Man strives to be a causal agent, to be the primary locus of causation for, or the origin of, his behavior; he strives for personal causation. (deCharms, 1968, p. 269)

According to deCharms, this basic desire to be in control of one's fate is a contributing factor in all motivated behavior, though it is the central force only for intrinsically motivated behavior.

In further discussing the notion of intrinsic motivation, deCharms used Heider's (1958) concept of perceived locus of causality:

> Whenever a person experiences himself to be the locus of causality for his own behavior . . . he will consider himself to be intrinsically motivated. Conversely, when a person perceives the locus of causality to be external to himself . . . he will consider himself to be extrinsically motivated. (de Charms, 1968, p. 328)

The postulate of a basic motivational propensity for self-determination is, of course, closely related to the postulate of a need for effectance. Angyal (1941), for example, suggested that human development can be characterized in terms of movement toward greater autonomy and that this movement depends in part on the continual acqusition of a variety of competencies. To be self-determining one must have the skills to manage various elements of one's environment. Otherwise, one is likely to be controlled by them.

Recent work on the psychology of control has indicated that people have a need to experience control over their environment or their outcomes. Although the need to control is not the same as the need for self-determination, evidence in support of the former is relevant to the latter. One set of studies focused on people's apparent desire or need to control the environment by showing that people believe they have more control than they actually do, particularly in situations where controllability cues are present (Langer, 1975). People, it seems, have such a strong desire for control that they may even project it into situations where they do not actually have it.

A more direct test of the hypothesis that people have a need for control was done by Schorr and Rodin (1984), who created experimental conditions in which people's intentional performance on one task would determine whether they, or others, would be in control of a future task. The researchers found, first, that subjects did display behavior which signified a need for control, and second, that to some extent the need for control was "for its own sake" rather than for increasing the likelihood of gaining prefered outcomes. It does appear, then, that people have a need to control aspects of their environment.

In reviewing research on control, Deci (1980) suggested that the intrinsic need that was operative for subjects in the various control studies was not a need to control the environment, but rather a need to be self-determining, that is, to have a choice. It is true, he said, that the need for self-determination is often manifest as a need to control the environment, so the previously cited research represents partial support for the need for self-determination, but there are very important differences between the concepts of control and self-determination. Control refers to there being a contingency between one's behavior and the outcomes one receives, whereas self-determination refers to the experience of freedom in initiating one's behavior. A person has control when his or her behaviors reliably yield intended outcomes, but this does not ensure self-determination, for the person can, in the words of deCharms (1968), become a "pawn" to those outcomes. In those cases the person's behavior would be determined by the outcomes rather than by choices, even though the person would be said to have control. It is true that a person needs control over outcomes to be self-determined in attaining them, but the need is for self-determination rather than for control *per se*. Further, we assert that people do not always want control of outcomes; indeed, they often prefer to have others take control. What they want is *choice* about whether to be in control. Thus, using the concept of a need for self-determination (i.e., of choice) rather than a need for control allows for the explanation of the fact that people need to feel free from dependence on outcomes over which they have control, and that people sometimes prefer not to control outcomes. These points will be elaborated in Chapters 6 and 7.

Support for the conception that the need for self-determination is basic to intrinsic motivation comes in part from research (to be reviewed in Chapters 3 and 4) that confirms that the opportunity to be self-determining enhances intrinsic motivation, and that denial of the opportunity to be self-determining undermines it. Further support comes from the work of Brehm (1966), who showed that when people perceive their freedom to be threatened, they experience reactance, whch is a motivation to restore the threatened freedom. With prolonged denial of freedom, Wortman and Brehm (1975) suggested, the reactance motivation will tend to diminish and people will fall into amotivation: they will feel helpless and their effectiveness will be impaired.

A wide range of evidence supports the view that the need for self-determination is an important motivator that is involved with intrinsic motivation and is closely intertwined with the need for competence. We conceptualize intrinsic motivation in terms of the needs for competence and self-determination. The two needs are closely related, but we refer to both to emphasize their mutual importance. Whereas White (1959) made competence the backbone of intrinsic motivation, it is important to emphasize that it is not the need for competence alone that underlies intrinsic motivation; it is the need for self-determined competence.

INTRINSIC MOTIVATION CONCEPTUALIZED

Human beings engage in a substantial amount of intrinsically motivated behavior, so theories of motivation must be able to explain behaviors that are motivated by "rewards that do not reduce tissue needs" (Eisenberger, 1972). This requires an adequate conception of intrinsic motivation and a general theory of motivation that includes intrinsic as well as other types of motivation. The conceptualizations of intrinsic motivation that have been proposed are summarized in Table 1. We saw that the attempts to integrate intrinsically motivated phenomena into Hullian drive theory and Freudian instinct theory proved inadequate. As Koch (1956) had predicted, it was necessary to posit the existence of a fundamentally different motivational source. At the physiological level this was done by arousal theories; at the psychological level it was done by incongruity theories and by theories that focus on the needs for competence and self-determination, or the emotions of interest and enjoyment. Drawing on these various works, we now offer a definition of intrinsic motivation.

Intrinsic motivation is based in the innate, organismic needs for competence and self-determination. It energizes a wide variety of behaviors and psychological processes for which the primary rewards are the experiences of effectance and autonomy. Intrinsic needs differ from primary drives in that they are not based in tissue deficits and they do not operate cyclically, that is, breaking into awareness, pushing to be satisfied, and then when satisfied, receding into quiescence. Like drives, however, intrinsic needs are innate to the human organism and function as an important energizer of behavior. Furthermore, intrinsic motivation may interact with drives in the sense of either amplifying or attenuating drives and of affecting the way in which people satisfy their drives.

The intrinsic needs for competence and self-determination motivate an ongoing process of seeking and attempting to conquer optimal challenges. When people are free from the intrusion of drives and emotions, they seek situations that interest them and require the use of their creativity and resourcefulness. They seek challenges that are suited to their

TABLE 1. Summary of Various Conceptualizations of Intrinsic Motivation along with the Primary Proponents of Each Approach

Approach	Proponents
Drive naming	
Exploratory drive	Montgomery, 1954
Avoid boredom	Myers & Miller, 1954
Manipulation drive	Harlow, 1953a
Sensory drive	Isaac, 1962
Visual exploration	Butler, 1953
Physiological arousal	
Optimal arousal	Hebb, 1955; Leuba, 1955
	Fiske & Maddi, 1961
Psychological incongruity	
Dissonance reduction	Festinger, 1957
Uncertainty reduction	Kagan, 1972; Lanzetta, 1971
Discrepancy from adaptation	McClelland, et al., 1953
Optimal incongruity	Dember & Earl, 1957; Hunt, 1965
Optimal arousal potential	Berlyne, 1971a
Psychoanalytic	
Instinct to master	Hendrick, 1942
Anxiety reduction	Fenichel, 1945
Ego energy	Hartmann, 1958; White, 1963
Competence and self-determination	
Effectance	Harter, 1978a; White, 1959
Self-determination	Angyal, 1941
Personal causation	deCharms, 1968
Competence and self-determination	Deci & Ryan (this volume)
Emotions	
Interest-excitement	Izard, 1977
Enjoyment and flow	Csikszentmihalyi, 1975

competencies, that are neither too easy nor too difficult. When they find optimal challenges, people work to conquer them, and they do so persistently. In short, the needs for competence and self-determination keep people involved in ongoing cycles of seeking and conquering optimal challenges.

A challenge is something that requires stretching one's abilities, trying something new. One way to conceptualize challenge is in terms of an incongruity between one's internal structures and aspects of the external world. Thus, to seek an optimal challenge is to seek an optimal incongruity. People seek incongruities in order to reduce them and to incorporate the discrepant elements into their existing structures. Intrinsically motivated behavior, behavior motivated by the needs for competence and self-determination, therefore can be seen to involve an ongoing process of seeking and reducing optimal incongruities.

Emotions are integrally related to intrinsic motivation. The emotion of interest plays an important directive role in intrinsically motivated behavior in that people naturally approach activities that interest them. Interest is, to a large extent, a function of optimal challenge, though there are other factors that also influence people's developing interests. The emotions of enjoyment and excitement accompanying the experiences of competence and autonomy represent the rewards for intrinsically motivated behavior. These rewards are not properly called reinforcements, of course, because they neither reduce a tissue deficit (Hull, 1943) nor are operationally separate from the activity itself (Skinner, 1953).

When people are intrinsically motivated, they experience interest and enjoyment, they feel competent and self-determining, they perceive the locus of causality for their behavior to be internal, and in some instances they experience flow. The antithesis of interest and flow is pressure and tension. Insofar as people are pressuring themselves, feeling anxious, and working with great urgency, we can be sure that there is at least some extrinsic motivation involved. Their self-esteem may be on the line, they may have deadlines, or some material reward may be involved.

In addition to the psychological definition, we need operational definitions for research purposes. First, we infer intrinsic motivation for an activity when a person does the activity in the absence of a reward contingency or control. This has been the basis of the so-called free-choice measure of intrinsic motivation that has been widely used in the experimental research that will be reviewed throughout this book. Like all operational definitions it is not perfectly correlated with the psychological definition, so it requires the use of some perspective in its application. A simplistic use of the operational definition, without proper judgment, has led to some confusing experimental findings. When applying this operational definition, it is useful to note subjects' affective reactions. For example, Ryan (1982) found that when subjects were ego-involved in an activity, when their self-esteem depended on their doing well, they experienced pressure and tension. If one observed subjects' feeling pressured and tense, even if they were behaving in the absence of any apparent "external" reward, one might suspect that there was some other motivational dynamic involved, and one would properly look deeper to understand the processes rather than naively infer intrinsic motivation.

Second, we sometimes look at the quality of performance or of outcomes as indicators of intrinsic motivation. Because intrinsic motivation has been associated with greater creativity (Amabile, 1983), flexibility (McGraw & McCullers, 1979), and spontaneity (Koestner, Ryan, Bernieri, & Holt, 1984), the presence of those characteristics can signify intrinsic motivation.

Finally, we use questionnaire measures of intrinsic motivation. For example, because intrinsic motivation involves interest and enjoyment, assessing subjects' interest and enjoyment allows us to infer intrinsic motivation. Higher levels of perceived competence and self-determination also imply intrinsic motivation and can be useful measures, particularly when used in conjunction with other measures. Again, with this operational definition it is important to employ perspective. For example, if subjects were rewarded and then asked how much they enjoyed the experience, they may say "very much." But did they enjoy the activity, or did they enjoy getting the reward? The former is relevant to intrinsic motivation; the latter is not.

SELF-DETERMINATION: A BRIEF HISTORY

The empirical exploration of intrinsic motivation has held importance for psychological theory because it has explicated the functioning of a class of behaviors that had not been well handled by drive or reinforcement theories. The study of intrinsic motivation has required the assumption that people are active organisms working to master their internal and external environments, and it has led to an examination of the importance of self-determination in a wide range of human behaviors and experiences. In fact it has led to the realization that self-determination is important in the development and exercise of extrinsic and intrinsic motivation. Consequently we shall attempt to show how the use of the concept of self-determination permits a more refined and elaborated conception of extrinsic motivation. In essence, extrinsic motivation refers to behavior where the reason for doing it is something other than an interest in the activity itself. Such behavior may, however, to a greater or lesser extent, be something the person feels pressured to do versus genuinely wants to do. Extrinsically motivated behaviors may range from being determined largely by controls to being determined more by choices based on one's own values and desires. In the latter case, they would be more self-determined.

Concepts related to self-determination have appeared in a variety of empirical and nonempirical psychological writings. Fundamentally, self-determination is an issue of choice and therefore necessitates a theory built on concepts such as volition, intentionality, or will. James (1890) was the first psychologist to discuss the importance of volition and in so doing to present a theory of will. However, since psychology became dominated by nonvolitional theories during the first half of the present century, these concepts were ruled out of consideration.

Around the middle of the century two important developments occurred that began to set the stage for self-determination to be considered. First, several theories posited fundamental tendencies for the developmental movement from heteronomy toward autonomy in the determination of behavior. And, second, the cognitive movement shifted attention from associative bonds to decisions as the central concept in the directionality of behavior.

Maslow (1943, 1955) for example, outlined a theory of motivation utilizing a concept that he, like Goldstein (1939), called *self-actualization*. All individuals, Maslow said, seek to actualize their unique potentials, to become all that they are capable of and to be autonomous in their functioning. A similar point was made by Rogers (1963), who argued that life activity can be understood in terms of the actualizing tendency, which is the organism's propensity to maintain and enhance itself. Although not the same as self-determination, the concept of self-actualization emphasizes the importance of choice and other self-related constructs.

Loevinger (1976a), in her theory of ego development, used a structural perspective and outlined the stages through which one moves in the developmental progression toward more unified, autonomous functioning. Shapiro (1981), also working in the psychoanalytic tradition, discussed autonomy in terms of the flexibility of psychological structures. Focusing primarily on the rigid structures that interfere with autonomy, Shapiro highlighted the notion of autonomy and its importance for understanding qualities of the ego's adaptation.

Lewin (1951b), who, along with Tolman (1932), was extremely influential in bringing about the cognitive movement in psychology, argued forcefully in support of intentionality and will as important motivational constructs. This led to the formulation of expectancy theories of motivation that explored the determinants of behavioral decision making (see Chapter 8), and to the empirical study of control that explored the importance of control over one's outcomes. Both of these developments within the cognitive movement were based on the assumption that behavior is a function of one's expectations about future outcomes, so the issue of whether or not one has control over outcomes is extremely important. Consequently, numerous researchers have studied the effects of one's beliefs about whether one has control on a wide variety of dependent variables.

Many of the studies have focused on the positive effects of enhanced perceived control over outcomes. For example, studies by Glass and Singer (1972) and by Miller (1980) demonstrated that when people believe they have or can gain control over aversive events in their environment, they perform more effectively than when they believe they cannot. Rodin, Solomon, and Metcalf (1978) and Langer and Saegert (1977) found that people with greater perceived control reported experiencing crowded spaces as less aversive than did people with less perceived control.

A related set of studies has demonstrated the negative effects of lack of perceived control over one's outcomes. Pennebaker, Burnam, Schaeffer, and Harper (1977), for example, reported that the lack of perceived control led to more reported physical symptoms, such as headaches. Seligman and his colleagues (Hiroto, 1974; Hiroto & Seligman, 1975; Seligman, 1968, 1975) have demonstrated repeatedly that lack of perceived control over outcomes leads to helplessness, in which case people display increased emotionality and impaired learning and performance.

Other studies have related control directly to health and well-being. For example, Schulz (1976) found that a sample of institutionalized aged people who were given greater opportunity to control outcomes was rated by staff members as becoming more psychologically healthy; showed evidence of being less physically ill; and had a lower mortality rate than a matched control group. Langer and Rodin (1976) reported similar results in a different institution for the aged. Follow-ups of these two studies (Schulz & Hanusa, 1978; Rodin & Langer, 1977) led to the important conclusion that long-term positive effects on people's well-being require that the people learn to accept greater personal responsibility for attaining their desired outcomes.

In general, then, considerable research suggests that greater perceived control over one's outcomes tends to be associated with a variety of positive effects, though some studies have shown that there are conditions within which perceived control can have negative consequences (e.g., Averill, 1973; Fegley, 1984).

As we mentioned earlier, the concepts of self-determination and control are not the same, though they are related. To be self-determining with respect to outcomes, people must have control over those outcomes, and not being able to control outcomes—which precludes self-determination—will have negative consequences, as the studies previously reviewed have shown. But having control does not ensure self-determination. If people feel pressured to attain certain outcomes or if they feel pressured to exercise control, they are not self-determined. Self-determination means that people experience choice. It will be in evidence either when they choose to exercise control and are free with respect to what outcomes they attain, or when they choose to give up the control. In either case, we predict positive effects. However, when people experience having to be in control or having to attain particular outcomes (i.e., when they are not being self-determining), the effects will be negative, just as they are when people cannot gain control.

Cognitive theories set the stage for the study of self-determination. By introducing the concepts of behavioral decision making (i.e., intentionality) and control over outcomes, they allowed self-determination theorists such as deCharms (1968) and Deci (1980) to point out that only some intended behaviors (namely, those with an internal perceived locus of causality) are self-determined, and that having control over outcomes does not ensure self-determination.

SELF-DETERMINATION CONCEPTUALIZED

Self-determination is a quality of human functioning that involves the experience of choice, in other words, the experience of an internal perceived locus of causality. It is integral to intrinsically motivated behavior and is also in evidence in some extrinsically motivated behaviors. Stated differently, self-determination is the capacity to choose and to have those choices, rather than reinforcement contingencies, drives, or any other forces or pressures, be the determinants of one's actions. But self-determination is more than a *capacity*; it is also a *need*. We have posited a basic, innate propensity to be self-determining that leads organisms to engage in interesting behaviors, which typically has the benefit of developing competencies, and of working toward a flexible accommodation with the social environment. This tendency toward adequate accommodation in the service of one's self-determination is central to the development of extrinsic motivation.

The psychological hallmark of self-determination is flexibility in managing the interaction of oneself and the environment. When self-determined, one acts out of choice rather than obligation or coersion, and those choices are based on an awareness of one's organismic needs and a flexible interpretation of external events. Self-determination often involves controlling one's environment or one's outcomes, but it may also involve choosing to give up control.

Although we define self-determination as a quality of human functioning, we also emphasize that it can be either supported or hindered by environmental forces, so we study it in part by exploring environmental influences. Further, we often speak of the opportunity to be self-determining, implying that when the environment supports self-determination, the person will be more self-determining. Technically, of course, we can only define self-determination with respect to the person's actual functioning.

Self-determination has also been operationalized for research purposes. Thus far this has been done with questionnaire measures, though it could be done with behavioral measures as well. In either case, we would look for evidence of persistence in the absence of immediate extrinsic contingencies and for a minimum of pressure, tension, and anxiety.

SUMMARY

In this chapter we have reviewed various approaches to the conceptualization of intrinsic motivation. The evidence is indisputable that intrinsic motivation exists and that it involves non-tissue-based, drive-independent needs. Early work focused on drive theory accounts, particularly drive naming. This approach proved inadequate, as did the drive theory accounts using secondary reinforcement and anxiety reduction. Another approach, which can be seen to be a neo-drive-theory approach, focused on the physiological level and posited that organisms need an optimal amount of arousal (i.e., nonspecific cortical bombardment) for effective functioning. Although interesting, this approach does not work very well for psychological theories.

An approach that received considerable attention focused on uncertainty or dissonance, that is, on incongruity between a cognitive structure and a stimulus input. Although it is clear that much behavior is directed toward the reduction of uncertainty or dissonance, it is also clear that much behavior is intended to increase uncertainty or dissonance. Several theorists considered both the reduction and induction of uncertainty or dissonance (i.e., of incongruity) by postulating that people have a tendency to approach stimuli that represent an optimal level of psychological incongruity.

We also considered the conceptualization of intrinsic motivation, which asserts that human organisms have needs for competence and self-determination. These needs have no appreciable effect on non-nervous-system tissues; they relate to the experience of being competent and self-determining and to the emotions of interest and enjoyment; and they motivate an ongoing interaction with the environment of seeking and conquering challenges that are optimal for one's capacities. The needs-for-competence-and-self-determination approach is the one that will be central for the remainder of this book.

Finally, we pointed out that although the quality of self-determination, characterized by psychological flexibility and the experience of choice, is inherent in intrinsically motivated behavior, it is also present in some extrinsically motivated behaviors. We briefly traced the emergence of the concept of self-determination and in so doing distinguished between self-determination and control. We suggested that the concept of self-determination is important for an understanding of the development of extrinsic motivation and accommodation to the social world.

II

SELF-DETERMINATION THEORY

Cognitive Evaluation Theory
Perceived Causality and Perceived Competence

Intrinsic motivation is the innate, natural propensity to engage one's interests and exercise one's capacities, and in so doing, to seek and conquer optimal challenges. Such motivation emerges spontaneously from internal tendencies and can motivate behavior even without the aid of extrinsic rewards or environmental controls. Intrinsic motivation is also an important motivator of the learning, adaptation, and growth in competencies that characterize human development. One would think from this description that intrinsic motivation is a ubiquitous phenomenon, and yet the examination of many settings suggests just the opposite. In factories and classrooms, offices and kitchens, one finds evidence of boredom, alienation, and inactivity. There appears to be a strong indication that people are prone to disinterest and stagnation.

In this and subsequent chapters we will review a wealth of data suggesting that these two apparently contradictory sets of observations are indeed reconcilable. Evidence indicates that intrinsic motivation is an inherent quality, and that people will tend to display manifestations of this when the circumstances permit. But this motivation, although strong and persistent, is also vulnerable to the continued encroachment of environmental forces that are perhaps all too common and often socially sanctioned. Evidence for our suggested reconciliation of the seemingly paradoxical observations has come from research on the factors and processes that tend to undermine rather than to enhance intrinsic motivation.

The research started with a straightforward question: If a person is involved in an intrinsically interesting activity and begins to receive an extrinsic reward for doing it, what will happen to his or her intrinsic motivation for the activity? For example, if a boy is rewarded for practicing the piano, what happens to his intrinsic motivation for piano playing? Is it enhanced, diminished, or left unaffected by the rewards?

Prior to the studies that have been designed within the last 15 years to explore this question, there had been only two reported, directly related studies, both from Harlow's primate laboratory. In those studies, monkeys manipulated a mechanical puzzle apparatus, and food was introduced into the situation for some of the monkeys. In one study, Davis *et al.* (1950) found that performance was better after this reward had been introduced and terminated than it had been before the reward was introduced. This suggests that the experience with food led the monkeys to imbue the activity with greater intrinsic value, so they were more interested in performing it well. However, the other study (Gately, 1950) showed just the opposite result. Following the removal of food rewards, the rewarded monkeys in the Gately study appeared to have lost interest in the activity, whereas the interest of the nonrewarded monkeys persisted. Although these studies used only small numbers of primate subjects, and their results were open to various interpretations, such as resistance to extinction, they were nonetheless provocative and suggested that there may be an interesting interaction between intrinsic motivation and extrinsic rewards. In spite of the importance of this issue, however, two decades passed before it was explored further.

The Effects of Monetary Rewards

The first published studies designed to consider the question directly were by Deci (1971). In the first of these he explored the effects of monetary rewards on intrinsic motivation. Subjects participated in three 1-hour sessions working on spatial-relations, block-building puzzles called Soma. Pilot testing had substantiated that these puzzles were highly intrinsically motivating for college-student subjects. During each of three sessions, subjects worked on four puzzles with a time limit for each. If they were unable to solve any of the puzzles within the allotted time, they were shown the solution so that the Zeigarnik (1927) effect (i.e., the tendency to return to uncompleted tasks) would not influence their subsequent motivation for the task. The only difference between the experimental and control groups in this study was that subjects in the experimental group earned $1 for each of the four puzzles they solved during the second session.

The subjects' intrinsic motivation was assessed during the first (baseline) and third (follow-up) session for the experimental and control subjects, using what has come to be called the free-choice measure of intrinsic motivation. This involved surreptitiously observing subjects' behavior during a free-choice period when interesting activities, in addition to the puzzles, were available, and there were no extrinsic reasons for working on the puzzles. It was reasoned that if subjects spent time working on the target activity when there was no extrinsic reason to do so, they were intrinsically motivated for it. Thus, the amount of time they spent with the target activity was used as a measure of their intrinsic motivation.

Comparisons were made between the changes in intrinsic motivation from the first to the third sessions for the experimental group relative to the control group, and the results indicated a decrease in the intrinsic motivation of the experimental subjects, relative to the control subjects. The experience of solving interesting puzzles for money seems to have decreased the experimental subjects' intrinsic motivation for this activity.

A second study, reported in the same article (Deci, 1971), was a field experiment conducted in a college newspaper office. Two staffs of headline writers were the subjects for this 16-week experiment, though they were not aware that they were being studied. One staff comprised the experimental group and one the control group. Subjects' baseline level of intrinsic motivation was taken during the weekly work meetings over the first 4 weeks. Then, during the 5th through 7th weeks, experimental subjects were paid $.50 for each headline they wrote. They were told that there was extra money in the budget that needed to be used up by the end of the year, so the editors had decided to pay staff members until it was used up. Finally, during the 8th through 10th weeks and again during the 15th and 16th weeks, subjects' intrinsic motivation was assessed. The paid, relative to nonpaid, subjects showed a significant decrease from the first 4-week period to the 3-week period subsequent to payment. This difference was still marginally significant in the follow-up period 8 weeks after payment had stopped. Thus, the field experiment replicated the laboratory experiment, and the two represent the first concrete evidence that extrinsic rewards can have a deleterious effect on intrinsic motivation.

Critics of this work (e.g., Calder & Staw, 1975a) have suggested that because subjects were paid during one period and then not paid during a subsequent one, they may have been angry at the experimenter for removing the rewards. If that were so, the apparent decrease in intrinsic motivation could have been merely an emotional reaction. This interpretation seems quite untenable, however, because in both studies subjects were told that the payments would be for a limited period, and they had originally begun the activity without expecting rewards. Further, no subject showed any evidence of emotionality when the rewards ceased.

There were two potential weaknesses to the laboratory experiment, however, that are worth noting. First, the experimenter was present in the room while the subjects were solving puzzles, so there is the possibility that he could have been giving subtle cues that influenced the subjects' subsequent free-choice behavior (Rosenthal, 1966). Second, as Scott (1976) pointed out, because the same experimenter took the free-choice measure, he knew what conditions the subjects were in and this could have biased his recording of time. To correct these two weaknesses, and to create a more efficient paradigm, one that required only one rather than three sessions, Deci (1972b) redesigned the procedure and replicated the results of the undermining of intrinsic motivation by monetary payments. Because this general paradigm has been used in numerous studies, we will outline it first and then discuss the particular experiments.

The General One-Session Paradigm. This paradigm employs an after-only design. Subjects participate for one hour, during which they work on intrinsically interesting activities. In several of the studies the Soma puzzles were used as the target activity, although other tasks, such as hidden-figures puzzles, computer games, art activities, and anagrams have also been used. The first experimenter meets each subject in a waiting room and the experimenter goes to an observation area outside the experiment room. Subjects know that the experimenter is watching them, and they communicate through an intercom. The instructions, spoken by the experimenter, typically indicate that this is an experiment to study problem-solving styles. The subject works on several puzzle problems, and if he or she is unable to solve a puzzle in the time allotted, the experimenter explains how to do it as the subject assembles it.

In each study, experimental subjects work with the puzzles under some condition of reward, feedback, constraint, or communication, whereas control group subjects do the same thing in the absence of the experimental manipulation. Of interest are the relative levels of intrinsic motivaton in the two groups subsequent to the experimental manipulation period. This paradigm is referred to as an after-only design because only one measure of intrinsic motivation is taken on each subject. Whereas the three-session paradigm employed a before-after design in which subjects' intrinsic motivation was assessed both before and after the experimental period, this paradigm was based on the assumption that, because of random assignment of subjects to groups, the average initial level of intrinsic motivation for each group would be the same. The differences in the group means following the experimental period could therefore be interpreted as if they represented changes. The assumption of comparable preexperimental levels of intrinsic motivation is a reasonable one if subjects are randomly assigned and cell sizes are adequately large.

To obtain the dependent measure of intrinsic motivation, the experimenter leaves his or her position for a period of, say, eight minutes under some credible pretext, such as going to the computer. This creates the free-choice period in which subjects are alone, have no extrinsic reasons for working on the activity, are unaware that they are being surreptitiously observed, and have other interesting things to do. The time they spend with the target activity during this period is used as the measure of intrinsic motivation. Various methodological precautions, such as closing the drapes over the one-way window and having a second experimenter do the free-choice observation through a crack in the drapes of a different window, are typically employed.

This general paradigm has now been used in dozens of published studies. The specifics have varied, of course—different activities have been used, the settings have been modified, and time limits have differed—but the overall concept of the design has been the same. We will now consider individual studies that have used this general paradigm, beginning with the replication of the monetary-rewards study described earlier.

Monetary Rewards. Just as in the three-session study, experimental subjects in this first one-session study (Deci 1972b) received $1 for each of the four puzzles that they were able to solve within the allotted time, whereas control subjects received no money. The results replicated those of the two payment studies described earlier: subjects who had been paid for working with an intrinsically interesting activity were less intrinsically motivated following their experience with the money than were subjects who had done the same activity without pay. An inspection of performance scores for the two groups revealed that there had been no differences in the average amount of time spent by the two groups of subjects working on the puzzles during the experimental period. Consequently, there is no indication that the free-choice behavior (i.e., the measure of subsequent intrinsic motivation) was differentially affected by performance, satiation, or fatigue (Deci, Cascio, & Krusell, 1975).

Calder and Staw (1975b) did a study in which some subjects were paid $1 for working on an interesting jigsaw puzzle, whereas other subjects were not. They found that subjects who received payments rated the puzzle activity as significantly less enjoyable than subjects who received no payments, thus replicating the Deci findings using a different task and a different dependent measure of intrinsic motivation. Further, Pritchard, Campbell, and Campbell (1977) did a study in which some subjects solved chess problems in an attempt to win money, whereas other subjects did the problems with no monetary incentives. Results revealed that in a follow-up session one week subsequent to the problem-solving session, those subjects who had worked for the financial incentives evidenced a significant decrement in intrinsic motivation (as assessed by the free-choice measure) relative to the subjects who worked without the incentives.

Several other studies have provided additional evidence that monetary rewards can decrease intrinsic motivation. Pinder (1976) found that paying male teenage subjects for working on a mechanical assembly task tended to decrease their expressed satisfaction and intrinsic orientation. Yoshimura (1979), who financially rewarded Japanese undergraduate males for doing jigsaw puzzles, found decrements in their intrinsic motivation and enjoyment. Anderson, Manoogian, and Reznick (1976) found that providing small financial incentives to 4- and 5-year-old children for working on an art task decreased their intrinsic motivation for the activity as measured by behavior during a subsequent free-choice period. And Eden (1975), in a survey study of male workers in an Israeli kibbutz, found a negative correlation between financial rewards and intrinsic motives.

The weight of evidence from these studies seems clear: when subjects received monetary rewards for working on a variety of activities, under a variety of circumstances in and out of the laboratory, their intrinsic motivation for the rewarded activity decreased. This phenomenon, which has been studied experimentally only recently, was illustrated amusingly somewhat earlier by the following fable:[1]

> In a little Southern town where the Klan was riding again, a Jewish tailor had the temerity to open his little shop on the main street. To drive him out of the town the Kleagle of the Klan sent a gang of little ragamuffins to annoy him. Day after day they stood at the entrance of his shop. "Jew! Jew!", they hooted at him. The situation looked serious for the tailor. He took the matter so much to heart that he began to brood and spent sleepless nights over it. Finally out of desperation he evolved a plan.
>
> The following day when the little hoodlums came to jeer at him, he came to the door and said to them, "From today on any boy who calls me 'Jew' will get a dime from me." Then he put his hand in his pocket and gave each boy a dime.
>
> Delighted with their booty, the boys came back the following day and began to shrill, "Jew! Jew!" The tailor came out smiling. He put his hand in his pocket and gave each of the boys a nickel, saying, "A dime is too much— I can only afford a nickel today." The boys went away satisfied because, after all, a nickel was money too.
>
> However, when they returned the next day to hoot at him, the tailor gave them only a penny each.
>
> "Why do we get only a penny today?" they yelled.
>
> "That's all I can afford."
>
> "But two days ago you gave us a dime, and yesterday we got a nickel. It's not fair mister."
>
> "Take it or leave it. That's all you're going to get!"
>
> "Do you think we're going to call you 'Jew' for one lousy penny?"
>
> "So don't!"
>
> And they didn't.

[1]Reprinted from *A Treasury of Jewish Folklore* (p. 440) by N. Ausable (ed.), (1976), New York: Crown Publishing Co. Copyright 1948, 1976 by Crown Publishing Company. Reprinted with permission.

Perceived Causality: Internal to External

To account for the effects of monetary rewards, Deci (1971, 1972b) used the ideas of deCharms (1968) and Heider (1958) to assert that the monetary payments had induced a change in the perceived locus of causality from internal to external, resulting in decreased intrinsic motivation for the activity. Whereas intrinsically motivated behavior has an internal perceived locus of causality: the person does it for internal rewards such as interest and mastery; extrinsically motivated behavior has an external perceived locus of causality: the person does it to get an extrinsic reward or to comply with an external constraint. With an external reward or constraint, an instrumentality develops such that the activity becomes a means to an end rather than an end in itself. The behavior is no longer something that is done because it is interesting; it is something that is done to get an external reward or to comply with an external constraint. This statement about the change in perceived locus of causality became part of what Deci (1975) referred to as cognitive evaluation theory. The theory along with its more recent extensions will be presented throughout this and the next chapter.

Deci and Ryan (1980a) elaborated the change in locus of causality statement, pointing out that Deci's earlier explanation had not adequately addressed the underlying *motivational* dynamics. We reiterated that intrinsic motivation is based in the need to be self-determining and suggested that rewards, which are widely used as instruments of control, can often co-opt people's self-determination and initiate different motivational processes. We describe this phenomenon as a change in perceived locus of causality from internal to external; however, we do not mean to imply that changes in intrinsic motivation are simply changes in perceptions. Rather, the perceived locus of causality construct is intended to reflect different motivational dynamics. The importance of this point will become clearer throughout this chapter and will be addressed directly in Chapter 7.

Other Extrinsic Rewards

If, indeed, the observed phenomenon of decreased intrinsic motivation due to payments is a result of an undermining of people's self-determination, with the concomitant change in perceived locus of causality, one would also expect other environmental events, such as rewards and constraints that impinge on one's self-determination, to undermine intrinsic motivation. A great variety of rewards and constraints has now been investigated.

Avoidance of Punishment. The avoidance of punishment is a common reward used to control people's behavior. Deci and Cascio (1972) explored the effects of this type of reward on intrinsic motivation using the one-session, Soma paradigm described earlier. Experimental subjects were given puzzles and told that if they were unable to solve a puzzle in the time allotted a buzzer would sound indicating that their time was up. They were given a very brief exposure to the buzzer so they would know it was noxious. Thus, the researchers created a situation in which the experimental subjects were implicitly threatened; but if they solved the puzzles in the allotted time they would be rewarded with the avoidance of the noxious buzzer. Control subjects did the same task without the buzzer.

Results of this study, although only marginally significant, showed that subjects who worked in order to avoid the noxious stimulus were less intrinsically motivated than subjects who did the puzzles without this added incentive. Again, it appears that their behavior had become somewhat dependent on the external contingency, thus undermining their self-determination. These results could, more easily than the reward results, be given alternative interpretations. For example, one could reasonably suggest that the threats are anxiety provoking, so the decrement in free-choice behavior could be a reflection of the anxiety. This is possible; indeed, external controls that decrease intrinsic motivation also create pressure and tension. Although the anxiety interpretation is often posed as an alternative interpretation, it is actually complementary.

Awards. Lepper, Greene, and Nisbett (1973) did the first intrinsic motivation study that used children as subjects. They had 3- and 4-year-old preschool children work with attractive magic markers and construction paper. Subjects in one group were told that they would receive a good-player award if they did some drawings for the experimenter. The award, which was to be placed on a bulletin board, contained the child's name, a gold star, and a red ribbon. For a second group, there was no mention of an award. In a free-choice situation, several days later, children who had received the award spent significantly less time with the art materials than did those who had not received the award.

In a follow-up study, Greene and Lepper (1974) used a similar procedure and replicated their previous results. In this study, some children who received awards were told that all children who did the task would receive the award, whereas other children were told that only the children who drew the best pictures would get the award. In both these groups, the awards decreased intrinsic motivation; the rewarded children spent less free-choice time with the art materials than did the children in the no-rewards, control group. The general finding was also replicated by Loveland and Olley (1979) using a very similar paradigm.

Anderson, Manoogian, and Reznick (1976), in their study with pre-school children, also had a good-player award condition. As with their money group, they found decrements in intrinsic motivation from the pre- to posttreatment, free-choice periods. These symbolic rewards, like money and the avoidance of punishment, seemed to decrease intrinsic motivation. We explain the results in terms of the rewards' co-opting self-determination and changing the perceived locus of causality from internal to external.

Tokens, Toys, Food, and Prizes. Greene, Sternberg, and Lepper (1976) utilized a token economy procedure to reinforce fourth- and fifth-grade children for doing math activities. There were three different experimental groups that received token rewards (credit toward certificates and trophies). In addition there was a no-tokens control group. Two of the three reward groups evidenced significant declines in time spent with math activities from pre- to posttreatment free-choice periods. For the third group, there was a small but nonsignificant decline.

Lepper and Greene (1975) did a study with preschoolers in which they rewarded the children with the opportunity to play with an attractive toy for doing a puzzle-solving activity. Solving the puzzles in order to play with other toys led to a significant decrement in their intrinsic motivation for the puzzle solving. Hom and Maxwell (1979) reported similar results with older subjects, using the opportunity to play a pinball machine as the reward.

Ross (1975) gave marshmallows as a reward to nursery school children for playing with a drum, and Ross, Karniol, and Rothstein (1976) used candy to reward first through third grade children for drawing. In both studies the food rewards decreased intrinsic motivation as measured by behavior in a free-choice period. In the Ross study, the effect was still evident in a four-week follow-up.

Harackiewicz (1979) reported that high school students who were rewarded with prizes for working on hidden-figure puzzles were less intrinsically motivated than their nonrewarded counterparts, and Lee, Syrnyk, and Hallschmid (1977) reported that developmentally delayed adolescents who were given desired prizes for playing with an interesting activity were less intrinsically motivated than subjects who were rewarded with less desirable prizes. McLoyd (1979) found the same results with normal children. Thus, the evidence that extrinsic rewards and contingencies can undermine intrinsic motivation is quite persuasive. The phenomenon has appeared with ages ranging from preschoolers to adults, rewards ranging from money to marshmallows, activities ranging from solving puzzles to beating a drum, settings ranging from psychology laboratories to a newspaper office, and cultures ranging from the United States to Japan.

Reward Salience and Expectancy

Several experimenters have attempted to understand the specific circumstances under which the undermining effect will occur. To do this, they have performed experiments that varied the type of reward structures and the type of tasks that were used.

Salience. Ross (1975) suggested that in order for rewards to have an impact on intrinsic motivation, the rewards must be salient in the subjects' experience while they are doing the activity. In his first experiment, he offered rewards to two groups. For one group, he provided a cue during the activity to keep the rewards salient, whereas for the other reward group there was no cue. The results revealed a decrement for the salient-reward group relative to a no-reward control group, but no decrement for the non-salient-reward group.

Reiss and Sushinsky (1975) criticized the studies that had reported decrements in intrinsic motivation caused by rewards. The authors asserted that the concept of intrinsic motivation was superfluous and that the reported results could best be understood in terms of a distraction effect. They suggested that the introduction of rewards distracts people from the task, so those people become less interested in the task, not because they lose intrinsic motivation for it, but because they do not attend to it. To explore this possibility and to get further data on his salience hypothesis, Ross (1975) did a second experiment with three reward groups. In one, he instructed subjects to think about the reward while doing the activity; in the second, he offered the reward and instructed the subjects to think about something else (snow) while doing the activity; and in the third, he offered the reward but gave no instructions about ideation. A fourth group was a no-reward, control group. Results indicated that the "think reward" group and the "reward without ideation" group both evidenced significantly less intrinsic motivation than the other two groups. From this he drew two conclusions. First, rewards need to be salient in order to undermine intrinsic motivation. The "think snow" group received the same rewards as the other two reward groups, but because the rewards were not salient, due to their thinking about snow instead of the rewards, the rewards did not undermine their intrinsic motivation. The second conclusion is that the undermining of intrinsic motivation is not simply a matter of subjects' being distracted from the task, because subjects who were distracted by thoughts of snow did not evidence decreased intrinsic motivation. A study by Smith and Pittman (1978) provided further evidence that the undermining effect is not simply a function of distraction.

Expectancy. Lepper *et al.* (1973) suggested that rewards will undermine intrinsic motivation only if the subjects expect, while performing the activity, that they will receive rewards for their performance. In their study, preschoolers in one group were told before they began the activity that they would receive a reward for doing it, whereas those in a second group received rewards unexpectedly after they had completed the activity. Relative to a no-reward control group, the expected-reward group showed significant declines in intrinsic motivation, whereas the unexpected-reward group did not. This finding was replicated by Greene and Lepper (1974). Actually, this finding can be seen as a special case of the salience hypothesis. Clearly, if no reward has been mentioned, it cannot be salient, and we saw that only rewards that are salient during task engagement undermine intrinsic motivation. Of course, if people repeatedly receive unexpected rewards for an activity, they may build up an expectation of being rewarded, even in situations where no reward is specifically offered, and this could lead to an undermining of intrinsic motivation.

One study has been reported that showed decrements in expressed enjoyment following unexpected rewards (Kruglanski, Alon, & Lewis, 1972); however, there was a pecularity to the experimental induction that makes the study difficult to interpret in relation to the question of expectancy. The experimenters gave unexpected prizes to grade school children who had won some group games. At the time the prizes were awarded, the experimenter stated, "As we said before, members of the winning team will be awarded special prizes as tokens of their victory." In fact, there had been no mention of it before. The rewarded subjects reported less enjoyment than the nonrewarded subjects, and the experimenters explained this in terms of the subjects' retrospectively misattributing their performance to the reward rather than to their interest in the games. However, the decrement may, for example, have been due to anxiety created by their believing they had been lied to or to confusion caused by their thinking they had misunderstood. As a result, there is no clear basis for interpreting this study as evidence that unexpected rewards decreased intrinsic motivation.

Staw, Calder, Hess, and Sandelands (1980) suggested that whether subjects believe payment is appropriate, in other words, whether there are norms for payment, is also a relevant factor in whether rewards will undermine intrinsic motivation. To test this, they used subjects from a university course, half of whom had been told at the beginning of the semester (and had been reminded later) that students are normally paid when they participate as subjects in an experiment. The other half had been told that payment is not normally given. Then, when they participated in the puzzle-solving study, half of the subjects in each group were told that they would receive $1 for participating. The results showed that money decreased enjoyment in the norm-for-no-payment group.

The opposite was true for the norm-for-payment group; those who received pay expressed greater enjoyment. Thus, the authors concluded that rewards will undermine intrinsic interest only if people receive salient rewards for activities in situations where the norm is for no payment.

We find these results interesting but the conclusions drawn from them inappropriate. In the norm-for-payment group, subjects went into the study expecting to be paid. Those who expected pay and did not get it evidenced less satisfaction and enjoyment than those who expected pay and did get it, presumably because they were upset over not having received what they expected. The difference in the enjoyment of the two norm-for-payment groups was a result of decreased enjoyment for the no-rewards group rather than increased enjoyment for the rewards group. The norm-for-payment conditions really represent a study of the effects on satisfaction of whether or not people's expectations about payment are fulfilled. If people begin an activity with expectations of being paid, they are likely to be more extrinsically motivated for the activity than intrinsically motivated. The addition of payments is likely to further decrease their intrinsic motivation (although they may be extrinsically satisfied by the payments), whereas no payment, if payment is expected, is likely to result in anger and dissatisfaction as well as a low level of intrinsic motivation.

Constraints and Other Extrinsic Factors

In the discussion so far we have focused on the effects of a wide variety of extrinsic rewards. These rewards have been found to decrease intrinsic motivation by making the activity dependent on the extrinsic reward, thereby decreasing self-determination, and changing the perceived locus of causality from internal to external. If rewards can function to induce a shift in the perceived locus of causality, it seems reasonable to expect that external demands or constraints would have a similar, if not stronger, effect. A variety of such factors has been explored by various researchers.

Surveillance. Lepper and Greene (1975) explored the effects of surveillance on the intrinsic motivation of preschool children for solving puzzles. To do this, the experimenters placed a television camera near the children and told them they would be watched through the camera. Results revealed that the surveillance led to a significant undermining of intrinsic motivation for the puzzle-solving activity. Plant and Ryan (in press) replicated the finding with college student subjects, and Pittman, Davey, Alafat, Wetherill, and Kramer (1980) extended the finding by showing that direct surveillance by another person also decreased children's intrinsic motivation for a play activity.

Deadlines. One might expect that because surveillance can be experienced as controlling and lead to a perception of external causality, deadlines would function similarly. In one's day-to-day life, deadlines are imposed on many activities, and they seem to create a pressure that leaves one feeling like a pawn to those forces. We would expect imposed deadlines to make salient a perceived external locus of causality and to undermine intrinsic motivation. Amabile, DeJong, and Lepper (1976) did an experiment that tested this hypothesis. They had college students work on interesting word games. Half the subjects were given deadlines for the activity, though the deadlines were ones that allowed adequate time to complete the task. The other half of the subjects made up two control groups. Neither was given deadlines, but one of the groups was asked to work "as quickly as you can." The results confirmed that the deadlines significantly diminished subjects' intrinsic motivation, relative to the two control groups, as measured by a free-choice period and a questionnaire.

Evaluation. Insofar as people's work is being critically evaluated by an external agent, it is possible that people will lose a sense of self-determination and experience a shift in the perceived locus of causality. Evaluations are the basis for determining whether people are complying with external demands, so evaluations themselves are likely to connote external control and therefore to undermine intrinsic motivation. Smith (1974) did a study in which college students learned about famous works of art. Some subjects were told that their performance would be evaluated and that they would receive written feedback. All experimental subjects received positive evaluations, and subsequently they displayed less intrinsic motivation in a free-choice period than did subjects who were not evaluated. It is important to note that it was the fact of the evaluation *per se* (as none of the evaluations was negative) that undermined intrinsic motivation. Amabile (1979) also found that performance evaluation had a deleterious effect on subjects' creativity.

This further supports the general point that when some aspect of the situation begins to control the person, to redirect the person's attention away from the task, and to interfere with his or her experienced freedom to engage in the task, that aspect will decrease the person's intrinsic motivation for the task.

Goal Imposition. In a study by Mossholder (1980), the effect of goal imposition on intrinsic motivation was explored. Subjects working on interesting assembly tasks either were told to do as well as they could or were assigned a goal that was very difficult. Previous work by Locke

(1968) had indicated that difficult goals tend to lead to better performance, so the Mossholder investigation looked at performance as well as
subsequent intrinsic motivation and satisfaction. The results yielded a
replication of the Locke effect in that the difficult-goal subjects performed
better than the no-goal subjects. However, the imposition of the goal
produced a decrement in subsequent intrinsic motivation and satisfaction. These findings, then, are quite consistent with those related to
evaluations. The imposition of goals implies an external evaluation, and
any imposition of outcomes, any pressure toward achieving externally
imposed standards, seems likely to undermine intrinsic motivation.

A study by Manderlink and Harackiewicz (1984) also explored the
effects of the imposition of goals on subjects' intrinsic motivation for an
interesting activity. They employed two types of goals, proximal goals
and distal goals, and found that only the proximal goals decreased intrinsic motivation. Because these immediate goals are more intrusive and
confining than the distant goals, they would be more likely to decrease
one's sense of self-determination and make the perceived locus of causality more external.

Competition. Many play activities involve trying to win, and people,
whether players or spectators, seem to be more interested in such activities when there is an explicit competition in progress than when there
is not. For example, one can play basketball without competing, but
people seem to want to compete at basketball—they want to have a
winner and a loser. One might think, therefore, that competition would
facilitate intrinsic motivation; however, we suggest that a focus on winning *per se* is typically an extrinsic goal. It may follow from competent
and self-determined behavior, but insofar as one undertakes the activity
specifically "to win" and/or "to avoid losing," one is doing the activity
for an extrinsic reason in much the same way that one is when one
undertakes an activity "to get money" and/or "to avoid punishment."
The case of competition may seem different from the case of monetary
payments, for example, because competition can be said to be endogenous to some activities; however, careful consideration allows one to
see that even for activities where competition is inherent in the structure
of the game there can be relative differences in the extent to which the
players focus on winning rather than on playing well. Trying to beat
someone else is exogenous to playing well, even though games such as
basketball are structured to include two competing teams. The real issue
here is the extent to which the person experiences pressure to win.
People's self-esteem gets easily tied up in winning, so people feel they
have to win to feel good about themselves. It is this pressure to win,
this being controlled by whether one's outcome is better than someone
else's, that leads competition to undermine intrinsic motivation.

Deci, Betley, Kahle, Abrams, and Porac (1981) predicted that instructing subjects to try to beat someone else in doing an interesting activity would decrease their intrinsic motivation for that activity. They had college students compete against an experimental accomplice who allowed them to win the competition, and the results revealed that those subjects had less subsequent intrinsic motivation for the activity than subjects who had done the activity in the presence of the accomplice without specifically competing. This undermining of intrinsic motivation by competition was particularly strong for females.

To some, this result may seem counterintuitive; for, they might say, winning makes people want to get back out there and do it again. This is probably true; but money works that way also. If you do something for a large reward, you are likely to want to do it again for the large reward. In the same way, the winner may want to do it again to win again, rather than for the inherent satisfaction of the activity. In both cases, the activity becomes an instrument, whether for making money or for winning. In Chapter 12, where we discuss intrinsic motivation and sports, we will return to this issue and address some of the complexities involved when the competitive focus is winning versus competence.

PERCEIVED CAUSALITY: EXTERNAL TO INTERNAL

Research has substantiated that extrinsic rewards and controls can affect people's experience of self-determination. In such cases, the events will induce a shift in the perceived locus of causality from internal to external, a decrement in intrinsic motivation for the target behavior, less persistence at the activity in the absence of external contingencies, and less interest in and enjoyment of the activity.

We now consider the possibility of enhancing intrinsic motivation by allowing, rather than restricting, one's self-determination. When people are self-determining, they make choices and have the opportunity to become more fully involved with the activity itself. At such times, the perceived locus of causality is internal; people understand the activity to be something they want to do for its own sake. A greater opportunity for self-determination frees people to be more intrinsically motivated and should strengthen their perceptions of internal causality.

Zuckerman, Porac, Lathin, Smith, and Deci (1978) tested this, using the one-session, Soma puzzle paradigm. Subjects in the self-determination condition were shown six configurations and allowed to select which three of the six they would work on. They were then allowed to apportion a total of 30 minutes of puzzle-solving time among the three puzzles.

Subjects in the control condition were yoked to subjects in the self-determination condition, so they worked on the same puzzles with the same time limits. The data showed that the self-determination subjects were more intrinsically motivated than control subjects on the free-choice measure as well as on questionnaire measures. Because the control group subjects in this study worked under the same conditions as control group subjects in the various reward studies discussed earlier, it seems reasonable to conclude that the difference was due to an increase in intrinsic motivation in the self-determination condition.

Swann and Pittman (1977) found similar results with children. In their study, some children were shown three play activities and told they could select the one they wanted. The experimenter then added that as long as they were sitting in front of Activity B, why didn't they begin with it. They wanted all children to work with the same activity, but they wanted the experimental subjects to feel more like they had a choice among the activities. The researchers found that the so-called illusion-of-choice subjects were more intrinsically motivated than the subjects who were not given the illusion of choice.

In another study, Simon and McCarthy (1982) found that giving actual choice to 5-year-old children enhanced their intrinsic motivation for the target activity. Thus, from these three studies we can conclude that environmental events that provide people with the opportunity for choice and allow them to feel self-determining, promote greater intrinsic motivation and a more internal perceived locus of causality.

PERCEIVED COMPETENCE: INCREASES

Intrinsic motivation is based in people's needs to be competent and self-determining. The two needs are so closely intertwined that we frequently refer to them together, although it is theoretically useful and operationally possible to keep them separate. The research reported so far involved experimental manipulations that affect people's self-determination with a resultant change in the perceived locus of causality and in intrinsic motivation. We turn now to studies related to competence. Simply stated, we would expect a close relationship between perceived competence and intrinsic motivation such that the more competent a person perceives him- or herself to be at some activity, the more intrinsically motivated he or she will be at that activity. This predicted relationship has two necessary conditions. First, the activity must be optimally challenging. Activities that are trivial or simple and therefore provide no challenge are not expected to be intrinsically interesting even if the person perceived him- or herself to be extremely competent. And second, for perceived competence to affect intrinsic motivation, the perceived competence must exist within the context of some perceived self-determination. In other words, if a person does well or poorly at an activity, that performance will affect intrinsic motivation only insofar as the person does not experience the level of performance to be wholly constrained by the situation. Before reviewing the evidence on the relationship between perceived competence *per se* and intrinsic motivation, we will report studies relevant to the optimal-challenge postulate.

Shapira (1976) found that when college students working on puzzles were free to choose their preferred difficulty level, they selected quite challenging puzzles, unless there were contingent extrinsic rewards involved, in which case they chose easy ones so that the probability of getting the rewards was higher. Danner and Lonky (1981) found that children also selected activities that provided challenges. When free to choose among a range of activities, the children went to ones that stretched their capacities slightly. These studies, then, document that people prefer to work on challenging activities when they are free to do so. Other researchers have studied the outcomes of subjects' working on activities that either were or were not optimally challenging. Harter (1974, 1978b) found that children expressed greater pleasure when working on moderately difficult (i.e., optimally challenging) anagrams than on ones that were very easy or very difficult. McMullin and Steffen (1982) found that when subjects worked on puzzles that got slightly more difficult on each trial, they displayed more subsequent intrinsic motivation than when the difficulty level remained constant at the initial level. This accelerating difficulty seemed to keep the challenge optimal for the subjects and thus maintained their intrinsic motivation for the activity. In sum, then, for an activity to be interesting, so that positive feedback will increase subjects' intrinsic motivation for it, the activity must be optimally challenging.

Several studies have explored the relationship between perceived competence and intrinsic motivation by considering the effects of positive feedback (sometimes referred to as verbal reinforcements) on intrinsic motivation for an interesting activity. Using paradigms similar to the one described earlier in the chapter, researchers have provided positive feedback to some subjects and no feedback to others. The basic comparison is between the intrinsic motivation of subjects who received positive feedback (and therefore presumably perceived themselves to be competent) and those who did not. In these studies the experimental tasks have typically been selected so as to meet the conditions of being optimally challenging and of being responsive to people's efforts, so that they can feel a sense of self-determination with respect to the outcomes.

The first such study was done by Deci (1971). In it, he found that subjects who received positive verbal feedback from the experimenter for working on Soma puzzles were more intrinsically motivated in a subsequent free-choice period than subjects who received no feedback.

Similar results were reported by Blanck, Reis, and Jackson (1984), who used several different tasks and found the same results. In still another study with college student subjects, Russell, Studstill, and Grant (1979) found not just that positive feedback was facilitative of intrinsic motivation, but that positive feedback that was self-administered by virtue of being inherent in the task led to an even higher level of intrinsic motivation than positive feedback that was administered by the experimenter.

Fisher (1978) explored the relationship between competence and intrinsic motivation in situations where the performance outcomes were either self-determined or constrained. She reported a significant correlation between competence and intrinsic motivation when there was personal responsibility for the outcomes, but no correlation when the outcomes were constrained. Her study, therefore, confirmed the second necessary condition that we outlined previously, namely that the perceived-competence, intrinsic-motivation relationship requires the context of some self-determination. Taken together, then, the studies with college students support that positive-competence feedback tends to enhance intrinsic motivation if the outcomes are self-determined. This effect seems to be particularly strong if the positive feedback is self-administered.

Several other studies have explored the effects of positive feedback on children's intrinsic motivation. In general, their findings corroborate those with adults. Anderson et al. (1976) found that verbal statements signifying competence enhanced the intrinsic motivation of their pre-school children relative to a no-feedback control group. Martin (1977) found that praising children for doing well at a target activity led them to prefer that activity to other comparable activities for which there had been no praise. Dollinger and Thelen (1978) compared the effects of verbal rewards to those of no rewards and to those of tangible rewards. The intrinsic motivation of the early-elementary-aged children who received verbal rewards did not differ from that of the no-reward control children; however, the intrinsic motivation of the verbal-reward group was greater than that of the tangible-reward group. In other words, verbal rewards (i.e., positive feedback) left intrinsic motivation unchanged in a situation where tangible rewards undermined it.

PERCEIVED COMPETENCE: DECREASES

So far, we have considered instances in which subjects received positive-competence feedback. The results generally supported the hypothesis that positive feedback for self-determined outcomes enhances intrinsic motivation. We now turn to negative feedback and perceived incompetence.

The simplest statement of this hypothesis is that negative feedback that implies incompetence will decrease intrinsic motivation. The hypothesis has received support from two studies by Deci, Cascio, and Krusell (1973). In the first, subjects self-administered negative feedback through failing at the puzzle-solving activity, and in the second the negative feedback was verbally administered by the experimenter. For example, subjects were told, "Although you did solve that one, your time was below average." In both studies, subjects who received negative feedback were less intrinsically motivated than subjects who received no feedback.

A study by Vallerand and Reid (1984) explored the effects of both positive and negative feedback on the intrinsic motivation of college students. They reported increases following positive feedback and decreases following negative feedback. In this study they assessed subjects' perceived competence and found that it also increased following positive feedback and decreased following negative feedback. The investigators then did a path analysis on their data and found that perceived competence mediated between feedback and intrinsic motivation.

There is an important question that arises from the findings of decreased intrinsic motivation following negative feedback, however, and that is whether all negative feedback is predicted to decrease intrinsic motivation. Because there has been relatively little research exploring the effects of negative feedback on intrinsic motivation, it is difficult to answer this question empirically. Our hypothesis is that any feedback that clearly signifies incompetence to the recipient will undermine intrinsic motivation, though all negative feedback need not imply incompetence. When working on an optimally challenging activity, for example, people will often make mistakes—in other words, they will get some negative feedback—and yet they remain highly intrinsically motivated for these activities. Indeed, many people feel challenged by modest amounts of negative feedback, particularly under conditions of internal perceived locus of causality for the behavior. With an external perceived locus of causality, even small amounts of negative feedback may decrease intrinsic motivation.

In sum, negative feedback that implies incompetence, whether derived from repeated failures or from persistent negative responses, is hypothesized to undermine intrinsic motivation, whereas negative feedback that facilitates one's future competence, because, for example, it is relatively mild in the context of an internal perceived locus of causality, is hypothesized not to be deleterious to one's intrinsic motivation.

Cognitive Evaluation Theory

Cognitive evaluation theory was first proposed by Deci (1975) to integrate the early empirical findings related to the effects of external events on intrinsic motivation. As the research continued, Deci (1980) and Deci and Ryan (1980a) elaborated and refined the theory, and Ryan (1982) extended it to include initiating and regulatory events inside the person as well as those that are external.

Cognitive evaluation theory describes the effects of events that initiate or regulate behavior on motivation and motivationally relevant processes. It suggests, as we saw in the preliminary literature review, that the important considerations in the characterization of initiating or regulatory events are the implications of those events for the person's experience of self-determination and competence. The theory has previously been presented as three propositions, although a fourth proposition that extends it to intrapersonal events will be presented in the next chapter.

Proposition 1

The first proposition is related to people's intrinsic need to be self-determining. It is stated in terms of the perceived locus of causality and has guided much of the research reviewed earlier under the perceived causality headings.

> *External events relevant to the initiation or regulation of behavior will affect a person's intrinsic motivation to the extent that they influence the perceived locus of causality for that behavior. Events that promote a more external perceived locus of causality will undermine intrinsic motivation, whereas those that promote a more internal perceived locus of causality will enhance intrinsic motivation.*

The perceived locus of causality is theorized to be a cognitive construct representing the degree to which one is self-determining with respect to one's behavior. Events that lead to an external perceived locus of causality and undermine intrinsic motivation are those that deny one self-determination, whereas events that lead to an internal perceived locus of causality and enhance intrinsic motivation are those that facilitate self-determination. We often say that the former events *control behavior,* whereas that the latter events *support autonomy.*

Events that control behavior generally lead people to comply with the controls, but they can also stimulate the opposite tendency to defy. Often people respond to a control by rebelling against it, perhaps doing just the opposite of what was demanded. These controlling events are also theorized to affect a variety of motivationally relevant psychological variables. For example, controlling events are hypothesized to stifle creativity, diminish cognitive flexibility, yield a more negative emotional tone, and decrease self-esteem, relative to events that support autonomy.

Proposition II

The second proposition relates to people's intrinsic need to be competent and to master optimal challenges. Stated in terms of perceived competence, it organizes the research reported earlier on the effects of challenge and feedback.

> External events will affect a person's intrinsic motivation for an optimally challenging activity to the extent that they influence the person's perceived competence, within the context of some self-determination. Events that promote greater perceived competence will enhance intrinsic motivation, whereas those that diminish perceived competence will decrease intrinsic motivation.

One's perceived competence is typically increased when one succeeds or gets positive feedback, so long as one feels some self-determination with respect to the activity. Perceived incompetence, however, tends to occur when activities are unmasterable. For example, noncontingencies between behavior and outcomes tends to promote perceived incompetence, as does persistent negative feedback or continued failures.

Whereas increases in intrinsic motivation associated with greater perceived competence occur only when the person feels self-determined with respect to the activity, decreases in intrinsic motivation associated with diminished perceived competence can occur within the context of control so long as the person perceives him- or herself to be responsible for the failures.

Proposition III

The third proposition relates to the fact that events relevant to the initiation and regulation of behavior have three aspects that may be differentially salient to different people or to the same person at different times. These aspects are labeled the *informational*, the *controlling*, and the *amotivating* aspects; and it is the relative salience of the three aspects to a person that effects changes in perceived causality and perceived competence, and that alters the person's intrinsic motivation.

The informational aspect provides effectance-relevant feedback in the context of choice; it promotes self-determined functioning. The controlling aspect pressures people to behave, think, or feel particular ways; it promotes control-determined functioning. The amotivating aspect signifies that effectance cannot be attained; it promotes amotivated functioning.

> *Events relevant to the initiation and regulation of behavior have three potential aspects, each with a functional significance. The informational aspect facilitates an internal perceived locus of causality and perceived competence, thus enhancing intrinsic motivation. The controlling aspect facilitates an external perceived locus of causality, thus undermining intrinsic motivation and promoting extrinsic compliance or defiance. The amotivating aspect facilitates perceived incompetence, thus undermining intrinsic motivation and promoting amotivation. The relative salience of these three aspects to a person determines the functional significance of the event.*

Although this proposition is stated in terms of the functional significance of an event for an individual perceiver, thus implying that the functional significance can be different for different people, we sometimes refer to events in terms of their average functional significance across groups of people. For example, we may talk about informational events, controlling events, or amotivating events on the basis of the average effect they have had on some groups of people. Technically, of course, an event can be properly labeled only with respect to its effect on an individual at a given time.

From the research reviewed thus far, we can conclude that choice (Zuckerman et al., 1978) and positive feedback (Deci, 1971) tend to be informational (i.e., on average the informational aspect is most salient); rewards (Deci, 1972b), deadlines (Amabile et al., 1976), and surveillance (Lepper & Greene, 1975) tend to be controlling (i.e., on average the controlling aspect is most salient); and negative feedback tends to be amotivating (i.e., on average the amotivating aspect is most salient).

Evolution of the Theory

Cognitive evaluation theory has changed in several ways from its earliest formulation (Deci, 1975). First, because research has led to a clarification of the relationship between self-determination and competence, this has been reflected in the theory. The first proposition now describes increases and decreases in intrinsic motivation related to the need for self-determination, and the second proposition describes increases and decreases related to the need for competence. This latter proposition now specifies the relationship of self-determination to the perceived-competence process. Second, the theory is stated as a more clearly motivational rather than cognitive theory; perceived causality and perceived competence are seen as concomitants, rather than causes, of the motivational changes. Third, the theory has been expanded to describe what happens when intrinsic motivation is undermined; people comply, defy, or become amotivated. Fourth, the theory refers to a variety of motivationally relevant psychological processes that accompany motivational changes. Finally, the theory has been expanded to include intrapersonal processes, though the proposition describing that extension will not appear until Chapter 4.

Cognitive Evaluation: Pre- and Postperformance. The 1975 version of cognitive evaluation theory stated that changes in the perceived locus of causality or changes in feelings of competence and self-determination produced changes in intrinsic motivation. This has often been interpreted to mean that all motivational changes result from evaluation that occurs subsequent to task engagement. We believe, however, that the changes in perceived causality or perceived competence are concomitant with, rather than causes of, the changes in motivation, and that the motivational changes can occur during or even prior to task engagement. We suggest that information from the person's internal states and from the environment are perceived and processed, either through what Arnold (1960) has called *intuitive appraisal:* an immediate, intuitive, precognitive processing; or *reflective judgment:* a more deliberate, thoughtful processing. The evaluative activity may be either conscious or nonconscious, and it is through this intuitive or reflective *cognitive evaluation*, which can occur prior to, during, or subsequent to task engagement, that an initiating event is experienced as informational, controlling, or amotivating. A study by Vallerand (1981) has demonstrated changes in intrinsic motivation following intuitive and reflective processing of information about competence.

Motivationally Relevant Processes

In discussions of cognitive evaluation theory by Deci (1980) and Deci and Ryan (1980a), we employed a concept called *motivational subsystems*, which was introduced to address the complex of cognitive, affective, and behavioral variables that are organized by motivational processes. For example, we suggested that the intrinsic motivational subsystem included an internal perceived locus of causality, perceived competence, flexibility in cognitive processing, a fuller experience of organismic needs and feelings, and so on. We do *not* use the term motivational subsystem any longer because the language tends to imply a mechanism or program that gets passively initiated by a stimulus, and thus would be contradictory to our active-organism, metatheoretical perspective. More recently, we have simply referred to intrinsically motivated processes, extrinsically motivated processes, and amotivational processes, rather than intrinsic, extrinsic, and amotivational subsystems, to reflect the organized nature of the complex of affective, cognitive, and behavioral variables. The coherence of these motivationally relevant processes remains an important emphasis for us, even though we do not use the term motivational subsystems.

The teleology of intrinsic motivation involves doing an activity for its own sake, that is, for its inherent interest and the spontaneous affects and cognitions that accompany it. As Csikszentmihalyi (1975) put it, intrinsically motivated behavior is autotelic. The teleology of extrinsic motivation involves doing an activity in order to attain an extrinsic reward or to comply with a demand. The shift from an intrinsic toward an extrinsic teleology is accompanied by a change in perceived locus of causality from internal to external and by a variety of other changes that have been explored in several recent investigations. We will now review these investigations. The basic idea is that the addition of a controlling event, such as a reward or a constraint, initiates extrinsic rather than intrinsic motivational processes, and dependent variables other than just free-choice behavior and interest/enjoyment are affected by the shift from an intrinsic to an extrinsic motivational organization.

Creativity, Recall, and Complexity. Amabile (1983) proposed what she called the *intrinsic motivation hypothesis* of creativity. In several studies she found support for the notions that people are more creative when they are intrinsically motivated, and that creativity is affected by variables similar to those that affect free-choice behavior and interest, particularly those related to the perceived locus of causality (Ryan, 1984). Controlling events seem to impair creativity, much as they do intrinsic motivation. In one study (Amabile, 1979), female college students worked on art projects; some of them worked with the expectation of being evaluated and some did not. The work of those who expected to be evaluated was subsequently judged to be less creative than the work of those who did not expect to be evaluated. In another study (Amabile, 1982a), competition was found to undermine creativity, as were extrinsic rewards (Hennessey, 1982). Koestner *et al.* (1984) did a study in which intrinsic motivation for an art activity and the creativity of artistic productions were used as dependent variables. They found that setting controlling limits on children's neatness with the art materials undermined both their intrinsic motivation and creativity, whereas informational limits did not. There was a significant correlation between intrinsic motivation, as assessed with the free-choice measure, and creativity, thereby supporting Amabile's (1983) hypothesis that intrinsic motivation underlies creativity. Koestner *et al.* also found evidence of more constriction and less spontaneity under controlling than under informational conditions.

Kruglanski, Friedman, and Zeevi (1971) found that when Israeli high school students were offered the valued reward of a tour through a university laboratory for working on a set of tasks, the students were less creative and exhibited poorer recall on these tasks, and they reported less enjoyment of the tasks than did students who were not promised the reward.

Pittman, Emery, and Boggiano (1982) reported a study in which preference for complexity was the dependent measure. They predicted and found that when subjects were rewarded for working on a moderately challenging activity, the reward induced a shift to extrinsic motivational processes and resulted in subjects' preferring easy tasks. A study by Kruglanski, Stein, and Riter (1977) yielded similar results. They found that when subjects were rewarded, they did what they had to do to get the reward, but they did nothing more. In other words, when extrinsically motivated, people tend to do the minimum amount of work that will yield the maximum reward.

Emotional Tone and Self-Esteem. In a study by Garbarino (1975), sixth-grade girls served as tutors for first-grade girls. Half the tutors were rewarded for their tutoring with movie tickets and half were not. Garbarino reported that the rewarded tutors were more demanding and more negative in their emotional tone than the nonrewarded tutors, and in turn that the students of the rewarded tutors learned less well and made more errors.

Here we see that extrinsic motivational processes, which have consistently been shown to be associated with less persistence during a free-choice period and with less interest and enjoyment, also tend to involve a more critical attitude and a more negative emotional tone than intrinsic motivational processes. Research by Ryan (1982) and Ryan, Mims, and Koestner (1983) has indicated that a central aspect of the negative emotional tone resulting from controlling extrinsic conditions is pressure and tension. Extrinsic rewards tend to be experienced as controlling, and people seem to feel pressure and tension when they are controlled.

A study by Deci, Nezlek, and Sheinman (1981) in public school classrooms revealed that the children of teachers who were oriented toward supporting autonomy had higher self-esteem and more intrinsic motivation than the children of teachers who were oriented toward controlling behavior. Apparently, controlling conditions that facilitate extrinsic responding not only have a short-term influence on one's emotional experience, they also appear to have a more lasting effect, as evidenced by the lowered self-esteem of the school children. Related findings were obtained by Ryan and Grolnick (1984), who found a significant relationship between children's experience of autonomy versus control in the classroom and their self-esteem.

Cognitive Flexibility. Two studies by McGraw and his associates have shown that monetary rewards to college students interfere with their flexible cognitive processing. In the first, McGraw and McCullers (1979) had college student subjects work with a type of problem activity originally used by Luchins (1942). In these problems subjects are given a set of jars holding different amounts of water. Their task is to isolate a specific amount of water in one of the jars by pouring water from jar to jar. For example, suppose Jar A can hold 4 ounces, Jar B can hold 15 ounces, and Jar C can hold 3 ounces. If one begins with Jar B full and Jars A and C empty and the problem is to end up with 5 ounces in Jar B, the solution would be (B-A-2C). In the study, subjects were given 9 consecutive problems all of which had the same solution. The 10th problem had a different, though simpler solution, and the question was how long it would take subjects to break set and find the simpler solution. Half of the subjects in the study were paid and half were not. The results revealed that those subjects who were paid had more difficulty breaking set than those who were not paid.

In a second study (McGraw and Fiala, 1982) subjects worked on a jigsaw puzzle and were interrupted during the activity. Much previous work by Zeigarnik (1927) and others has shown that subjects tend to return to uncompleted tasks. In this study, half of McGraw and Fiala's subjects expected a monetary reward for working on the puzzle and half did not. The researchers found that those subjects who expected a reward were less likely to return to the uncompleted task than those subjects who did not. This led the authors to conclude that rewarding the performance of a task can lead to premature cognitive disengagement with the task, so one will not observe the same cognitive processes that are evident with a fuller, intrinsically motivated engagement.

Grolnick and Ryan (1985) did a study that extended this conclusion to conceptual learning. Their experiment, which will be presented in more detail in Chapter 9, showed that children's conceptual learning was poorer under extrinsic conditions than under intrinsic conditions. Conceptual learning seems to require the cognitive flexibility that has been shown to be associated with intrinsic motivation.

Undermining Attitudes. When intrinsically motivated, people tend to perceive the locus of causality for their behavior to be internal, and they are guided more by their internal states. When extrinsically motivated, however, they tend to perceive the locus of causality to be external, and their behavior is more a function of external controls. This, as we have seen, has ramifications for their internal states. Benware and Deci (1975) applied this analysis to attitude change, as illustrated in the following example. Suppose a man attempts to persuade his neighbor to support a referendum blocking the construction of an expressway through a nearby game preserve. If he did it because he believed strongly in wildlife conservation, the perceived locus of causality would be internal. However, if he had a neutral attitude but was hired by the Conservation Society to campaign for the referendum, the perceived locus of causality for the behavior would be external. In the former case, the perceived cause for the persuasion was his own attitude; in the latter case, it was the money from the Society.

Now suppose he was a believer and also was hired to espouse his belief. This is analogous to being paid for doing an intrinsically motivated activity. The question is, What would happen to his attitude if he were paid to espouse it? The addition of payment could lead to the experience of the persuasive behavior's being extrinsically motivated, and thus instrumental for getting the reward rather than being the expression of one's own beliefs. It seems plausible that with this shift in the perceived locus of causality from internal to external, the person would become less favorable toward the espoused position, because he would not need to hold to the attitude to justify the behavior and because people are often paid as a way of getting them to do things they do not believe in.

In the Benware and Deci (1975) study, two groups of subjects were asked to argue in favor of a position that they believed in. Their initial attitudes had been assessed as part of a battery of placement tests that they had taken three months prior to the experiment. During the experiment each subject argued in favor of students' having inputs to college course offerings. They argued the position five times, speaking into an intercom system and believing they were presenting the argument to five different listeners. Half the subjects were paid $1.50 for each presentation, thus earning $7.50, whereas the other half received no pay. Results showed a significant change in attitudes away from the espoused position for the paid subjects relative to the unpaid subjects.

In another study, Kiesler and Sakamura (1966) also explored the effects of monetary rewards in pro-attitudinal advocacy. They found that payments for espousing a belief-consonant position made subjects' beliefs more vulnerable to change during a subsequent period when they read an argument that was counter to their beliefs. In sum, it appears that when the expression of an attitude becomes instrumental to reward attainment, one's committment to the attitude is weakened.

Defiance: Reactance. As we said, people respond to controlling events either by complying with what is demanded of them or by rebelling against the demand. The tendency to defy has also been explained by reactance theory (Brehm, 1966), which states that if some event removes or threatens to remove a behavioral option that is important and was believed to be available, the person will experience reactance against this loss of freedom and will be motivated to restore the freedom (Brehm & Brehm, 1981). People may attempt to restore the freedom in a variety of ways: they may inflate the value of the forbidden option and work hard to attain it; they may refuse to do what they are being forced to do; or they may do what they are forced to do but sabbotage it in some other way. Research by Brehm and Sensenig (1966) and others has demonstrated these phenomena experimentally.

We suggest that the research reported earlier on the effects of rewards implies that rewards, which typically are thought of very positively, can actually limit people's freedom. They do not necessarily remove a specific behavioral option, which Brehm said was necessary to initiate reactance, but they do limit people's freedom by tending to make them dependent on the rewards. They control through seduction rather than force, and although people tend to comply with the demands, there is the complementary tendency to defy, to refuse to be controlled, and to do the opposite of the prescribed behavior.

Our position differs from Brehm and Brehm's (1981) in that we assert that most reactance behaviors do not actually restore freedom. When a person distorts cognitions, rebels against an authority who offers a reward, or does the opposite of what is demanded just because it is demanded, the person is still being controlled. Those responses may reduce discomfort, but they do not restore freedom, for freedom can come only through choice, not through automatic defiance. According to reactance theory, the loss of freedom sets up a motive to restore freedom. We suggest that the response that is thus motivated may or may not restore freedom. If the person chooses behaviors that return lost options or that yield the most desired outcomes under the circumstances, the person will be self-determined. But insofar as the response is distortion and defiance, it is control-determined rather than self-determined. Automatic distortion and defiance represent the complementary tendency to compliance in situations of being controlled.

Ryan (1982) observed compliance and reactance in response to controlling feedback. In that study, subjects worked on interesting hidden-figure puzzles; half of them were given controlling feedback—that is, feedback that pressured them by emphasizing how well they should be doing—and half were given noncontrolling feedback. Later, subjects were asked how much effort they had expended. The results revealed that those subjects who were controlled rated themselves as expending significantly less effort than those subjects who were not. Further, their performance tended to be worse. It may be that those subjects who had been controlled with the evaluative feedback superficially complied by doing what was asked, but they also reacted against the controls by putting in less effort and doing more poorly than the subjects who got informational feedback.

Let us recapitulate. Reactance, according to Brehm (1966), is a phenomenon that occurs when a specific behavioral option that the person believes to be available is threatened. We have presented a somewhat broader interpretation, suggesting that reactance may occur following any limitation of one's freedom, including that which results from being extrinsically rewarded. If it does, the person may become defiant and rebel against the demand, thus displaying control-determined behavior.

External, controlling events vary in the degree to which they pressure people to respond, thereby threatening their freedom. Controlling events that are less forceful, we hypothesize, will tend to seduce people into compliance, whereas those that are more forceful will tend to produce reactive defiance. We do not know of any test of the hypothesis, though such a test does seem warranted.

Amotivation: Helplessness. According to cognitive evaluation theory, when environments allow neither self-determination nor competence for a given behavior, people will become amotivated with respect to that behavior. This may be accompanied by such affective and cognitive states as listlessness, helplessness, depression, and self-disparagement. As we said earlier, a situation will be amotivating when it is interpreted as unmasterable, that is, when one perceives oneself to be incompetent to attain one's desired outcomes. This would typically occur when one receives persistently negative feedback about one's performance, when one repeatedly fails, or when one believes that outcomes are noncontigently delivered.

Seligman and his colleagues (Garber & Seligman, 1980; Seligman, 1975) have done a great deal of work on noncontingency as the cause of learned helplessness. As originally stated (Seligman, 1975), the helplessness hypothesis asserted that situations of response-outcome independence, in other words, situations where outcomes are not contingent on the organism's behavior, will produce the state called helplessness. Later Abramson, Garber, & Seligman (1980) reformulated the hypothesis to include two types of helplessness, personal and universal, and to explain when helplessness will generalize across time and situations. Personal helplessness results from the expectation that one cannot achieve a desired outcome but that relevant others can, whereas universal helplessness results from the expectation that neither oneself nor the relevant others can achieve the outcome. In the expanded version of the theory, uncontrollability of outcomes does not necessarily lead to amotivation and self-disparagement; there are a variety of ways that one can understand or rationalize an incident, particularly if the noncontingency is unstable (i.e., not likely to occur again) or specific (e.g., related to a very narrow set of circumstances).

The newer statement of helplessness theory describes the conditions where a noncontingency is likely to plunge a person into amotivation and those where the person will be able to resist feeling helpless. Non-contingent environments, like other amotivating events, stimulate the tendency toward amotivation and the experiences of helplessness and self-disparagement. Under various conditions, however, such as those where the person learns how to regain control, or where the person can rationalize the event, amotivation and helplessness can be forestalled and the person will remain motivated as before.

Reactance and helplessness have both been hypothesized to result from a person's perceiving that he or she does not have control in a situation. Two different formulations have outlined the conditions within which not having control will lead to reactance versus helplessness (Roth, 1980; Wortman & Brehm, 1975). In essence, these formulations suggest that a person will be reactive and strive to regain control when that seems to be possible (for example, following only a brief experience of noncontingency), but that the person will plunge into helplessness when his or her attempts to regain control seem fruitless. The main point of these formulations, like that of the revised helplessness theory, is that amotivation and helplessness result from lack of perceived control only when one believes that all one's attempts to regain control, whether through actions or cognitive distortions, will fail. In short, amotivation results when one perceives oneself to be incompetent to achieve intended outcomes.

REWARD ADMINISTRATION AND TYPES OF TASKS

Throughout the chapter we have spoken of rewards without addressing the procedures through which they were administered, and we have reported research only on activities that were initially intrins-ically interesting. There have been several studies that have addressed the type of reward administration and also the type of task. We will now review these two groups of studies.

Reward Contingencies

Rewards can be delivered on the basis of varying criteria. For instance, people can be rewarded for occupying particular roles quite independ-ently of what they do in those roles; they can be rewarded for completing a task; they can be rewarded in a way that ties rewards to the effectiveness of their performance; or they can be rewarded for performing better than someone else. This aspect of reward structures has been explored using the concept of reward contingency. The reward contingency literature had become quite confusing until Ryan *et al.* (1983) provided a taxonomy that allowed for a consistent interpretation of the findings.

The issue of contingency first appeared in a study by Deci (1972a) in which the effects of contingent rewards ($1 paid for each puzzle that a subject solved), noncontingent rewards ($2 paid for participating in the experiment), and no rewards were compared. He reported that contingent rewards decreased intrinsic motivation relative to noncontingent rewards and no rewards. Subsequently, several other investigators explored the contingency issue, and in 1977, Condry reported that the results were inconclusive. Since that time, still other studies have been done and the results appear at first glance to be even more disparate, although with the Ryan *et al.* (1983) taxonomy, the results can be seen to be quite consistent. We will begin by presenting their standardized terminology.

First, the term *task-noncontingent rewards* is used to mean that rewards are given to people for participating in an experimental session, independent of what they do in that session. They are paid simply for their presence, so the rewards are not contingent on doing the task. In many previous writings (e.g., Deci, 1972a; Pinder, 1976) this type of reward structure was referred to simply as noncontingent. Ryan *et al.* introduced the term task-noncontingent to avoid confusing this reward structure with the type of noncontingency that leads to amotivation and helplessness. Task-noncontingent rewards are essentially comparable to the real world circumstance in which people are paid for being on the job, rather than for particular behaviors or levels of performance.

Second, the term *task-contingent rewards* is used to mean that a reward is given for actually *doing* (i.e., completing) the task. In experiments with children (e.g., Lepper *et al.*, 1973) the reward has typically been offered for doing an activity, such as painting a picture or beating a drum. These are activities that all children are able to complete, and all the children received the same reward. In experiments with adults, the reward has more often been offered specifically for completing the task, so the level of the reward varied somewhat from one subject to another. For example, in the Deci (1971) study, subjects were offered $1 for each puzzle they completed, and different subjects completed different numbers of puzzles. The task-contingent payments system is roughly comparable to the piece-rate system in the real world and is what Deci (1972a) originally referred to as contingent rewards.

Third, the term *performance-contingent rewards* is used to mean that a reward is given for a specified level of effective performance. The focus here is on the quality of one's performance relative to some type of normative information or standard, so the rewards convey competence information. There is no common real-world pay structure that is clearly analogous to these rewards, although certain types of bonus or incentive systems would be considered performance-contingent. Of course, task-contingent rewards can also convey competence information; for example, when rewards are administered for each unit of production, more rewards mean that one is performing better. However, without specific reference to the quality of performance or to normative levels of performance, they would not be considered performance-contingent. If a person were offered $1 for each task completed, it would be a task-contingent reward; if he or she were offered $1 for each task that was completed faster than 70% of the people who had done it, it would be performance-contingent.

Finally, some studies have used the term contingency to refer to zero-sum situations in which two or more people compete for a reward. Winning, and thus receiving the reward, demonstrates competence and therefore represents a kind of performance contingency; however, the competition introduces additional considerations that make the situation somewhat different. We use the term *competitively contingent rewards* to refer to situations where people compete directly with others for a limited number of rewards that are fewer than the number of competitors.

With the taxonomy, we will now review the literature on the effects of various reward contingencies on intrinsic motivation for initially interesting tasks, in other words, for tasks that are optimally challenging, responsive to one's initiations, have some feedback built into them, and are not typically done for extrinsic rewards. Some of the studies on tangible rewards have used males, some females, and some both sexes. There is no evidence of an interaction between any reward administration and sex. Similarly, different studies have employed different-aged subjects, ranging from preschool children to adults, and there is no indication of an age-by-administration interaction. Consequently, neither sex nor age will be treated as an independent variable in this review.

Task-Noncontingent Rewards. Three studies have examined the effects of task-noncontingent rewards on intrinsic motivation, and none has shown a detrimental effect. Deci (1972a) offered college student subjects $2 for participating in a puzzle solving experiment and found that their intrinsic motivation following the puzzle solving did not differ from that of nonrewarded subjects. Pinder (1976) replicated the finding with college students, and Swann and Pittman (1977) reported similar results with children for whom the effects of task-noncontingent, good-player awards were compared to the effects of no rewards. Task-noncontingent rewards appear not to decrease intrinsic motivation because they do not create an instrumentality and are not experienced as controlling. In studies by Ross et al. (1976) and Okano (1981) subjects were rewarded for waiting before beginning a task. In neither study did the rewards decrease intrinsic motivation. This could be expected because the rewards are functionally equivalent to task-noncontingent rewards: in both types of administration the reward is extraneous to doing the task and therefore has no effect on subjects' intrinsic motivation for the task.

In two other studies, researchers reported having compared non-contingent rewards to no rewards (Calder & Staw, 1975b; Weiner & Mander, 1978), although, according to our definitions both reward administrations were actually task-contingent. Calder and Staw offered a reward to subjects for participating in the experiment; however it was placed on the table at the end of a set of puzzle pieces and subjects were told, "When you finish you can have that dollar over there." This statement made the reward task-contingent because it explicitly stated that the subjects needed to finish the task to get the reward. In the Weiner and Mander study, the so-called noncontingent reward was offered for "continued involvement in the task," which is really the meaning of task contingency.

Task-Contingent Rewards. In several studies the effects of task-contingent rewards (those given for actually doing or completing the activity) have been compared with no rewards or with task-noncontingent rewards. Task-contingent rewards are generally administered in the absence of additional effectance-relevant feedback from the experimenter because such information is not inherent or necessary in this reward structure. The studies on task contingency reported here involve no explicit feedback unless otherwise noted.

Deci (1971, 1972b) reported that task-contingent monetary rewards, given for completing puzzles, decreased subjects' intrinsic motivation for the puzzles, relative to no rewards. Similar results were reported by Weiner and Mander (1978), who actually used both kinds of task-contingent rewards—those given for doing a task and those given for completing the task—and found that both decreased intrinsic motivation, though the undermining by rewards that required completing the task was more extreme than the undermining by rewards that merely required working on the task. Pittman, Cooper, and Smith (1977) and Smith and Pittman (1978) also found that task-contingent monetary rewards decreased subjects' intrinsic motivation for game activities. In those studies, as in the Deci (1971, 1972b) studies, subjects' rewards depended to some extent on their performance; however the rewards were classified as task-contingent rather than performance-contingent because the rewards were not contingent on how well subjects performed relative to some type of standard for performance, such as normative information. Better performance led to greater rewards, but subjects had no way of knowing how well they were actually performing. Daniel and Esser (1980) reported similar results when rewards were offered in a way that implied more rewards for better performance. Finally, Calder and Staw (1975b) and Luyten and Lens (1981) reported that task-contingent rewards, offered for "completing" puzzles, decreased subjects' intrinsic motivation.

Numerous researchers have reported that offering task-contingent rewards merely for doing an activity decreased subjects' intrinsic motivation relative to no rewards. These findings have resulted from offering money to college students (Wilson, Hull, & Johnson, 1981); prizes to high school students (Harackiewicz, 1979); candy to elementary school children (Ross, Karniol, & Rothstein, 1976); and good-player awards to preschool children (Greene & Lepper, 1974; Lepper *et al.*, 1973). Danner and Lonky (1981), Dollinger and Thelen (1978), Fazio (1981), Loveland and Olley (1979), McLoyd (1979), Morgan (1981), and Ross (1975) have all provided further support for the hypothesis that task-contingent rewards, offered to children for working on an intrinsically interesting activity, decrease the children's intrinsic motivation for the activity. Ross (1975) demonstrated that the rewards have to be salient to have this effect; McLoyd (1979) showed that the rewards have to be desirable to the children to have the effect; Danner and Lonky (1981) found that the task has to be optimally challenging (i.e., intrinsically interesting) for the rewards to undermine intrinsic motivation; and Fazio (1981) showed that the undermining effect can be forestalled by reminding the children that they were initially interested in the target activity. Loveland and Olley (1979) observed the undermining effect 1 week after the children were rewarded with a good-player award, although the effect had worn off by 7 weeks.

The evidence makes it clear that task-contingent rewards, whether given for working on or completing an activity, decrease intrinsic motivation relative to no rewards, if the task-contingent rewards are administered without additional explicit performance feedback. In a study by Deci (1972b), task-contingent rewards were combined with verbal feedback and compared to a condition of no feedback and no rewards. Whereas task-contingent rewards alone decreased intrinsic motivation relative to no rewards, the addition of positive-competence feedback averted this effect, such that there was no significant difference between the no-reward/no-feedback group and the task-contingent reward/verbal feedback group. Harackiewicz (1979) and Swann and Pittman (1977) also compared task-contingent rewards plus positive feedback to no rewards and no feedback. Both studies found that the two groups did not differ. Thus, these studies indicate that the effects of task-contingent rewards and positive feedback may offset each other.

Direct comparisons of the effects of task-contingent rewards and task-noncontingent rewards (rather than the separate comparison of each to no rewards) have yielded less clear results, although there is some support for the hypothesis that task-contingent rewards are more detrimental than task-noncontingent rewards. Deci (1972a) reported a clearly significant difference between groups given the two kinds of rewards, and Phillips and Lord (1980) found this effect on a self-report measure though not on a behavioral measure. Pinder (1976) found marginal support for the hypothesis that task-contingent rewards are more detrimental than task non-contingent rewards. Farr, Vance, and McIntyre (1977) reported results that tended to support the hypothesis (although they interpreted their data as being largely nonconfirmatory), and Farr (1976) reported no difference between task-contingent and task-noncontingent groups.

The explanation for why task-contingent rewards are more detrimental to intrinsic motivation than task-noncontingent rewards is based in the degree of control conveyed by the two types of rewards. If someone must complete a task to get a reward, the task is more likely to be seen as instrumental to the reward. The task is something one must do to get the reward, so the reward is more controlling than a task-noncontingent reward, which one gets independent of whether one finishes the task. However, the fact of the reward's being given for completion of a task could provide some competence feedback, but with most tasks, completion *per se* (without normative information) provides minimal effectance-relevant feedback. Although a task-contingent reward could in some instances be relatively informational, in most instances it is relatively controlling, so intrinsic motivation tends to be undermined to a somewhat greater degree than with task-noncontingent rewards.

Performance-Contingent Rewards. Performance-contingency goes one step further than task-contingency in making potentially more salient the informational and the controlling aspects of the reward. By requiring a specific level of performance, the reward is more controlling, but it could also increase the informational value of the reward considerably. In considering the effects of performance-contingent rewards we begin by comparing performance-contingent rewards to no rewards. One important issue to keep in mind is that performance-contingent rewards, by definition, provide competence feedback that is generally quite positive. This necessitates distinguishing between no-reward comparison groups for which there is comparable feedback and those for which there is not comparable feedback. First, we consider no-reward groups with positive feedback.

Karniol and Ross (1977) did a study with 4- to 9-year-old children who received either performance-contingent rewards or received no rewards but got positive feedback. Their results showed no difference between the performance-contingent rewards group (that received implicit, positive-competence feedback) and the no-reward/positive-feedback control group. Rosenfield, Folger, and Adelman (1980) compared what they called a contingent-reward/positive-competence feedback group (in essence, a performance-contingency group) with a no-reward/positive-competence feedback group. There was no difference between the two groups in terms of subsequent intrinsic motivation, although in their study the competence feedback was based on performance during a practice period rather than during the actual puzzle solving period, so it is difficult to apply their results to the question under consideration. Finally, both Harackiewicz (1979) and Ryan et al. (1983) demonstrated convincingly that subjects who received performance-contingent rewards displayed less intrinsic motivation than those who received no rewards but got positive feedback comparable to that conveyed by the performance-contingent rewards. It appears, then, although the results are somewhat mixed, that performance-contingent rewards do undermine intrinsic motivation relative to situations without rewards but with the same degree of positive feedback as that inherent in the reward administration. Apparently, the performance contingency per se is often experienced as controlling.

The relationship between a performance-contingent reward condition and a no-reward condition without positive feedback is more complex. Both Harackiewicz (1979) and Ryan et al. (1983) investigated this. In both studies there were two types of performance-contingent administrations: one that highlighted the informational aspect of the reward and one that highlighted the controlling aspect. This suggests that the interpersonal context within which the performance-contingency is administered can make the reward informational or controlling. As we indicated previously, performance contingency has the potential for making either aspect salient, and it seems that the interpersonal style of administering the performance contingency is an important determinant of whether it will be informational or controlling. In both studies performance-contingent rewards that were informational (i.e., conveying choice and freedom) enhanced intrinsic motivation relative to those that were controlling (i.e., pressuring people and thus denying freedom). Further, in both studies the intrinsic motivation of the no-reward, no-feedback control group was midway between that of the two types of performance-contingent reward groups. Thus, performance-contingent rewards can either enhance or diminish intrinsic motivation relative to no rewards without positive feedback, depending on whether they are informationally or controllingly communicated. However, both types of performance-contingent rewards undermine intrinsic motivation relative to no-reward situations that do provide positive feedback comparable to that conveyed by the performance-contingent reward.

Performance-Contingent versus Task-Contingent Rewards. As with no rewards, task-contingent rewards can be delivered either with or without accompanying competence feedback. First, consider a comparison of performance-contingent rewards to task-contingent rewards with comparable feedback. From cognitive evaluation theory, one would predict that if the feedback accompanying the two groups is comparable (so that the information is the same), then performance-contingent rewards are likely to be more undermining than task-contingent rewards because, as we said, the performance contingency highlights the controlling nature of the rewards by making good performance on the task directly instrumental for attaining the reward. There is only one study that included both of these groups. Harackiewicz's (1979) results showed that controllingly administered performance-contingent rewards decreased intrinsic motivation relative to task-contingent rewards with positive feedback, although informationally administered performance-contingent rewards did not differ significantly from task-contingent rewards with positive feedback.

The more complex comparison is between performance-contingent rewards and task-contingent rewards that are administered without positive feedback. Because the performance contingency can increase the controlling aspect of the reward but can also convey positive feedback, it has counteracting effects relative to a task contingency. Luyten and Lens (1981) reported a nonsignificant tendency for performance-contingent rewards to lead to higher intrinsic motivation than task-contingent rewards without feedback, and Boggiano and Ruble (1979) found that performance-contingent rewards led to significantly greater intrinsic motivation in children than task-contingent rewards without feedback. Enzle and Ross (1978) found the same significant results for college students. In the Enzle and Ross article, the authors used atypical terminology, which is important to recognize in interpreting their results. They referred to the group that we call performance-contingent as *criterion-contingent* because their rewards depended on a specified performance criterion, and they referred to the group that we call task-contingent, interchangeably as *task-contingent, task-performance-contingent,* and *performance-contingent.* Thus, for example, in their table of results, the group they labeled criterion-contingent is the group that we call performance-contingent and the group they labeled performance-contingent is the group that we call task-contingent. Nonetheless, the results show clearly that, using our terminology, the performance-contingent group was more intrinsically interested than the task-contingent group that did not get feedback.

Harackiewicz (1979) and Ryan *et al.* (1983) both included a task-contingent group with no feedback and two performance-contingent reward groups. As we said, both studies included an informationally administered performance-contingent group and a controllingly administered performance-contingent group, although as Ryan *et al.* (1983) pointed out, Harackiewicz used terminology that was different from ours. In that report she used the term *informational reward* to refer to what herein would be labeled a controllingly administered performance-contingent reward. When the terminology is standardized, both studies reported the same results. Performance-contingent rewards that were informationally administered (i.e., administered in the absence of undue pressure) enhanced intrinsic motivation relative to task-contingent rewards without feedback, whereas the intrinsic motivation of the controllingly administered performance-contingent rewards group did not differ from that of the task-contingent group. The positive feedback inherent in the performance-contingent reward was offset by the clearly controlling nature of the administration.

Competitively Contingent Rewards. Finally, we turn to a review of the effects of competitively administered rewards. Pritchard *et al.* (1977) reported that when a $5 reward was made contingent on doing better than the other people in one's group (of about six people) the rewards decreased intrinsic motivation relative to no rewards. This type of contingency is competitive. Only one person could win the reward, so the other people in the group had to lose. The competitive contingency is highly controlling, because winning (rather than just doing well) is instrumental to attaining the reward. In fact Deci, Betley *et al.* (1981) reported that this type of direct, face-to-face competition decreased subjects' intrinsic motivation even when there were no rewards involved.

Greene and Lepper (1974) did a study in which one group of children received task-contingent rewards and another group received what we interpret as competitively contingent rewards. These latter children were told that only a very few of the children in their class, those who drew the very best pictures, would get a good-player award. The intrinsic motivation of these two groups did not differ.

Thus, although Greene and Lepper did not refer to the one type of reward as competitively contingent, the results indicated that there was no difference between competitively contingent and task-contingent rewards, whereas other studies had shown that performance-contingent rewards lead to more intrinsic motivation than task-contingent rewards (e.g., Boggiano & Ruble, 1979). The additional control induced by the competition offset the effects of the positive feedback that was inherent in doing well.

In summation, any reward administration that carries positive-performance feedback tends to enhance intrinsic motivation because of the feedback. However, all contingent rewards, themselves, apart from the inherent feedback, tend to decrease intrinsic motivation. Competitively contingent rewards are the most controlling, performance-contingent less so, and task-contingent even less than performance-contingent. The complexity of the results has to do with the counter-acting effects of positive feedback and of the control inherent in rewards. Therefore, precision about exactly what groups are being compared is very critical. The results of the various reward effects are summarized in Table 2.

The Nature of the Task

By and large, the studies that have investigated the effects of rewards and controls on intrinsic motivation have employed initially interesting puzzle or play activities. These studies have enumerated conditions under which external factors either increase or decrease subjects' intrinsic motivation for an initially interesting activity. A few studies have used the type of task as an independent variable to assess the generalizability of the phenomena across activities.

Arnold (1976) suggested that although several studies that used interesting activities found decrements in intrinsic motivation following the introduction and subsequent removal of rewards, this phenomenon ought not occur if the activities are extremely interesting. To test this, he recruited people to participate in a game; no mention was made of its being an experiment. The task was a highly interesting computer game, for which subjects either were not paid or were paid $2. The results confirmed that on the various dependent measures, intrinsic motivation was either unchanged or enhanced by the payments. However, in interpreting these results there are several points that need to be made. First, the rewards were task-noncontingent; subjects simply received $2 regardless of what they did. Second, the first mention of money occurred just before performance began, after a 10-minute video-taped introduction and a brief question-and-answer period. Thus, subjects had been fully oriented toward the game without any mention of money, so the rewards were nearly comparable to unexpected rewards. The rewards, therefore, were essentially task-noncontingent and unexpected, both characteristics being ones that lessen the likelihood of the

TABLE 2.   A Summary of the Results of Representative Studies That Have Explored the Comparative Effects of Various Types of Reward Contingencies on Intrinsic Motivation. (See *Note* below.)

	No reward (no feedback)	No reward (positive feedback)	Task-contingent (no feedback)	Task-contingent (positive feedback)	Performance-contingent (informational)
Task-noncontingent (no feedback)	Did not differ (Deci, 1972b)		Increased (Deci, 1972b)		
Task-contingent (no feedback)	Decreased (Deci, 1971)				
Task-contingent (positive feedback)	Did not differ (Deci, 1972a)	Decreased (Harackiewicz, 1979)	Increased (Harackiewicz, 1979)		
Performance-contingent (informational)	Increased (Ryan, et al., 1983)	Decreased[a] (Ryan, et al., 1983)	Increased (Enzle & Ross, 1978)	Did not differ (Harackiewicz, 1979)	
Performance-contingent (controlling)	Decreased (Harackiewicz, 1979)	Decreased[a] (Ryan et al., 1983)	Did not differ (Ryan, et al., 1983)	Decreased (Harackiewicz, 1979)	Decreased (Ryan, et al., 1983)

Note: The table should be read as follows: Begin by reading a row label (i.e., a label on the left); then read the verb in a box of that row. That tells the effects on intrinsic motivation of the row label relative to the column label (i.e., the label at the top of that particular column). For example, the box that is second from the top in the first column would read as follows: *task-contingent* rewards with no feedback decreased intrinsic motivation relative to a no-reward, no-feedback condition (as demonstrated by Deci, 1971).

[a] These two cells showed the decrease in intrinsic motivation relative to a no-reward group that received positive feedback that was comparable to that of the reward group (i.e., that was either informational or controlling, respectively).

undermining effect. A true test of Arnold's hypothesis would necessitate the use of task-contingent, expected rewards. We see no reason to expect highly interesting activities to be impervious to the negative effects of extrinsic rewards, although the effects may be slower in appearing and ceiling effects may mask changes in underlying motivational processes.

Several studies have included uninteresting tasks as well as the conventional, intrinsically interesting tasks. Calder and Staw (1975b) varied task interest, having subjects work on either an interesting or a dull jigsaw puzzle activity. Half the subjects in each condition were rewarded with $1 and half were not. Results revealed an interaction, such that with interesting puzzles the money led to less expressed enjoyment on a postexperimental questionnaire, whereas with dull puzzles the money led to greater expressed enjoyment. Thus, whereas the undermining effect was replicated when an interesting task was used, the opposite effect, often called a reinforcement effect, occurred when a dull task was used. Calder and Staw interpreted this as evidence that rewards enhance intrinsic motivation for a dull task.

We disagree with their interpretation. If a task is dull there are no appreciable intrinsic rewards in doing the activity. However, people may be more satisfied and may enjoy the experience more if they are paid for it. But that does not mean that they are more intrinsically motivated for it. The satisfaction and enjoyment come from the activity's being instrumental to the receipt of rewards, not from the intrinsic properties of the activity. The satisfaction and enjoyment are extrinsic rather than intrinsic. Making a lot of money at an activity can be quite satisfying and enjoyable, but that does not make the activity intrinsically interesting; it makes it extrinsically gratifying. People typically do not do dull, boring activities unless they are rewarded or forced, so dull tasks tend to be associated with extrinsic factors. The receipt of the expected reward may satisfy people, but it does not motivate them intrinsically.

Kruglanski, Riter, Amitai, Margolin, Shabtai, and Zaksh (1975) pointed out that extrinsic rewards are sometimes inherent in the activity itself. For example, when flipping a coin for money, the money is endogenous to the activity, whereas when doing puzzles for money, the money is exogenous to the activity. In their experiments, they used both types of tasks and found that when money was exogenous to the activity, paid subjects expressed less interest in the activity than unpaid subjects, whereas when money was endogenous to the activity, paid subjects expressed greater interest in the activity than unpaid subjects.

This interaction is similar to the interaction obtained by Calder and Staw (1975b) and to one obtained by Staw et al. (1980). In the Kruglanski et al. study, payments interacted with the exogenous/endogenous variable; in the Calder and Staw study, money interacted with the interesting/

dull variable; and in the Staw *et al.* study, money interacted with the norm-for-payment/no-norm-for-payment variable mentioned earlier in the chapter. When money is endogenous to the activity, when the activity is dull and boring, or when the activity is one for which there are norms for payment, the activity is an extrinsic or instrumental activity, and subjects are more satisfied when they are rewarded for an extrinsic activity than when they are not. Although the three sets of authors interpreted this as evidence that the rewards increased intrinsic motivation in those situations, we interpret the results merely as evidence that subjects are more extrinsically satisfied and would prefer to continue to do the activity for rewards. In none of the three studies mentioned was there a behavioral, free-choice measure of intrinsic motivation. All the significant findings were with attitude measures, and with those it is difficult to sort out intrinsic motivation from extrinsic satisfaction. Further, a study by Daniel and Esser (1980), which used both a behavioral and an attitudinal measure, found that rewarding subjects for doing an uninteresting activity left both dependent measures unchanged; they failed even to replicate the attitudinal results.

There is some support for our interpretation in two studies. Pinder (1976) used both dull and interesting tasks and crossed that with payments versus no payments. As a dependent measure, he asked subjects, "How satisfying did you find the task itself (independent of the pay you received)?" He reported that paid subjects expressed marginally less satisfaction with the task itself regardless of whether the task was dull or interesting. When the satisfaction associated with pay is removed, so that the expressed satisfaction is with the activity itself, there is no indication that rewards will enhance intrinsic interest or intrinsic motivation. Deci, Porac, and Shapira (1978) used the same coin-toss activity as Kruglanski *et al.* (1975) and found, as did Kruglanski *et al.*, that rewards increased satisfaction with the experience; however, there was no increased intrinsic motivation as measured by a free-choice measure. In sum, extrinsic rewards can generally be expected either to have no effect or to decrease intrinsic motivation for dull, boring, extrinsic tasks. On the other hand, extrinsic rewards may increase enjoyment by increasing extrinsic satisfaction.

The effects of rewards on the enjoyment of interesting versus dull tasks can be seen to be parallel to the effects of rewards on one's performance of interesting versus dull tasks. Numerous studies reviewed by McGraw (1978) have shown that task-contingent rewards impair performance on interesting (complex or conceptual) tasks but they improve performance on dull, repetitive tasks. When people are rewarded for doing interesting activities, the rewards decrease their intrinsic motivation and enjoyment and hinder their performance. When they are rewarded for doing dull activities, the rewards increase their enjoyment and improve their performance, but their intrinsic motivation remains at the same low level.

SUMMARY

In this chapter we have organized studies that have investigated the effects of various initiating and regulatory events on intrinsic motivation. We interpreted all of the results in terms of cognitive evaluation theory, suggesting that self-determination and competence are the fundamental issues involved in intrinsic motivational processes. The theory analyzes initiating and regulatory events in terms of their effects on a person's perceived locus of causality and perceived competence, suggesting that events can have three different functional significances. Events such as choice and positive feedback that facilitate self-determined competence have an informational significance and were found to enhance intrinsic motivation. Events such as rewards, deadlines, and surveillance that pressure people toward specific outcomes have a controlling significance and were found to undermine intrinsic motivation. These events, we suggested, tend to promote extrinsic compliance or defiance. Finally, events such as negative feedback and noncontingencies that signify one's inability to reliably attain intended outcomes have an amotivating significance and have also been found to undermine intrinsic motivation.

In presenting cognitive evaluation theory, we traced the elaborations and refinements that have followed its first presentation (Deci, 1975), and we discussed its relationship to psychological reactance (Brehm, 1966) and human helplessness (Garber & Seligman, 1980). The motivational organization of cognitive and affective variables, such as creativity, cognitive flexibility, emotional tone, and self-esteem was presented, and research on reward-contingencies was organized using the Ryan *et al.* (1983) taxonomy of contingencies. Competitively contingent rewards were seen to be most controlling (and thus most undermining of intrinsic motivation); whereas, in descending order, performance-contigent, task-contingent, and task-noncontingent rewards were less controlling, relative to appropriate no-reward control groups that include comparable feedback. Finally, research on the nature of the task was interpreted within the context of the theory.

Cognitive Evaluation Theory
Interpersonal Communication and
Intrapersonal Regulation

The convergence of results reported in the last chapter represents an important step in understanding the impact of external events on people's motivational processes. The research reviewed in that chapter focused primarily on the events themselves, the presence or absence of surveillance and the nature of the reward structure, for example, and explored their average effects on people's motivation and on related variables. According to cognitive evaluation theory, however, the impact of an event on motivational processes is determined, not by the objective characteristics of the event, but rather by its psychological meaning for the individual. The perceived locus of causality and perceived competence are descriptors of a person's experience with regard to a behavior, rather than a property of the environment. They reflect the individual's organization of reality. Similarly, whether an event will be interpreted as informational, controlling, or amotivating is an issue of the relative salience of these aspects to the perceiver, and is affected by his or her sensitivities, background, agendas, as well as by the actual configuration of the event. In short, environmental events are affordances that are used by the perceiver in the internal construction of motivationally relevant inputs.

When we focus our analysis at the level of the recipient's experience, three important ramifications have proven empirically useful. First, it suggests that the interpersonal context within which an event is experienced could be an important determinative factor in the effect of the event on the perceiver. Second, it suggests that individual differences in the perceiver of an event may play an important role in determining how the event is experienced and, therefore, what its effects are. And third, it allows for the possibility that the events that initiate and regulate some behaviors may be largely or wholly within a person and therefore relatively independent of situational events. This has led to an exploration of the relationship of various types of internal regulatory events to self-determination. We will now discuss each of these three topics in turn.

INTERPERSONAL CONTEXTS

The traditional language of empirical psychology suggests, and indeed research has shown, that environments play an important role in the determination of behavior. However, when one considers what constitutes an environment, one realizes that the most salient aspects are rarely concrete events such as rewards or feedback, but are usually the other people who are dispensing the rewards and feedback. For example, when you feel controlled at work, you are not likely to experience yourself as controlled by the reward structure itself, but rather by your employer through the reward structure. Similarly, if you were to receive positive feedback for your performance, the meaning of that feedback would be grounded in the interpersonal context of that communication as much as in the words *per se.* As Watzlawick, Beavin, and Jackson (1967) put it, the analog aspect or metamessage of a communication often carries as much or more weight as the digital aspect or literal content. Similarly, we suggest that the interpersonal context within which an event such as a reward or feedback is administered will meaningfully influence the impact of that event; in other words, the interpersonal context gives the event its metamessage. First, we will consider research relevant to rewards and then move on to feedback.

Performance-Contingent Rewards

Ryan *et al.* (1983) suggested that the interpersonal administration of performance-contingent rewards could be either informational or controlling and that the rewards would have a markedly different impact on intrinsic motivation and affect in these two different contexts. They reviewed a previous study by Harackiewicz (1979) interpreting her results according to their hypothesis and then conducted a study to confirm the hypothesis.

In the Harackiewicz study two groups of subjects were offered performance-contingent rewards. One group was told that they would receive a reward if they performed well enough, but there was no mention of the standards nor was there any indication during the performance period whether they were doing well. A second group was given norms for performance so they would have some indication of how well they were doing during the performance period. Ryan *et al.* (1983) suggested that the withholding of information during the performance period of the first group may have been experienced by subjects as very controlling and would thus have induced pressure, tension, and evaluation apprehension. Indeed, Harackiweicz reported that the withholding of norms did vitiate any enhancing effect of the positive feedback that was ultimately conveyed to the subjects through the reward. In fact, although rewards administered in the norms condition tended to enhance intrinsic motivation relative to no rewards/no feedback, rewards administered in the no-norms condition caused a level of intrinsic motivation that was significantly less than that evidenced in the no-reward/no-feedback group.

In the Ryan *et al.* study, there were also two performance-contingent reward groups. Subjects in one group were told that they would receive rewards "if they performed well," and those in the other group were told that they would receive rewards "if they performed well, *as they should.*" The italics indicate the phrase that was hypothesized to create a controlling rather than informational context for the reward. Subjects in both groups received positive feedback as they proceeded through the task. As predicted, subjects in the controlling, performance-contingent reward condition were less intrinsically motivated than subjects in the informational, performance-contingent reward condition. Further, the controlling-rewards group reported experiencing significantly greater pressure and tension than the informational-rewards group. As in the Harackiewicz study, the no-rewards, no-feedback group displayed a level of intrinsic motivation that was midway between the two performance-contingent reward groups. From these two studies, then, we can see that the same event, in this case a performance-contingent reward structure, can be either informational or controlling depending on the interpersonal dynamics prompted by the rewarder.

In the Ryan *et al.* study there were also two groups of nonrewarded subjects who received the same informational versus controlling positive feedback as that received by the subjects in the performance-contingent reward groups. One group received the positive feedback (without rewards) within an informational context and the other received it within a controlling context. Consequently, the two positive feedback groups were directly comparable to the two performance-contingent reward groups, the only difference being the absence of the rewards. Results showed, consistent with the general conclusion presented at the end of the last chapter, that both types of performance-contingent rewards undermined intrinsic motivation relative to that of the comparable positive-feedback/no-reward groups. Additionally, even without rewards, the positive feedback that was embedded within an informational context resulted in greater subsequent intrinsic motivation than the same positive feedback within the controlling context.

Finally, a recent study by Harackiewicz, Manderlink, and Sansone (1984) suggested that the interpersonal evaluation that is implicit in a performance-contingent reward structure is the component of the structure that is controlling. Thus, if that were removed, the reward could serve the function of highlighting the informational aspect of the reward structure. In their study, subjects who received a performance-contingent reward for performing better than 80% of the previous subjects displayed greater subsequent intrinsic motivation than subjects who were told before they began that they would be evaluated and were told after they finished that they had done better than 80% of the previous subjects. The reward, separate from the implicit evaluation that accompanied it, seems to have highlighted their competence (they must be very competent if others are willing to reward them for it), and therefore made the performance-contingent reward structure more informational than the evaluation structure. Although Harackiewicz *et al.* did not manipulate the interpersonal context *per se*, they did demonstrate that one component of an interpersonal context that makes it controlling is the fact of people's being evaluated in it.

The Harackiewicz *et al.* study was an interesting and important demonstration of the fact that the effects of rewards depend on the meaning of the rewards to the recipients. We would add only one caveat to their discussion, namely, that although interpersonal evaluation is one factor that can make rewards controlling, there are others as well. Particularly in the real world people may need rewards for other reasons (to buy food for their children, for example) and in so far as they have to have the rewards they will tend to experience them as controlling independent of (i.e., in addition to) the evaluation that is implicit in them.

In sum, the research studies above have led to the following conclusions. First, interpersonal factors emanating from the rewarder can lead performance-contingent rewards to be experienced as either informational or controlling. If controllingly administered, they tend to undermine intrinsic motivation relative to no rewards and no feedback, and if informationally administered (i.e. administered in the absence of conveyed pressure or control), they tend to enhance intrinsic motivation relative to no rewards and no feedback. Second, regardless of the interpersonal context, performance-contingent rewards tend to undermine intrinsic motivation relative to conditions in which comparable positive feedback is given in the absence of rewards, unless the positive feedback is given in the context of subjects' being evaluated, in which case the performance-contingent rewards could lead to greater subsequent intrinsic motivation than the evaluative feedback, because the rewards would be relatively less controlling. This leads to the dual conclusions that it is the meaning of a reward to the recipient, rather than the reward itself, that impacts on motivation, and that the interpersonal context, particularly as it relates to issues of control and evaluation, is an important factor in determining the meaning of the reward.

A study by Pallak, Costomiris, Sroka, and Pittman (1982) suggests that the history of one's experiences with rewards (i.e., the interpersonal contexts within which one has previously received rewards) will also affect how a reward is experienced in the present situation. They found that good-player awards were interpreted informationally (and thus increased intrinsic motivation) when given to children in schools where symbolic rewards were regularly used to signify competence, whereas they were interpreted controllingly (and thus decreased intrinsic motivation) when given to children in schools where they had not been typically used.

Positive Feedback

Since 1971 when Deci first demonstrated that positive-performance feedback could enhance intrinsic motivation, numerous studies have been conducted to explore the general issue of positive feedback. The results of these studies, which seem at first blush to be complex, even contradictory, can, in fact, be nicely integrated using the information-control distinction of cognitive evaluation theory.

Smith (1974) reported that positive feedback decreased the intrinsic motivation of college student subjects, but Weiner and Mander (1978) reported an increase. These findings, although apparently inconsistent, resulted from different experimental paradigms. In the Smith study, subjects learned about art history and were told before they began that their performance would be evaluated. Subsequently, they all received positive feedback. In the Weiner and Mander study, subjects were not told that they would be evaluated; they merely received the positive feedback following their performance. Thus, the Smith procedure had set up an evaluation apprehension, similar in kind and similarly controlling to the one created in the no-norms condition of the Harackiewicz (1979) performance contingency study. In the Weiner and Mander (1978) study, the interpersonal context was non-evaluative, so the positive feedback was apparently experienced as informational rather than controlling, thereby resulting in the increase rather than decrease in intrinsic motivation. This interpretation received some support from the Smith study itself, which had included a second verbal rewards (i.e., positive feedback) group. Those subjects had not, however, been told that their performance would be evaluated, and they did not evidence the decrease in intrinsic motivation.

The important point is that even positive, competence-affirming feedback can be interpreted as either informational or controlling and will have a markedly different effect on intrinsic motivation and related variables depending on the interpretation. Emphasizing evaluation made the interpersonal context more controlling and thus resulted in decrements in intrinsic motivation. Two studies have explored this information–control issue directly.

In the first, Pittman, Davey, Alafat, Wetherill, and Kramer (1980) gave positive feedback to college student subjects who spent 15 minutes working with a puzzle activity. In the informational-feedback condition, subjects were given the puzzles and asked to work on them, doing as well as they could. After 6 minutes, they were told that they were doing well, and after 15 minutes they were stopped and told that they had done well. In the controlling-feedback condition, feedback was given in a way that represented pressure toward performing well. The experimenter told the subjects initially that it was important for them to do well because their data were needed to complete the study. After 6 minutes they were told that they were doing well, and that if they kept it up, their data would be very helpful. Finally, after 15 minutes they were stopped and told that they had done well and that their data would be useful. The important difference in the two conditions was that, in the controlling condition, the experimenter appeared to have an investment in the subject's performance outcomes, and that investment heightened the controlling nature of the feedback; it pressured them toward specific outcomes. As expected, the controlling feedback led to significantly less intrinsic motivation than the informational feedback.

Ryan (1982) also demonstrated that controlling feedback decreased intrinsic motivation relative to informational feedback. In his study, which employed college students working with hidden-figures puzzles, feedback was made controlling through the use of the term "should"; subjects were told how they should be performing. For example, subjects in the controlling condition were told how their performance compared to the maximum and average performance, and then they were given an evaluative statement, such as, "Good, you're doing as you should." Subjects in the informational feedback condition were simply told how their performance compared to the maximum possible performance and to the average performance for that puzzle. Ryan found the same results as

Pittman *et al.*: when competence was made controlling by indicating that there are outcomes that subjects should attain, the feedback undermined intrinsic motivation relative to informational feedback.

Self-Administration

Thus far, all of the reported research has explored the effects of interpersonal communications in the form either of tangible rewards or of positive feedback that was administered by some significant other, such as an experimenter. Results have shown that, on average, rewards tend to be experienced as controlling and to undermine intrinsic motivation, whereas positive feedback tends to be experienced as informational and to enhance intrinsic motivation. However, research has shown that both tangible rewards and positive feedback can be either informational or controlling, depending on subtle elements of the interpersonal context. Accordingly, the same reward or feedback will have a different effect on intrinsic motivation resulting from these different quality contexts.

There has been the suggestion by various writers that the self-administration of rewards or feedback would allow greater self-determination with respect to the rewards or feedback and would therefore have a more positive effect on intrinsic motivation. This suggestion has to some extent paralleled the shift in focus among reinforcement theorists from other-administered to self-administered reinforcements (e.g., Bandura, 1977b; Kanfer, 1975). In terms of the present line of research, this leads to the question of the relative effects on intrinsic motivation of other-administered versus self-administered rewards and feedback.

Several studies have included a self-administered reward or feedback condition. In one, Dollinger and Thelen (1978) found that when children self-administered good-player awards, their subsequent intrinsic motivation was significantly decreased relative to no rewards and to other-administered good-player awards. Although one might argue that self-administered should be less detrimental because it allows subjects to be more self-determining, hence less controlled, this study indicated that the self-administration was even more controlling. Perhaps the children felt unsure about what constituted rewardable performance, or perhaps they felt controlled to reward themselves as well as controlled to do the target activity.

A study by DeLamarter and Krepps (1982) found that the self-administration of tokens by college students for working on interesting Soma puzzles also led to decreased intrinsic motivation relative to a no-reward group. This study did not, however, have an other-administered token group, so there was no basis for comparing self- versus other-administration of the same reward.

In contrast to the two studies just mentioned, two others have found that self-reinforcement procedures averted the undermining effect. Margolis and Mynatt (1979) found that when fifth- and sixth-grade children self-administered monetary rewards (taken from a bowl of nickles) for playing with toys, their subsequent intrinsic motivation was comparable to a no-reward group and was significantly greater than that of a second reward group whose rewards were administered by the experimenter. Enzle and Look (1979) reported similar results with college students. From these four studies, it seems unclear whether the self-administration of rewards will make the rewards more informational, more controlling, or no different from the other-administration of the same rewards.

Noting the inconsistency of these results, Ryan (1982) suggested that self-administered rewards or feedback, like other-administered rewards or feedback, could be either informational or controlling. The key factor, he suggested, is not so much the type of administration (self versus other) as it is the meaning or functional significance of the administration, whichever type it is. Ryan had college students self-administer feedback for their performance on hidden-figures puzzles. Half the subjects self-administered controlling feedback and the other half self-administered informational feedback following each of three hidden-figures puzzles. The self-administration of feedback was accomplished by having subjects record their own performance on an experimenter-provided norms sheet and to compare it to the maximum possible performance and the average performance of previous subjects (actually the stated average was somewhat lower than the true average so subjects would get positive feedback). In addition, controlling subjects selected a "should" statement (e.g., "Good, I'm doing just as I should") that they thought best described their performance, and read it to themselves a couple of times.

In this study there were also comparable other-administration conditions in which the experimenter administered either the same informational or the same controlling feedback as in the self-administration conditions. A yoking procedure ensured that the feedback—which was, on average, moderately positive—was the same across administration conditions. The results revealed a main effect for type of feedback; controlling feedback undermined intrinsic motivation relative to informational feedback regardless of whether it was self- or other-administered. There was no effect for the type of administration. Regardless of whether competence feedback is self- or other-administered, it seems to decrease intrinsic motivation if it pressures people toward specific outcomes and to increase intrinsic motivation if it merely provides effectance affirming information.

The Meaning of Controlling

We have defined controlling events as those that are experienced as pressure to think, feel, or behave in specified ways. The experience of pressure, no matter how subtle the source, facilitates an external perceived locus of causality. From the various studies, a number of factors have emerged that seem to make a communication controlling.

First, we have seen consistently that structuring the situation in a way that makes an activity instrumental for receiving a desired outcome is a necessary condition for control. In fact, a recent study by Lepper, Sagotsky, Dafoe, and Greene (1982) demonstrated that the mere fact of creating an instrumentality between an activity and an outcome can lead to a reorientation in one's engagement with the activity. In that study, two groups of preschool children were asked to work with two different, though equally attractive, drawing activities. In the experimental group, subjects were told that they could "win a chance" to draw with the second set of materials by drawing two pictures with the first set. In the other group, subjects were simply given the two sets of materials in the same order as had been used for the experimental subjects. They were asked to draw pictures, much as the experimental subjects had been asked, but the first drawing was not made instrumental for a chance to use the second set of materials. Several weeks later, the children were observed in a free-choice situation in which both sets of materials were available. The results revealed that children in the experimental condition spent less time with the first (instrumental) activity than with the second activity, relative to the children in the other, noninstrumental condition. It appears, then, that the imposed contingency implied control. The children's behavior was controlled by the adults' having made performance on the first activity instrumental to having a chance to engage the second activity.

Of course an instrumentality does not always imply control, but the research suggests two things. First, instrumentality seems to be a necessary condition for control (and hence for the undermining of intrinsic motivation) because, as we saw in Chapter 3, task-noncontingent rewards, which do not create specific instrumentalities, tend not to undermine intrinsic motivation. And second, instrumentalities do, on average, tend to imply control, as numerous studies reviewed herein have suggested. Thus, a rewarder or communicator should be sensitive to the issue of control when creating structures for rewarding or communicating. When instrumentalities are involved, one must work to make them informational rather than controlling.

Another finding that has emerged clearly from the research is that factors that imply evaluation tend to pressure people and therefore to be experienced as controlling. In the Smith (1974) study the fact of explicit evaluation decreased intrinsic motivation even though the evaluations were positive, and explicit evaluation also had a negative effect on creativity in a study by Amabile (1979). Even the implicit evaluation inherent in statements about how people should perform has been shown to be highly controlling in studies by Ryan and colleagues (Ryan, 1982; Ryan et al., 1983).

Finally, when the situation implies that one's behavior is for someone else's purposes rather than for one's own, the situation is likely to be experienced as more controlling. This was demonstrated by the Pittman et al. (1980) study in which subjects lost intrinsic motivation when the experimenter expressed his or her investment in the subjects' doing well. It apparently became unclear to the subjects whether they were doing well for the experimenter or for themselves.

The Meaning of Informational

We have defined informational events as those that allow choice (i.e., that are free from unnecessary pressure) and that provide information that is useful for a person in his or her attempts to interact effectively with the environment. Informational events are thus not experienced as attempts to control behavior but rather as supports for autonomy.

There is, however, an important distinction between an informational environment and a permissive environment, both of which could in a certain sense be described as allowing autonomy. Permissive environments are ones that are not only without controls, but are also devoid of structure. Thus, functionally, they amount to neglect. Whereas informational environments provide some type of feedback, or structures that allow one to derive one's own feedback, permissive environments do not contain the effectance-relevant information that is necessary for developing competencies and guiding action.

The importance of the type of environmental responsiveness that provides effectance-relevant information was illustrated by an inadvertent finding in the Anderson et al. (1976) study of preschool children. In their study, one group was designed to be a no-feedback, control group. An experimenter was in the room with each child while the child was working on the target activity, though in the no-feedback group the experimenter was instructed to ignore or not respond to the child.

The researchers reported that this condition, which was supposed to serve as a comparison group, evidenced the lowest levels of intrinsic motivation of any of their conditions, including one with extrinsic rewards. It seems clear that a permissive, nonresponsive environment, although it may not specifically obstruct autonomy, is not what we call informational. Indeed, it is probable that it is amotivating because it seems to interfere with the development of competence and may lead subjects to experience the situation as unmasterable.

A study by Koestner *et al.* (1984) has shown how even setting limits on children's behavior can be done so as to serve the function of an informative structure rather than a control. In the former case, one would of course expect greater intrinsic motivation than in the latter. In their study, first- and second-grade children worked with paints and paper and the question of interest was the effects of the imposition of limits around neatness on their intrinsic motivation for painting.

Being informational in setting limits is more complicated than merely providing choice and positive feedback, however. There is likely to be a conflict between what the limit requires and what the child would like to do. For example, telling a child to be neat may conflict with his or her desire not to be neat. Therefore, to make limits informational, there must be the additional elements of an acknowledgement of the potential conflict and an explanation of why the limits are important in that situation. These factors, which are central to Ginottian limit setting (Ginott, 1961; Orgel, 1983), when combined with the provision of as much choice as possible and some effectance-relevant feedback will help to maintain the subjects' experience of self-determination and an internal locus of causality. Controlling limits, by comparison, pay little attention to the child's needs or feelings and merely convey what the child has to do.

In the Koestner *et al.* study there were three groups of children. For one group, no limits were imposed on the children's neatness. For the second group, there were informational limits: these children were told that although it is often fun to be messy with the paints, this is a time when it is important to be neat so that the materials will remain in good order for the other children. For the third group, there were controlling limits: these children were told that they should be neat so the materials will remain in good order for the other children.

The results revealed a main effect on both a free-choice behavioral measure and an enjoyment measure. Children who were given informational limits were significantly more intrinsically motivated than children who were given controlling limits; the no-limits children were comparable to the informational-limits children. It appears, therefore, that controlling limits undermine intrinsic motivation, whereas informational limits do no. The structure that is provided by the informational limits and the concern for the children that they convey seem to offset the detrimental effects of the limits themselves. In fact, the informational-limits children expressed somewhat greater enjoyment of the activity than the no-limits children. Koestner *et al.* also investigated the creative quality of the children's paintings and found, using Amabile's (1982b) method for assessing creativity, that the controlling limits significantly undermined creativity as well as intrinsic motivation.

From the various studies we can derive the factors that make an event informational. First and foremost is choice, in other words, the absence of unnecessary controls, so that one can experience a sense of self-determination. Second, there must be some type of effectance-relevant information vis-à-vis one's performance on an optimally challenging activity. And, finally, if the event somehow conflicts with a person's needs or feelings, this implicit conflict must be acknowledged.

The Communicator and the Context

We have pinpointed several specific factors in the interpersonal context that tend to lead communications (for example, rewards or feedback statements) to be experienced as controlling versus informational. Other research has shown that the intent or orientation of the communicator can also affect whether communications are experienced as informational or controlling, and hence increase or decrease intrinsic motivation. In a field study, Deci, Nezlek, and Sheinman (1981) studied the orientations of fourth- through sixth-grade classroom teachers along a "supporting autonomy" to "controlling behavior" continuum. They suggested that teachers may be oriented toward supporting the autonomy of the children in their classrooms or they may be oriented toward controlling the behavior of the children. These researchers predicted that the teachers who were oriented toward controlling would reward and communicate accordingly, thereby depleting the intrinsic motivation of their children, relative to teachers oriented toward supporting autonomy, who were expected to reward and communicate in a more informational fashion. The researchers then measured the intrinsic motivation and self-esteem of the children in the 35 classrooms using measures developed by Harter (1981b, 1982) and correlated them with the teachers' orientations. They found a significant correlation indicating that children in classrooms with teachers oriented toward supporting autonomy had higher intrinsic motivation and self-esteem than the children in the classrooms of teachers oriented toward controlling.

In a follow-up study, Deci, Schwartz, Sheinman, and Ryan (1981) preselected three classrooms with teachers oriented toward controlling and three with teachers oriented toward supporting autonomy. On the second day of the school year and again seven weeks later, they measured the intrinsic motivation and self-esteem of the children in those classes. They reported evidence that within the first 2 months of the school year the children in the autonomy-supporting classrooms had become more intrinsically motivated and had higher self-esteem relative to the children in the more controlling classrooms.

These studies suggest that characteristics of the communicator may affect whether the context of the communication is experienced as primarily informational or primarily controlling. This difference, as we saw, resulted in differences in intrinsic motivation, self-esteem, creativity, and other relatied variables.

CHARACTERISTICS OF THE PERCEIVER/RECIPIENT

Two different lines of research have explored variables in the perceiver or recipient of a reward or communication, as they affect the informational versus controlling meaning of the event. The first relates to the gender of the perceiver, and the second, to psychometrically assessed individual differences in the perceiver.

Sex Differences: Information and Control

In Chapter 3 we reported that when, in the context of self-determination, people perceive themselves to be competent at a challenging activity, they become more intrinsically motivated. Positive-competence feedback frequently leads people to perceive themselves as more competent and has generally been shown to enhance intrinsic motivation in children and adults alike. Although this has been the general finding, the issue is actually somewhat more complex. First, as we saw earlier in this chapter, when feedback is administered in an interpersonally controlling or evaluative context, it can decrease rather than increase intrinsic motivation. Second, we will now see that males and females often respond very differently to positive feedback.

The informational aspect of positive feedback affirms people's self-determined competence. The controlling aspect of positive feedback controls people's behavior by capitalizing on their need to be liked. When people want praise, praise can be used to pressure them toward specific outcomes. Several studies have indicated that females may be more susceptible to being controlled by praise than are males. Females therefore seem more likely to experience praise as controlling, and males to experience it as informational.

Deci *et al.* (1975) found that when male and female college students were praised by either a male or female experimenter for working on Soma puzzles, the praised males displayed greater subsequent intrinsic motivation then nonpraised males, whereas praised females displayed less subsequent intrinsic motivation than nonpraised females. This dramatic finding had also been present, though less clearly, in a previous study (Deci, 1972b), and had been supported by the results of a study by Carone (1975), in which praise decreased females' intrinsic motivation, and a study by Deci (1971), in which praise increased the intrinsic motivation of a group of subjects that was about 90% male.

In interpreting these results, Deci (1975) suggested that the informational aspect of praise may be more salient for males (leading to increased intrinsic motivation), whereas the controlling aspect may be more salient for females (leading to decreased intrinsic motivation) because of traditional sex-role socialization practices. Boys have been encouraged to be more independent and achievement oriented, whereas girls have been encouraged to be more dependent and interpersonally sensitive. Thus as adults men may be more attuned to the informational aspect of praise because their socialization has oriented them toward looking for evidence of independent achievement rather than evidence of having pleased the provider of the praise. On the other hand, women may be more attuned to the controlling aspect because their socialization has oriented them toward looking for evidence of having pleased the provider. Functionally, praise for men amounts to competence information, whereas for women it is a source of control. This interpretation received some support from a study by Alegre and Murray (1974) in which females were found to condition more readily to verbal reinforcement than were males.

In a subsequent study, Blanck *et al.* (1984) found that positive feedback enhanced the intrinsic motivation of both male and female college student subjects. These researchers used the same paradigm and the same task as that used by Deci *et al.* (1975), and they used undergraduate subjects from the same university. The only apparent difference between the two studies was that the data from the Blanck *et al.* study were collected at least 6 years later than those from the Deci *et al.* study (1978 versus 1972). Blanck *et al.* argued that during that period there had been considerable change in people's beliefs about sex roles. There are more independent, achievement-oriented, career women serving as role models and setting the stage for more equality in the socialization of boys and girls around the issues of independence and achievement. These changes may have led the women in their study (who attended a highly competitive eastern university) to be more independent and achievement oriented. If so, the informational aspect of the positive feedback would have become relatively more salient for them than was the case for their counterparts several years earlier. This could explain the difference in the results of their study and that of Deci *et al.* (1975).

Because the Blanck *et al.* study is the only recently reported exploration of sex differences and praise in adults, it is difficult to know just how pervasive the effects of the change in sex-role orientation may be. The question is particularly accute because the population of women in the Blank *et al.* (1984) study may be somewhat atypical in that they came from a very highly achievement-oriented setting.

Two recent studies of children suggest that the apparent change, reflected in the Blanck *et al.* data, may not be very widespread. In the first, Zinser, Young, and King (1982) gave three levels of verbal rewards to second- and third-grade boys and girls. Some got no verbal rewards, some got a low level of verbal rewards, and some got a high level of verbal rewards. Using a free-choice measure of intrinsic motivation, the authors reported an interaction between verbal rewards and gender. As the level of reward got higher, the boys' intrinsic motivation increased, whereas the girls' intrinsic motivation decreased.

In an elaborate study that focused specifically on informational versus controlling aspects of verbal rewards, Kast (1983) found results complementary to those of Zinser *et al.* (1982) and Deci *et al.* (1975). First, using a rating procedure, she created two pools of feedback statements: one informational and one controlling. The controlling statements included references to such things as doing well "for me" (i.e., the experimenter). As expected, and consistent with the findings of Ryan (1982), Kast found that the controlling feedback significantly lowered the intrinsic motivation of boys and girls relative to the informational feedback. Second, however, she then gave feedback that included both informational and controlling elements to boys and girls in the third, fifth, and eighth grades. She found that girls tended to interpret this mixed feedback as controlling, whereas boys tended to interpret it as informational. This was evidenced by the girls' displaying less subsequent intrinsic motivation than the boys. The girls' intrinsic motivation following mixed feedback was comparable to what it had been following controlling feedback, whereas the boys' intrinsic motivation following mixed feedback was comparable to what it had been following informational feedback. Apparently, in the Deci *et al.* (1975) study, the nature of the feedback was sufficiently ambiguous that females read control into it and males read information into it. The conclusions from the Kast (1983) study seem to be that it is possible to give positive feedback to females in a way that will be experienced as informational by carefully avoiding statements that include references to doing well for others or to how well they should be doing, but females seem to be more ready to interpret positive feedback as controlling than are males. Verbal feedback that is clearly controlling, of course, tends to be detrimental to the intrinsic motivation of both genders, whether they be children (Kast, 1983) or adults (Ryan, 1982).

In a study by Haddad (1982), sex differences also emerged in response to verbal feedback. Her study was designed to explore the effects of informational versus controlling feedback on children's desire for self-determination. Citing Deci's (1980) assertion that intrinsic motivation provides the energy for the processes of self-determinaton, Haddad hypothesized that if people are given controlling feedback and are subsequently given the opportunity to be self-determining, they may display less self-determination than if they had been given informational feedback. She hypothesized that controlling feedback will undermine people's desire to make their own choices. In her experiment, 10- and 11-year-old children were given either informational or controlling positive feedback for working on anagram problems. Subsequent to that, the children were told that they would be working on four more anagrams; that they could choose all four by themselves, that they could choose some and let the experimenter choose the rest, or that they could have the experimenter choose all four for them. The results revealed that girls in the controlling group wanted to choose fewer of their own than girls in the informational group, but there was no such difference for boys in the two groups. The experience of receiving controlling feedback seems to have undermined the girls' self-determination more dramatically than the boys'.

On balance, the set of studies reporting sex differences indicates that females tend to be more sensitive to the controlling aspect of verbal feedback. When praised, females tend to experience the communication as more controlling than do males, and there is a tendency for positive verbal feedback to have a more detrimental effect on their intrinsic motivation and self-determination.

Individual Differences in the Perceiver

Only a few studies have considered psychometrically measured differences in the perceiver as a mediator of the effects of initiating or regulatory events on intrinsic motivation. All but one of these studies have used the locus of control as the individual difference variable. Although the concept has been used differently by different authors (see Chapter 6 for an extended discussion of the concept), the basic notion is that people have generalized beliefs about the control of desired outcomes. Those who are said to have an internal locus of control believe that outcomes are more under their own control, whereas those who are said to have an external locus of control believe that outcomes are delivered by chance or by some other force wholly out of their control (Rotter, 1966).

Baron and Ganz (1972) suggested that this variable may have relevance to intrinsic and extrinsic motivation. They reported that children with an internal locus of control worked better with intrinsic rewards, whereas children with an external locus of control worked better with extrinsic rewards.

Lonky and Reihman (1980) and Earn (1982) have applied the variable to the information-control distinction. They argued that people high on internal locus of control—believing themselves to be more in control of outcomes—will be more likely to interpret rewards and communications as informational, whereas people who are low on internal control will be more likely to interpret them as controlling. Lonky and Reihman studied the effects of verbal praise on the intrinsic motivation of children high and low on internal locus of control, as measured by the Bialer (1961) scale. They found that when children high on internal locus of control were praised, they showed an increase in intrinsic motivation from the pre- to posttreatment assessment, whereas children low on internal locus of control who were praised showed a decrease over the comparable period.

Earn (1982) looked at the intrinsic motivation of college students who worked on puzzles. He argued that if the controlling aspect of a reward were made salient, it would tend to undermine the intrinsic motivation of all subjects; if it were left ambiguous, then internal locus of control people would be likely to interpret the reward informationally, whereas external locus of control people would be more likely to interpret it controllingly. He reported two studies in which students, either internal or external on locus of control, were given no reward, a $2.50 reward, or a $5 reward, for working with puzzles. In one study, the controlling aspect of the rewards was made quite salient and the rewards tended to undermine the intrinsic motivation of all subjects. However, in the other experiment, the controlling aspect was more ambiguous, and Earn found that for internals, the larger the reward, the more their subsequent intrinsic motivation, whereas for externals, the larger the reward, the less their subsequent intrinsic motivation. This, of course, suggests that when the controlling aspect was ambiguous, externals interpreted the reward as controlling, whereas internals interpreted it as informational.

The final study that considered individual differences was by Boggiano and Barrett (1984). In it they explored the effects of both positive and negative feedback on the intrinsic motivation and performance of children who were either intrinsically oriented or extrinsically oriented, as assessed by Harter's (1981b) scale of extrinsic versus intrinsic orientation in the classroom. These researchers found, first, that success feedback increased the intrinsic motivation of intrinsically oriented children, but not that of extrinsically oriented children. The intrinsically oriented children apparently interpreted the positive feedback as more informational, and the extrinsically oriented children, as more controlling. For the latter group, the positive feedback seems to have strengthened their extrinsic responding but did not increase their intrinsic motivation. This finding provides a nice parallel to the results of the Ryan (1982) study reviewed earlier. Ryan created informational versus controlling positive feedback by modifying the interpersonal context, whereas Boggiano and Barrett found that the same feedback, administered in the same way, was differentially experienced as informational versus controlling because of the orientations of the recipients. In both cases, positive feedback that was experienced as controlling led to significantly less intrinsic motivation than positive feedback that was experienced as informational.

Boggiano and Barrett (1984) also explored the intrinsic motivation of intrinsically and extrinsically oriented children following failure feedback. They found that negative feedback to intrinsically oriented children apparently represented a challenge and therefore increased their intrinsic motivation for the activity; whereas negative feedback to extrinsically oriented children seemed to represent evidence of their incompetence and therefore decreased their intrinsic motivation and plunged them into a state of amotivation and helplessness. The conclusion about amotivation and helplessness comes from the fact that their subsequent performance on other activities was significantly impaired.

The finding that negative feedback plunges extrinsically oriented people into amotivation is a very important one, for it establishes a theoretical connection between extrinsic motivation and amotivation. Neither represents self-determination, and people can pass from extrinsic motivation to amotivation on the basis of their perceptions of incompetence. Being extrinsically oriented makes one particularly vulnerable to amotivation and helplessness when feedback does not continue to affirm one's competence.

To summarize, research has indicated that factors in the recipient of an interpersonal communication, whether the communication takes the form of a tangible reward or an intangible statement, play an important role in the way the communication is received and interpreted. Thus far, this has been demonstrated with respect to the recipient's gender, locus of control, and motivational orientation.

Intrapersonal Regulation: Information and Control

Throughout this chapter, we have explored the effects of various situational factors that are relevant to the initiation and regulation of behavior. Yet in everyday life, many events are initiated and regulated not by external events such as commands or promises of a reward, but by events inside oneself—for example, pressures, needs, feelings, expectations—that may be quite independent of the current external circumstances. Similarly, rewards, if one gets them at all, are often self-administered (e.g., one buys oneself a present), and may even be wholly inside the person (e.g., one says to oneself, "Gee, I did that really well").

Increasingly in recent years behavioral psychologists have turned their attention to internal events, with corresponding discussions of self-management, self-control, and self-reinforcement (see, for example, Bandura, 1977b; Kanfer, 1975; Mahoney, 1974; Skinner, 1974). The idea is that self-control leaves the person in charge of him- or herself, and in the words of Kanfer and Karoly (1972), can be "a means of counteracting alienation, powerlessness, and loneliness" (p. 237).

The idea of self-control would seem to bear relationship to our concepts of internal causality and self-determination; in fact, people have often used the various terms interchangeably. However, we understand the term self-control to mean something quite different from self-determination. The issue revolves around whether all regulatory events that are inside the person constitute internal causality and self-determination.

Self-control is a concept that has emerged from the cognitive-behavioral perspective (e.g., Kanfer, 1975), a perspective that focuses on people's expectations about reinforcements. Within that framework, *self-control* refers to the process in which one (1) sets one's own reinforcement contingencies (e.g., "I will buy myself a present and aggrandize myself if I work for six hours tomorrow"); (2) monitors one's own behavior (e.g., timing my working); and then (3) reinforces oneself (e.g., buying myself the present and telling myself what a good person I am). This process of self-control is contrasted with control by others, in which the contingencies are set, the monitoring is done, and the reinforcements are delivered by an external agent such as a boss, a teacher, or a parent.

Although self-determination may involve controlling one's own reinforcement contingencies, the central issue in self-determination is the experience of choice or freedom from pressure, rather than who administers the reinforcements. (Indeed, self-determination is most apparent in situations that are free of reinforcement contingencies, whether external or internal.) We suggest that the idea of control (whether by oneself or others) implies pressure toward specified outcomes. Insofar as one is monitoring and reinforcing oneself, one is likely to be pressuring oneself (i.e., controlling oneself), and, if so, this does not represent self-determination. Although we believe that self-control is in many ways preferable to being controlled by others, we suggest that being controlled by oneself can be fully as uncomfortable and detrimental to intrinsic motivation and related processes as being controlled by another. One can be as tyrannical toward oneself as others can be. The issue is not so much whether the source of control is oneself or another, but whether or not one is being controlled.

The important distinction that we wish to highlight is between events that initiate and regulate behavior in an informational fashion (thereby allowing freedom from pressure) and those that initiate and regulate behavior in a controlling fashion (thereby pressuring one toward specific outcomes). These events can be outside the person, or they can be wholly within the person. The issue of whether one's behavior is regulated by oneself or regulated by another is an important one; however, a more differentiated analysis, one that distinguishes between modes of self-regulation, is necessary. To regulate oneself informationally is quite different from regulating oneself controllingly. And we hypothesize that controlling oneself can have the same type of negative consequences as being controlled by others: a negative emotional tone, the experience of pressure and tension, and the loss of intrinsic motivation.

We use the terms *internally informational* and *internally controlling* to refer to those initiating or regulating events that occur within the person and whose nature is either informational or controlling, respectively. In this regard, the information–control distinction for events inside the person parallels exactly the information–control distinction for events outside the person (i.e., in the environment). Internally informational regulation represents self-determination; internally controlling regulation does not.

By way of explication, consider this example. An adolescent girl was taking guitar lessons. Each week, as the time to meet with her instructor approached, she focused on the need to practice. Even though the instructor did not force her to practice, the thought of not practicing evoked in her a sense of guilt and anticipatory anxiety. She experienced having to practice, so she practiced. When she finished, she was relieved and experienced satisfaction in being prepared. However, had she failed to practice, the guilt and bad feelings would have been exacerbated. Here practicing was regulated by internally controlling events. She created intrapsychic contingencies with affective consequences.

By contrast, imagine a scenario in which the girl focused on the satisfaction that would accrue from improving. In thinking about the week's practicing, it was not thoughts that she should practice that motivated her, but rather the anticipation of meeting a challenge, or mastering a new chord or rhythm. Even though the practicing may not have been intrinsically enjoyable, she was self-determined in it; she practiced because she personally valued getting better on the instrument. The regulation of her practicing was internally informational.

Now imagine that the guitar lessons stopped for several weeks while the instructor went on vacation. The instructor left no homework or lessons, so the girl was on her own and free to do as she pleased. Under which of the scenarios do you imagine the girl would have been most likely to play the guitar spontaneously? We suggest that if the regulation had been internally controlling, the girl would have been less likely to play during the vacation. Indeed, she may have been relieved of the tension and burden that she generally experienced each week before her lesson. By contrast, if the regulation had been internally informational, the girl, having not had the backdrop of conflict and pressure, would have continued to be task-involved and motivated to play her guitar.

It is important to see that the behavior that occurred is not the distinguishing factor. In both cases the behavior was the same: the girl practiced before each lesson. But the experience and the underlying psychological processes that regulated the behavior (i.e., the practicing) were quite different. In the first case, she motivated herself to practice by focusing on the guilt or anxiety that might accrue if she failed to do so—an example of internally controlling regulation. In the second case she wanted to improve, so she engaged in the behavior willingly. This is an example of internally informational regulation.

Proposition IV

Ryan (1982), who first introduced the concepts of internally informational and internally controlling regulation, hypothesized that internally informational events facilitate intrinsic motivation, whereas internally controlling events undermine it. By broadening the hypothesis and including the concept of internally amotivating events, we have extended cognitive evaluation theory by adding a fourth proposition.

> Intrapersonal events differ in their qualitative aspects and, like external events, can have varied functional significances. Internally informational events facilitate self-determined functioning and maintain or enhance intrinsic motivation. Internally controlling events are experienced as pressure toward specific outcomes and undermine intrinsic motivation. Internally amotivating events make salient one's incompetence and also undermine intrinsic motivation.

Experimental Investigations

Ryan (1982) did the first study that explored the effects of internally informational versus internally controlling events on intrinsic motivation and on the experience of pressure and tension. He used the ideas of ego-involvement and task-involvement to operationalize the concepts of internally controlling and internally informational, respectively. DeCharms (1968) had likened ego-involvement, that state in which one's self-esteem is "on the line," to extrinsic motivation and an external perceived locus of causality. When ego-involved, he suggested, people become invested in, and pressure themselves toward, particular outcomes. They evaluate themselves in terms of the outcomes they attain. In discussing creativity, Crutchfield (1962) asserted that ego-involvement means working with an ulterior motive and Frank (1941) suggested that this state involves the experience of pressure and tension. Task involvement, by comparison, can be likened to intrinsic motivation and an internal perceived locus of causality. A person becomes involved with the activity at hand not because of self-esteem issues but because he or she is focused on the interesting aspects of the activity. Without an investment in particular outcomes and without ulterior motives, one experiences less pressure and tension and may be more creative in doing the activity.

Ryan (1982) had subjects work on hidden-figures puzzles. Half the subjects were told that the activity involved breaking down and reorganizing perceptual fields and that one's performance at the activity was a reflection of creative intelligence. "In fact," he added, "hidden figures problems are used in some IQ tests" (which is true). This was intended to get college student subjects ego-involved in the activity. The subjects' concern about intelligence and academic performance, he reasoned, would be likely to hinge self-evaluations on performance, and would therefore be likely to engage the activity in an internally controlling manner. The other subjects were given similar inductions highlighting aspects of the task, but nothing was said about intelligence. By comparison, then, these subjects would be expected to be more task-involved, operating in an internally informational manner. The results revealed that ego-involved subjects were less intrinsically motivated (as measured by their activity in a subsequent free-choice period) than task-involved subjects. Further, ego-involved subjects also reported experiencing greater pressure and tension than task-involved subjects.

This later finding is an interesting complement to one from the Ryan *et al.* (1983) study. They found that subjects who were given either controlling positive feedback or controllingly administered, performance-contingent rewards reported experiencing greater pressure and tension than subjects who were given informational feedback or informationally administered, performance-contingent rewards. Thus, it appears that controlling events, whether initiated from within or without, decrease intrinsic motivation and induce greater pressure and tension than informational events.

It is important to recognize that all subjects in the Ryan (1982) study got positive feedback. Thus, the ego-involved subjects accomplished their goal; they proved to themselves that they were intelligent. If they had not known that they did well, they might have persisted at the activity under considerable pressure and tension to achieve their extrinsic though internal goal of preserving their self-esteem. Having accomplished their ego-involved goal, they were no longer extrinsically motivated, and the experience appears to have undermined their intrinsic motivation.

In another study (Plant & Ryan, in press), an internally controlling state was induced differently. These researchers used the work of Duval and Wicklund (1972) on objective self-awareness to suggest that when people focus on themselves "as objects" by looking at themselves from the outside, they will be in a controlling mode vis-à-vis themselves. Objective self-awareness is a state not unlike being observed or surveilled by another and is likely to facilitate internally controlling self-regulation. Lepper and Greene (1975) showed that surveillance by others undermined intrinsic motivation, so it seems reasonable to predict that surveillance by oneself would do the same.

Based on the earlier work by Duval and Wicklund (1972), Plant and Ryan used three levels of what they, like Carver and Scheier (1981), called self-awareness. Subjects who comprised the control group worked in the absence of a self-awareness manipulation, and subjects in the other two groups worked in front of either a mirror or a video camera. Video surveillance had in the past been shown to create the type of self-focused attention called public self-awareness, which is the state of viewing oneself as if through the eyes of another, and the presence of a mirror had sometimes been shown to have this same effect, though the mirror effects had been less clear-cut. In the Plant and Ryan study, half the subjects in each self-awareness condition were given a task-involvement induction and half were given an ego-involvement induction. Thus, they had attempted to facilitate internally controlling regulation in three ways: with a mirror, a video camera, and an ego-involving induction. Results of the study confirmed their predictions. First, they replicated Ryan's (1982) task versus ego results with a main effect that showed the undermining of intrinsic motivation by ego-involvement. Second, they found that self-focused attention, when created either by a mirror or by a video camera, led to decreased intrinsic motivation. The effect for the video camera, which more closely approximated external surveillance, was stronger than that for the mirror, though both effects were evident.

Carver and Scheier (1981) have also discussed research on dispositional self-focused attention and experimentally manipulated self-focused attention. Referring to a psychometric instrument developed by Fenigstein, Scheier, and Buss (1975), they suggested that qualitatively distinct attentional styles may be involved in self-regulation. Public self-consciousness refers to the trait-like tendency to be aware of oneself, or in other words to focus attention on oneself, as if viewed from the outside. Private self-consciousness, on the other hand, refers to the tendency to be aware of one's internal states, in other words, the private aspects of oneself.

Plant and Ryan (in press) suggested that the disposition of public self-consciousness has a close relationship to regulation by internally controlling events, so they predicted that it would be negatively related to intrinsic motivation. Private self-consciousness, on the other hand, has a less clear relationship. Since both internally controlling and internally informational events are private, a person could be aware of either one when his or her attention is focused privately. Thus, although public self-consciousness was predicted to be negatively related to intrinsic motivation, private self-consciousness was not. Results of their study confirmed the predictions. Public self-consciousness was strongly negatively related to intrinsic motivation as assessed by the free-choice measure in the Plant and Ryan study. Private self-consciousness, however, was unrelated to intrinsic motivation. This finding, then, provides evidence for our contention that regulation through attention to events inside oneself does not ensure self-determination. Only when those events are informational can one expect self-determined behavior or high levels of intrinsic motivation. Furthermore, both public self-consciousness (the trait) and public self-awareness (the state) may represent internally controlling regulation.

Thus far we have addressed the concepts of internally informational and internally controlling events. It is also possible to classify some events as *internally amotivating*. These would be events that occur within the person that signify one's inability to master some situations or events, such as self-deprecation or hopelessness. Although there is no work that has explored the effects of internally amotivating events directly, there are two studies of noncontingencies that are relevant. Brown and Inouye (1978) have shown that helplessness can be induced simply by having people observe others doing poorly, and DeVellis, DeVellis, and McCauley (1978) reported similar results when people observed others behaving in an uncontrollable setting but were not actually in that setting themselves. From these studies, we conclude that if a mere observation of someone acting in an uncontrollable situation can leave people feeling helpless, the observation must have stimulated an internal dynamic, a set of beliefs about themselves, that might be called internally amotivating. This suggests therefore that the effects of such events would parallel the effects of amotivating events outside oneself, just as the effects of internally informational and internally controlling events parallel the effects of informational and controlling events outside oneself.

SELF-DETERMINATION AND CAUSALITY

We have used the concept of internal versus external perceived locus of causality widely in our previous writings as well as in Chapter 3 of this book. Let us now integrate those concepts into the present discussion. An *internal perceived locus of causality* exists when a behavior is experienced to be initiated or regulated by an informational event, whether the event occurs inside or outside the person. On the other hand, an *external perceived locus of causality* exists when a behavior is seen as being initiated or regulated by a controlling event, whether that event occurs inside or outside the person. This shows clearly that the referent of the internal-external causality distinction is not the boundary created by one's skin. Instead the appropriate line of demarcation is one's sense of self. Activity that is perceived as having an internal locus of causality is congruent with or emanates from one's sense of self, whereas activity with a perceived external locus of causality is seen as being brought about by events or pressures outside of one's integrated sense of self. Thus even though an internally controlling event occurs inside the person, it is not regulated by processes that could be thought of as being internal to one's sense of self, so it is not self-determined and would be described as having an external perceived locus of causality.

Although self-determination is a descriptor that is applied to behavior, it is the psychological processes underlying the behavior that distinguish self-determined from non-self-determined behaviors. The same behavior can be either. To infer whether or not a behavior is self-determined, one would look for qualitative aspects of the behavior and the situational circumstances within which it occurs. A central feature of self-determined functioning is flexibility, whereas a central feature of non-self-determined functioning is the experience of pressure and tension. By assessing such qualitative aspects of the behavior, as well as considering the presence or absence of various situational controls, one can begin to make inferences about the extent to which a behavior is self-determined.

Intrinsically motivated behaviors are by definition self-determined. One follows one's interests, one seeks challenges, and one makes choices. The choices are relatively unconflicted and unselfconscious. There are no demands or rewards determining the behavior; one simply engages in behaviors that interest one and that one expects to be accompanied by spontaneous feelings of effectance. We have also seen that when behavior is regulated internally and informationally, the behavior is self-determined, and in the next chapter we will present a framework explicating more generally when non-intrinsically motivated behaviors are self-determined.

Summary

In Chapter 3 we suggested that events that initiate and regulate behavior—things like the offer of a reward, the imposition of a deadline, or the provision of feedback—will be experienced by the recipient as being one of three sorts: informational, controlling, and amotivating. In that chapter we reviewed research indicating how commonly occurring events, like rewards and feedback, tend on average to be experienced. In the present chapter, we found that, although there are tendencies for events to be experienced in certain ways, the interpersonal context within which an event occurs will affect how it is experienced and thus influence its effect on motivational processes. We saw, for example, that although rewards tend to be experienced as controlling and thus to decrease intrinsic motivation, they can be offered in a way that will lead them to be experienced as informational and will, therefore, exhance intrinsic motivation. Similarly, positive feedback, which tends to be experienced as informational, can be made controlling by mentioning how the recipient's performance compares to what it should be.

Further, we reviewed evidence suggesting that variables in the recipient of a communication will affect how it is interpreted and thus its motivational impact. Gender, locus of control, and motivational orientations were all found to mediate whether certain events were experienced as informational, controlling, or amotivating.

Finally, we presented an extension of cognitive evaluation theory which suggests that behavior may be regulated or affected by events wholly within the person; that these events can vary in their functional significance, such that they can be variously experienced as informational, controlling, or amotivating; and that their effects on motivational processes will parallel the effects of their interpersonal counterparts. This extension to the theory was the basis for discussions of the meaning of internal versus external causality and of self-determination.

Toward an Organismic Integration Theory
Motivation and Development

Organismic theories in psychology are constructed around two core notions: that behavior is regulated in part by internal structures that are elaborated through experience; and that human beings are by nature active. There is no place where these assumptions are more critical than in the area of development, for as we will see they are essential to an understanding of the ubiquitous phenomenon of children working eagerly and continually to master their internal and external environments.

THE NATURE OF DEVELOPMENT

The term *development* is etymologically derived from the concept of unfolding, or opening out, thus implying a process of one's potentials becoming manifest or actualized. This is perhaps what Rogers (1963) had in mind when he described development in terms of an "actualizing tendency." As he put it, the organismic tendency toward its own maintenance and enhancement "is the very nature of the process we call life" (p. 3). Piaget (1971) viewed it similarly when he stated that "the very nature of life is constantly to overtake itself," (p. 362). So basic is the concept of development to the nature of organisms, that these authors invoked the concept of life itself in describing it.

From these quotes one can also infer that the concept of development does not encompass all human change. Whereas change refers to any type of alteration in structure, whether progressive, accretive, or entropic, the term development is reserved for those changes that involve progressive organization of organic or psychological structure (von Bertalanffy, 1968). Thus, the study of human development entails an exploration of the transformations through which internal structures are increasingly elaborated and unified. Change that does not represent increased complexity and coordination of structure would not properly be termed development. This point is an especially important one, for it highlights the difference between mechanistic theories, which tend to view the issue of development in accretive terms, as a mere adding on of behaviors (or associative bonds that are said to determine behaviors), and organismic theories, which view it in terms of the elaboration of hierarchically organized structures.

The central process through which humans develop has been described in structural terms by several theorists. Piaget (1971), for example, spoke of "temporal transformation of structures in the double sense of differentiation of substructures and their integration into totalities," (p. 71), and Werner (1948) argued more broadly that the fundamental law of organic development is its tendency toward increased differentiation of elements and hierarchical integration of those elements. In the same vein, we suggest that development follows a general pattern in which one distinguishes specific elements of one's internal and external environments and then brings those elements into harmony with one's existing structures, thereby elaborating and refining the structures. We use the term *organismic integration* to refer to this general process.

Structural theories of development suggest that, through differentiation and integration, an invariant sequence of hierarchically organized stages emerges. The structures of each sequential stage build on and encompass the prior structures, and yet at each stage there is an organization or logic that gives relative stability and coherence to its form of functioning. It is in this sense of an emerging sequence of stages that we can give meaning to the term unfolding, from which development was etymologically derived.

One can easily be lead astray, however, by phrases like "an invariant sequence of stages," for it seems to connote a preprogrammed progression in which characteristics automatically emerge. Development is anything but preprogrammed, however. It emerges as the organism actively contends with the environment; it emerges from a dialectical struggle between the organism and the environment.

Accordingly, an explication of development requires more than just structural concepts; it requires the concept of activity. It is by acting on their surroundings, by exploring, testing, succeeding, and failing, that children develop their capacities and construct ever more elaborate and refined internal structures, which are the basis for future actions. Activity is, of course, implicit in many structural theories, because it is said that the nature of structures is to function and, through functioning, to transform themselves. We suggest, however, that the mere assumption of activity is not adequate for describing the energization of development. It is here that intrinsic motivation, which is the energic basis of the active organsm, is directly relevant. Simply stated, intrinsic motivation plays its major role in development as the energizer of the organismic integration process, as well as, in many instances, of the behaviors that promote that integration.

Both the concept of inherent activity and our assertion that development is intrinsically motivated imply that the locus of causality for natural development is internal. It does not require the impetus of external reinforcers, as the mechanistic theories have asserted, but will occur as an outcome of the organism's striving for competence and self-determination, providing, of course, that the environment does not prevent or forestall it.

The organismic theories that are currently dominant in developmental psychology emphasize the structural rather than the energetic aspects of development. They address the *what* rather than the *why* of development. Piaget's (1952) theory of cognitive development, Loevinger's (1976a) theory of ego development, and Kohlberg's (1969) theory of moral development, for example, all focus on sequences of stages, and although they assume an inherent activity through which the transformations occur, they tend not to address its dynamics.

By positing the intrinsic motivation of development rather than merely having activity be an inherent aspect of structures, we are in a better position to explicate the agency that we believe to be central to development. To some extent, we assert, one's development is something that one does to satisfy one's needs, rather than something that just happens when structures inherently function. Given our interest in self-determination (i.e., in human agency), we will focus more on the motivational than the structural aspects of development.

Motivational concepts are relevant to the constancies or invariants in development; in other words, the natural developmental progression is motivated. However, motivation takes on particular significance with respect to individual differences in both the rate and the extent of development. By considering motivational variables we have the opportunity to provide at least a partial answer to the questions of why some people develop faster than others and why some people's development progresses or stalls in certain domains. Furthermore, motivational variables are useful mediating constructs for organizing research and theory related to the issue of what environmental conditions facilitate versus hinder effective and reliable developmental change.

We maintain that the distinction between intrinsic and extrinsic motivation is critical for an understanding of development. We begin with the assertion that intrinsic motivation, one's basic needs to be competent and self-determining, is the primary energizer of the developmental (i.e., the organismic integration) process. However, the behaviors that constitute the inputs to development may be either intrinsically or extrinsically motivated. In other words, the development of some capacities and structures results from doing things that are interesting (i.e., from intrinsically motivated action), but the development of other capacities and structures results from behaviors that are not themselves interesting but are instrumental for adaptation to the social world (i.e., from extrinsically motivated action). The central developmental issue involved with extrinsically motivated behaviors is the internalization of their regulation, in other words, their integration into one's internal, organized structures.

Viewing the process of internalization as an aspect of the organism's quest for more competent, self-determined functioning has led to the theory of internalization that will be presented later in the chapter. As we will see, it moves beyond the other empirical theories to describe the motivational basis of internalization and to distinguish between types of internalized regulation by using the concept of self-determination. Viewing internalization as a function of the organismic integration process has also allowed us to apply the principles and findings acquired in the study of intrinsic motivation toward an understanding of the motivational conditions that promote versus forestall internalization and the development of integrated self-regulation.

THE ORGANISMIC INTEGRATION PROCESS

Internal structures develop toward greater elaboration and unity, and the more elaborated, unified structures provide the basis of more effective and autonomous functioning. The dual processes underlying this movement toward increasingly refined and wholistic structures are, as we have said, the differentiation of substructures and their integration into the larger unified structure. Taken together, we refer to them as the organismic integration (or simply, the integrative) process, which we have asserted is itself intrinsically motivated. Before addressing the motivational aspects of development, which are our central concerns, we will elaborate the general integrative process from a structural perspective by considering differentiation and integration in turn.

Differentiation involves the exercise of existing capacities in such a way that a relatively global aspect of one's internal structure becomes broken down into more specific elements. Differentiation is perhaps easiest to see with respect to perceptual development in which the child continually detects properties and patterns in the environment that had previously elicited no response. But differentiation is evident in personality development as well. For example, consider the baby who has achieved the sense of mother as an entity separate from him or herself. The baby gradually learns through experiences that mother both gratifies and frustrates, thus differentiating mother into good mother and bad mother—the good mother gratifies and the bad mother frustrates.

In Piaget's theory, the phenomenon that we are calling differentiation occurs through the operation of the assimilation schema, which he referred to as "the basic fact of psychic life" (Piaget, 1952, p. 41). When organisms encounter environmental stimuli that are moderately discrepant from their existing cognitive structures, these inconsistencies activate the assimilatory schema, which involves the two processes of assimilation and accommodation.

Assimilation is the process through which the organism incorporates aspects of the environment into its preexisting cognitive structures. This includes, for example, repeating or reproducing past actions and generalizing them to new situations or objects, thereby enlarging the range of one's existing capacities. Assimilation entails discriminating situations to which a schema will and will not apply, thereby affording a more differentiated understanding of reality. Frequently, however, one's existing cognitive structures are not sufficient to incorporate all the nuances of a situation. Thus, grasping the novel or unknown aspects of a situation may be necessary. This requires *accommodation*, the process through which the organism changes or elaborates its existing cognitive structures to include more aspects of the situation.

The processes of assimilation and accommodation are inseparably intertwined in life, and together they constitute the assimilation schema through which cognitive structures are elaborated. This basic schema, which serves the function of adaptation, builds on one's existing structures and, together with the organism's tendency toward organization, transforms existing structures into increasingly complex ones.

Piaget's theory suggests that the organism is continually operating on the environment and obtaining information through the exercise of the existing schemata. The exercise of schemata involves the ever challenging and interesting task of assimilating more and more of what the environment affords, as well as accommodating to what it affords. Through continual interactions with the environment, the child's schemata grow in complexity as he or she constructs new ways of organizing and integrating the environment. But differentiation does not occur only with respect to the child's mastery of the external world. It also concerns mastery of what Greenspan (1979) labeled *internal boundaries*. In other words, differentiation of capacities is also relevant to drives and affects. Variables such as physiological inputs, self and object representations, and emotions can be conceptualized as stimulus nutriments that children are intrinsically motivated to master, just as they are intrisically motivated to master form boards, pots and pans, and other tangible objects at their external boundaries. The differentiation that occurs at the internal boundaries results from the operation of the assimilatory schema and provides the basis for stable and flexible interactions of one's internal milieu with the interpersonal world.

Greenspan pointed out that the assimilations that occur with respect to the internal versus the external boundaries may proceed on different timetables. For one thing, the stimulus nutriments serving as inputs for structural development at the internal boundary are highly variable and complex. Furthermore, they are much less likely to be optimal when compared to activities in the impersonal world of objects; in other words, they often overwhelm the existing structures, being too far beyond the optimal challenge.

Psychodynamic theorists, such as Rapaport (1967) and White (1963), have also discussed the importance of differentiation of capacities at the internal boundaries. Rapaport suggested that people can be considered active when their structures regulate drives and emotions, whereas they would be considered passive when drives or emotions overpower structures. Differentiating elements of one's drives and emotions is part of the process of developing adequate structures, ones that will regulate the drives and emotions rather than be overpowered by them. Structural regulation of the internal as well as the external environment is the hallmark of autonomous ego functioning.

Elkind (1971), in the tradition of Piagetian thinking, elaborated the differentiation process in describing what he called *cognitive growth cycles*. These cycles, Elkind suggested, accompany the development of each cognitive ability and its associated behaviors. Cognitive growth cycles have several phases, beginning with the child's seeking stimulus inputs that provide the nutriments for further growth. Children can nourish their cognitive growth through a wide variety of stimulus inputs, and the ones that they encounter may be the basis for developing long-term preferences.

According to Elkind, children work with stimulus nutriments in characteristic ways that involve repeating actions, gating out irrelevant stimuli, storing relevant information, and playing with a newfound skill. When children have acquired a new cognitive ability, they tend to use it repeatedly until they grow tired of the activity. At that point, differentiation will be complete and the growth cycle will terminate.

It would of course be misleading to represent development as the simple elaboration of isolated capacities, because these capacities must be consistent and coordinated with one another if adaptive action is to occur. Developmental change, from an organismic perspective, represents synthetic alterations of structure, and *integration* is the process through which this synthesis occurs. In the example of the baby who differentiated mother into good and bad, the differentiated elements must move toward harmony for the growing child to develop the concept of mother as a person.

As with the concept of differentiation, we find multiple supports for the concept of integration among developmental theorists. Piaget proposed a second functional invariant of structural transformation that functions to integrate differentiated elements. He referred to this as *organization*, suggesting that the organism must be conceived of as a totality, within which there is a coordination of elements. Piaget (1952) stated it as follows:

> In short, the uniting of accommodation and assimilation presupposes an *organization*. Organization exists within each schema of assimilation. . . . But there is above all total organization; that is to say, coordination among the various schemata of assimilation. Now, as we have seen, this coordination is not formed differently from the simple schemata, except only that each one comprises the other in a reciprocal assimilation. (p. 142)

Through *reciprocal assimilation*, formerly separate schemata unite to form a new totality, superordinate to the previous one. The process is both microscopic and macroscopic because the organism tends toward increasing coordination within each element and among all the elements. It represents a holistic tendency within the organism.

In psychoanalytic theory, as well as in Piagetian theory, integration has a central place. Here it is generally referred to as the *synthetic function*. Freud (1923) introduced the construct in explicating what he saw to be the ego's remarkable tendency toward unity, though it received more specific attention from Nunberg (1931), who discussed how ego activity shows a pervasive tendency toward unification. This, he pointed out, can be seen in the ego's attempting to produce harmony among psychic structures and strivings; in its intolerance of contradiction; in the tendency toward causal thinking and organization of reality; and in creative activities, such as science and art. Nunberg suggested that the yardstick of psychological health is the degree to which the ego has developed unity among its elements.

Hartmann (1939), following Nunberg, gave the synthetic function a superordinate role in development. Adaptation, he suggested, results from the coordination of all one's functions. Through structuring the differentiated elements of one's inner and outer world, one is developing a personality that helps to define the range of responses available to one (i.e., one's competencies), and the range of environments that one is likely to seek and explore.

The notion of personality development as the product of the synthetic function has been recently explicated in the work of Loevinger (1976a), who adopted a structural view of personality that is akin to Piaget's theory of cognitive development. Loevinger portrayed ego development as the progressive structuralization of drives, affects, and cognitions into a stable unity. "The organization of the synthetic function is not just another thing that the ego does, it is what the ego is" (1976a, p. 5). More recently, Loevinger (1984) stated that, in retrospect, she might better have referred to this functioning structure as the self than the ego, thereby further emphasizing its centrality.

Indeed, we suggest that it is the synthesis of elements into a unified superordinate structure that provides the sense of identity and coherence that we refer to as the *self* and that is the basis for self-determined functioning. We use the term integration to refer to those functions that Piagetians labeled organization and psychodynamic theorists called synthetic, and we use the term *integrative process* to refer to that ongoing process of differentiating and integrating one's experience into a unified sense of self.

INTRINSIC MOTIVATION AND DEVELOPMENT

We believe it is useful to view the integrative process as being intrinsically motivated. Although other organismic theories have not done this explicitly, the assertion is congruent with and an elaboration of their perspectives. As Greenspan (1979) explained, Piaget maintained that structures are "self-motivating"; in other words, it is in the nature of structures to function. Particularly germane to our point would be that it is in the nature of the assimilation schema to function, because integration results from the operation of the assimilation schema. Although, as Flavell (1963) pointed out, Piaget paid relatively little attention to the motivational or energization aspects of development, a translation of this latter statement into motivational terms would be consistent with our position. Further, Piaget (1981) suggested that the affective aspect of assimilation is interest, and that the assimilation schema functions with respect to optimally incongruous stimuli. Interest, of course, is central to our conception of intrinsic motivation, and the idea that organisms work to assimilate optimally incongruous stimuli is closely related to our hypothesis that intrinsically motivated activity involves seeking and conquering (i.e., integrating) optimal challenges. By failing to make the motivational aspect of the process clear, however, and by treating the developmental process as occurring naturally or automatically, Piaget and other structural theorists have not fully captured the sense of personal agency or intentionality that we believe to be involved in development. Organisms work hard to differentiate and integrate aspects of their experience.

Elkind (1971) was more explicit about motivation than Piaget, and suggested that cognitive growth cycles are motivated by intrinsic growth forces. Once a cycle has been completed and the new structure fully developed, he added, the corresponding behaviors will no longer be intrinsically motivated and will generally require extrinsic motivation to operate. Elkind, like Flavell and Wohlwill (1969), suggested that competence (i.e., development) should be distinguished from performance. The former has to do with the development of structures and is clearly intrinsically motivated, whereas the latter has to do with the utilization of fully differentiated structures and therefore generally requires extrinsic motivation. This implies that, for an activity to be intrinsically motivated, it must serve to promote developmental growth.

White (1963), working within the psychoanalytic tradition, had the concept of effectance motivation at the heart of his discussion of development. He suggested that the ego has independent energies, which he referred to as effectance motivation, and that there are natural satisfactions (i.e., feelings of efficacy) that result from the exercise of all one's capacities, including the synthetic function. Loevinger's (1976a) statement that "the striving to master, to integrate, and make sense of experience is . . . the essence of the ego" (p. 59) is of course congruent with, though less motivationally explicit than, White's statements.

In sum, we have seen that the various organismic theories all provide a central, though generally not explicit, place for intrinsic motivation in the differentiation and integration of organismic capacities. Indeed, the integrative process may be the prototype of the spontaneous activity, both psychological and behavioral, that occurs in the absence of extrinsic inducements.

Intrinsically Motivated Behavior

Thus far we have focused our attention on the integrative process itself. However, the functioning of the integrative process is intertwined with behavior; it requires behavior to provide nutriments for the development of competencies. Children learn through behaving—through thinking and acting—and much of this behavior, as well as the integrative process itself, is intrinsically motivated.

Children's natural curiosity leads them to engage in a wide range of exploratory, manipulatory, and experimental behaviors. Without prods or incentives, indeed frequently in the face of open discouragement, children work determinedly to figure out how things go together or what actions produce what effects. They are fascinated by the novel, and persistent in their attempts to make it familiar. Learning has often been said to be the central business of childhood.

Closely related to curiosity-based behaviors, in the sense of being active and natural, is play. Although play serves an important adaptive function, adaptation is not the goal of play. Indeed, a defining characteristic of play is precisely its absence of any goals (Garvey, 1977). Play is compelling and satisfying in its own right; it is, as Csikszentmihalyi (1975) put it, autotelic. It needs neither direction nor reinforcement; in fact, if it is not self-determined it is not play. Flavell (1977) said that to ask why a child plays is akin to asking why a child breathes. Children play for enjoyment, but this activity often has the side benefit of developing competencies.

Curiosity and play are fundamental features of children's behavior. They are involved in what Elkind (1971) called cognitive growth cycles, and they are classic examples of intrinsically motivated behavior. They are spontaneous, emanating from interest and internal proneness, and their occurrence requires no outside compulsions or constraints.

Discussions of curiosity and play are so intertwined with discussions of the integrative process throughout the developmental writings of organismic theorists that they are virtually inseparable. It is exploration, manipulation, and play that are the actions that produce much of the differentiation and integration. We have separated them here only so that we will be able to show how the intrinsically motivated integrative process is also germane to many extrinsically motivated behaviors. That point will be explicated in the second half of the chapter.

The Effects of the Environment

If we are correct in our assertions that the integrative process that characterizes development is intrinsically motivated, and that much of the child's development results from intrinsically motivated behaviors, it would follow straightforwardly that the principles of cognitive evaluation theory are directly applicable at both levels of developmental phenomena. Cognitive evaluation theory suggests that environments that provide optimal challenge, competence-promoting feedback, and support for autonomous activity will facilitate intrinsic motivation. They should accordingly facilitate development as well.

Optimal Challenge and Perceived Competence. One condition that is critical for effective development is adequate stimulation in the form of optimal challenges, given the child's capacities. In Piaget's words, the child must encounter stimuli that are moderately assimilable. When children are intrinsically motivated, they seek out optimal challenges, and their engagement with those challenges contributes to the continuing differentiation and integration of existing capacities and structures. The concept of optimal, when applied to challenge, must always be understood with respect to one's existing structures. As Montessori (1965) described it, the developing child needs to find stimulation in the environment that is *"organized* in direct relation to his internal organization which is developing by natural laws" (p. 70). Optimal challenge, therefore, involves elements that are slightly discrepant from, and can be assimilated into, one's existing, organized structures.

The principle of optimal challenge has also been discussed by Hunt (1966, 1975a) under the rubric of the "problem of match." His view suggests that the situations that are most intrinsically motivating are those that contain information relevant to structures already stored and mastered but that are discrepant enough to call forth adaptive modifications. Overly familiar or excessively repetitive tasks and tasks that greatly exceed existing capacities will call forth boredom and distress, respectively. They do not generate the feelings of competence or interest that are so essential to intrinsic motivation.

An empirical test of the hypothesis that challenges that provide an optimal level of incongruity are intrinsically motivating was provided recently by the Danner and Lonky (1981) study reviewed in Chapter 3. They used the Piagetian model for defining the cognitive complexity of three tasks intended to vary in difficulty: dichotomous sorting, class inclusion, and combinatorial reasoning. Children were pretested on their classification-ability levels and then divided into three groups on the basis of that assessment. The children were then introduced to the classification tasks and finally left alone with the tasks. The amount of time spent by each child on each task was recorded unobtrusively, and an additional interest rating for each was obtained. This free-choice time and interest rating served as measures of intrinsic motivation. The results demonstrated that children in each of the cognitive-ability groups spent the most time with and rated as most interesting the tasks that were one step ahead of their pretested skill level. The results supported the prediction, based on Deci's (1975) cognitive evaluation theory and Piaget's (1977) equilibration model, that children would choose to work on tasks that provide optimal stimulation for cognitive development.

Harter (1974) reported the complementary finding that children derived greater pleasure from optimal challenges than from ones that were too easy or too hard. When the children worked on tasks that were moderately difficult given their capacities, they smiled more and expressed greater enjoyment of the task than when they worked on tasks that were either more or less difficult.

Under normal conditions, children self-regulate the optimal level of challenge. If an activity is not sufficiently challenging, the child will move to one that is more challenging, and if it is too challenging, the child will move to one that is easier. Children tend to engage in non-optimal activities only through the provision of external pressures. Organized environments, such as schools, often use external pressures rather than optimal challenges to motivate children to learn, and pressure motivates a different, and generally inferior, type of learning. It does not encourage the natural, integrative process; instead, it tends to encourage the adding on of facts.

Closely related to the idea of optimal challenge is that of perceived competence. Harter (1978a) emphasized the importance of perceived competence for effectance motivation, and Harter and Connell (1984) used structural modeling to support the view that children's perceived competence affects their level of intrinsic motivation, and thus, we would add, their development. To a large extent, perceived competence comes from success experiences and from positive feedback. When children are working with optimally challenging activities, perceived competence will tend to come naturally, for they will be having the experiences of success following concerted effort that lead to the perceptions of competence.

For infants, a positive sense of competence and intrinsic motivation seem to come primarily from the responsiveness of the environment. In research with infants, Yarrow, Klein, Lomonaco, and Morgan (1975) found that the responsiveness of both the inanimate and social environments was related to subsequent exploration. Lewis and Goldberg (1969) reported complementary findings from a study of mother–infant interactions, and both sets of authors concluded that environments that respond to infant's initiations will foster a sense of competence and mastery that will fuel further development.

It seems, then, that much of the necessary feedback for children's perceived competence can come directly from the responsiveness of tasks or people in their environments, yet specific positive feedback from others if often important as well. Several lines of research, much of it reviewed in Chapters 3 and 4, provide support for this later point. Experimental studies by Boggiano and Ruble (1979) and numerous others, for example, have demonstrated that positive feedback to children tends to enhance their intrinsic motivation, although as we saw repeatedly, when the positive feedback takes on controlling tones, it can have a detrimental effect on intrinsic motivation.

The Interpersonal Context. Our view of human development leads to the assertion that differentiation and integration processes will occur naturally in interpersonal environments that are informational rather than controlling, environments where adults avoid controlling the child's intrinsic activity. Untimely interference and direction by adults can be a disturbing influence on a child's developing mastery, and the use of rewards, deadlines, and controlling communications will undoubtedly be detrimental. These influences are likely to take children away from the tasks that are optimally challenging and thus necessary for natural development, and they are also likely to undermine the children's intrinsic motivation even if they are working at an optimal level.

The former point was demonstrated in a study by Shapira (1976), although he used college student subjects. He found that when subjects were free from the offer of rewards, they selected challenging activities, but when rewards were introduced, they selected very easy ones. The second point, that rewards to children for working on optimally challenging tasks will decrease their intrinsic motivation for those tasks, was confirmed by Danner and Lonky (1981). They reported that when children were rewarded for working on the optimal activities that they had selected themselves, they lost intrinsic motivation for the activities, relative to children who were not rewarded.

It appears, then, that rewards may be detrimental to development because they tend to be experienced as controlling and to foster an external locus of causality, thereby undermining intrinsic motivation. A similar point can be made for all interpersonal communications. The more controlling they are, the more likely it is that they will impede the developmental process. Two studies of family interactions provide support for this conclusion. In the first, Grolnick, Frodi, and Bridges (1984) observed mothers interacting with their babies and rated the mothers' behaviors in terms of the degree to which they were controlling (versus oriented toward supporting autonomy). The researchers then assessed the mastery motivation of the babies using a procedure developed by Morgan, Harmon, Gaiter, Jennings, Gist, and Yarrow (1977) and found that the babies of controlling mothers tended to display less persistence and competence than those of the mothers who were less controlling.

Chandler (1981), in a cross-sectional investigation of children's motivational orientations, also examined the impact of parental intervention on children's motivation for mastery oriented behaviors. Among the types of behaviors included in her measures were building something with toys, playing a ball game, playing with friends, and reading books.

In general, children had reported that they tend to do these activities for fun, interest, and challenge.

Chandler obtained self-report data from mothers of the 121 children in her sample concerning their parenting interactions. Of present interest is mothers' reports about how they and the fathers respond to their children's successes and failures on each of these mastery behaviors. From factor analyses, Chandler found that following both successes and failures there was a factor that she labeled instruct and model. She then examined the relationship between these responses and the intrinsic motivation of children for the mastery behaviors. For failure experiences the instruct-model style had no significant effect on children's intrinsic motivation; however, modeling and instruction following success had a significant detrimental impact on the children's intrinsic motivation. This apparently untimely intrusion of instructing a child after he or she has just succeeded at a mastery attempt impeded continuing intrinsic interest and exercise of structures.

The results of the Grolnick *et al.* and the Chandler studies are, of course, congruent with a host of data and with the general conclusion that undue control or pressure will decrease intrinsic motivation and negatively affect related affective, cognitive, and behavioral variables. These two studies are particularly important, however, in that the data were obtained from actual family interactions.

Are we suggesting that parents and educators stay out of the way completely? Not wholly so, of course. Chandler's data suggested that following failure, instruction was not detrimental, and may have been helpful, for intrinsic motivation. Further, cognitive evaluation theory suggests, and numerous studies have confirmed, that effectance-relevant information is important for intrinsic motivation, so long as it is made available within the context of self-determination or choice (e.g., Fisher, 1978). In other words, the children must feel free (rather than pressured) to use the competence-relevant information. Furthermore, there are also times when intrinsic development could lead to socially intolerable activities. Children may love to paint, bang pots and pans, play with hot water spigots, and do a variety of annoying and perhaps dangerous (but intrinsically motivated) actions. In such situations, limit setting may be entirely appropriate, and as the Koestner *et al.* (1984) study described in Chapter 4 revealed, limits can be set effectively without undermining intrinsic motivation if they are conveyed in a manner that does not threaten the child's self-determination and self-esteem.

As a general rule, of course, parents do need to be involved with their children. They need to show concern and to provide informational structures. Limit setting is one aspect of providing the needed informational structures, and as Coopersmith (1967) concluded, when the limits are clear and provide the opportunity for choice they will tend to promote high self-esteem. Further, from the Koestner *et al.* study, we can conclude that limit setting will tend to support children's intrinsic motivation, if the limit setting includes three important elements. First, it needs to provide as much choice as possible and refrain from conveying unnecessary pressure—even the pressure that is implicit in the word *should*. Limits need to allow the child to be as self-determining as possible. Second, they need to include some mechanism that provides non-evaluative feedback, feedback that does not call the child's self-esteem into question. Third, because setting limits invariably presents the child with a conflict between what he or she wants or feels and what the limits require, it is important that the child's needs or feelings be acknowledged and accepted so the child will be able to integrate the seemingly conflicting elements. Otherwise, the conflict will tend to diminish the child's self-esteem and forestall a self-determined accommodation to those limits.

The Development of Intrinsic Motivation

Babies are interested in a wide range of novel stimuli, and as they develop into young children they seem interested in learning about all aspects of their environment. Their general need for competence and self-determination operates globally, and they orient to all sorts of inputs. Gradually, however, they develop preferences and behave more selectively, and their competencies tend either to flourish or to atrophy depending on whether they are accompanied by interest.

The processes through which one's interests (in other words, one's intrinsic motivation) develop are, we suggest, the same as those through which all development proceeds. At the beginning interests are relatively undifferentiated, and gradually through accumulated experiences they become more differentiated. Deci (1975) spoke of this as the differentiation of motives, because the term *motive* describes where one's energy is directed and pertains to one's interests and competencies (i.e., to structures).

Deci (1975) suggested that the differentiation of activities that people find intrinsically motivating is the function of two things: what Woodworth (1918) referred to as a child's native equipment (i.e., innate abilities); and the experiences that the child has with various activities. The first of these will certainly have a strong influence. There are clear differences in children's innate talents, and children seem more interested in things they are able to master than things they are not. However, as Hunt (1975b) suggested, there is a wide "range of reaction" in the expression of innate abilities, and the areas where one applies one's competencies will depend on what is available and on the quality of the circumstances that surround what is available. Thus one's innate capacities are intertwined with experience, and the two begin to interact very quickly to influence the expression of one's inherent capacities. In this interaction, the factors that affect the differentiation of interests are hypothesized to be those described by cognitive evaluation theory.

The interaction of capacities and environments begins with innate abilities that affect one's mastery attempts, resulting in successes and failures that in turn affect one's perceived competence and intrinsic interest. Further, the ambient opportunities that are available to offer optimal challenges will also be important in one's developing preferences. Only some types of activities are available to children—music, for example, is widely available in some homes and not at all in others—and this availability is surely a factor in the development of their interests and capacities. A boy who grows up on a small island is more likely to become interested in and competent at fishing than basketball, though the opposite is likely to be true for the boy brought up in a city. The environment presents affordances, and the child goes to the optimally challenging ones. Furthermore, children tend to use affordances to do the activities that they observe to be socially valued. Thus, for example, the children of the Dakota tribe described by Erikson (1950) chased roosters in mimic of the hunt—an activity that was clearly valued by their elders.

Finally, although challenging affordances affect the differentiation of intrinsic interest, they are not the only factors that do. All boys in the island village do not become interested in fishing, for example. Another significant factor that we hypothesize to affect the differentiation of interests is the degree to which one's opportunity to interact with the affordances is self-determined. The pressures and controls of adults, as we have seen over and over, can alienate the developing interests even for talented children. One wonders, for example, how many potential Arthur Rubensteins have turned away from the piano to preserve their sense of self-determination when their lessons become overly controlled.

The interaction of the environment and one's innate capacities is thus central to the development of intrinsic motivation. The differentiation of one's interests is, like other developmental processes, an opening out or unfolding that is influenced by what the environment affords and permits. Difficult as it may be for parents and educators to provide the conditions that will allow this natural developmental process to occur with respect to things children find intrinsically interesting, the difficulties are even far greater when they face the task of promoting the development of regulations for behaviors that have no inherent interest. There, the issues become more complex and necessitate the use of extrinsic motivators to facilitate the developmental process.

EXTRINSIC MOTIVATION AND DEVELOPMENT

Although differentiation and integration occur naturally with respect to activities or inputs that interest children, there are many behaviors that do not naturally interest them but that the social world deems necessary for them to learn. As children grow older, the social environment, and particularly caretakers, place increasing demands and limits on the exercise of their capacities. Caretakers feel the need to prohibit or redirect children's activity so that children will engage in behaviors that they would not otherwise do, but that ensure their safety, conform with cultural values, or in some way gratify the caretakers' needs.

There is, therefore, an expectable but critical opposition between children's active nature and the values and conditions of social life, a developmental conflict (or series of conflicts) often described as *socialization*. The concept of socialization gives recognition to the fact that there are many behaviors, attitudes, and values that are neither natural nor intrinsically motivated, but that are important for effective functioning in the social world. Similarly, there are many behaviors that children find intrinsically interesting but that adults find painful, intrusive, or disagreeable. In both cases, the adults are faced with the responsibility of externally regulating the children's behavior so the children will do certain things that are neither spontaneous nor intrinsically motivating. Caretakers, however, are not merely interested in eliciting those behaviors, they generally desire that the children accept responsibility for them. This shift in the locus of regulation for those behaviors frees the adults of the responsibility and prepares the children for participation in the cultural milieu.

Because these new behaviors—whether they be acquisitions or abstentions—do not occur spontaneously out of interest, they require the provision of extrinsic factors if they are to occur at all. The problem, then, is one of regulating a child's behavior with extrinsic contingencies in such a way that the regulating will gradually be accepted by the child as his or her own and the use of the controls will not have detrimental effects on related, intrinsically motivated behaviors. Thus, an important problem for adaptation and development is the promotion of a shift from regulation by external factors to self-regulation by internal factors in a variety of behavioral domains. This is the issue of internalization.

The term *internalization* refers to the process through which an individual acquires an attitude, belief, or behavioral regulation and progressively transforms it into a personal value, goal, or organization. It is the developmental process by which a child integrates the demands and values of the socializing environment.

The concept of internalization is by no means new. It has enjoyed currency in psychology for most of this century, though different psychologists have treated the concept quite differently. Hartmann and Loewenstein (1962), for example, used the term to describe regulations that were initially based in interaction with the external world and have become internal, whereas Schafer (1968) defined it as the process by which subjects transform real or imagined external regulations into internal regulations. Numerous authors outside of psychoanalytic theory (e.g., Collins, 1977; English & English, 1958) have also used the term to describe the change from outer to inner regulation.

In our view internalization is an active process. Transforming an outer regulation into an inner one requires that one reorganize one's capacities and propensities, and it may require that one shift one's perspective or values. Such modifications, like all developmental acquisitions, require active work. When the organism is passive or resistent, the modifications are unlikely to occur. We therefore believe that internalization is an aspect of the active-organism side of the organism–environment dialectic. As such, internalization is not something that gets done to the organism by the environment, it is something the organism does actively to accommodate the environment, unless the environment overpowers the organism.

Because the domain of internalization consists of all those behaviors that do not occur spontaneously but are required by the social world, the process of internalization involves developing the capacities for mastering external demands and, in appropriate instances, for taking them on as one's own. This in turn allows for greater autonomy and more effective functioning (e.g., Ryan, Avery, & Grolnick, 1985).

We are now in a position to assert that the process by which this internalization occurs is not different in kind from the integration of capacities that were differentiated through purely intrinsic motivation. It is, however, more complex, for it involves the resolution of the inherent conflict between what one would do naturally and what one is being asked to do. It requires a greater degree of accommodation. The basic similarity is the tendency for the integrative process to function—in this case resulting in the integration of extrinsically motivated regulations—in the service of one's movement toward greater competence and self-determination. Whether in the case of intrinsically motivated behaviors

or extrinsically motivated behaviors, the natural (i.e., intrinsically motivated) processes of differentiation and integration will function toward
the development of structures that allow competence and self-
determination. With intrinsically motivated behaviors, we emphasized
the differentiation aspect because the opening out metaphor applies and
the integration occurs quite naturally. With extrinsically motivated
behavior, however, we will emphasize the integration aspect because
the taking in of a conflicting force requires substantial integration. Still,
differentiation and integration are necessary within both classes of
behaviors.

Internalization, then, is asserted to be a constructive process aimed
at allowing one to be more competently self-determining in the social
world, even though the goals of the specific behaviors are extrinsic. The
concept of self-determination is particularly important with respect to
internalization, because the intrinsic need for competent self-
determination is theorized to motivate the internalization process, and
because the concept of self-determination describes the ideal outcome
of the internalization process. As we saw in Chapter 4, not all forms of
internal regulation constitute self-determination. Ego-involvement, for
example, is often the basis for regulation that is inside the person but
that neither represents self-determination nor has an internal locus of
causality. Internalization poses the important problem not merely of
moving the regulation of extrinsically motivated behavior inside the
person, but of integrating external motivation into a unified system of
structures and motives so that the extrinsic regulation that is internalized
will eventually be experienced as self-determined. It is only when the
cultural values become the child's values and are smoothly and uncon-
flictfully exercised that internalization is complete.

Let us summarize our argument thus far. The organismic tendency
toward expanded harmony (i.e., the intrinsically motivated integrative
process) leads children to master and incorporate many behaviors that
are not themselves intrinsically motivated but are valued by the social
environment and thus are instrumental for the children's long-term
effectiveness. Behaviors that the organism would not do naturally will
have to be extrinsically motivated, but these behaviors may be integrated
into the realm of self-determination (i.e., they can be valued and done
willingly), even though they will never become intrinsically motivated.

Our assertion that the process of internalization is part of the organismic integration process implies, of course, that one should see the
process occurring naturally (unless the environment impedes it), and
thus that one would observe more internalized regulation as children
grow older. Because this represents an essential part of our argument,

we will review evidence in support of this hypothesis before moving on to a more detailed description of the internalization process and to a consideration of the role played by the environment.

Evidence for Internalization

Chandler and Connell (1984) investigated the hypothesis that extrinsically motivated behaviors would exhibit a developmental trend toward increasingly internalized regulation. They studied chore behaviors (things like following parental requests, picking up one's room, doing homework, and going to bed on time), that were initially disliked by children and were in need of extrinsic, parentally provided supports for their occurrence. They asked children of ages from 6 to 13 to describe the reasons why they did these target behaviors, and the children's responses were recorded verbatim. A pretested coding system with high reliability was then used to classify their responses into various categories. For our current purposes there were two categories of particular interest. The *extrinsic* category included those motivational responses that indicated that the behavior in question could be elicited only by extrinsic cues (e.g., an extrinsic reward or punishment). The extrinsic response category included gaining or maintaining peer or sibling approval; avoiding peer or sibling disapproval; gaining or maintaining adult approval; avoiding adult disapproval; gaining or losing a specific tangible reward; and following specific rules. The *internalized* category included motivational responses that indicated that the child had an understanding of the internalized consequences of performing a behavior, thus indicating that the behavior was self-motivated, though of course not intrinsically motivated. These were achievement of a self-selected goal; avoidance of a self-selected consequence; and altruism. Altruistic responses were included here because they tend to reflect an internalized goal of making someone else happy, although they had a very low frequency of occurrence.

Chandler and Connell reported that extrinsic responses were negatively correlated with age, whereas internalized responses were positively correlated with age. This supports our hypothesis of a developmental process leading to an internalized orientation for performing behaviors such as chores. One can assume that when children first begin learning how to do chores, they are likely to be motivated to perform them only by extrinsic factors administered by parents. With development, children incorporate the parental values and standards such that they become internalized values and standards. The data gathered here suggest that, when children are able to understand and accept that the consequences of performing behaviors such as chores can be beneficial to their own goals, internalization can be said to have occurred. The children would then be expected to motivate themselves to engage in these chore behaviors. Further research, particularly longitudinal rather than cross-sectional and including children younger and older than those in the Chandler and Connell sample, would aid in adding detail to an understanding of the internalization process. But their data are among the first to demonstrate the developmental process of extrinsic regulation moving toward self-determined regulation.

There was an important attitude change that accompanied the change in motivational orientation across these ages. Older children rated the chore behaviors as more important than younger children, and the attitude of importance was significantly related to the children's use of internalized responses. The more the children felt it was important to do chores and to follow parental rules, the more likely they were to give internalized reasons for performing them, and the less likely they were to give extrinsic reasons. These two findings suggest that an aspect of the developmental process of internalizing the regulation of specific behaviors is their becoming valued or viewed as important by the children.

Evidence that relates to our hypothesis of a developmental trend from heteronomy toward autonomy with respect to extrinsic motivation can also be inferred from Loevinger's (1976a,b) research on ego development. Through the use of various psychometric instruments she has traced the stages of ego development, noting a progression from depending entirely on the environment for regulation, toward autonomous regulation through the use of what she called *mature conscience*. This type of regulation, which is free of guilt and self-condemnation, represents the archetype of self-determined responding. Although her research indicates that few people function in that manner a great deal of the time, the developmental trend is clearly toward autonomous self-regulation.

Internalization and the Integrative Process

A basic premise of organismic integration theory is that there is developmental movement from the nonregulation of behaviors that do not interest one, toward self-determined regulation of the subset of those behaviors that are useful for one's effective adaptation. Having reviewed some preliminary evidence in support of this, we move on to a more detailed description of the internalization process.

Nonregulation of behavior is most clearly evident in newborns. Insofar as caretakers desire anything that does not come naturally for the infant, they must make it happen. Caretakers move the child by picking him or her up; they give the child a bottle or breast; and they bathe and change the child. Regulation of nonspontaneous activities is not mediated by processes internal to the child, for the child does not have the necessary capacities. The regulation itself is impersonal with respect to the child, even though it may occur in response to the child's having cried or signaled. During these early months the child lacks the requisite capacities for mastering social demands.

Perhaps the most fundamental skill that must be differentiated for such mastery to occur is anticipation, a skill that is likely to have developed by the time of the child's first birthday (Hunt, 1965). The child will have engaged in a number of actions and perceptual activities in which contingent relationships occurred between his or her actions and a response from the environment. Observation of children in activities such as peek-a-boo or playing with mobiles suggests that contingently responsive environments are stimulating and interesting for the child and foster development of the capacity for predicting outcomes where contingencies exist. In fact, a number of researchers, such as Ainsworth, Blehar, Waters, and Wall (1978) have shown that responsive environments are extremely important for children's effective development in general. When children are deprived of regularity, lawfulness, and contingency in their environments, they tend to lag developmentally.

A second capacity necessary for mastery of external demands is control of one's own actions and affects, at least in a primitive form. The initiation and inhibition of action, which is essential for all voluntary behavior, becomes increasingly involved in a child's behavior as the child progresses through the second half of his or her first year. Thus, by the end of the first year, most children will have developed the two most critical skills that constitute the groundwork for internalization.

Internalization, then, begins with the child's using his or her primitive capacities to respond to external demands. Initially, this means that the child applies the developing functions of *anticipation* and *self-control* to respond to external cues. Thus, for example, a boy, as early as in his second year, might anticipate his mother's angry response as he reaches for an expensive glass elephant on the end table and then control (inhibit) his behavior. This would be an early form of what we call *external regulation*, which is the most basic form of extrinsic motivation; the child behaves (i.e., refrains from touching the elephant) in order to attain or avoid immediate consequences administered by another. This external form of self-regulation becomes increasingly refined during the first few years of life as the child becomes more adept at anticipating consequences and controlling him or herself, even when the consequences are more distant and there are other potentially distracting stimuli in the immediate situation.

In a recent study by Vaughn, Kopp, and Krakow (1984), children between 18 and 30 months were asked to display self-control. Either their mothers asked them to pick up some toys or the experimenter asked them to refrain from touching attractive objects, and in both cases the degree to which they complied was measured. Results indicated that the behaviors indicative of self-control increased with age over this period, thereby indicating a greater mastery of the skills necessary to engage in what we have called the external form of self-regulation.

External regulation, then, involves the imposition by another person of external contingencies to which the child responds. Often these have tangible consequences for the very young child; they might, for example, be avoidance of a scolding or receipt of a reward such as food or physical contact. With time, however, the focus of interest for the child is increasingly social. What matters, and therefore what motivates external self-regulation, are social rewards and contingencies. Such factors as praise, disapproval, and esteem from others become progressively more potent sanctions that promote certain otherwise nonspontaneous behaviors. At this point the external self-regulation is a reflection of primitive internalization. The behaviors are maintained (unstably) through external supports, but they are internalizations by virtue of the fact that the child anticipates the consequences of action, and self-regulates with respect to what is anticipated. What has been internalized is a conception of the external regulatory forces as they still exist.

We have said several times that the important developmental problem for self-regulation is not merely one of learning and responding to external contingencies however, it is one of moving beyond external regulation to the point where one takes on the control of those behaviors and can perform them in the absence of immediate external consequences. Ultimately, of course, the issue is promoting self-determination of those behaviors.

According to organismic integration theory, the developmental movement beyond external regulation can be described with three processes and three corresponding types of self-regulation. After children have learned to regulate themselves in the presence of relatively immediate extrinsic contingencies, one sees increasing evidence of their being able to do those behaviors when the contingencies become more and more distant and are eventually removed. This occurs following the process of introjection.

We use the term *introjection* to refer to the process whereby a regulation is internalized in essentially its original form; children regulate themselves by carrying on a relationship with an internal representation of the previously external contingencies. That is, children establish an internal representation (i.e., a structure) that is essentially isomorphic with the formerly external controls, and then act in accord with the now internalized demands. They then apply approval and disapproval to themselves, contingent on their actions. Consider for instance the example of a boy just learning to regulate the expression of his play. He finds his red rubber ball on the floor and experiences the impulse to throw it, but he inhibits the action. The inner form of the inhibition might be a thought or maxim such as, "Good boys don't throw balls in the house." Through introjection, the boy has established an internal version of his mother's contingent evaluation of his behavior (i.e., a self-administered version of what was originally her approval and disapproval). The child is now engaging in *introjected self-regulation*. In practice, the regulatory thoughts are usually not so explicit, and the regulation is more affective than cognitive, but the explicit cognitions presented above describe the form of the regulation.

In a sense, introjected self-regulation represents the first evidence of what might properly be termed self-control, as that term has come to be used in the cognitive-behavioral literature (e.g., Kanfer, 1975), for the child is doing the monitoring and is administering the sanctions to him or herself.

Introjected regulation involves the management of conflicting impulses (to do or not to do; to refrain or not to refrain) and requires the superordinate support of cognitive-affective consequences. Introjected regulation is, of course, more stable than external regulation because it does not require the presence of external contingencies; the contingencies are now within the child and thus continuously present. However, introjected regulation does share many characteristics with external regulation, most notably the conflictful controller–controlled relationship and all that that entails. Whereas with external regulation, the controller and the controlled are separate people, with introjected regulation they are now aspects of the same person. In both cases, however, there is the tension inherent in being controlled.

An example of introjected regulation that has persisted beyond the point where it is age-appropriate can be seen in what Ryan (1982) and Nicholls (1984) have called ego-involvement, where people regulate their performance in anticipation of either disparaging or inflating self-attributions about their abilities. More appropriate, in a sense, would be the term *superego-involvement*, because internal evaluation accompanied by affective consequences is more a function of what psychoanalytic theorists call the superego than of the ego. In children, however, where the concept of ability is not well differentiated, the specific state of ego-involvement may not apply, but analogous forms of contingent self-evaluation with affective consequences (i.e., superego controls) do apply. Shame and guilt are the most common hallmarks of introjected regulation.

In our theory, introjected self-regulation is not self-determined, for it lacks the unity of action that characterizes self-determination. The next point along the internalization continuum, however, moves the child a step closer to self-determination with respect to internalized regulation. Gradually, as the child works to master the demands of the social world, he or she will increasingly identify with the behavioral outcomes (e.g., with keeping one's room clean) and with the regulations that yield them. Through *identification* the child accepts the regulation as his or her own. Thus the conflict is largely dissipated, and we find integration within this differentiated element of self-regulation. With introjected self-regulation a boy might clean his room because "children should—good children have clean rooms," but with self-regulation through identification he might clean it because "I like my room clean—it lets me find things easier."

The concept of identification has been used widely in the psychological literature. In areas as diverse as psychoanalytic theory (e.g., Hartmann & Loewenstein, 1962) and attitude change (e.g., Kelman, 1961) the focus of one's identification is always another person. For us, however, although identification may very well involve internal representations of another person, the focus of identification is the regulation and its outcome rather than the person. One values the outcome (i.e., the clean room) and feels that it is important to do the behavior that produces the outcome. The need for self-determination is the force that gives value to the self-regulation of those outcomes that have social utility. By focusing on the regulations, values, and outcomes rather than significant others as that with which one identifies, we are in a better position to explain why children internalize some, though not all, of the regulations and values held by the significant others.

Developmentally, introjections may, but do not necessarily, move on to the level of identification. As we will see later in the chapter, this is hypothesized to depend on the environmental conditions within which the introjection occurred; on the internal conditions (e.g., the level of anxiety) that accompany the introjections; and on the environmental conditions that exist as the child functions with those introjections.

As the child identifies with a regulation, the support of cognitive and affective consequences such as self-aggrandizement and self-disparagement become increasingly less essential. The child experiences less pressure and greater flexibility, the two being inversely related. We do not mean to imply that a regulation with which a child has identified involves a total absence of conflict. There may be some conflict between it and other aspects of the child's internal structure, but there is a relative absence of conflict within the regulatory schema itself.

The final step along the internalization continuum is necessary before the conflict will be fully minimized and the person will be fully self-determined with respect to the nonspontaneous, but now chosen, behavior. This involves integration of the regulation into one's developing sense of self. Here we see the integrative process being completed, as the self-regulation becomes integrated with other identifications into a coherent, conflict-free hierarchy. With identification there is consistency within a regulatory schema and with integration there is consistency between it and other regulatory schemata with which one has identified. At this point, one's internal unified structure will actually have been transformed rather than merely added onto, and one's self-regulation will be fully self-determined. If, as the boy in our earlier example grows older, he achieves integration with respect to not throwing the ball in the house, he would understand the consequences of his actions (e.g., refraining would prevent things from getting broken) and believing that to be important, he would choose to refrain. When a regulation has been integrated, previously conflicting thoughts like, "It's fun to throw the ball in the house," and "My mother gets upset when I throw the ball in the house," could exist in pressure-free juxtapostion, and neither one would determine his behavior. Instead, his behavior would be determined by choices made flexibly on the basis of consequences and values. He would typically choose to refrain, but he might choose to throw the ball in the house if the circumstances were appropriate and he was willing to accept responsibility for whatever consequences might occur.

According to organismic integration theory, integrated self-regulation is the natural outcome of internalization that is not impeded or thwarted by environmental influences. It represents the true meaning of socialization; one does not simply do what one thinks the social values dictate, one behaves, feels, and thinks in a way that is congruent with the social values because one has accepted them as one's own. The internalization continuum appears schematically in Figure 1.

To summarize, our theory suggests that in addition to the nonregulation characteristic of infancy there are four styles of regulating nonspontaneous behavior. The first, involving the presence of external contingencies, is external regulation; it follows from the processes of anticipation and self-control. The second, based in internal prescriptions, is introjected regulation; it results when external regulations have been introjected. The third, involving less internal conflict, is self-regulation through identification; it occurs when the child has identified with the

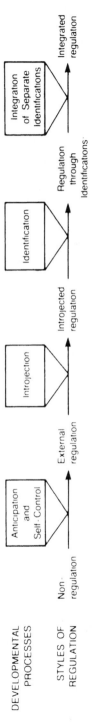

FIGURE 1. The internalization continuum of organismic integration theory representing the movement from nonregulation to fully self-determined regulation, as well as the developmental processes involved in the transitions.

behavioral outcome and its regulation. And the fourth, representing full self-determination, is integrated self-regulation; it results from the integration of the identification into one's unified sense of self.

Previous theories of internalization, particularly in the social-cognitive tradition of empirical psychology (e.g., Collins, 1977; Lepper, 1983) have typically failed to differentiate the degree to which an internalization has been integrated into the self and therefore represents self-determination. Further, cognitive-behavioral theories of self-control (e.g., Bandura, 1977b; Kanfer, 1975) have made no attempt to distinguish among the different forms of self-regulation that result when the internalization process has achieved different degrees of integration. Consequently, our theory represents a more differentiated (and, we hope, integrated) view of the internalization process and the styles of self-regulation that accompany different degrees of internalization.

Individual Differences in Children's Self-Regulation

Thus far, in presenting the organismic integration view of internalization, we have focused on the natural, or average, expectable developmental progression through infancy and childhood. We intended to convey that different styles of regulation require the development of certain competencies and that these competencies develop sequentially as the child grows older. This does not, however, imply that every internalized regulation goes through each phase invariantly. When children are older or when there is less inherent conflict between regulations and the children's desires, for example, internalization may be easier and may essentially bypass the earlier emerging modes of regulation. In essence, then, the developmental emergence of capacities represents a set of prototypes for regulatory styles.

We further suggest that children progress through these phases of development at different paces and achieve different degrees of integration, both within and between regulatory schemata. Thus, one can view regulatory styles as an issue of individual differences in children as well as an issue of development. The cross-sectional study of individual differences can help to shed light on the developmental process, though of course longitudinal work is necessary for a truly satisfactory study of development. Furthermore, the cross-sectional study of individual differences in motivational orientations (i.e., regulatory styles) can be the basis for inferences about environmental influences on the development of individual differences, though longitudinal work would be the most satisfactory way of studying this issue as well.

In this section, we will review the first steps in the empirical validation of the organismic integration view of internalization by describing cross-sectional research done with a new scale to assess self-regulatory styles in children. We will then move on to a discussion of environmental influences.

The new scale was developed by Connell and Ryan (1985) to assess children's internalization in the domain of schoolwork. Because it was thought that the 8- to 12-year-old children for whom the scale was developed would not yet have achieved a full integration of the regulations regarding schoolwork, the scale did not include the full-integration style of regulation. Thus, it assesses the degree to which regulation for school work is extrinsic (i.e., external), introjected, and identified-with. In addition, the scale assesses children's intrinsic motivation for school work, as that is also relevant to learning (Connell & Ryan, 1984).

The Connell–Ryan self-report questionnaire focuses on why children do various aspects of their school work. In completing the scale, children indicate the degree to which they do school-related behaviors for various reasons that are grouped into the categories labeled extrinsic (e.g., to get praise), introjected (e.g., to avoid guilt), and identified (e.g., to understand the material better), corresponding to the three types of self-regulation relevant to internalization. Although all three styles actually represent different forms of extrinsic motivation, the label extrinsic regulation refers to the case where actual external contingencies are perceived to be the reasons for the behavior. It is what, in this chapter, we have called external regulation. The fourth subscale, measuring the intrinsic regulatory style, included items like doing homework because it is interesting or fun. To validate the scale, Connell and Ryan related children's scores on the various subscales to theoretically relevant constructs. We will now focus on the three subscales representing degrees of internalization and explore their relationship to various aspects of adjustment and performance.

Consider first the extrinsic style of regulation. Various data sets from fourth- through sixth-grade children in urban and suburban schools indicate consistently negative relationships between extrinsic regulation and mastery motivation (Harter, 1981b), or intrinsic motivation as measured by the Connell–Ryan questionnaire. Further, the more extrinsically oriented the children were, the less competent they saw themselves in the cognitive domain and the lower their perceived self-worth (Harter,1982). Consistent with this has been the findings of a positive relationship between extrinsic regulation and anxiety (Buhrmester, 1980), anxiety amplification (Tero & Connell, 1983), and the importance of being liked. In terms of school work, the extrinsic style of regulation involved poorer conceptual learning (Grolnick & Ryan, 1985) and lower standardized achievement scores (Ryan, Connell, & Deci, 1985).

To the degree that the children had introjected the regulatory processes, they apparently pressured themselves to do as they should, for there were positive correlations between introjection and various anxiety measures. Children who had introjected the regulatory process no longer saw powerful others as responsible for their achievement outcomes (Connell, in press), but rather reported more internal control over outcomes. Further, introjection was unrelated to mastery motivation and to perceived competence and had a slightly negative relation to self-esteem. Presumably the instability of having one's esteem hinged on success is a somewhat negative factor, and may be responsible for the negative relationship.

Self-regulation through identification implies that the conflict inherent in the controller–controlled relationship has dissipated, and accordingly Connell and Ryan found no correlation between regulation through identification and the measures of anxiety and negative coping. Instead, they found a relationship with positive coping (i.e., with doing something active to cope with failure), and with perceived cognitive competence, general self-worth, and mastery motivation. Apparently, as a child's identifications become stronger, his or her sense of self and action strategies are clearer and less conflicted.

Although extrinsic regulation was negatively related to learning, neither introjection nor identification was. Parenthetically, the intrinsic orientation was positively related to learning. It appears that looking to extrinsic factors for regulating one's learning behaviors interferes with effective learning. We would also speculate that as the introjected regulation becomes increasingly less age appropriate, it too would be negatively related to learning.

Looking over the pattern of results we can draw some interesting conclusions, tentative though they be, about social adjustment and the development of self-esteem. White (1963) linked self-esteem to a sense of competence, suggesting that it springs from one's successful attempts to make the environment respond. The current results emphasize how important it is for those competent interactions to be self-initiated. Repeatedly, we have seen positive correlations between intrinsic motivation and self-esteem (e.g., Harter, 1982), and now we see that the more internalized one's extrinsic motivation, and thus the more self-determined, the more it seems to contribute to positive self-esteem. Strong and stable self-esteem seems to emanate from a strong sense of self, which motivationally means intrinsic motivation and more integrated internalization of extrinsic motivation. In general, then, the picture that emerges is one in which, as children accept the regulation of nonspontaneous behaviors as their own, they are developing a stronger sense of self, are more internally motivated for those behaviors, and perceive themselves to be more competent. Their anxiety about school dissipates somewhat and they are less worried about how much they are liked. These findings of course reflect exactly what we would expect given our theoretical analysis of internalization. Further, the pattern of correlations among the subscales supports the continuum quality of the internalization process.

Internalization and the Environment

The internalization processes described in Figure 1 represent the paradigmatic case of development in which a child progresses toward self-determined regulation. Many regulations are never integrated; however, they are internalized only to the degree represented by one of the less developmentally advanced styles of regulation. How, then, is one to account for differences in the degree to which any particular regulation is internalized? The answer to this question falls straightforwardly out of our motivational analysis. Recall that the movement of regulation away from external contingencies and towards self-determination is a function of integration, and that theoretically the integrative process is itself motivated by the intrinsic need for competence and self-determination. This suggests, then, that individual differences in the integration of values, goals, and regulations is a function largely of whether the environment supports or thwarts the integrative process as it functions with respect to those values, goals, or regulations. Stated in this way, we can apply and extend our previous work on environmental influences to the question under current consideration. Specifically, we hypothesize that the outcome of the developmental process toward integrated internalizations is a function of three classes of factors: the first relates to competence; the second, to the conflict between the organism and the behavior requested; the third, to the degree that the situation is controlling.

Competence. The factor of competency is a significant though not particularly controversial one. The integration of various cultural regulations, for example, involves various degrees of cognitive complexity, and the developing child will be able to integrate only that material for which he or she has the requisite structures. It would be impossible, for example, to internalize and integrate even a primitive sense of mutual responsibility without a minimum of concrete operational reasoning, and a full understanding would require formal operations. Motivationally, this point would be stated in terms of optimal challenge. The internalization of regulations, like any other intrinsically motivated activity, necessitates a challenge that is optimal given the person's competencies. There must be a match between what the person is able to do and what is required of him or her by the task at hand. A person cannot integrate a regulation if the regulation is not sufficiently close to his or her existing structures for the natural developmental processes to incorporate it.

In addition to having optimal challenge, positive-competence feedback is hypothesized to be extremely important for the internalization process. Because the child has no inherent interest in the behavior itself, the feeling of support and recognition that comes from the feedback would perhaps be more important than if the behavior itself were intrinsically motivated. Inasmuch as the behavior is extrinsically motivated and is done because the social world requests it, recognition of one's effectiveness by that social world is important.

The nature of negative feedback is also, of course, important for internalization. Negative feedback decreases intrinsic motivation if it implies incompetence; but if it provides useful, nonevaluative information about how to do better next time it will typically not be detrimental to intrinsic motivation, for it can facilitate one's having an effective impact on the environment. One can learn from that type of feedback. Thus, we suggest, the internalization process will be facilitated by positive feedback or by the type of supportive negative feedback that helps a person learn how to do better.

Conflict. The second issue regarding the degree to which a value and regulation will be internalized relates to the inherent conflict between the required behavior and relevant organismic tendencies. We addressed this issue in its simpler form earlier in the chapter when we discussed limit setting around intrinsically motivated activities, and pointed out that limits typically create a conflict between what the child would like and what is being asked. Because these natural inclinations conflict with what is being requested, the conflict needs to be acknowledged and accepted so that the child can develop a harmony between seemingly conflicting forces. Otherwise, the child may resort to blocking the conflicting needs or feelings from awareness, believing that he or she is worthy only when he or she wants and feels what is expected. Alternatively, the child may end up defying the request and devaluing the social context. Neither outcome, of course, is desirable.

When the issue involves internalizing the regulation of a behavior that is not intrinsically interesting, the issue becomes even more complex, for it raises the question of whether the behavior is congruent with one's organismic nature. Clearly, organisms are not infinitely maleable, and thus some behaviors are not integratable. Neither prodding nor support will lead to the integration of regulations such as "boys must not cry" or "people must not feel sexual," for these regulations are inherently conflictful with the nature of people. It is in people's nature to cry and to feel sexual.

Further, we do not expect that people will identify with empty, meaningless jobs, nor do we expect them to value ideals that are contradicted, exploited, or consumerized in other aspects of the culture. Regulations that are foreign to one's organismic nature will never be integrated. At most, they will be introjected and will result in the types of rigidities, inflexibilities, and fragmentations that characterize internally controlling regulation in adults.

It may be that one way to understand human nature is to look at those values and regulations that never get fully integrated or self-determined. From that, one could understand those aspects of culture that are alien to human nature and therefore productive of ill-being. Given the mechanistic metatheory that has characterized American psychology, this issue has been irrelevant. It seems to us, however, that it is an interesting and important, albeit politically controversial, issue, and that, contrary to popular opinion, it is empirically researchable. By developing and improving methods for studying the integration of regulations and values, we may have the possibility of exploring aspects of human beings' organismic nature.

Control. The final set of factors that affects the degree to which a regulation will be internalized is the extent to which the external regulator pressures the child to engage in the behaviors. Because we have asserted that the internalization process (although not the particular behavior being regulated) is intrinsically motivated, it follows that the internalization process will function satisfactorily only in those conditions that facilitate the intrinsic motivation that underlies the process. The key to this, of course, is the absence of undue pressure and control, so the child can gain an experience of self-determination. Surplus social controls exacerbate conflict and tend to result in either compliance or defiance, both of which forestall development and preclude integration. With reactive defiance, one does not even get the desired behavior, and with compliance, one gets the behavior but not the desire to become self-determined with respect to it.

Although introjection is part of the natural developmental progression toward integration, its occurrence in the presence of too much social control could arrest the natural progression. For integration to occur, the child must be free to try out the self-regulaton, to succeed or fail, and to understand its utility experientially. The child must experience self-determination with respect to the regulation.

Lepper (1983), in an interesting essay, made a similar point. Referring to the "minimal sufficiency principle," he suggested that internalization of a regulation (rather than mere compliance with the external control) is more likely to occur when the social control surrounding the behavior is just sufficient to elicit the behavior but is minimally coersive so that the child can come to experience the behavior as chosen. Although Lepper did not distinguish between introjected, identified, and integrated internalizations, he reviewed evidence from social psychology experiments where persistence in the absence of contingencies (hence internalization) was found to be greater following minimal justification for the non-intrinsically motivated behaviors than following coersion.

Although a precise specification of the conditions that are likely to arrest the internalization of a particular regulation at some point along the continuum short of integration is premature, we can derive theoretically, with the help of indirect evidence, some hypotheses. The most extreme and erratic forms of external control, ones involving punishments and considerable inconsistencies, may leave the child passive and amotivated. The nonintentional behavior that occurs would reflect nonregulation. In less extreme cases, controlling events that are more consistent, though still severe, may lead to the understanding and anticipation of contingencies, though the regulations would tend not to be internalized. These would result in external regulation. Controlling events that are more socially oriented, emphasizing approval and disapproval, may facilitate introjection, but if they are overly controlling and evaluative they may not allow further internalization. Only in conditions where the salience of controlling events is minimal, only when one feels the affirmation of one's self and then is allowed to experiment with regulating one's behavior as is required by the social milieu, are we likely to observe identification and integration of social regulations.

Connell and Ryan (1985) presented data that are inferentially consistent with the above suggestions. They administered the internalization scale and also Connell's (in press) perceived-control scale to fourth-through sixth-grade children. They found that children's perceptions that powerful others control their outcomes (hence, presumably, reflecting strong external control in their lives) were strongly positively correlated with extrinsic regulation, less strongly correlated with introjected regulation, and uncorrelated with regulation through identification. One can extrapolate (speculatively) from this that when there is less perception of control by powerful others there will be a greater tendency to move toward integration of a regulation.

In summation then, we suggest that the environmental circumstances, particularly those created by parents, that will facilitate internalization are those that support autonomy, accept feelings, and recognize competence. Although this has not been studied directly, various pieces of indirect evidence point to its validity. Further, there are some studies of parental practices that are consistent with, though not direct tests of our hypothesis. Noteworthy among these is a study by Baumrind (1971) of the relation between parenting practices and children's self-reliance and self-control. She classified parenting practices into three categories: authoritative, authoritarian, and permissive, and reported that the authoritative style was most strongly related to child behaviors that reflect internalization. The authoritative style, which includes parent behaviors such as warmth, rationality, consistency in limits, and support for self-expression, bears similarity to our characterization of the conditions that facilitate integrated internalizations. As such it represents indirect support for our hypothesis.

SUMMARY

In this chapter we have outlined in preliminary form a general organismic integration view of human development. By development we mean not just change but rather the differentiation and integration of structure that transforms one's capacities in the direction of elaboration, flexibility, and unity. The elaboration of structures represents mastery or competence with respect to both the external boundary of objects and the internal boundary of drives and emotions. Theoretical accounts of the integrative process of development require the postulate of intrinsic motivation as the energy source for integration. Such a concept suggests a spontaneous, natural tendency toward differentiation and integration that does not necessitate prods and pushes from the environment. Of course all change is not intrinsically motivated, only change that is developmentally significant, in other words, change that represents differentiating and integrative activity, whether with respect to knowledge, skills, or interests. Competence and unity are the resultants of structural development. Capacities, when differentiated and synthesized, tend to be flexible, spontaneous, and conflict-free. Unity of structure is thus a hallmark of healthy functioning.

Not only does intrinsic motivation energize development, but structures differentiate so that intrinsic motivation gets directed toward different activities. This has been referred to as the development of intrinsic motivation. Further, we discussed the development of extrinsic motivation, focusing on the internalization of regulations for behaviors that are not themselves intrinsically motivating but that are required by socializing agents. We outlined an internalization continuum progressing from the nonregulation of nonspontaneous behaviors; to external regulation by immediate contingencies; to introjected regulation, in which an external regulatory process has been incorporated as a control, thus maintaining the inherent controller–controlled dichotomy and conflict;

to regulation through identification with the goals and values of the regulation, in which case the inherent conflict will be largely dissipated; to integrated regulation where the regulation itself has become integrated with other regulations into the unified sense of self that is the basis for true self-determination. We hypothesized that internalization is actually a function of the intrinsically motivated integrative process and we discussed the environmental conditions that facilitate integrated internalization. Our foci were perceived competence and optimal challenge, the recognition of inherent conflicts between the person's organismic tendencies and the required behaviors, and the minimization of controls and pressures.

6

Causality Orientations Theory
Personality Influences on Motivation

Throughout the book, we have made varied references to three broad classes of behaviors and motivationally relevant psychological processes, generally referring to them as self-determined, control-determined, and amotivational.

Self-determined behaviors are initiated and regulated by choices, based on awareness of one's organismic needs and integrated goals. Using information from internal and external sources, one chooses how to behave in anticipation of achieving self-related goals and satisfying organismic needs. As we have indicated, there are two types of self-determined behaviors. In Chapters 3 and 4 we focused on intrinsically motivated behaviors, which represent the classic case of self-determination, and in Chapter 5 we saw that extrinsically motivated behaviors can also be self-determined, if they are regulated by integrated internalizations. In other words, if the behaviors are chosen, based on one's needs and integrated goals, they are self-determined, even if they occur in the context of rewards or constraints. Research on self-determined behaviors, particularly intrinsically motivated ones, has shown that they tend to involve greater creativity (Amabile, 1983; Koestner *et al.*, 1984), more cognitive flexibility (McGraw & McCullers, 1979) and an internal perceived locus of causality and enhanced perceived competence.

Control-determined behaviors are initiated and regulated by controls in the environment or inside the person. Rather than being regulated by one's own choices, they are determined by controls such as reward contingencies or internally controlling states. Like self-determined behaviors, they are purposive, but in control-salient responding the intentionality is determined by demands rather than by choices and personal goals. One "decides" to do something feeling like one has no choice. An example would be students who make the decision to study because they believe they have to rather than because they genuinely choose to.

Control-determined responding is nonintegrated, extrinsically motivated behavior that may take the form either of compliance with the control or rebellion against it. Where there is compliance, there is the polar tendency for defiance, and vice versa. They are complementary responses to being controlled, although in most instances one or the other tends to be dominant. From the research reviewed in previous chapters, we concluded that control-determined responding involves greater pressure and tension and is less creative and flexible than self-determined responding. Its perceived locus of causality tends to be external.

Amotivated behaviors are initiated and regulated by forces wholly beyond the person's intentional control. Behaviors are neither intrinsically nor extrinsically motivated in the sense that they are not intentional. The individual feels unable to regulate his or her behavior in a way that will reliably yield desired results, so the person tends to lose control to the unmanageable forces. Amotivation is particularly evident and widely studied as personal helplessness (Abramson *et al.*, 1978), which results from environmental forces that are neither predictable nor controllable. This is amotivation at the external boundary, the boundary between the person and forces in the world. Amotivation can also be experienced with respect to the internal boundary, in which case people are overwhelmed by forces inside themselves. A person, for example, may be overcome by rage or jealousy and behave in a way that is wholly uncontrollable. The person did not intend the behavior and there is no identification with it. He or she may even dissociate from the behavior by distorting or forgetting it. Amotivation at the internal boundary means that the person does not have adequate structures to regulate the drives or emotions, whether they be structures of the integrated self that regulate self-determined functioning, or internally controlling structures that regulate control-determined functioning. Thus, the drives or emotions overwhelm the structures leaving the person amotivated and helpless with respect to those forces.

It is important to recognize the difference between rebellion and amotivation at the internal boundary. In the former case, the reactance to control leads the person to act against the controls in a deliberate or intentional way; the person endorses the behavior and is deliberately directing (albeit conflictfully) any emotions or drives that get expressed. In amotivation, the forces overwhelm the person and there is no intentionality, no endorsement of the behavior, and no directing of the forces.

Behaviors and Initiating Events

The research reported in Chapters 3 and 4 was concerned primarily with the relationship between initiating or regulatory events and the various types of behaviors and processes just described. From that research we were able to categorize initiating or regulatory events as having one of three functional significances: informational, controlling, and amotivating, on the basis of an analysis of two descriptive dimensions: whether they are perceived to support autonomy versus control behavior; and whether they are perceived to be effectance-enhancing versus effectance-diminishing. Informational events, which support autonomy and provide effectance-enhancing feedback, tend to promote self-determined behavior. Controlling events, which pressure people toward particular outcomes, tend to promote control-determined behavior. And amotivating events, which ensure that the person cannot competently attain desired outcomes, tend to promote amotivated behavior.

The exploration of the effects of initiating and regulatory events was done primarily with experimental studies in which independent variables were manipulated and their effects on intervening and dependent variables were documented. The analytic sequence or model of causality that is implicit in this work can be represented as: Stimulus → Organism → Response; or S–O–R, for short. A stimulus is interpreted or evaluated by the organism and a response (i.e., a behavior, a cognition, or an affect) follows. Because people (i.e., organisms) differ, stimuli may be differentially interpreted by different people or by the same person at different times, but still the analytic sequence begins with the stimulus.

An alternative viewpoint suggests that the analytic sequence could usefully begin with the organism rather than with the stimulus. In other words, people can be seen as selecting and interpreting stimuli in accordance with their needs and orientations. Stimuli are not seen as impinging on the person so much as they are seen as affordances (Gibson, 1979) that the person can attend to and interpret. The person selectively attends to stimuli, interprets stimuli more on the basis of his or her personality than on the subtleties of the stimuli, and projects characteristics onto the stimuli. In a sense, the person actively constructs stimuli rather than passively receives them. This perspective suggests a different analytic sequence, one that begins with the organism rather than the stimulus. The organism selects, or projects stimuli and then interprets and responds to them. The sequence would be: O–S–O–R.

With this view of the analytic sequence, our research focused not on whether a "stimulus event" itself tends to be interpreted as informational, controlling, or amotivating, but rather on whether people are oriented in such a way that they are likely to seek out, create, and interpret events as informational (inputs to the choice process); controlling (pressures to behave in specific ways); or amotivating (forces beyond their intentional control). In doing that research we were not suggesting that the objective properties of a stimulus event and the interpersonal context within which it occurs are irrelevant to people's interpretation of the event. Indeed, Chapters 3 and 4 reviewed the studies that have shown how important those factors are. What we are suggesting is that most stimulus situations contain sufficient ambiguity that one's orientation can play a significant role in what one attends to and how one interprets the salient events. Some variance in the regulation of behavior is predicted to be accounted for by the person side of the person–environment dialectic.

People use stimulus events for their own purposes, in accord with their own needs and orientations. To some extent, they define the stimulus event to be what they want it to be. For example, consider a graduate student who asks a professor to suggest a research project. Suppose the professor makes a suggestion, which is merely a suggestion (i.e., the professor is being informational) and the student takes it as a control, and responds in a control-determined fashion. This would be an instance in which the response is not a function of the stimulus but rather of the student's needs and orientations. If the student had a choice of professors, he or she might well select the one who would be controlling in answering the question, and even if the student did not, he or she would be likely to treat what any professor said as a control. The student's orientation would account for a significant portion of the student's behavior.

In this chapter, we explore the utility of beginning the analytic sequences with the organism rather than with a stimulus event. We do this by reporting research that was concerned primarily with whether person variables can themselves account for significant amounts of variance in motivationally relevant behaviors and processes. Because our exploration of self-determination and competence led to the tripartite characterization of initiating events, we structured the exploration of orientations in a way that involves three orientations that parallel the three classes of initiating events.

CAUSALITY ORIENTATIONS

The research reported in this chapter was based on the speculation that people are oriented to some extent to interpret (i.e., to seek, create, and evaluate) events as informational, to some extent to interpret them as controlling, and to some extent to interpret them as amotivating. We hypothesized that, because of their own orientations, people will relate to events as if they were one of the three types, and they will display the kinds and qualities of behaviors, cognitions, and affects that we have found to be associated with the corresponding type of initiating or regulatory event. This hypothesis can also be expressed in terms of self-regulation. We suggest that the three orientations lead people to regulate themselves as if they were in an informational environment, a controlling environment, or an amotivating environment, respectively.

We refer to these orientations as *causality orientations* and have labeled the three orientations the *autonomy* orientation; the *control* orientation; and the *impersonal* orientation. We hypothesize that everyone is to some extent autonomy oriented, to some extent control oriented, and to some extent impersonally oriented; that it is possible to measure the strength of each orientation within a person; and that the strength of these orientations will allow predictability of a wide range of psychological and behavioral variables.

Deci (1980) first introduced the concept of causality orientations. Using terminology developed by Heider (1958) and deCharms (1968), he labeled the three orientations internal, external, and impersonal, to reflect the fact that the perceived locus of causality is internal for the first, external for the second, and impersonal for the third. Deci and Ryan (1985) changed the names of the first two from internal and external to autonomy and control for two reasons. First, because the terms internal and external have been widely used in the locus-of-control literature, their use to describe causality orientations seemed to create undue confusion. The locus-of-control and locus-of-causality concepts are very different. Second, people typically understand the term internal causality to describe behaviors that are regulated by any events inside the person, but we had intended it to describe only behaviors that are regulated by events internal to one's integrated sense of self. This, too, created confusion.

Thus, the autonomy orientation describes the tendency for behavior to be initiated and regulated by events internal to one's sense of self and by events in the environment that are interpreted as informational. In both cases the perceived locus of causality is internal. The control orientation describes the tendency for behavior to be initiated by events in the person that are external to one's integrated sense of self (i.e., introjected regulations or internally controlling events) and by events in the environment that are interpreted as controlling. In both cases the perceived locus of causality is external.

In Deci's (1980) discussion of causality orientations, he spoke of people having one of the three orientations. For example, a person might have been classified as being internally (autonomy) oriented, and hence a highly self-determining person. Alternatively, the person might have been classified as being either externally (control) oriented, or impersonally oriented, and thus not self-determining. On the basis of empirical work and additional consideration we concluded that it is not efficacious, in fact it is often misleading, to classify people as types. Rather, it seemed to make more sense to assume that people are, to some extent, oriented in each of the three ways and to assess the strength of each orientation. Although there may be people who are very high on one orientation (say, control) and very low on the other two (autonomy and impersonality), so that it would be reasonable to classify them as being oriented in one way (control oriented), we do not typically attempt to do so, nor do we advocate it. By assessing the degree to which people are oriented in each of the three ways, the strength of the relevant orientation (or a combination of orientations) can be used in predicting various behaviors, cognition, and affects.

This modification in the conception of causality orientations represents a shift away from the *categorical* view of personality, in which people are seen as being of a particular type, for example, internals versus externals (Rotter, 1966) or introverts versus extroverts (Jung, 1928), and toward the *dimensional* view, in which people are described in terms of their placement on two or more dimensions. Some investigators, such as Wundt (1903), used the intersection of dimensions to develop categories; however, as we said, we propose to retain the three dimensions rather than to use them in forming categories of people. This elaboration of the causality orientations concept is an important one, for it portrays the personality as a system of interacting characteristics. Having made these preliminary remarks, we now turn to a fuller description of the three orientations.

The Autonomy Orientation

Central to this orientation is the experience of choice. When autonomy-oriented, people use available information to make choices and to regulate themselves in pursuit of self-selected goals. Whether intrinsically motivated or extrinsically motivated, behavior based on choice is self-determined and emanates from the integrated sense of self that underlies the autonomy orientation.

When we use the term *choice*, we intend it to be a motivational, as opposed to cognitive, concept. This point has several related implications. The first is that only some behaviors are truly chosen. Whereas the cognitive theories make the explicit or implicit assumption that all behavior is chosen on the basis of expectancies about reinforcements (e.g., Bandura, 1977a; Vroom, 1964), we assume that many behaviors are automatic and do not involve genuine choice. For example, reinforcement-determined (i.e., control-determined) behaviors are not chosen and thus not self-determined; they are controlled by the reinforcement contingencies. This leads to the second implication, which is that choice is not synonymous with decision. In other words, from a cognitive perspective, the concept of choice applies whenever someone decides to do something, whereas from a motivational perspective, the concept of choice applies only when the person experiences a sense of freedom or choice with respect to the action. For example, at the beginning of the chapter we mentioned students who decided to study because they felt they had to. From a motivational perspective, this would not be considered genuine choice for it bears the markings of control-determined rather than self-determined behavior.

Choice may, though it need not, be deliberate or analytical. In other words, a person does not need to make a conscious, deliberate decision for there to be choice. Choice may, in some cases, be intuitive and spontaneous. The flow experience discussed by Czikszentmihalyi (1975) and reviewed in Chapter 2 is the archetypical intrinsically motivated experience; the person is fully involved with the activity. When so motivated, the person is not making deliberate choices, but rather is flowing freely in his or her actions and experiencing self-determination as he or she does so. Conversely, rigid, inflexible, conditioned behavior would not be considered self-determined or autonomous even if the person made a deliberate decision to do it. The fact of the inflexibility, with the accompanying pressure and tension, implies that it was not a real choice, but instead was a control-determined decision.

Experientially, one way to know whether a behavior was genuinely chosen is whether the other options were (or could have been) fully entertained. We assert that a behavior is truly chosen only if the person could (whether intuitively or deliberately) seriously consider not doing it. The inflexibility of a person's having to do a behavior and not being able to seriously consider other options suggests that the behavior does not represent true choice, even if it was decided on. Instead, it was probably initiated by an internally controlling event. Consider this example. Many undergraduates go to college without ever having considered not doing so. It had always been expected of them by parents, friends, and society, so they learned to expect it of themselves—they introjected the expectation. They might report that they decided to go to college and claim that they are there by choice, but we suggest that if they had not and could not fully entertain the alternative of not going, they have not genuinely chosen to go. In many instances, giving consideration to not being in college is so anxiety provoking that people are unwilling or unable to do it. The causality orientation that lies behind deciding to be in college under such conditions would not be the autonomy orientation, for the autonomy orientation involves making a genuine choice and being willing to experience whatever anxiety might be involved in giving serious consideration to the discarded option (i.e., to not being in college).

By suggesting that rejected options need to be fully considered, we are not implying that the choice has to be conscious or deliberate; it can, as we said above, be intuitive and spontaneous. The point is really one that relates to the flexibility of psychological structures and processes. The autonomy orientation involves making flexible choices, whether intuitively or deliberately and whether consciously or preconsciously.

In addition to choice, the autonomy orientation is characterized by the awareness of one's organismic and integrated needs and feelings. Perls (1973) defined awareness as a relaxed attending to some aspect of the organism, and it is the sense of nonpressured attending that is the mark of self-determination. Thus, an anxious, pressured attending to some internal event is not true awareness; instead, it is characteristic of an internally controlled attentional style—pressure being a defining characteristic of control.

Use of the words *organismic* and *integrated* to describe the needs of which one is aware is also an important aspect of the autonomy orientation. Implicit in it is the assertion that only some needs are integrated. Integrated needs refer to innate, organismic needs and needs that have differentiated out of these; in other words, needs that have been integrated into one's sense of self. For example, the intrinsic need for self-determined competence is an innate need, whereas the need to play the piano might be a more specific intrinsic need that has differentiated out of the global intrinsic need. Both of these would be considered organismic (assuming that the need to play the piano had been fully integrated rather than merely introjected). However, some needs are acquired as substitutes for organismic needs that have not been adequately satisfied; these would not be considered integrated needs, so they would not imply an autonomy orientation. For example, the seemingly insatiable need to eat is often said to be a substitute for an inadequately gratified need for love or acceptance. This need for food would be a substitute need rather than an organismic need, although, of course, the basic hunger drive is an organismic need. These distinctions have been discussed in greater detail by Deci (1980).

The awareness of organismic needs leads to a condition that might be termed *organismic congruence*, in which there is a consistency among one's behaviors, thoughts, feelings, and needs. In dynamically oriented psychotherapies, the therapist often looks for inconsistencies between the verbal and nonverbal communications as a cue to the organismic disturbances that result when one blocks one's organismic needs or feelings from awareness and operates with what we refer to as substitute needs.

The autonomy orientation is also characterized by what might be called choiceful accommodation. When the active, autonomous person encounters situations that are nonresponsive and cannot be changed, he or she may accommodate the situation (rather than inflexibly persisting at it) and thus direct his or her activity to situations that will be responsive. Choiceful accommodation is really just a matter of using information effectively, of dealing with environmental events as if they were informational. By using inputs to get a realistic sense of what is possible, one is able to choose the goals that yield the best possibilities for satisfying the needs that are motivating the activity. Integration (rather than compliance) is the developmental process that underlies choiceful accommodation.

Behaviorally, a strong autonomy orientation may be manifest in a variety of ways. It leads people to seek out opportunities to be autonomous, so that, for example, a person selecting a job would seriously consider whether the setting allows autonomy. Further, it would lead people to initiate more in the situations they are in. In essence, this means that they interpret environments as informational and use the information to make informed choices about when and where to initiate. It will also make people more resilient and less susceptible to losing intrinsic motivation and self-determination in controlling environments. If a person has integrated regulations that were initially extrinsic, the person will be more able to remain self-determining in the presence of extrinsic controls.

The Control Orientation

The control orientation is based in a concern with controls. It involves experiencing initiating events as pressure to perform accordingly and not experiencing a real sense of choice. One's functioning is, to a large extent, determined by controls in the environment or by internally controlling imperatives, such as *should, have to, ought to,* and *must.* The motivational consequences for the internally controlling regulation are self-aggrandizement following success and guilt or shame following failure.

At the heart of the control orientation is a conflict or power struggle between the controller and the controlled. In some instances the conflict is played out interpersonally, between two people or between a person and an organization or structure, but in many instances the battle is played out intrapsychically, with the controller and the controlled inside the same person. In these cases, the controls would have been introjected and would function as a set of internally controlling events.

The control conflict may be suppressed, in which case the person would be compliant without actively experiencing the sense of conflict, but also without experiencing a true sense of choice; or it may be actively conscious, in which case the person would be either compliant and riddled with tension or openly rebellious, doing the opposite of what was demanded. Whether the person responds primarily with compliance or primarily with defiance, the sense of freedom or self-determination is lacking. The rebellious one, who claims to be free, "doth protest too much." He or she is behaving largely in opposition to the controls because they are controls, so the person is really being inversely controlled. This phenomenon is the basis for the use of paradoxical intentions (Watzlawick *et al.*, 1967), or more colloquially, "using psychology" to get someone to do something. In many instances rebellion is healthier than compliance, because it is the desire for autonomy that is doing battle with the controls, but the battle itself implies control rather than self-determination. The action is unintegrated and thus not autonomous.

With the control orientation awareness is also restricted. People attend to themselves in much the same way that others attend to them, by observing their behavior and aligning their internal states with the behavior. Bem (1972) referred to this as self-perception, although we emphasize that it is the control-oriented way of knowing one's inner states and is the antithesis of true awareness. When control-oriented, people attend to internal events that are related to control—things like proscriptions, demands, and needs that are substitutes for unsatisfied organismic needs.

The control orientation involves cognitive consistency rather than organismic congruence. People tend to rationalize and reduce dissonance by aligning their thoughts with their actions and with the controls. But in doing so, it is only their thoughts that are being aligned, and they are, in a sense, deceiving themselves by blocking their organismic needs and feelings from awareness. This control-oriented, cognitive consistency is a prime example of the organismic incongruence picked up by therapists, in which the nonverbal communications belie the verbal expressions. The consistency is not organismic, it is a consistency of cognitions that is aimed at the reduction of anxiety or discomfort.

The control orientation may be associated with a high level of competence (though it is not self-determined competence) in adults. Through learning how to achieve desired, contingently offered love and approval, a person becomes competent and effective. But the person's sense of self-worth typically gets hinged on continued good performance, so the person becomes heavily ego-involved in performing well—the very process that Ryan (1982) found to undermine intrinsic motivation. With the control orientation and the accompanying ego-involved achievement come self-judgments that will typically parallel the judgments that were made by the significant caregivers whose love and approval were contingently dispensed.

With the control orientation, if we assume a predominance of compliance rather than rebellion, accommodation is everywhere evident, but this is not the choiceful or healthy accommodation inherent in the autonomy orientation. Rather, it is an accommodation that denies one's self and places the demands of the environment ahead of one's own needs and feelings. Being external to one's integrated sense of self, the control orientation involves regulation in accord with demands and controls rather than with one's self and one's organismic condition. The integrated self is underdeveloped and the organismic condition is to a great extent suppressed.

Behaviorally, the control orientation often leads people to seek and select controlling situations and to look for control in situations that objectively would tend to be described as informational. This phenomenon was illustrated earlier in the chapter by the example of the graduate student who asked the professor for a suggestion and took the suggestion as a demand.

The Impersonal Orientation

The impersonal orientation is based in a sense of one's being incompetent to deal with life's challenges. Impersonal functioning is erratic and nonintentional, for one does not have the necessary psychological structures for dealing with external and internal forces. The impersonal orientation involves the beliefs that behavior and outcomes are independent and that forces are uncontrollable, and it results in the experience of incompetence. This orientation supports amotivation at the external and internal boundaries.

Seligman's (1975) work on the environmental circumstances that promote helplessness explored noncontingent outcomes, those that are delivered by fate, chance, caprice, or malevolence. Formulated differently, this can be seen as the unmasterability of forces at the external boundary. The person, being unable to master the forces that determine his or her desired outcomes, develops a sense of personal helplessness, a sense that he or she is unable to cope with these forces in the world. At the internal boundary, the impersonal orientation means that the person has never learned to manage the forces of drives and emotions; he or she has not developed structures for managing these forces. Whereas the autonomy orientation is characterized by flexibility and an integrated sense of self, and the control orientation is characterized by the inflexibility of introjects and internal controls, the impersonal orientation involves inadequate structures of either sort, so the person is buffeted about by forces in the environment and the forces of drives and emotions. Often people become immobile, perhaps unintentionally appearing passive-aggressive (deliberate or intentional aggression, whether it be active hostility or passive spite is characteristic of the control rather than the impersonal orientation).

Behaviorally, the impersonal orientation may lead people to behave without intentions. They might, for example, follow precedents because they have not learned to be purposive. Often, amotivated behavior will be driven by nonconscious forces, so people may engage in addictive behaviors and feel helpless with relation to them. In general, the impersonal orientation will be accompanied by a high level of anxiety.

Jones and Berglass (1978) introduced the concept of self-handicapping strategies to describe people's deliberately doing badly or presenting themselves poorly. Although there is a superficial relationship between this strategy and the impersonal orientation, self-handicapping is more a strategy of the control orientation, when one's competence and confidence are shakey, than of the impersonal orientation. As Jones and Berglass said, the self-handicapping strategy is typically employed when one's self-competence is precarious rather than entirely negative. With impersonality, one's self-competence and self-worth tend to be strongly negative. The precarious self-image is the result of a control orientation that has fared marginally well in its attempts to gain the desired contingent love and approval. In difficult situations, the control orientation of a person with a precarious ego may use a self-handicapping strategy to protect that ego. The impersonal orientation also underlies self-defeating behaviors, but these result from the person's hopelessly giving up intentionality and not acting on his or her own behalf. The self-handicapping strategy is a more active manipulation, whereas hopelessness is a form of passivity.

The Development of Causality Orientations

In the early weeks following birth, children are active and impulsive. Their behavior is motivated by biological urges and intrinsic energy, without any self-regulatory mediation. There is, however, the innate, natural tendency toward organismic integration.

Erikson (1950) described how the central concern for children during their first year is learning to trust, which results from the environment's both impinging on and responding to them in predictable ways. Trust

is the affective experience that accompanies the development of anticipation and self-control that we discussed in the last chapter. As we said,
there must be some established order in the child's experience of the
world for the child to learn the anticipation and self-control that are
necessary for self-regulation and trust. Noncontingent, unpredictable
responses to the child prevent this development. For example, if when
a child cries, he or she is sometimes loved, sometimes ignored, and
sometimes punished, the child will never be able to develop a mastery
of the environment. Similarly, if the child is always punished no matter
what he or she does (in other words, he or she continually fails in a
contingent environment), the child will also be unable to develop a
mastery of the environment. Both types of environmental events are
amotivating and neither permits the development of the anticipation
and self-control that are necessary for primitive forms of what are referred
to as external regulation. Research by Yarrow, Rubenstein, and Pederson
(1975) has shown that noncontingent (i.e., amotivating) environmental
events do in fact impair the motivation and competence of infants.

Erikson (1950) pointed out that learning to trust the environment
is accompanied by a developing trust of oneself. As one develops anticipation and self-control at the external boundary, one will also be developing anticipation and self-control at the internal boundary. An inability
to develop the former prevents one from developing the latter, and the
failure to develop anticipation and self-control at these boundaries means
that the organismic integration processes will tend to be thwarted at the
level of nonregulation, which characterizes early infancy (Figure 1,
p. 139). This nonregulation is, we suggest, the prototype of the impersonal orientation, and thus, as it persists beyond its developmentally
appropriate point, it becomes the basis for a strong impersonal orientation. Then, as one encounters amotivating environments in later years,
the impersonal orientation that began in the first year will be crystalized
and strengthened. In short, the impersonal orientation develops to the
degree that amotivating environments both undermine intrinsic motivation and thwart the organismic integration that permits even external
self-regulation.

Contingent, masterable environments are necessary for movement
away from impersonality, but contingent events in such environments
may be either controlling or informational. The sense of controlling environments is that they deliver outcomes when the person complies,
whereas the sense of informational environments is that they deliver
outcomes when the person initiates. This distinction is perhaps especially important when the child moves into his or her second year and
faces what Erikson (1950) called the autonomy conflict, but it is important
throughout development. Insofar as the contingencies are demanding

and controlling, we hypothesize, they will foster dependence on the outcomes and will tend to undermine intrinsic motivation and to thwart internalization at the levels of external regulation and introjection. Introjection, when it is rigid and persists beyond its developmentally appropriate point, is referred to as internally controlling regulation, and because regulation by external events and by internally controlling events constitutes the control orientation, we conclude that controlling environments are the developmental antecedents of the control orientation.

The controlling events that are perhaps most pervasive and detrimental are those that contingently administer love and acceptance. When a child is loved and accepted only when he or she performs well, in other words, only when he or she is "a good boy or girl," the child learns to value him- or herself only when he or she performs properly. Simply stated, the child's self-worth becomes hinged on performing well, and this contingent self-regard is a central underpinning of the control orientation. With the contingent administration of love, the control orientation develops if one is generally able to perform competently and thus to achieve love and acceptance with some predictability. Conditions of contingent love that cannot be met, however, conditions that leave the child feeling incompetent and unable to achieve the desired love in a predictable way, are psychologically equivalent to amotivating conditions and, as we said, strengthen the impersonal orientation.

Rogers (1951) emphasized the importance of unconditional acceptance and love for the development of a healthy personality. He suggested that personal regard should be based on one's existence rather than on the appropriateness of one's behavior. Within the context of this unconditional acceptance of the child by adults, adults need to be contingently responsive to the child's initiations. In general terms, this is what we have in mind by informational environments.

Being informational and thus supporting a child's autonomy involves more responding to the child's agendas and less imposing agendas on the child. It conveys to the child that he or she has choice and is effective. It allows the child to maintain intrinsic motivation and to identify with and integrate regulations and values. These are the basis of a strong autonomy orientation.

To summarize our brief discussion of the development of causality orientations, the impersonal orientation involves amotivation and nonregulation of behavior, which result from experiences with amotivating environments; the control orientation involves external responding and internally controlling regulation, which result from experiences with controlling environments; and the autonomy orientation involves intrinsic motivation and the integrated internalization of regulations, which result from informational environments.

The General Causality Orientations Scale

To assess the empirical utility of the causality orientations concept it is necessary to have a means of measuring the strength of people's orientations. Toward that end Deci and Ryan (1985) developed the first causality orientations scale. We reasoned that although the strength of one's orientations may differ from one domain to another (for example, from the work domain to the domain of social relationships), the empirical utility of the concept for a general theory such as self-determination theory depends on its capturing sufficient variance to allow predictability across domains. Thus, we began with a general, cross-domain scale.

The scale was constructed to assess the degree to which a person is oriented toward each of the three causality orientations. Its reliability and internal consistency were established and the subscales were found to be relatively independent. The autonomy and control subscales were uncorrelated, whereas the control and impersonal subscales were modestly positively related ($r = .27$) and the autonomy and impersonal subscales were modestly negatively related ($r = -.25$). The scale was then used in various research projects that included establishing its place in a nomological network of constructs. We will now review that research by considering the various constructs in turn. In so doing we will be further explicating the three orientations.

Self-Determination

Heider (1958) described a continuum from personal causation to impersonal causation that was used to reflect the degree to which an observed effect was caused by personal versus impersonal forces. Effects that were intended imply personal causation, and those that were not imply impersonal causation. This descriptive continuum bears relationship to the degree to which the behavior producing those effects is self-determined, with personal causation relating to self-determination and impersonal causation relating to non-self-determination. Deci (1980), in discussing the relationship of the causality orientations to Heider's personal-impersonal continuum, suggested that a high level of the autonomy orientation (which he then called the internal orientation) represents the paradigmatic case of personal causation, whereas a high level of the impersonal orientation represents the paradigmatic case of impersonal causation. A high level of the control (or external) orientation, he suggested, because it shares the characteristics of perceived behavior-outcome dependence and intentionality with the autonomy orientation, tends to be closer to personal causation than to impersonal

causation. The earlier mentioned correlations among the causality orientation subscales suggest, however, that this may not be so. The control
(or external) orientation is more closely related to the impersonal orientation than to the autonomy orientation. Thus, although the control
orientation involves intentionality as a mediator in control-determined
behavior, empirical results indicate that the control and impersonal orientations represent non-self-determination. Whether one feels controlled by contingencies and demands or buffeted about by impersonal
forces, one is likely to be lacking a sense of self-determination. In neither
instance is there an experience of real choice; instead one tends to experience pressure, tension, and anxiety. Even the intentionality involved
in the control orientation is a pressured intentionality rather than an
interested, relaxed one.

The concept of self-determination bears relationship to that of ego
development, as discussed by Loevinger (1976a). A high level of ego
development refers to greater organismic unity and autonomous functioning, which are characteristics of the autonomy orientation. Given
this similarity, we predicted and found a positive correlation ($r = .43$)
between the autonomy orientation and ego development, using Loevinger's measure. On the other hand, because the control orientation
and the impersonal orientation represent failures to achieve a sufficiently
unified sense of self to promote self-determined functioning, they were
predicted to be negatively related to ego development. The impersonal
orientation was, of course, hypothesized to be more deficient than the
control orientation because the control orientation does involve intentional action. These predicted relationships did appear: the control orientation was slightly negatively related ($r = -.22$) and the impersonal
orientation, more strongly negatively related ($r = -.32$). These correlations support the view that high levels of the three causality orientations can be differentially described in terms of the degree to which they
reflect self-determined functioning.

Self-Actualization

The concept of self-actualization, as discussed by Maslow (1970), is
used to describe people who have developed to the point of utilizing
their full potentials in an integrated and unconflicted way. The concept
includes such notions as self-reliance, present-centeredness, and spontaneity. Because these descriptors have theoretical relevance to the causality orientations, we explored the relationship between self-actualization
and the autonomy, control, and impersonal orientations, expecting positive correlations of self-actualization with autonomy; slightly negative

relationships with control; and highly negative relationships with impersonality.

Shostrom (1966) developed a widely used measure of self-actualization, called the Personal Orientations Inventory, which we employed to test our predictions. The scale has 2 central ratio subscales: self-supporting versus reliance on others; and present-centered versus dwelling on the past or future. In addition there are 10 other subscales assessing different aspects of self-actualization. Our data revealed that the self-support ratio was positively correlated with autonomy (.31), modestly negatively correlated with control ($-.20$), and highly negatively correlated with impersonality ($-.39$). The self-supporting ratio showed the same pattern of results, as did the spontaneity dimension. Correlations for each of the other 9 subscales were also ordered in the expected way, with some of the correlations being highly significant and others nonsignificant. Overall, then, there was clear evidence for the concept of self-actualization also being descriptively useful for explicating the nature of the three causality orientations.

Self-Esteem

As we said earlier, self-determined functioning, as represented by an autonomy orientation, is theorized to be based in a strong sense of self, and thus to be associated with a high level of self-esteem. The control orientation, however, involves one's self-esteem being based on one's performance as viewed by controlling elements of the external world, or its internally controlling counterpart. And the impersonal orientation involves an inadequate representation of self that is accompanied by low self-esteem. We predicted and found a positive relationship between the autonomy orientation and self-esteem ($r = .35$) using the Janis and Field (1959) measure of self-esteem. We also predicted and found no correlation between the control orientation and self-esteem. With the control orientation, self-esteem is theorized to be based in external evaluations, and because the normative nature of these evaluations yields a split between positive and negative evaluations, there should be no direct link between the strength of one's control orientation and the level of one's self-esteem. Finally, as predicted, the impersonal orientation was negatively correlated with self-esteem ($r = -.61$).

Parenthetically, because ego development, self-actualization, and self-esteem are all positive and highly valued characteristics, and because all are positively related to the autonomy orientation, one might wonder whether responses to autonomy items are affected by self-presentation. To test this we related the autonomy orientation to social desirability

(Crowne & Marlowe, 1964) and found no correlations, so the scale does not seem to be confounded by self-presentation.

Locus of Control

The term *locus of causality* used in conjunction with causality orientations is not the same as *locus of control* as explicated by Rotter (1966). The term locus of control refers to whether people believe that outcomes are controllable, in other words whether outcomes are believed to be contingent on one's behavior. Research on the locus of control developed out of a social learning perspective, within which behaviors are understood to be controlled by expectancies about reinforcements, so the critical questions revolve around who or what is believed to control those reinforcements or outcomes. Locus of causality, on the other hand, refers to the perceived source of initiation and regulation of behavior. Research on locus of causality and causality orientations developed out of a motivational analysis of behavior in which the critical questions revolve around what factors energize and direct behavior and how those factors relate to self-determination. Simply stated, locus of control is concerned with what controls a person's outcomes; locus of causality is concerned with why a person behaves as he or she does. Although the locus of control of outcomes undoubtedly affects the initiation and regulation of at least some behaviors, it is but one among many factors that do. Others include such things as people's needs, feelings, and habits.

Rotter distinguished internal and external control on the basis of people's beliefs about the relationship between behavior and outcomes. Internal control refers to the belief in behavior-outcome dependence; people expect that if they behave in certain ways, they will be able to attain desired outcomes. The control of reinforcements is said to be internal to the person because, although the contingencies or demands are set by outside agents, the person believes that he or she can reliably attain (or control) the reinforcements by doing what the contingencies require. External control, on the other hand, refers to the belief in behavior-outcome independence; people expect that outcomes are delivered by fate, luck, or the unpredictable whims of some outside agent, so there is no way that they can reliably attain the outcomes. The control of reinforcements is external.

There are two major reasons why an internal locus of control is not directly related to one of the three causality orientations. The first relevant difference between the locus of control concept and the locus of causality concept is that locus of causality is used in a theoretical system that recognizes that some behaviors are not aimed toward the attainment of reinforcements. These intrinsically motivated behaviors are rewarded or maintained by the spontaneous thoughts and feelings that accompany them. This means that there are many behaviors involved with the autonomy orientation (hence an internal locus of *causality*) that are not even acknowledged by the internal locus of *control* concept, which focuses on reinforcements. The second difference is reflected in the fact that the locus of control concept does not distinguish between extrinsic behaviors that are, versus are not, self-determined. Thus, there is no distinction between behaviors that are controlled by extrinsic rewards and those that are extrinsic but are truly chosen. These, of course, are behaviors that are based in integrated internalizations. The former class of behaviors is control-determined, whereas the latter class is self-determined. The former class would be associated with the control orientation, whereas the latter class would be associated with the autonomy orientation. In the locus-of-control literature, however, both classes would be considered to have an internal locus of control. Given these two major differences there were no predicted relationship between locus of control and either the autonomy or the control orientations.

The external locus of control does, however, have a direct, theoretical relationship with the impersonal orientation. Developmentally, the experience of reinforcements' not being reliably attainable (hence the belief in an external locus of *control*) impairs intentionality and fosters an impersonal orientation toward causality. Consequently, we expected a strong correlation between external control and impersonal causality. Results reported by Deci and Ryan (1985) showed that, as predicted, external locus of control was strongly positively related to impersonal orientation scores ($r = .52$). Further, external control was modestly correlated with our control orientation ($r = .29$). It appears, therefore, that although Rotter's external locus of control is conceptually intended to measure beliefs in behavior-outcome independence (i.e., in the noncontingent delivery of outcomes), it also to some extent measures people's experiences of being controlled by external demands when outcomes are contingent on their behavior.

This fact may have been the basis for Levenson's (1972, 1973a,b) extending the locus-of-control concept to include three dimensions: internal control, control by powerful others, and chance. Those people who believe in what Rotter called an external locus of control may see their outcomes being controlled by powerful external agents (parents, teachers, bosses) or by chance. This elaboration was paralleled in Connell's (in press) three-dimensional measure of children's perceived control over successes and failures.

There has been confusion in the locus-of-control literature, and the closely related perceived-control literature, over the meaning of external control. This revolves around whether external control refers to the perceived noncontingency of outcomes or to perceived contingency with an external controlling administration. As we said, Rotter used the term to refer to perceived noncontingency of outcomes; Levenson used the term to refer to the perception that either powerful others or chance controls one's outcomes (the former implies contingency and the latter implies noncontingency); and Weiner (1972) and other attribution theorists have used the term to refer to people's believing that their outcomes are determined by any factor outside themselves. An example of the latter use of the term would be someone's believing that he or she failed an exam because it was too hard; the outcome was controlled by the test's difficulty.

Self-Consciousness

Fenigstein *et al.* (1975) introduced an instrument to assess aspects of self-consciousness. They suggested that one's style of attending to oneself can take three general forms. One can attend to private aspects of oneself—one's thoughts, feelings, and needs—in which case one would be privately self-conscious. One can attend to public aspects of oneself, as if seen through the eyes of another, in which case one would be publicly self-conscious. Finally, one can attend to oneself with a high level of anxiety about how one is being perceived by others, in which case one would be socially anxious.

Conceptually, one's attentional style can be seen to be related to causality orientations. Private self-consciousness means that one attends to one's internal states, whatever they are. All three of the causality orientations are accompanied by internal states: relaxed interest for the autonomy orientation; pressure and tension for the control orientation; and anxiety and helplessness for the impersonal orientation. As any orientation becomes stronger, one would be more likely to attend to its private components. Research indicated that private self-consciousness was modestly correlated with all three orientations ($r = .21$ for autonomy; $r = .23$ for control; and $r = .24$ for impersonal).

Public self-consciousness is theorized to be a component of the control orientation. To be oriented toward controls, whether one behaves compliantly or rebelliously, means that one is likely to be aware of oneself as the controllers would be aware of one. This is very much congruent with the idea of public self-consciousness. Further, public self-consciousness would also be expected to be related to the impersonal orientation, because one's ineffectance and belief in outcomes being determined by impersonal forces would have one concerned with (perhaps even making projections about) other people's negative evaluations of one. As expected, public self-consciousness was correlated with both the control and the impersonal orientations ($r = .22$ for control; $r = .41$ for impersonal).

Finally, social anxiety would be expected to relate to one's social ineffectiveness and thus, like public self-consciousness, to be related to the impersonal orientation. In fact, social anxiety and impersonality were very strongly correlated ($r = .58$).

Research reported by Plant and Ryan (1985), found results that are congruent with several of the above mentioned relationships between self-consciousness and causality orientations. In their experimental research Plant and Ryan found a negative relationship between public self-consciousness and intrinsic motivation. Public self-consciousness, tending to be controlling in nature, seems to undermine intrinsic motivation, just as controlling, extrinsic events do. Social anxiety was also found to be negatively related to intrinsic motivation, as would be expected. Finally, private self-consciousness did not affect intrinsic motivation, because as the previously mentioned correlations suggest, private self-consciousness is equally related to a high level of each of the causality orientations and thus, for example, to intrinsic motivation and to extrinsic motivation or amotivation.

Other Constructs

There are numerous other psychological constructs that are theoretically related to one or another of the causality orientations. We will briefly mention several of these.

Supporting Autonomy. Deci, Schwartz, Sheinman, and Ryan (1981) developed a measure of adults' orientations toward supporting children's autonomy versus controlling their behavior. This measure of adults' orientations was found to be related to the intrinsic motivation and self-esteem of the children who were involved with those adults. We would expect that adults who are oriented toward autonomy in their own functioning would be concerned about the autonomy of the children they relate to; consequently we predicted that autonomy-oriented adults (on the causality orientations scale) would be oriented toward supporting children's autonomy. This relationship, as reported by Deci and Ryan (1985), was very strong ($r = .55$).

Conceptually, one would expect that adults who are control-oriented themselves would also be oriented toward controlling children's behavior. In terms of measurement, however, the causality orientations scale was constructed in such a way that the autonomy subscale and the control subscale were independent; but the scale measuring adults' orientations toward children was bipolar, so that supporting children's autonomy was perfectly negatively correlated with controlling children's behavior. Therefore, the positive correlation between the autonomy orientation and the tendency to support autonomy in children tended to preclude a relationship between the control orientation and the tendency to control children's behavior. The Deci and Ryan (1985) research found no correlation between the two.

Type-A Behavior Pattern. Being controlled by external events such as extrinsic rewards has been shown to be related to the experience of pressure and tension (Ryan *et al.*, 1983). Similarly, being controlled by internally controlling events such as ego-involvements has been found to be related to pressure and tension (Ryan, 1982). It stands to reason then that being controlled by one's own control orientation would also be associated with pressure and tension. Because the Type-A, coronary-prone behavior pattern (Jenkins, Rosenman, & Friedman, 1967) is characterized by the experience of being pressured and driven, we predicted and found the Type-A pattern to be correlated with the control orientation ($r = .26$).

Self-Derogation. The impersonal causality orientation, which involves the inability to achieve desired outcomes predictably and therefore to develop and actualize intentionality, entails the experience of personal helplessness and the self-blaming that accompanies it. The self-derogation scale was developed by Kaplan and Pokorny (1969) to assess self-blaming, so we predicted that it would correlate with impersonal causality. The scale included ten items, each with a binary response, though we changed the response format to utilize 7-point rating scales so we would get greater variability. As expected, self-derogation was strongly positively related to impersonality ($r = .38$) and slightly negatively related to autonomy ($r = -.20$). The more strongly autonomy oriented and the less strongly impersonally oriented one is, the less likely one is to engage in self-derogation.

The issue of self-derogation is another place where we find divergence between the perceived control (i.e., locus of control) and the causality orientations concepts. For example, in Connell's (1984) scale of perceived control over outcomes, children would be ascribed internal control for failures if they blamed themselves for the failures. In the causality orientations conceptualization this could be a concomitant of impersonal causality. The autonomy response to failure is an interested, open-minded questionning of what one could do to achieve the desired outcome next time.

Depression. Depression is widely believed to be related to people's experience of ineffectance and amotivation. Consequently, we would expect people with a high impersonal orientation to be particularly susceptible to depression. To test this we administered the Beck Depression Inventory (Beck & Beamesderfer, 1974) to 80 subjects who had completed the causality orientations scale. As predicted, there was a significant correlation (.29) between impersonality and the tendency to be depressed, and no relationship between the other two orientations and depression.

Emotions and Attitudes

All of the research reported previously related the three causality orientations to other personality constructs. Other research has explored the types of emotions and attitudes subjects report while in experimental settings. Ryan (1982) had subjects complete the Differential Emotions Scale (Izard, Dougherty, Bloxom, & Kotsch, 1974). This scale consists of 30 individual emotional descriptors (e.g., downhearted, contemptuous, shameful, joyful),and subjects indicated, on a 5-point scale, the extent to which they felt each. The responses were then factor analyzed, and the eight factors that emerged—two hostility factors, enjoyment, fear, shame, interest, surprise, and guilt—were correlated with the autonomy, control, and impersonal orientations.

The strongest relationships were with the impersonal subscale. The impersonal causality orientation is based in ineffectance, the belief that one cannot reliably attain desired outcomes. Associated with this chronic experience of ineffectance, as one might expect, is a generally negative emotional tone. Impersonality was somewhat related to hostility, though it was primarily related to fear, shame, and guilt, the feelings that can be interpreted as hostility directed toward oneself (correlations ranged from .21 to .38). The control subscale, on the other hand, was correlated with the hostility factor that represents hostility directed outward ($r = .21$). The autonomy subscale tended to be inversely related to hostility and guilt (r's $= -.16$ and $-.26$, respectively). In another data set, the autonomy orientation was positively related to the interest factor.

In the Ryan (1982) study, subjects also filled out a postexperimental attitude questionnaire. Their responses on this questionnaire were also correlated with their autonomy, control, and impersonal scores. The results revealed that the impersonal subscale was negatively related to the degree of being relaxed ($r = -.36$) and positively related to felt pressure ($r = .30$). The control subscale was positively related to the item, "it was important for me to do well on the puzzle activity," (.27) though, interestingly, it was also negatively related to reports of "how hard I tried" ($-.19$). "Having to do well" is conceptually related to the control orientation; doing well at an achievement task, particularly one assigned by someone else (in this case the experimenter), is a characteristic of the compliance component of the control orientation. However, the negative relationship of control with "try hard" seems at first blush to be anomolous. It is probable that this correlation reflects another characteristic of the control orientation, namely, a defensive self-presentation. In being control oriented, people want to look good to the controllers or evaluators, so they might report not trying hard as a way of maximizing their image. If they do well, people will think especially highly of them for doing well without trying, and if they do poorly, not trying hard provides an excellent excuse.

Kernis (1982) also did an experiment in which subjects completed the causality orientations scale and the differential emotions scale. Kernis' results were very similar to Ryan's in that there was a very strong relationship between people's impersonality scores and their reports of experiencing the negative emotions. In his study, Kernis also created an informational, a controlling, and an amotivating experimental condition and related the autonomy, control, and impersonal scores to the emotions in each of the three conceptually relevant conditions. He reported evidence of an interaction between personality, as represented by the causality orientations, and environment, as represented by the three experimental conditions. There was a negative relationship between the control orientation and joy, and a positive relationship between the control orientation and fear in the informational context, but a positive relationship between the control orientation and joy, and a negative relationship between the control orientation and fear in the controlling context. When people are high on the control orientation they seem to be happier and less fearful in controlling environments than in informational, autonomy-supporting environments.

Behaviors

We have just begun to relate causality orientations to behaviors. In general, we predict that the three causality orientations will relate to behaviors in ways that parallel how the three classes of initiating events relate to behaviors. A strong autonomy orientation should tend to relate to the types and qualities of behavior that emerge from an informational context; a strong control orientation, to those from a controlling context; and a strong impersonal orientation, to those from an amotivating context.

Exam Performance. Eighty-eight students from a personality lecture course completed the causality orientations scale. During the semester, they took an exam, and results revealed that there was a significant negative correlation between the control orientation scores and grades. The more control oriented people were, the poorer they performed. Wheeler (1984) reported a similar finding, in which subjects' performance on a hidden-figures task was negatively related to their control orientation. These findings are congruent with research showing that the introduction of controlling events, such as extrinsic rewards, into a learning situation tends to lead to poorer performance on heuristic activities, such as conceptual learning (Grolnick & Ryan, 1985; McGraw, 1978). A focus on controls, whether because there are extrinsic rewards or because people are control oriented, leads to decrements in performance.

The exam from the personality class mentioned previously included short-answer questions and a highly unstructured essay that asked students to discuss some topic from the course that interested them. After students got their grades they rated the fairness of the two different parts of the exam. These ratings were then predicted in a hierarchical regression procedure, in which the variance due to grades was removed and the causality orientations scores were entered. The strongest of the relationships that emerged was between autonomy scores and fairness ratings on the unstructured part. The more autonomy oriented a student was, the more the student found the unstructured question fair. With a strong autonomy orientation, one tends to learn out of interest rather than obligation, so these students felt more comfortable with the less structured question focused on their interests.

Attachment Patterns. A recent study by Bridges, Frodi, Grolnick, and Spiegel (1983) employed the causality orientation scale in an exploration of mother–child attachment patterns. Ainsworth *et al.* (1978), as well as numerous other investigators, have studied attachments using the strange-situation paradigm and the A, B, C classification system. This classification system describes three general types of attachment patterns: the A pattern is based in an insecure attachment in which the baby tends to avoid contact with the mother; the B pattern is based in a secure attachment; and the C pattern is based in an insecure attachment in which the baby is resistant and ambivalent toward the mother. The strange-situation paradigm involves a series of separations and reunitings of the baby with the mother and with a stranger.

In the Bridges *et al.* study, mothers completed the causality orientations scale and participated in the strange-situation paradigm with their 1-year-old infants. Mothers were classified in terms of their attachment relationships and then the averages of the autonomy, control, and impersonal scores were computed by attachment classifications. The mothers of avoidant babies (the A pattern) had higher scores on the impersonal subscale than the mothers in the other two classifications; the mothers of the securely attached babies (the B pattern) had higher scores on the autonomy subscale than the mothers in the other two categories; and the mothers of the resistant babies (the C pattern) had higher scores on the control subscale than the mothers in the other two classifications. Although the overall significance of the pattern of results was only marginal because of having so few pairs with the A and C

attachment patterns, the results do suggest some interesting specula-
tions. It may be that mothers' tendencies toward impersonality, with
the associated anxiety and passivity, result in their babies' being avoidant, and that mothers' tendencies toward control, which presumably
lead them to be intrusive and controlling with the babies, result in the
babies' being ambivalent and resistant.

Coping with Surgery. King (1984) studied 50 patients prior to, and
following, voluntary cardiac bypass surgery. She measured the degree
to which they viewed the experience as a challenge, thus focusing on
the potential benefits, versus as a threat, thus focusing on fears and
negative aspects. Their scores were then predicted from their causality
orientations scores and from their scores on seven coping measures.
Results revealed that the greatest amount of variance in the appraisal
of the experience as a challenge was accounted for by their autonomy
orientation score. And this was the only predictive variable that remained
predictive from pre- to postsurgery. People who are more autonomy
oriented seem to view difficult situations more as challenges than as
threats.

Occupations. One hundred and two professionals from a large corporation completed the General Causality Orientations Scale. Nineteen
were research scientists who worked in the company's "think tank" and
83 were engineers who worked in the manufacturing organization. These
data revealed that the engineers were significantly more control oriented
than the researchers, whereas the scientists had higher, though not
significantly different, autonomy scores. It seems that people's causality
orientations may play a role in the types of jobs they select.

Summary of Scale Development

The general causality orientations scale has been shown to be tem-
porally stable and internally consistent and to fit appropriately into a
nomological network of motivationally relevant constructs. Further, it
has been shown to relate to emotions, attitudes, and behaviors in a
theoretically meaningful way.

The general scale was constructed to crosscut domains and to include
a wide range of responses and reactions. This was done to assess the
general utility of the construct. Because its validity has been confirmed,
domain-specific scales are being constructed to deal with narrower classes
of responses, and the results of one investigation that employed the
causality-orientations-at-work scale will be reported in Chapter 11. It is
generally expected that the domain-specific scales will allow greater predictability of behaviors, because the construct will be assessed with respect

to the particular class of events under investigation. A recent investigation by Paulhus (1983) revealed that when perceived control was partitioned into domains and instruments were developed to assess each, the specific scales predicted their own domains well, relative to scales that measured the same construct in other domains. This suggests that predictions of behavior will be enhanced by domain-specific causality orientation scales.

Summary

A great deal of research reported in Chapters 3 and 4 has confirmed that the three classes of behaviors and motivationally relevant processes that we have referred to as self-determined, control-determined, and amotivational are facilitated, respectively, by the three classes of initiating and regulatory events: informational, controlling, and amotivating. Research reported in this chapter suggests that people's relatively enduring orientations toward causality are also reliably related to these three classes of behaviors and psychological processes. We described three orientations: autonomy, control, and impersonal. The autonomy orientation involves the tendency to select or interpret initiating and regulatory events as informational and is theorized to be associated with intrinsically motivated behaviors and those extrinsically motivated behaviors that are based in integrated internalizations. In short, a high degree of autonomy orientation facilitates self-determined functioning. The control orientation describes the tendency to select or interpret initiating and regulatory events as controlling and is hypothesized to be associated with control-determined behaviors. And the impersonal orientation, which involves experiencing situations as unmasterable, relates to amotivation at the internal and the external boundaries.

The causality orientations have been shown to be relevant for understanding adult developmental concepts, such as self-actualization and ego development, and they were shown to be related to a wide range of other constructs, such as self-consciousness, self-derogation, self-esteem, and the Type-A coronary prone behavior pattern. The research is particularly important for our organismic theory of self-determination because it shows that characteristics of the organism as well as characteristics of initiating and regulatory events play an important determinative role in motivationally relevant human functioning.

III

ALTERNATIVE APPROACHES

Operant and Attributional Theories

Early in this century, American psychology rallied around the study of overt behavior, as had been suggested by Thorndike (1913) and Watson (1913). This perspective, which had its roots in the philosophy of logical positivism, demanded the use of operational definitions that were specified in terms of overt, observable behaviors. The most influential spokesperson for this position was undoubtedly Skinner (e.g., 1938), who proposed and elaborated an operant theory of behavior. Although the perspective is no longer as central to empirical psychology as it once was, there are still a number of psychologists who subscribe to a relatively orthodox operant perspective, and the field of applied behavior modification is firmly rooted in operant theory.

During the decades of the 1960s and 1970s, many people who had worked in the operant tradition shifted their focus away from a strictly operant perspective toward a cognitive perspective. This involved studying the relationship between people's cognitions (i.e., their expectations and attributions) and their behavior. Whereas operant theory was formulated largely in terms of objective characteristics of people's past reinforcements, cognitive theories tended to focus on people's attributions about why they engaged in past behaviors and their expectations about future reinforcements.

Our own work uses neither the operant nor the cognitive perspective, although it has been informed by each. Instead, we focus our analysis deeper in the organism, at the level of motivations and emotions rather than at the level of behaviors and cognitions. This allows us to consider behaviors and cognitions in our analysis, but it also allows for the exploration of a variety of phenomena that have not been dealt with adequately by behavioral or cognitive theories.

Still, numerous investigators have explored some of the same phenomena that we have explored and have interpreted them within either an operant or a cognitive framework. Therefore, we will present the alternative viewpoints, highlighting what we believe to be their strengths and weaknesses.

OPERANT THEORY

Operant psychology (Skinner, 1953) has, in essence, been concerned primarily with the explication and application of the law of effect (Thorndike, 1913). It has detailed changes in response rates that occur in the presence and absence of reinforcements. The core of the empirical findings (e.g., Keller, 1969) is summarized in Figure 2 in the form of a response-rate curve, with four distinct phases. An operant behavior has an initial level of frequency of occurrence in the absence of reinforcements; this level, which is called baseline, is represented as phase I. The introduction of an external reinforcement, such as food or water, will increase the rate of responding, assuming the organism has been deprived

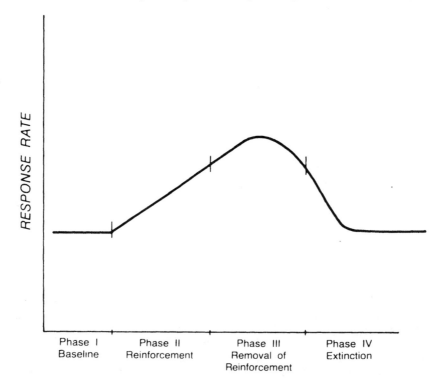

FIGURE 2. The relationship of response rates to the introduction and withdrawal of reinforcement.

of the reinforcing substance long enough so that it will effectively reinforce a response. This increased responding is represented as phase II.
When the reinforcements are terminated, the response rate increases
rather markedly for a short time, then peaks and subsides, returning to
the response rate that was evident at the time the reinforcement was
terminated. It is as if the organism tries harder to get the reward until
it learns that the reward is not forthcoming. This period is labeled phase
III in the figure. With continued withholding of the reinforcements, the
response rate continues to decline until it reaches the initial baseline. It
then levels off and remains at that rate; the effect of the reinforcement
has worn off. This return to baseline is labeled phase IV. During this
period, which is referred to as extinction, there may be brief periods of
spontaneous recovery in which the rate of responding has a temporary
increase, as if the organism were checking to see if the reward had been
reinstated.

Much of the operant research has investigated how different schedules of reinforcement affect this curve. What might be the shape of the
curve if the organism were reinforced after every third response rather
than after every one? Or, what would be the effect if 2 responses out
of every 10 were reinforced on a random schedule? The answers are
that these different schedules would affect the shape and durations of
the second through fourth phases of the curve. For example, phase III
would last longer and the return to baseline in phase IV would take
longer if the reinforcements were intermittent rather than continuous.

The bulk of the research related to operant theory has been done
with animals, such as rats, pigeons, and monkeys. Thus, the response-
rate curve in Figure 2 applies most directly to the behavior of these
animals. With humans, whose cognitive capacities often allow them to
understand immediately that reinforcements have been terminated, the
shape of the curve may be quite different. In such cases there would
not be a phase III, because the person would not need to discover
whether reinforcements had been terminated, and the so-called return
to baseline should occur very quickly, in fact immediately. This would
mean, then, that the curve would move directly from phase II to phase
IV and that the slope of the initial segment of phase IV of the curve
would be steeper.

Rewards and Response Rates

Operant psychology does not postulate about motivation; it concerns itself with observable behaviors and observable reinforcements.
All behaviors are said to be under the control of some reinforcement
contingency. Thus, there is believed to be no such thing as intrinsic

motivation. Behaviors that we call intrinsically motivated are said either to be operants at the baseline level of activity or to be under the control of unidentified reinforcement contingencies.

Nonetheless, the research reported in Chapter 3 is directly relevant to operant psychology, for it would imply that, for humans, the introduction and subsequent removal of rewards or controls has an effect that amounts to a rate of responding in phase IV that is different from the initial baseline. If this were so, it would call into question several important foundations of operant psychology.

People frequently say that the decrease in free-choice period responding that we presented in Chapter 3 and use as evidence of the undermining of intrinsic motivation is counter to the operant prediction that reinforcing a behavior strengthens that behavior. This, however, is deceptive, and one must be careful to specify what point in the reinforcement curve one is addressing. The research that we have reviewed thus far has attempted to assess intrinsic motivation subsequent to the termination of reinforcement. Thus, we would be talking of either phase III or phase IV responding. Because the research was all done with humans who knew that the reward had terminated, operant theory would lead us to expect subjects to go immediately into phase IV when the reward was terminated and to return very quickly to baseline. The free-choice behavior from which we infer the level of intrinsic motivation would not, according to operant theory, be stronger following the cessation of the reward than it was prior to the introduction of the reward. Rather, it would be expected to be the same. Any deviation from baseline during the postreward period would be counter to the prediction derived from operant theory.

Several operant-behavioral or cognitive-behavioral theorists have discussed and criticized the emerging literature on intrinsic motivation and its relation to external rewards. There have been three lines of attack. First, some writers have claimed that the undermining phenomenon does not exist, that its demonstration has resulted from artifacts or inappropriate methodological procedures. The burgeoning literature in which the phenomenon has been replicated dozens of times across ages, cultures, tasks, and conditions, makes that a difficult position to defend. A second group of critics has accepted that the phenomenon exists but has asserted that it is inconsequential. The final group has accepted its existence and has attempted to explain it within behavioral theory. Let us now review this work.

"Failures" to Replicate

Feingold and Mahoney (1975) reported a study that, they asserted, casts doubt on the existence of an undermining effect. In it, 5 second-grade children went through a series of sessions in which they worked with dot connection drawings. Following the assessment of baseline activity, a token economy was established in which the children were reinforced with tokens (redeemable for prizes) for performing above baseline. As expected, their response rate increased. In subsequent, no-reinforcement periods, the children's responding decreased, though it did not return to a level as low as baseline.

In interpreting these results, there are two important points to be noted. First, there were only 5 subjects in the experiment, so one must use considerable caution in generalizing these results. Second, and more important, there was no control group that did the same activity without reinforcements. The true test of an undermining effect would consider changes in responding from baseline (phase I) to extinction (phase IV) for a rewarded group as compared to changes for a nonrewarded group. That would allow for the control of extraneous factors, such as practice effects that could affect extinction-period responding. It is possible, for example, that the comparable extinction-level responding of a no-reward control group would have been higher than that displayed by the rein-forcement group in the Feingold and Mahoney study. If that had been the case, their data could have been interpreted, in a relative sense, as support for the undermining effect, so there is no way of knowing what conclusions are warranted.

Hamner and Foster (1975) also did a study that they claimed failed to support the undermining phenomenon. In it, subjects worked at coding questionnaire data from a sexual attitudes survey. They were paid either task-contingently (5¢ per questionnaire) or task-noncontingently (75¢ for 20 minutes of work), or not paid. The authors then measured their output, claiming that that was a measure of intrinsic motivation. The results revealed that the subjects who received task-contingent payments performed more than the other two groups, which did not differ from each other.

There are two important points to be made about this study. First, one can question whether the activity of transcribing numbers from a questionnaire to a computer coding sheet is an intrinsically interesting activity (even if the questionnaire does relate to sex). More problematic, however, is the fact that the rewards were still in effect when the output was measured. The subjects who were paid 5¢ per questionnaire coded more questionnaires than subjects who either got no pay or task-noncontingent pay. We would, of course, make the same prediction and would assert that it says nothing whatsoever about intrinsic motivation. It is merely a demonstration of something that has been demonstrated hundreds of times before, namely, that contingent reinforcements increase organisms' response rates on this type of nonconceptual task while the contingency is in effect. For intrinsic motivation to be inferred, the researchers would have had to look at coding behavior following the removal of the payments.

Brennan and Glover (1980) did an experiment in which students from a course were asked to work on puzzles and either were rewarded with a 10-point bonus on one of their exam grades or received no reward. Pre- to posttreatment behavioral measures indicated no differences between these two groups. The authors presented it as evidence against the undermining phenomenon. There are a number of methodological difficulties with this experiment also. For example, as long as the exam had not yet occurred and the experiment was related to the course, the reward contingency was, in a sense, still in effect. However, leaving aside the methodological problems, one need merely recognize that the rewards in that experiment were task-noncontingent, which, as we saw in Chapter 3, is the type of reward structure that is least likely to produce a decrement.

Competing Responses and Boredom

Reiss and Sushinsky (1975) criticized the early studies that claimed to show the undermining of intrinsic motivation for using such a brief reinforcement period and for using only single-trial reinforcement procedures. They suggested that with a more extended reinforcement period, the undermining effect would not appear. They then reported two studies with young children as subjects: one employed the single-trial reinforcement procedure and replicated the undermining effect previously shown by Lepper et al. (1973); the other employed a multiple-trial procedure and failed to replicate the effect. Reiss and Sushinsky suggested that the effect observed in single-trial experiences was actually due to a distraction effect. The rewards, they suggested, interfere with subjects' attending to the target activity and therefore lead them to be less interested in that activity.

In replying to this critique, Lepper and Greene (1976) made a number of interesting comments. First, in the Reiss and Sushinsky study, there was not a control group that received no reinforcements; the design was a within-subject design. Therefore, this study, like that of Feingold and Mahoney (1975) discussed previously, failed to control for a variety of possible extraneous factors. Further, there were no attractive alternative activities available to the children during the free-choice period, and unfamiliar adults were in the room recording the children's behavior. Given these conditions, it is questionable whether their dependent measure has any relevance to intrinsic motivation.

Smith and Pittman (1978) did an elaborate study that was specifically intended to test the distraction or competing response hypothesis. In it,

Smith and Pittman reproduced the distraction effect that wore off with repeated trials, as Reiss and Sushinsky had suggested it would. However, they also found that the undermining of intrinsic motivation occurred and became stronger with repeated trials, even after the distraction effect wore off. We can conclude that although rewards may produce a distraction effect, this effect does not provide a reasonable account of the phenomenon that we refer to as an undermining of intrinsic motivation.

Mynatt, Oakley, Arkkelin, Piccione, Margolis, and Arkkelin (1978) also emphasized the importance of extended baseline and reinforcement periods. They did a study using first-grade children who were observed for 29 consecutive school days working on educational games. Baseline observations lasted 9 days, reinforcements lasted 11 days, and follow-up observations were done over an additional 9 days. They reported that a rewarded (with candy) and a nonrewarded group evidenced substantially reduced on-task behavior during the follow-up period relative to the baseline period; however, the two groups did not differ from each other during the follow-up. They concluded that there was no evidence of rewards undermining intrinsic motivation; instead, both groups appeared to have become satiated with the target activities.

It does appear that both groups became bored with the activity, and by the follow-up period both groups had such a low level of target activity that a floor effect may have prevented the appearance of an undermining effect. As with the distraction hypothesis, we would certainly agree that children will become satiated with activities, even ones that are initially very interesting. That fact, however, does not provide an account of the decreased, posttreatment responding of rewarded groups (relative to nonrewarded groups) who have not worked on the task long enough to have become satiated with it. In other words, it does not represent an adequate explanation of the frequently demonstrated undermining of intrinsic motivation by external rewards or constraints.

The Focus of One's Analysis

Lepper and Greene (1976) made another interesting point, namely, that the concerns of Reiss and Sushinsky seemed to be different from theirs. Behaviorists, who tend to focus their attention on a functional analysis of behavior, have typically eschewed any theorizing about the internal regulation of behavior in the absence of specific reinforcement contingencies. Indeed, several authors (e.g., Scott, 1976) have specifically asserted that intrinsically motivated behaviors are simply behaviors

for which the controlling, external contingencies have not yet been identified (Sidman, 1960). This difference in focus, of course, has been evident in the studies mentioned previously where, for example, Hamner
and Foster (1975) attempted inappropriately to measure intrinsic motivation while the reinforcement contingencies were still in effect.

When one begins with the assumption that there is no intrinsic
motivation (Scott, 1976), when one is unwilling to consider that intrinsic
motivation is fundamentally different from drive-based motivation
(Mawhinney, 1979), or when one begins with the assertion that reinforcement theory (or one of its recent variants) is the only appropriate
analysis for behavior, then there is no way to elucidate intrinsically
motivated processes. The focus is altogether different.

Scott (1976) argued that reinforcement theory is adequate for
explaining any of the behaviors that were observed in the intrinsic motivation studies, though he also asserted that the studies were fraught
with methodological problems that made their findings suspect. He suggested that if there were a phenonemon to be explained, the explanation
would revolve around the complex interaction of multiple reinforcing
events.

Mawhinney (1979) also advocated a reinforcement analysis beginning with Premack's (1971) version of reinforcement theory. The theory
is based on the concept of reinforcement value. When a more valued
activity is made contingent on doing a less-valued one, the former is
defined as extrinsic with respect to the latter, the latter being defined
as intrinsic. If food is more valued than water, and if drinking is instrumental to eating, then drinking would be considered an intrinsic behavior and eating an extrinsic one. Mawhinney then used Dunham's
notion that individuals have preferred durations for activities, and he
explained what we call the undermining of intrinsic motivation in terms
of "extrinsic" activities interrupting the optimal duration of "intrinsic"
activities.

From considering these discussions one can see clearly the difference in focus of their work and ours. First, their concept of an intrinsic
behavior is completely different from ours. And second, although we
have used the response-rate curve of Figure 2 to explain where, in an
operant analysis, one would look to see the undermining of intrinsic
motivation, our concern is not primarily with response rates. Instead,
our concern is with an exploration of intrinsic motivation and its various
ramifications—phenomena that reinforcement theorists tend to obfuscate.

To explore intrinsic motivation, one must begin with the assumption
of its existence as a real motivational propensity, different in kind from
drives and understandable in terms other than the level of reinforcement

value. This assumption seems quite tenable given the research reviewed in Chapter 2 and given its utility for the integration of all the research presented in Chapters 3 and 4. Therefore, if one uses the concept, one must look to measure it in a way that is congruent with its meaning. As Lepper and Greene (1976) stated, one must, for example, pay attention to subjects' probable situation-specific expectations about the presence of extrinsic rewards if one is attempting to assess intrinsic motivation for some activity. If, in a situation, they expect that a reward might be forthcoming, their behavior cannot reasonably be used to infer intrinsic motivation. Even when their behavior occurs in the absence of reinforcement contingencies, if they (wrongly) expect that the contingencies are operative, their behavior is not a reflection of their intrinsic motivation. The definition that states that intrinsically motivated behavior is behavior that occurs in the absence of any apparent reward contingencies is merely an operational definition; it is not a psychological definition. Thus, it needs to be used with judgment if it is to represent meaningfully the psychological construct of intrinsic motivation.

A final behavioral critique of our work was made by Williams (1980). He suggested that rewards do not undermine intrinsic motivation unless they constrain one's behavior. Thus, he said, rewards have both a rewarding aspect and a constraining aspect. The rewarding aspect enhances post-manipulation activity, whereas the constraining aspect decreases post-manipulation activity because the constraint is comparable to a punishment. Williams then did a study in which fourth- and fifth-grade children were rewarded with either desirable or undesirable rewards for working with various games. In addition, there was a group (called the constraint group) that was asked to work on the target activity and a group (called the control group) that was simply left to work with the activity.

The study employed a before-after design in which free-choice activity was assessed prior to and after the manipulation period. Results showed that the undesirable reward and the constraint groups showed a decrease in free-choice activity from pre- to posttreatment, whereas the desired reward group showed a slight increase. Williams interpreted this in terms of an increase in free-choice activity caused by the reward value of the desired reward. However, what was left unmentioned was that the control group increased from pre- to posttreatment considerably more than the attractive-reward group. Relative to the control group, then, the attractive-reward group evidenced a small decrement in free-choice activity, so that, although the author reported an increase for the attractive-reward group, the conclusion was unwarranted and misleading.

We find the reward-value/constraint-value distinction to be confusing. First, what Williams failed to recognize is that all extrinsic rewards have a constraining aspect, what we refer to as a controlling aspect. Second, to speak of reward value, independent of needs, leaves the concept incomplete. In other words, something is rewarding only if it satisfies a need, so without explicating what the concept of reward value means, he has failed to shed any new light on the phenomena. Further, to say that reward value increases subsequent activity is illogical and inconsistent with behavioral theory. Rewards increase subsequent activity only if people expect that rewards will continue to be forthcoming.

We maintain that the informational-versus-controlling distinction deals adequately with each of these points. First, we suggest that all external rewards have a controlling aspect (i.e., all external rewards, to some extent, constrain behavior). Second, the informational aspect of rewards provides what might be called reward value for one's intrinsic needs for competence and self-determination. They let one know that one is competently self-determining. And they could be predicted to increase subsequent activity, because if one feels competent and self-determining in relation to an activity one may undertake it again with the expectation of experiencing further intrinsic satisfaction.

Summary

We have used a response-rate curve to show where one would look for the undermining of intrinsic motivation if one were using the operant framework and to suggest that studies that have reported failures to replicate have frequently attempted to measure intrinsic motivation at the wrong place in the response-rate sequence. When reinforcement contingencies are still in effect one cannot infer intrinsic motivation, for it is intertwined with extrinsic motivation.

Some behaviorists have criticized the concept of intrinsic motivation as being too vague. We suggest that the so-called vagueness is due to the fact that the behavioral manifestations of intrinsic motivation may be different in different situations, and that a logical analysis of the concept and the situation usually allows one to be quite precise in predicting behavioral manifestations. What one gains from using a concept that is psychological rather than behavioral is a richness of theory that allows for more comprehensive theorizing and considers human experience as well as human behavior. This, of course, points to the fact that our concerns are somewhat different from those of behavioral or response-rate theorists. We are less concerned with responses, and more concerned with human psychological (especially motivationally relevant) processes and their various ramifications. Behavior represents one place to focus and make predictions, but it is by no means the only place and not necessarily the most important.

COGNITIVE APRROACHES

The cognitive perspective has had an influence in the area of motivation, just as it has in most other areas of psychology. In motivation, the approach has been brought to bear in two general ways. First, it acted to shift the analysis of behavior from past reinforcements to expectations about future reinforcements. People's thoughts or expectations were given a causal role in the explanation of human action. Whereas operant theory asserts that people respond to stimuli because they were reinforced for responding to those stimuli in the past, cognitive theory suggests that people respond to stimuli because they expect to be reinforced in the future. The operant approach focuses on what has happened; the cognitive approach focuses on what people believe will happen. Of course, what has happened in the past will have a major impact on people's expectations, but in cognitive theory the past is said to play a role by influencing expectations rather than by determining behavior. In cognitive theories, one's expectations and decisions, rather than one's reinforcement history, are given determinative status.

The second major influence of the cognitive approach has been a focus of attention on a postbehavioral, self-analysis of one's behaviors and their causes. This work, which is generally referred to as self-attribution, suggests that, following people's behavior, people analyze why they did what they did. The results of this analysis are said to be fed into the information-processing system in a way that affects their subsequent motivation, attitudes, and feelings.

The focus on postbehavioral, self-related inferring can be understood as an offshoot of attribution theory, originally proposed by Heider (1958) and elaborated by Jones and Davis (1965) and by Kelley (1967). Whereas the original theory was proposed to describe the way people infer the internal states of others, the more recent focus has been on the way people infer their own internal states. In other words, the self-attribution approach suggests that people analyze their own behavior and infer their own internal states in much the same way that they analyze the behavior and infer the internal states of others.

In the remainder of this chapter and in the next, we will review the cognitive approach as it relates to motivation. In this chapter we will focus on the attributional work because that is most relevant to cognitive evaluation theory and the results reported in Chapters 3 and 4. We will begin with interpersonal attribution theories and move on to self-attribution theories.

INTERPERSONAL ATTRIBUTIONS

As first discussed by Heider (1958), attribution involves the linking of some event with the conditions that prompted it, through a process of considering personal and environmental forces. This process of attribution stems from people's desire to understand their world as somewhat ordered and nonrandom. People can, through attributions, predict and control their own relation to the world.

We suggest that the process of making attributions is an intrinsically motivated process because it helps people master their environments and to feel a sense of competence and self-determination. People make attributions so they can figure out the world and be effective in relating to it. Attributing is part of the process of learning and part of the process of mastering new situations. It allows people to make predictions (correctly or incorrectly) and it helps them achieve desired outcomes if their predictions are correct. The fact of the attributional process being so integral to learning and effective functioning in the world suggests that it is intrinsically motivated, just as learning itself is intrinsically motivated; yet it too, like learning, can be extrinsically motivated. People will make attributions if rewarded for doing so, and they will make attributions that are instrumental to goal attainment. It is a basic human process that is naturally intrinsically motivated but frequently will be extrinsically motivated.

Heider (1958) distinguished between phenomenal and causal descriptions of perception. He proposed that attributions are phenomenal or immediate, and that there is not an elaborate cognitive processing involved in making attributions. He stated, "[In] person perception [the observer] not only perceives people as having certain spatial and physical properties, but also can grasp even such intangibles as their wishes, needs, and emotions by some form of *immediate apprehension*" (Heider, 1958, p. 22, italics added). More recent models, particularly that of Kelley (1967), portray the attributional process as being much more analytical. He proposed that people make attributions in a way that is much like the scientist's analytic procedures of exploring causal relationships. Presumably, both types of attributing are done. People speak of having intuition or an immediate sense about some event; they attribute phenomenally. But they can also be quite deliberate and calculating in their attempts to get to the bottom of causal relationships; they are sometimes analytical in their attributing.

Attribution Theories

According to Heider, behaviors and their outcomes can be accounted for by personal forces and by environmental forces. Personal forces include trying and power. Trying is of course a motivational concept and is determined by intentions and exertion; power is essentially synonymous with ability. Environmental forces include barriers to the occurrence of behavioral outcomes, typically referred to as task difficulty and luck. It follows that whether people can cause outcomes to occur depends on whether their power outweights the barriers. Whether they do achieve a desired outcome depends on one of two sets of circumstances: either that they can and they try; or that they are lucky. The first set of circumstances typically involves personal causality: their power outweighed the barriers, and they tried to bring about the outcome. In the second set of circumstances, it makes no difference whether they have power or not, or whether they tried hard or not; the environment delivered the outcome. There was impersonal causality.

When people fail to bring about an outcome, it may mean that their power was inadequate given the barriers; that they did not try; or that they were unlucky. The first and third cases are impersonal causality, and the second is personal.

Intention is the most critical factor in personal causality. According to Heider, there cannot be true personal causality without intention. Even if a failure were due to one's lack of ability (a personal force), rather than to the overwhelming size of the barrier (an environmental force), without intention, the outcome would not be a case of personal causality. Personal causality assumes intention to produce the observed effects; that is, it involves one's being motivated to achieve the observed end state. It is typically assumed that people do not intend to fail.

Jones and Davis (1965) expanded Heider's work in their theory of correspondent inferences. Their theory begins with the observation of one action (which may, of course, have many effects) and attempts to account for the attribution of that action to a particular intention and subsequently to a dispositional characteristic of the actor. They asserted that for an action to be attributed to a disposition of the actor, and thus to involve personal causality, an observer must infer intentionality on the part of the actor. To do this the observer must believe that the actor had the ability to cause the effect and had knowledge that the behavior would lead to the effect. If there were not ability and knowledge, there would be no intention, so the Jones and Davis model would not be applicable. Their model, then, attempts to predict which personal cause will be attributed when personal causation appears appropriate; it is not intended to determine whether or not personal causation will be attributed.

The attribution of causality in their model is determined by the desirability of an effect. They assert that an observer will pick the most desirable effect of an action as the reason for the action (i.e., as the actor's intended outcome). Then that intention will be used to infer a disposition. The more unique the effect (i.e., the less common the effect), the more likely that the behavior will be attributed to a disposition. For example, if a woman ran to her office, the observed effects might be that she arrived at her office on time and was out of breath. It would be inferred that her intention was to arrive at her office on time, because being out of breath is less desirable and therefore not considered the intent. According to the model, the observer would then determine how unusual that effect is. If it were quite unusual, the attribution would be quite strong; if it were rather usual, the attribution would not be so strong. The reasoning for this is that if one is doing something quite ordinary and socially appropriate, it does not tell us much about one's dispositions. On the other hand, unusual behaviors tend to say more about the person. Arriving at one's office on time is not too unusual, so the dispositional attribution would not be very strong.

Kelley (1967, 1971) took quite a different approach to expanding and elaborating Heider's theory. His version of the attributional process was patterned after an analysis-of-variance framework. Kelley's model differed from that of Jones and Davis (1965) in two primary ways. First, Kelley's analysis allowed for making attributions not only to the personal dispositions of the actor (e.g., the woman's compulsive promptness), but also to the entity in question (e.g., a strict boss) or to the particular circumstances (e.g., there was an important meeting that day). To determine which of these potential causes will be inferred, the observer is said to analyze what factors covary with the behavior. If the woman is always on time everyplace she goes, the behavior would be attributed to her because we know that everyone is not always on time; the behavior covaries with the person. If the woman is always on time getting to the office but not to other places and everyone else who works for her boss is also always on time, the behavior can be seen to covary with the boss. If the woman is not always on time to the office, then her being on time that day would be attributed to the specific circumstances.

Kelley referred to this analysis in terms of the *covariation principle* of attributions and suggested that all people use *consensus* information (whether all people are likely to do the target behavior), *distinctiveness* information (whether the behavior is likely to occur in situations other than the target situation), and *consistency* information (whether the behavior occurs consistently in the target situation) to determine what factor covaries with the target behavior.

We can see from this that Kelley's model is more general, in that it attempts to account for environmental (entity or circumstances) attributions as well as personal ones. The Jones and Davis model provides a more detailed means of assigning causality to a particular personal cause, whereas Kelley's model allows for causality to be assigned to other causes. Jones and Davis' model would not be applicable if the evidence suggested an environmental cause.

As we said, the Jones and Davis model is primarily concerned with the uniqueness of effects. The more socially desirable the effect is believed to be (i.e., the less unique the effect), the less confident would be the dispositional attribution. Because most people get to their offices on time, the Jones and Davis model would assign a disposition with low confidence. The Kelley model, however, would go further and try to see whether the woman really is usually on time in this and other situations and whether others around her are also. Then it would lead one to attribute causality for the behavior to the factor that it covaried with.

The use of Kelley's covariation principle requires repeated observations with respect to the target behavior. Kelley (1971) recognized, however, that people often cannot make repeated observations and have only minimal data available. Consequently he offered two other principles to explain how people make attributions when they have observed only one instance of a behavior.

The *augmentation principle* asserts that if a behavior occurs in the presence of inhibiting environmental forces, the personal attribution will be augmented. For example, if the woman in the example had to run three miles through very cold weather (inhibiting environmental forces), the personal attribution would be stronger than if the weather were beautiful and she had to run only one mile through the park. The latter case would be one of facilitating environmental forces, so there is greater ambiguity in determining the cause.

The *discounting principle* proposes that when behavior occurs in the presence of multiple plausible causes, the attribution will be discounted, that is, the observer attributes the effect less to any one cause than he or she would if only that cause were plausible. The attributor will be less confident about the attribution and will make a less extreme attribution than he or she would make if there were only one plausible cause. This implies that if a behavior occurs in the presence of a facilitating environmental force, internal factors will be discounted. For example, if the woman were on time and ran through the beautiful park in nice weather, the attribution to her disposition would be discounted.

Enzle, Hansen, and Lowe (1975) reported evidence suggesting that environmental forces tend to take precedence over personal ones as attributed causes. Thus, if both personal causes and environmental causes are plausible explanations, there is causal ambiguity and the cause will most likely be attributed to the environmental force.

Attributing Motivation

Intrinsically motivated behaviors are ones for which the rewards are internal to the person. The actor engages in them out of interest and to feel competent and self-determining. Extrinsically motivated behaviors are ones that the actor performs to receive some extrinsic reward. If a man typed a manuscript to make money, he would be extrinsically motivated; if he did it because he enjoyed typing and felt competent and self-determining while typing, he would be intrinsically motivated.

In either case the behavior would be the same, but the desired effect would be different. In the extrinsic case, the desired effect would be the receipt of money, whereas in the intrinsic case, the desired effect would be to have a satisfying engagement with the activity.

The issues involved in the attribution of intrinsic versus extrinsic motivation are more complex than might be thought at first blush. Both cases seem to involve intentions to bring about desired effects and would therefore, according to Heider's theory and to Jones and Davis' theory, be considered cases of personal causation. However, deCharms (1968) argued that when one's behavior is directed toward the attainment of extrinsic rewards, the person tends to become a pawn to those extrinsic rewards and to the person or system dispensing them. This was shown to be true in numerous studies reported in Chapter 3. DeCharms introduced the concepts of internal causality and external causality to describe the nature of attributions in cases of intrinsic motivation versus extrinsic motivation, and we incorporated those concepts into cognitive evaluation theory and causality orientations theory.

In causality orientations theory the autonomy orientation is said to have an internal locus of causality and to represent the paradigmatic instance of personal causation; the control orientation is said to have an external locus of causality; and the impersonal orientation is said to involve impersonal causality. Research reported in Chapter 6 indicated that the control orientation, which represents external causality, was more closely related to the impersonal orientation (i.e., impersonal causation) than to the autonomy orientation (i.e., personal causation). This finding supports the distinctions offered by deCharms' analysis and suggests that these further distinctions are relevant for the attribution theories of Heider and of Jones and Davis. They would consider extrinsically motivated behavior to represent personal causation, but it seems to have aspects of personal and impersonal causation and to tend more toward impersonal causation than personal causation.

Deci (1975) referred to intrinsically motivated behavior as involving personally caused intentions, and to extrinsically motivated behavior as having environmentally caused intentions, as a way of stressing that extrinsically motivated behavior tends to be controlled by the extrinsic rewards. This same point is more generally and more accurately made, however, in the distinction we currently make between self-determined behavior and control-determined behavior. Not all intentional behavior is self-determined and thus does not represent pure personal causation. Extrinsically motivated behavior is often not self-determined (although we saw in Chapter 5 that it can become integrated and thus be self-determined) and therefore may not represent pure personal causation. Even when one acts intentionally in accord with one's introjected regulations in the absence of extrinsic controls, there tends not to be pure personal causation.

Kelley's theory allows for behavior to be attributed to external sources in cases of extrinsic motivation, although he was not concerned with the issue of personal causation *per se*. Using Kelley's covariation principle, if a man did a particular task only when he was paid for it and was always willing to do it when offered money, the behavior would covary with the money so the attribution would be to the money. He would be said to be highly extrinsically motivated (at least for that particular task) and his intrinsic motivation would be discounted. If, in addition to doing this task only when paid, the man did most things only when paid, he would be seen as being generally controlled by money and as being highly extrinsically motivated.

Deci, Benware, and Landy (1974) reported research that explored the conditions within which an observer would attribute intrinsic or extrinsic motivation to an actor. They reasoned, in line with Kelley's discounting principle, that if people engage in an activity for no apparent external cause (i.e., no apparent extrinsic reward), they will be perceived as intrinsically motivated. Conversely, if they receive large extrinsic rewards for performing the activity, they will be perceived to be more extrinsically motivated and less intrinsically motivated. In the latter case, given a plausible external cause that is sufficient to justify the behavior, there is no need to attribute intrinsic motivation. Further, because rewards are so frequently used to motivate people to do things that do not interest them, observers may well operate with an association between extrinsic rewards and being uninterested in the activity.

Deci *et al.* also reasoned that the behavior itself, in addition to the external conditions (i.e., the level of reward), would influence the attributions made by an observer. If a man is producing some commodity or performing some service, the number of units he produces or the number of services he renders is likely to affect the attributions an observer makes about his motivation. If the person receives a set amount of payment (i.e., a salary, as opposed to piece-rate payments) and performs under constant conditions, his output might be expected to be a direct reflection of his intrinsic motivation. The more he produces, the more intrinsically motivated he would be perceived to be.

Now consider attributions of extrinsic motivation and recall that an extrinsically motivated person is someone who engages in the behavior in order to get a reward. If there is no reward, there will be no behavior. If a man is getting a set smount of pay that cannot be affected by his output, he will be likely to produce as little as he can get by with. Performance does not get him rewards, so he may not perform much. Hence, low output suggests high extrinsic motivation. On the other hand, if his output is high, he will be seen as low in extrinsic motivation, because he would not be producing so much if he were motivated primarily to get money. This leads to the prediction that a person will attribute greater intrinsic motivation and less extrinsic motivation to performers who produce a high level of output than to ones who produce a low level of output, when rewards are the same and are not tied directly to output.

Deci *et al.* (1974) tested these two predictions. The subjects were each given a booklet that described an experiment alleged to have been conducted the previous semester and that purportedly tested the developmental trend of color perception in humans. It was explained to the subjects exactly what procedural steps these color-perception subjects (to be called *actors*) had gone through. The subjects were told that the actors had been given a large stack of uncolored pictures and asked to color pictures for three hours, coloring as many pictures as they wished and the kinds of pictures they liked best.

The two manipulated variables in this study were a) the amount of monetary reward ($2.50/hr. versus $.50/hr.) received by the actor, and b) the level of output produced by the actor (25 pictures completed in 3 hours versus 5 pictures completed). All subjects were told that the average number of pictures completed by all actors was 15, although each actor had had 100 different pictures available to color. In summary, the four experimental conditions were low output, low reward (5 pictures, $1.50/3 hours); high output, low reward (25 pictures, $1.50/3 hours); low output, high reward (5 pictures, $7.50/3 hours); and high output, high reward (25 pictures, $7.50/3 hours). Subjects were randomly assigned to the four conditions by being provided with one of the four different booklet forms corresponding to the four conditions. Each subject was asked to judge the probable motivation of one actor after having been provided with reward/output information peculiar to that actor.

The predictions that there would be a direct relationship between level of reward and extrinsic motivation and that there would be an inverse relationship between level of reward and intrinsic motivation were supported. Subjects attributed greater extrinsic motivation and less intrinsic motivation to actors who had received $7.50 than to those who had received $1.50.

The predictions that there would be a direct relation between level of output and intrinsic motivation and that there would be an inverse relation between level of output and extrinsic motivation were also supported. Subjects attributed greater intrinsic motivation and less extrinsic motivation to subjects who completed 25 pictures than to those who completed 5. There was no interaction between output and reward on either dependent variable. The predictions, therefore, received strong support from the data. It appears that when people perform a task for large extrinsic rewards they will be perceived by an observer to be more extrinsically motivated and less intrinsically motivated than when they perform a task for small extrinsic rewards. Further, when they produce high output on the task they will be perceived to be more intrinsically motivated and less extrinsically motivated than when they produce low output.

The experiment just presented considered the effects of monetary rewards on attributions of intrinsic and extrinsic motivation. What might be the effects of other external events? Kite (1964) did a study that allows a partial answer to this question. His study showed that when one person punished another by fining him for poor performance, attributions about the causes of the compliance behavior were very highly environmental. The cause of the behavior was attributed to the punishment. In another condition where subjects were rewarded with monetary payments for doing well, attributions were also environmental, that is, the cause of the behavior was in large part attributed to the reward. However, in the punishment condition the causality was more strongly attributed to the external control than in the reward condition.

Combining these results with those of the Deci et al. (1974) study, one would expect that not only extrinsic monetary rewards, but also other external controls, would lead to decreased attributions of intrinsic motivation.

Reward Contingency. The monetary rewards said to have been administered in the first Deci *et al.* (1974) experiment were hourly payments that were not contingent on output (i.e., were task-noncontingent). Imagine now a situation where extrinsic rewards are made contingent on output. A set amount of reward is paid per unit of output, so the greater the output the greater the rewards and the lower the output the lower the rewards; the rewards would be task-contingent. What attributions would an observer make about the motivation of a performer in a task-contingent payment situation?

An important piece of information to be considered in making predictions about the attributions in task-contingent versus task-noncontingent situations is the fact that in a contingent situation the rewards are, to a much greater extent, under the control of the performer. The performer determines the magnitude of his or her monetary payments by the level of performance, whereas in the task-noncontingent situation the rewards are fixed and the performer has no effect on them.

To derive the predictions for the attributions of motivation in a task-contingent and task-noncontingent situation, consider a 2×2 experimental design with high output/high reward and low output/low reward on one dimension and noncontingent and contingent payments on the other. Imagine that the task-contingent payment is set in such a way that output and rewards are the same for the contingent payment group as for the noncontingent group, at each of the two levels of output/ rewards. It would then be possible to compare performers whose output and rewards are the same but whose basis of rewards is different. Because rewards are a direct function of output when they are task-contingent, rewards and output will necessarily covary. Hence, to make meaningful comparisons between the task-contingent and task-noncontingent conditions, rewards and output would have to covary in the task-noncontingent conditions as well.

Deci *et al.* (1974) did a second study which employed the 2×2 design just mentioned. Half the subjects were told that the actor, to whom they were making attributions, had been paid task-contingently (\$.30 per picture colored), and the other half were told that the actor had been paid by the hour. The high versus low output was the same as in the prior study (5 versus 25 pictures colored). Thus, subjects were told that contingently paid actors in the high output condition earned \$7.50, which is the same amount that was earned by the high producer in the task-noncontingent condition who received \$2.50 per hour. In the low output condition, the actor was said to have colored five pictures and therefore received \$1.50, which was the same amount as that earned by the actor who received $.50 per hour. Thus, the amount of output and rewards was the same in the two high output/high reward conditions, and also in the two low output/low reward conditions. The only difference was that in two conditions payments were contingent on performance, and in the other two they were not contingent.

Now let us consider the predictions for attributions of intrinsic motivation and extrinsic motivation in these four conditions. First, consider extrinsic attributions in the case where the output and rewards were low. When people are contingently paid they are likely to be perceived as less extrinsically motivated than those who are noncontingently paid because the contingently paid people *chose* to get the low rewards—it was under their control. Presumably, they would have worked more if they had been extrinsically motivated, so they must be relatively low in extrinsic motivation. Although the noncontingently paid people also received low pay, they did not determine their own level of pay; although they should be perceived to be relatively low in extrinsic motivation (as shown in the first Deci *et al.* study just reported), it is not likely to be as low as for the contingently paid people, because they did not determine their own level of pay.

Now consider the high-output/high-reward conditions. The contingently paid people are likely to be perceived as more extrinsically motivated than the noncontingently paid people, because they determined their own high level of reward. They worked hard to get the high payments, so they are probably highly extrinsically motivated. Thus, the researchers predicted an interaction between the output/reward variable and the contingency variable such that the high-output/high-reward contingent cell would be most extrinsic, the low-output/low-reward contingent cell would be least extrinsic, and the two noncontingency cells would be moderately extrinsic.

Finally, consider the predictions for attributions of intrinsic motivation and look first at the high-output/high-reward conditions. In the noncontingent cell the rewards are fixed so the performers' output does not affect their rewards. It would be clearer that their high output was a reflection of their intrinsic interest in the activity. However, when the rewards were contingent on output, it would not be so clear whether the high output stemmed from their intrinsic interest in the activity or from the instrumental value of the activity for attaining the rewards (multiple plausible causes). Thus, people in this condition are likely to be perceived as less intrinsically motivated than people in the noncontingent condition. Now for the low-output/low-reward conditions; when actors are paid noncontingently, their rewards do not depend on their output, so low output suggests low intrinsic motivation. For contingently paid actors, however, it is not clear whether low output is due to low intrinsic motivation or to a lack of interest in making money (i.e., low extrinsic motivation). Thus, the attributions to intrinsic motivation are likely to be low, but not so low as in the noncontingent condition. The researchers, therefore, predicted an interaction between the output/reward variable and the nature-of-payment variable such that high-output/high-reward, noncontingent rewards would lead to the most intrinsic attributions and low-output/low-reward, noncontingent rewards would lead to the least intrinsic attributions.

The data support all of the predictions. Subjects attributed greater extrinsic motivation to the performer in the high-output/high-reward conditions when payments were task-contingent than when they were task-noncontingent, and less extrinsic motivation to the performer in the low-output/low-reward condition when payments were task-contingent than when they were task-noncontingent. Further, subjects in the high-output/high-reward conditions attributed greater intrinsic motivation to the performer when rewards were task-noncontingent than when they were task-contingent, and subjects in the low-output/low-reward conditions attributed less intrinsic motivation when rewards were noncontingent than when they were contingent. Both interactions were highly significant.

SELF-ATTRIBUTIONS

Over the years since attribution theory was introduced, cognitively oriented social psychologists have increasingly used an attributional analysis to study how people perceive their own internal states. Bem's (1967, 1972) self-perception theory, which was developed out of operant theory, has been the most widely discussed self-attributional theory and has been used in the interpretation of research on such topics as attitude change, emotions, intrinsic motivation, and socialization.

In essence, the self-attribution approach asserts that people know their own internal states in much the same way that they know others' internal states: through inferences. By observing their own behavior and the circumstances within which it occurred, people are said to logically derive what they must be feeling, wanting, or believing. A feeling, motive, or belief is, according to this approach, an attribution made to oneself by oneself, and the rules by which attributions are made to oneself are said to be essentially the same as those by which attributions are made to others. One looks for plausible external causes for a behavior, and in the absence of external causes that are sufficient to justify the behavior, one attributes internal causes. For example, if a woman were forced at gunpoint to hit her child, she would justify the deviant act in terms of having been forced to do it; she would not be likely to see herself as angry at her child or as an abusive parent. There was adequate external justification, so she would be able to attribute the more desirable internal states to herself—she could continue to see herself as a loving mother. However, if she did it following the mere suggestion, "Why don't you hit him?" the attributions would be different. The external cause (viz., the suggestion) would probably not be seen as adequate justification for the behavior, so the woman would be more likely to attribute anger to herself and to be critical of herself as a parent. The important point is that the self-attributional approach asserts that the anger and negative self-thoughts are postbehavioral inferences made to oneself on the basis of assessing the prior occurrence.

In research on self-attribution, as in research on interpersonal attribution, the discounting principle and the augmentation principle (Kelley, 1972) are widely used to interpret results. The intrinsic motivation research reported in Chapter 3 has been frequently discussed in terms of the self-attributional approach (Kruglanski, 1975; Lepper et al. 1973). These authors have focused on the undermining of intrinsic motivation by external events, which in the self-attribution literature has been called the overjustification effect. The reasoning goes as follows: when people have been rewarded or controlled for working with some interesting target activity, they will, postbehaviorally, assess the situation, noting that there was a strong external cause. They will then attribute causality for their behavior to the external cause and discount any plausible internal cause, namely, intrinsic motivation. Thus, they will attribute less intrinsic motivation to themselves than they would if there had been no plausible external cause. There was more than enough justification (i.e., there was overjustification) so they will discount the internal justification. Analogously, if there seems to have been insufficient justification or if they did the activity in spite of barriers, they will augment the internal cause and attribute greater intrinsic motivation.

It is important to note that this type of theory is not a theory of motivation, but rather a theory of self-inferring. It is relevant to motivation insofar as it deals, albeit after the fact, with inferences about motivation, but it is not a motivation theory, for it does not deal with the central motivational questions of the energization and direction of behavior. Its applicability has been solely to the explanation of changes in intrinsic motivation following behaviors that occurred in various situations.

Empirical Considerations. First, we will assess the validity of the self-attribution theories for dealing with the phenomenon of the undermining of intrinsic motivation by reviewing studies that are relevant to this question. There are two key issues in whether a self-attributional analysis is a useful approach for explaining the undermining phenomenon. We will address each of these and then move on to the broader issue of whether the attributional approach can account for all the changes in intrinsic motivation (undermining and enhancing) that were reported in Chapters 3 and 4 and were explained by our motivational theory.

The first issue, as pointed out, for example, by Sandelands, Ashford, and Dutton (1983), is whether people actually engage in the conscious inferencing process that is implied by the self-attributional explanation. Zajonc (1980) reported a series of studies that speaks to this issue, although they were not actually studies of intrinsic motivation. He explored subjects' preferences among various stimuli and found, for example, that prior exposure to stimuli led people to prefer those stimuli over others to which they had not been exposed. In many instances the prior exposure had been subliminal, so subjects had no awareness of having seen the stimuli previously, but still they preferred them. Zajonc's conclusion was that people's affective experiences (in this case their preferences) do not need conscious, attributional mediation.

Applying Zajonc's work to our present discussion, we assume that changes in intrinsic motivation (like the development of preferences) do not require the intermediary step of self-attribution. The processes go on at a level deeper in the organism than mere thoughts. These processes are very likely occurring prior to, during, and after task engagement.

The second issue is whether the discounting process must occur (whether consciously or nonconsciously) in order for the undermining phenomenon to occur, because discounting is the attributional process that is said to yield the phenomenon. The possibility for testing this came from some interesting developmental research done by Smith (1975), Schultz, Butkowsky, Pearce, and Shanfield (1975), Karniol and Ross (1976), Kun (1977), and Di Vitto and McArthur (1978). These investigators reported that the use of the discounting principle is observed first at a developmental stage that begins around 8 years of age. Prior to that, children tend either to infer internal causality in a relatively random fashion or to augment internal causality (rather than discount it) in the presence of external forces.

Using this fact, Morgan (1981) reported a study that was specifically designed to test the self-attributional interpretation of the undermining phenomenon. His strategy involved identifying children who had developed the discounting schema and children who had not. Half of the children in each of those two groups were rewarded and half were not. Then the subsequent intrinsic motivation of the children in each group was assessed. In the first of two studies, Morgan used different-aged children, 5 versus 11 years old, to create the groups of discounting, and nondiscounting children, as 5-year-old children do not use discounting, whereas 11-year-old children do. In the second study, Morgan used only 8-year-old children, 8 being the age around which children tend to acquire the discounting schema. He then tested the 8-year-olds for the schema and separated them according to those who had acquired the schema and those who had not.

All children in both studies worked on jigsaw puzzles, and half the subjects in each group, from both experiments, were rewarded with their choice of desirable foods (candy, marshmallows, etc.) and half were not. The primary dependent measure was the standard free-choice measure, taken 2 to 4 weeks after the experimental manipulation. Results revealed that, in both studies, the extrinsic rewards led to decreases in intrinsic motivation for all children regardless of whether they employed the discounting schema. In other words, the self-attributional process of inferring one's own level of intrinsic motivation by using the discounting principle was shown not to have mediated the undermining of intrinsic motivation.

Another study, by Ransen (1980), also failed to find any support for the discounting principle as the basis for the undermining phenomenon. His study, which used a template-matching procedure, was inconclusive about what exactly were the mediating processes, though it did indicate that self-attribution was not and that personal causation was somehow involved.

On the basis of these studies we can conclude that attributions are not necessary for the occurrence of the undermining of intrinsic motivation by external initiating or regulatory events. This does not, however, imply that attribution cannot affect subsequent intrinsic motivation. In fact, a study by Pittman et al. (1977) has indicated that self-attribution can affect intrinsic motivation. These investigators used false physiological feedback to lead subjects to think that they were either more intrinsically motivated or more extrinsically motivated. Half the subjects were rewarded for working with an interesting game and half were not. Results, from a free-choice period, revealed that although the rewards decreased intrinsic motivation for false feedback groups and a no-false-feedback, control group, the intrinsic-cue group showed the smallest decline. In other words, by affecting subjects' postbehavioral attributions, they were able to have an impact on the subjects' subsequent intrinsic motivation. Porac and Meindl (1982) reported conceptually similar results using a very different paradigm.

Taken together, these and other studies suggest that although attributions become more external when people are rewarded (e.g., Brockner & Vasta, 1981; Phillips & Lord, 1980), and although self-attributions can affect intrinsic motivation, they are by no means necessary mediators for changes in intrinsic motivation to occur. What is required, therefore, is a theory that can take account of the affects of self-attributions but does not place them at the center of changes in intrinsic motivation. Our motivational theory is such a theory.

According to our theory, the interaction of people's needs and perceptions of the environmental affordances lead them to engage in an activity in a way that is either intrinsically motivated or extrinsically motivated. This means that the "effects of external events" can occur prior to, and after, task engagement. The mere presence of a controlling reward, for example, may have shifted people's motivation for the task away from intrinsic and toward control-determined, extrinsic motivation even before they began doing the task. Then, if people are successful at the activity, they may experience being effective at getting rewards. This postbehavioral experience may further strengthen their extrinsic motivation and further undermine their intrinsic motivation. The success experience could, in the words of deCharms (1968), make them more competent pawns rather than more competent initiators.

The recognition that some of the change in motivation for the task can come before the behavior begins is important for interpreting the results of research showing that people's performance on heuristic or conceptual activities is poorer and their creativity less when they are rewarded than when they are not (Amabile, 1983; McGraw, 1978). If the intrinsic motivational decrements occur after the behavior, as self-perception theory suggests, the performance results could not be explained by the same theory as the intrinsic motivation results.

To summarize our perspective on this issue, controlling events and the individual's tendency to be controlled (i.e., the control orientation) lead to an extrinsic engagement with the activity. The process of engaging in that way strengthens the individual's tendency to be controlled; in other words, it strengthens extrinsic motivation and weakens intrinsic motivation. On the other hand, informational events and the person's tendency to interpret events as information (i.e., the autonomy orientation) lead to an intrinsic engagement with the activity. Here, the person is self-determining, in which case success, and even rewards, could serve to affirm one in one's self-determination. The process of choosing is strengthened and the person becomes more intrinsically motivated.

Theoretical Considerations. Self-attribution theories look first to external forces that either facilitate or hinder people's performance. If the forces facilitate the behavior, internal causes are discounted, and if they hinder the behavior, internal causes are augmented. One of the primary theoretical problems with this approach, however, is its inability to deal with qualitatively different internal regulatory events. For example, internally controlling regulation is very different from internally informational regulation, even though they would both be called internal causes. Internally controlling events initiate behavior in a way that is relatively independent of external events, but the quality of one's engagement with an activity that is internally controlled is more similar to the quality of one's engagement when controlled by external events than to the quality of engagement initiated by internally informational events. It is the fact of the initiating event's being controlling versus informational, rather than the fact of its being outside the person versus inside the person, that carries the greater variance in the quality and impact of one's activity. Both types of distinctions are important, of course, so a theory must take account of the nature and effects of each.

Attributing one's own behavior to an internal cause is said to be done on the basis of the presence or absence of plausible external causes, the social desirability of the effect, and other such nonpersonal considerations. This type of self-attributional theorizing does not allow one to distinguish between two very different processes, such as doing something because you feel you have to and are afraid of the guilt and self-incrimination that would follow if you did not do it; and doing something because it interests and challenges you and provides you with excitement and stimulation. In both instances, activity could be initiated and sustained in the absence of external, supporting contingencies, in fact the activity could be sustained in spite of inhibiting forces. Thus, self-attribution theory would suggest that one would make internal attributions of being intrinsically motivated and self-determined in both cases; but they are not both instances of intrinsically motivated or self-determined behaving.

In a similar vein, the self-attribution theories either ignore or downplay awareness or personal knowledge. Attribution theory, when applied to interpersonal perception, is appropriate because observers have no direct access to the actor's internal states and must therefore infer them, but it is less appropriate when applied to intrapersonal perception because people do have (or at least can gain) access to their own internal states. The self-attribution view of "knowing oneself" facilitates a confusion between knowing what one wants or feels through awareness of one's organismic condition and thinking that one wants or feels what is believed to be appropriate in that situation.

We do believe that self-attributional processes occur; people do look to external sources to figure out what they want or feel, but this process of attributing to oneself must be placed in theoretical juxtaposition to the process of direct awareness of one's internal states. In Chapter 6 we distinguished between the autonomy orientation and the control orientation. The autonomy orientation involves knowing one's internal states through personal knowledge or direct apprehension; one experiences one's feelings and needs directly and internally. The control orientation, however, involves knowing one's internal states through inference; one wants or feels what one thinks that one should want or feel. In most instances, this phenomenon is probably an aspect of psychological defenses involving blocked awareness.

Perceiving Intrinsic Motivation in Oneself and Others

Another issue that we will address in our comparison of cognitive theories with our motivational theory concerns the clear parallels that have been shown to exist between perceptions of oneself and of others. For example, considerable research has shown that monetary rewards decrease people's intrinsic motivation, and also that observers infer less intrinsic motivation in people who are paid for an activity. Here we see a parallel between what happens to a person's internal states and what is inferred by observers to happen. There are at least two possible explanations for this parallel. One is provided by the cognitive, self-attribution theories (e.g., Bem, 1972), and the other, more encompassing account, is provided by our motivational theory.

Bem's self-perception theory asserts that people know their own internal states by making attributions to themselves based on observations of their own behavior and the circumstances in which it occurs. When people are rewarded or controlled for working on an initially interesting activity, the self-perception approach suggests that they will see themselves doing the activity for the reward or control and will assume that that is the reason why they are doing it. Consequently, they will infer low intrinsic motivation, because external causes plus intrinsic motivation would be seen as overly sufficient justification. As Bem (1972) pointed out, this requires the assumption that strongly apparent external contingencies will imply to people that they did not want to do the task for its own sake. On the other hand, when people see themselves doing the activity with no salient rewards or controls, they will infer that they must be intrinsically motivated. Why else would they be doing the activity?

It is interesting to note that the task itself plays a relatively unimportant part in the process. People are said to infer liking for an activity on the basis of their behavior and the contingencies of reinforcement. The process would be the same for dull or interesting tasks. People look for extrinsic justification; if they find it they infer low intrinsic motivation, and if they do not, they infer high intrinsic motivation.

With this theory, it is easy to account for the observed parallel between what actually happens to people's internal states and what is attributed to them. The principles by which people know themselves are said to be the same as those by which they know others. Presumably, through social learning they come to know what feelings or needs are appropriate, expected, and normative for certain situations, and then they use this knowledge to attribute feelings, motives, and attitudes to themselves just as they attribute them to others.

The alternative explanation begins with self-knowledge and asserts that people make interpersonal attributions partly on the basis of what they know about themselves. When people observe others, they make causal attributions to those others primarily by knowing what their own internal states would be in that situation. They perceive in others what exists in themselves.

DeCharms (1968) and Bridgman (1959) have discussed the relationship between perceiving motivation in oneself and in others. Bridgman argued cogently that the process of verifying one's own motivation is separate from the process of inferring someone else's motivation. One need have no observation of one's own behavior in order to know that one is motivated. But observations are the primary data for making inferences about other people's motivation. Bridgman pointed out that people may make observations of their own behavior and internal states, but that this is less common than knowing one's internal states from direct personal knowledge. DeCharms elaborated Bridgman's position by adding that personal knowledge may be useful in assessing others' internal states. It is that position that we are elaborating here by suggesting that the basic element in inferring others' internal states is one's own personal knowledge. One comprehends others' motivations largely by projecting what one's own motivation would be in that situation.

Of course, people will not always attribute to others exactly what would be true for them; it is merely the starting point for our analysis. Other perceptual and motivational factors come into play and operate in systematic ways to produce differences in knowledge of self versus others.

There has been some research on the differences between attributions made by actors to themselves and by observers to actors. Jones and Nisbett (1971) reviewed a number of studies indicating that actors tend to attribute their behavior more to external than to dispositional causes, whereas observers tend to attribute actors' behavior to their personal dispositions. Actors' accounts of their behavior tend to focus more on the initiating circumstances in the situation, whereas the observers' accounts tend to focus on stable characteristics of the actors. Jones and Nisbett suggested that this is due in part to the fact that actors have more information about themselves, but it is due largely to the fact that different types of information are differentially salient to the actor and observer. For observers, the behavior itself and the actor doing the behavior are the primary focus of their observation. Until the behavior has been observed, the circumstances are irrelevant to the observer.

Those circumstances would be important only retrospectively when the observer attempts to account for a behavior, but by then they are unavailable to the observer, so the observer attributes in terms of the actor's dispositions. For the actor, all of the circumstances leading up to a behavior are salient aspects of the behavioral unit. Actors never actually observe the behavior, for they are acting; their focus is outward to the situation, so that their attribution is likely to be in terms of the situational factors that led them to behave in that way.

Jones and Nisbett focused on perceptual differences, though there are also motivational factors that influence the attributions that people make to themselves versus those they make to others. For example, people typically like to see themselves in favorable ways and like to see themselves as being in control of situations, even of ones that may be determined by chance (Langer, 1975). Considerable research, reviewed by Zuckerman (1979), has shown that people tend to attribute positive attributes to themselves when they succeed, whereas they tend to blame the environment when they fail.

Observers are also motivated by their own best interests. When the actor fails (or is involved in some other unfortunate occurrence), the observer may need to hold the actor accountable. If observers were to attribute the cause to external situational factors, then the observers would be acknowledging that they themselves might also fall prey to those forces. Not wanting to see themselves as susceptible to failure, they may attribute causality to the actor. On the other hand, if the outcome is positive they may be less likely to see the actor as responsible because they will not want to see the actor as more capable than they see themselves.

The points are that the attributional process is itself motivated; that there is a basic tendency to attribute to others what one believes would be so of oneself in that situation; but that other motivational factors affect the attributional process and may lead people to attribute different causes to other people's behavior than they do to their own.

METATHEORETICAL CONSIDERATIONS

Perhaps the most critical and central differences between our motivational theory and the cognitive theories revolve around metatheoretical considerations. We begin with different philosophical assumptions about the nature of people than do the cognitive theorists, and we work to explicate the interaction between the possibilities for human freedom and the limitations to that freedom. Cognitive theorists have not been concerned with this dialectic, and therefore their theories suffer from an important lack of context.

When the process of self-attribution is viewed within the context of the interplay of freedom and boundedness, self-attribution can be seen to be more a concomitant of boundedness than of freedom. People need to infer their own internal states only to the extent that they have blocked direct awareness of their internal states. This, we assert, signifies non-self-determination rather than self-determination.

Furthermore, self-attribution may actually be involved in the process of people's limiting their freedom. For example, when children attribute to themselves the feelings that are appropriate given the situation, they may experience conflict between what they actually feel and what they have attributed to themselves (i.e., what they think they should feel). This conflict can, in turn, lead them to block awareness of the true feeling as a way of reducing the conflict. As a result, they will feel what is appropriate by continuing to make self-attributions, and in so doing they will be contributing to their own lack of self-determination.

One is free to the extent that one's behavior follows from true choice rather than from external controls and internally controlling events. One may use information from external or internal events in choosing how to behave, in which case one would be self-determined, but to the extent that the determination of one's behavior shifts to the controls and away from choice, one has lost some of one's freedom. The process of self-attribution is hypothesized to accompany this loss of freedom. As one's behavior is more determined by controls and less determined by choices, one is likely to be less aware of one's internal states, so one is more likely to infer them through self-attribution.

The most extended discussion of freedom from a cognitive perspective was recently presented by Brehm and Brehm (1981) within the context of reactance theory. For them, freedom means having behavioral options, and according to their theory, a motivational condition is set up whenever one's freedom is lost or threatened. This motivational condition, referred to as reactance, is aroused when someone expects an important behavioral outcome and that expectation is threatened. The motivational condition then leads one to "restore one's freedom" by problem solving, rebelling against the threat, or distorting one's cognitions.

Although freedom to attain outcomes is of concern to us and is dealt with in our theory, we are more concerned with freedom as a characteristic of psychological flexibility. Automatic rebellion or cognitive distortion in the experience of reactance indicate a lack of cognitive flexibility and, as we said in Chapter 3, do not actually restore freedom. They merely relieve the tension created by reactance.

The difference between the behavioral freedom emphasized by reactance theory, which is an example of a cognitive theory, and the psychological freedom emphasized by our motivational theory can, perhaps, be detected in this quote from Brehm and Brehm: "Having to exercise a freedom that one does not want to exercise"(1981, p. 389). According to our theory, one is not free when one has to exercise a behavioral option. "Having to exercise a freedom" is a contradiction in terms. Having a particular possibility may be preferable to not having it, even if one has to exercise it, but that can not be the focus of a theory of psychological freedom, for it is not the essence of freedom. "Having to" implies lack of freedom, even if that "having to" comes wholly from one's own thoughts.

The key to the difference once again revolves around the distinction between internally informational and internally controlling regulation. To be free of external force is, of course, generally desirable, as is getting an outcome that one expects. But being robot-like, that is, being controlled by internal scripts in exercising one's behavioral options, or in rebelling against the loss of a behavioral option, does not represent freedom. It is more a case of being bound by internal forces than it is of being free. One can be bound by external forces or internal forces. The cognitive theories have been able to deal with the issue of freedom with respect to external forces, but they have missed the fundamental issue of freedom with respect to internal forces.

A similar issue can be seen with respect to control. Cognitive theorists generally speak of the advantages of people having perceived control over situations. However, as we have said before, control is different from self-determination. Self-determination involves choice, and people may choose to take control or to give up control. The basic intrinsic need is not to be in control of situations or of outcomes; it is to choose, to be self-determining with respect to situations or outcomes. Of course, the opportunity to gain control is a prerequisite to choosing to control, but it does not guarantee self-determination. Having to control is just like having to exercise a freedom; it does not represent freedom or self-determination. On the other hand, if one does not have the opportunity to gain control one cannot choose to control, but one can exercise one's self-determination by making an adequate (integrated) accommodation to the lack of control. Presumably, then, one would find the opportunity to exercise control elsewhere.

Our concept of psychological freedom is of course more difficult to study than the concept of behavioral freedom, for one cannot easily observe whether a person's compliance or defiance is chosen or controlled. However, we have been increasingly able to study such impalpable phenomena. By using a metatheory of the freedom–boundedness interaction and a theory that is based in motivational processes, one can use ingenuity to study such phenomena.

In sum, we have suggested that much of the difference between our approach and the cognitive approaches can be traced to differences in metatheory. By starting with a concern for freedom, as represented by psychological flexibility, one can account for the phenomena described by cognitive theories while at the same time placing them in a larger perspective.

Summary

In this chapter we briefly presented operant theory through an analysis of a response-rate curve. This allowed us to point out that if one were looking for "changes in intrinsic motivation" due to reinforcements one would compare the difference between baseline responding and extinction responding of the reinforced group to the same difference in an appropriate control group. We reviewed studies that had reported failures to replicate the undermining of intrinsic motivation by extrinsic rewards, and we saw that each one either used data from the wrong phase in the response rate curve or failed to use an appropriate control group. We also reviewed research indicating that behavioral explanations of the undermining effect—explanations such as distraction—did not hold up under empirical scrutiny.

Attribution theory was then introduced and a distinction drawn between its application to interpersonal perception and self-perception. Research on the interpersonal attribution of intrinsic and extrinsic motivation was reviewed. We then raised the issue of whether self-attributional theories could adequately explain the undermining of intrinsic motivation. Empirical work confirmed that the self-attribution approach could not adequately explain the phenomenon, though research has shown that self-attributions can affect intrinsic motivation. The use of a self-attributional versus motivational explanation of the observed parallels beween the changes that occur in people's internal states and the attributions made by others about those changes were also discussed. The chapter closed with a brief discussion of the metatheoretical differences between a cognitive and motivational analysis of intrinsic motivation and self-determination.

8

Information-Processing Theories

Cognitive theories are generally organized in terms of the processing of information and have frequently used the flow chart as a tool for explication. When applied to the study of motivated behavior they are often referred to as expectancy theories, for they are based on the assumption that people's behavior is a function of their expectations about achieving desired outcomes. By processing information about behavior–outcome relationships, people are said to form expectations and make decisions about what behaviors to engage in.

Cognitive theories of motivated behavior can be traced to the pioneering work of Tolman (1932, 1959) and Lewin (1936, 1938, 1951a). Tolman worked primarily with learning phenomena, whereas Lewin was more concerned with social behavior, yet the essence of each motivational system was similar and is summarized in Figure 3. Both theories begin with an energy source. Tolman referred to it as *drive stimulation*, by which he meant internal conditions that might loosely be termed needs. Lewin spoke of *tensions* as the energy source, and although he (Lewin, 1951b) at one point traced the energy to underlying drives, he focused his analysis on the tensions that get set up by cognitive events such as the formulation of an intention. As Heider (1960) explained in discussing Lewin's theory, a tension can be set up in someone merely by one's being asked to perform a task.

Tolman and Lewin agreed that these energy sources lead to the establishment of goals. Tolman said that drive stimulations have value-giving properties; they set up both positive and negative goals. Lewin also used the term goals and introduced the concept of *valence* to refer to the psychological value of a particular goal or end state.

When one has established a goal, one will engage in behaviors that are expected to lead to the goal and thus to reduce the drive stimulation or tension. The direction of the behavior, according to Tolman, will be toward a positive terminal stimulus (i.e., toward a positive goal) and,

FIGURE 3. The basic elements of a cognitive model of motivation.

according to Lewin, will be toward regions in one's "life space" that have positive valence. The basic meaning of the two formulations is essentially the same, which is that people behave so as to approach goals that they expect will decrease drive stimulation or tension.

The cognitive theories of Lewin and Tolman differed in two fundamental ways from the drive theories of that period (e.g., Hull, 1943). First, although Lewin and Tolman considered drives to be very important, their theories were organized around the pull of desired outcomes rather than the push of drives. This allowed them to interpret the issue of energization more broadly than the drive theorists. Second, they gave cognitions an important mediating role in the determination of behavior. The direction of behavior, rather than being a matter of associative bonds or habits, was explained in terms of people's selecting goals. Tolman introduced the concept of purposiveness suggesting that people (and rats) behave with purposes, and that these cognitive factors represent the central elements in the motivation of behavior.

Several theorists have utilized a cognitive approach to explain various aspects of the motivational process. These have tended to focus either on the expectancy determinants of behavior or on the processes of regulating planned behavior. Interestingly, however, although both Lewin and Tolman began their theories with an energy source, the newer cognitive theories (e.g., Bandura, 1977a; Rotter, 1966; Vroom, 1964) have generally not dealt with human needs or comparable motivational concepts. Rather than exploring the needs that give valence to outcomes, the theorists have focused on the valence of outcomes from a functional perspective. Outcomes are said to be valent if people's expectations about achieving them affect their behavioral decisions. As we said earlier, the lack of attention to energy puts these cognitive theories more in the operant tradition than in the motivational tradition. This is perhaps most clearly evident in Bandura's (1977b) theory where he used the term reinforcements rather than outcomes and maintained that the concept of human needs is too vague to be useful. Atkinson's (1964) theory is an exception in that he used the concept of needs, but that was only with respect to achievement-related needs.

In part because they fail to consider human needs, many cognitive theorists begin the analytic sequence with stimuli. In other words, they are structured in a way that makes behavior stimulus-bound. As Weiner (1972) stated it, when presenting his own cognitive theory, a cognitive model of motivation involves antecedent stimuli, mediating cognitive events, and behavior. This sequence, which in Chapter 6 we referred to as an S–O–R model, begins with stimuli rather than with the organism, and as such portrays the organism as inherently passive, behaving only when prompted by a stimulus event. What is missing is the notion that, because of their needs and other characteristics, organisms seek out stimuli rather than wait for them; they act on the environment as well as react to it. Their action is, we assert, frequently prompted by internal, organismic activity—needs becoming salient, images being formed, memories coming into awareness. Organismic initiation begins with human needs; it is the needs of the organism that prompt activity and orient the organism toward stimuli. As we have said, the term "affordances" is perhaps better than "stimuli" as a descriptor of the external events that the organism seeks or attends to in playing out its internally initiated activity. The problem with the term stimuli is that it connotes that the organism is reactive rather than active.

EXPECTANCY THEORIES

Having made these preliminary remarks, we turn to a presentation of several cognitive theories of motivated behavior. We will begin with Vroom's theory, which was developed for use primarily in the field of industrial motivation to predict people's work-related behaviors.

Vroom's Model

Vroom's (1964) theory was represented as a set of algebraic formulae that allow one to quantify what Vroom called "force toward action" (i.e., the motivation to engage in a particular behavior). He asserted that any action could potentially lead to a wide range of outcomes and that the force toward that particular action (F_i) is determined by the valence of each of these outcomes (V_j) and the expectancy that the action will lead to each of the outcomes (E_{ij}). Expectancy is a subjective probability ranging from 0 to 1. The specific proposition is that the force toward the ith action is a function of the algebraic sum of the valence of each outcome (V_j) multiplied by the expectancy that action i will lead to outcome j:

$$F_i = f \left[\sum_{j=1}^{n} E_{ij} \times V_j \right]$$

Although expectancy is simply a probability estimation, the determination of valence is somewhat complicated. It is here that we observe the great importance that Vroom placed on extrinsic motivation, for outcomes are said to have valence in accord with whatever other outcomes they are intrumental for attaining. More specifically, valence of an outcome (V_j) is determined by the valence (V_k) of all other outcomes (call them second-order outcomes), which outcome j might help one achieve, and the instrumentality of outcome j for achieving each second-order outcome k. Specifically, the model asserts that the valence of outcome j is a function of the algebraic sum of the valence of each outcome k multiplied by the instrumentality of outcome j for achieving each outcome k:

$$V_j = f\left[\sum_{k=1}^{n} V_k \times I_{jk}\right]$$

The instrumentality can take on values between -1 and $+1$. It represents a person's belief about whether or not the first-order outcome will help him or her attain some second-order outcome. In other words, Vroom has asserted that outcomes have valence only in relation to other outcomes to which they lead. An outcome's valence depends on the consequences of that outcome.

The formal statement of Vroom's model is somewhat complex, so let us consider an example: suppose we are interested in assessing the motivation (i.e., force toward action) of a man who works in Wisconsin to apply for a job in the psychology department at Campus X of the University of California. We would begin by enumerating all of the possible outcomes that could follow from his action. It could lead to (1) his getting that job, (2) his getting a free trip to California for an interview, (3) his department chair learning that he wants to leave Wisconsin, (4) his spending some time and money on the application procedure, etc.

Once these are enumerated, we must assign valence to each of these first-order outcomes, which we do in accord with the consequences of these outcomes. Take as an illustraton the first-order outcome of getting a free trip to California. What are the potential consequences (i.e., second-order outcomes) of this first-order outcome? Perhaps they are (1) meeting famous psychologists at the California university, (2) missing the opportunity to participate in a symposium in Wisconsin, (3) having a chance to visit with friends in California, (4) getting a few days away from Wisconsin snow to enjoy California sunshine, (5) avoiding an unpleasant meeting that will be held while he is away, etc. Now, each of these second-order outcomes has a valence, and the first-order outcome (getting the interview trip to California) is instrumental to each of the second-order outcomes. For example, it may not be a certainty that he would get to visit friends, since they may be out of town or his own trip may have to be too short; perhaps the instrumentality is .80. This would be multiplied by the valence of the second-order outcome of seeing his friends. Then the procedure would be repeated for each of the other second-order outcomes that could follow from getting the interview trip. After all the second-order outcomes have been assigned valence and the instrumentalities have been determined, it is possible to determine the valence of the first-order outcome of "getting a free trip to California for an interview." We would then proceed in a similar fashion to determine the valence of the other first-order outcomes, such as getting the job, etc.

Finally, when the valences of all first-order outcomes have been determined, we could determine the motivation to make the application by using the first equation. To do that, we would need to determine the subjective probabilities that making application would lead to each outcome. For example, the probability of getting the job may be .12, of getting an interview trip, .19, etc. Then, the contribution of the outcome "getting the job" to the force toward applying is the product of the valence of getting the job and the probability of getting the job. When this has been computed for each first-order outcome, the summation of those quantities is a numerical representation of the motivation to perform the action of applying.

There are a number of points that could be raised about this model. First, there is no mention of the intrinsic value of the attainment of first-order outcomes. Galbraith and Cummings (1967) have suggested that Vroom's model could be modified to include the notion of intrinsic rewards. This suggests that the valence of first-order outcomes would be determined by the function proposed by Vroom, plus a function of the valence of the intrinsic rewards. This proposal has received relatively little attention, but it does at least point to the importance of including both intrinsic and extrinsic outcomes in a cognitive model of motivated behavior.

A second point about the Vroom model is that there is no discussion of how second-order outcomes acquire valence. It is possible that a first-order outcome in one situation could be a second-order outcome in another situation, so when it is a first-order outcome the valence is computed in the complex way mentioned above, but when it is a second-order outcome one apparently is supposed to know its valence. The other possibility (aside from knowing the valence) is that second-order outcomes take on valence in the same manner that first-order outcomes do. But if this were so, we would end up with an infinite regression of valences and instrumentalities. As it turns out, this problem is more a conceptual one than an applied one. In studies using the Vroom model, the valence of second-order outcomes has generally been assessed quite easily with self-report scales. Whereas it may be that these second-order valences are due in large part to their own instrumentality for attaining still other outcomes, people seem to have a sense of the valences of the second-order outcomes. Mitchell (1974) reviewed several studies that have tested the Vroom model and concluded that researchers have been able to measure these concepts satisfactorily.

Atkinson's Model

Atkinson (1957, 1964, 1974) has specified the mathematical relationship between what he considers to be the various determinants of achievement behavior. His theory asserts that the tendency to approach (or avoid) an achievement-related situation (T_a) is the resultant of the tendency to approach success (T_s) and the tendency to avoid failure (T_{af}). In other words, the tendency to approach is equal to the tendency to succeed minus the tendency to avoid failure. Because the tendency to avoid failure always works out to be a negative number, the formula is actually written $T_a = T_s + T_{af}$.

One's tendency to approach success is a function of the motive for success, the probability of success, and the incentive value of success. The motive for success (M_s) is simply one's need for achievement, that is, one's need to match some standard of excellence. This is a relatively stable personality characteristic which, according to McClelland (1965), develops from the bonding of achievement cues to positive affect. It is generally assessed by scoring story responses to the Thematic Apperception Test (Murray, 1943) for achievement imagery (see Atkinson, 1958). Because it is a characteristic of a person, the value of M_s in Atkinson's theory is a constant within a person and across situations. It will be manifest when the situation allows the person to feel responsible for the outcome (i.e., when outcomes are personally caused rather than environmentally caused), when there is feedback of results, and when there is some risk of failing.

Probability of success (P_s) is one's expectancy of achieving the goal, which as Atkinson (1964) pointed out, is a concept that derives from Tolman's notion of expectancy of goal. A person's expectation about reaching a goal through a given behavior will be based on whatever information is available, including his or her experience in similar situations in the past. Expectation is represented by a subjective probability of success and takes on values from 0 to 1, representing certainty of not succeeding, on the one hand, and certainty of succeeding, on the other.

Incentive value of success (I_s) relates to the pride a person will feel in achieving the goal, which is said to depend on the difficulty of the goal. The accomplishment of a difficult goal has greater incentive value than the accomplishment of an easy goal. Representing this numerically, Atkinson proposed that incentive value of success is equal to 1 minus the probability of success ($I_s = 1 - P_s$). This shows quite clearly the importance of achievement *per se*, in Atkinson's theory. For Lewin, Vroom, and others, the valence of a goal is a general term referring to the psychological value of a goal, which according to their theories may be unrelated to or related in only a small way to the difficulty of the goal. But for Atkinson, the valence of the goal is a direct function of the probability of success rather than of other outcomes that may follow goal attainment.

Combining the elements of the tendency to approach success (T_s) yields $T_s = M_s \times P_s \times I_s$. It should be noted that, since I_s is equal to $(1 - P_s)$, T_s will be greatest when $P_s = .5$. This is because $(.5)^2$ is greater than $P_s(1 - P_s)$ when P_s takes on any other value between 0 and 1. If the theory is correct, it means that people will have a strong tendency to try to succeed in moderately risky situations, and that this tendency will be particularly pronounced in people with high motives for success. These predictions have received some support from a study of risk-taking behavior in children (McClelland, 1958).

The second major component in Atkinson's theory of the resultant tendency toward achieving is one's fear of failure, or tendency to avoid failure (T_{af}). This tendency leads people to avoid rather than approach an achievement situation. Like the tendency to approach success, the tendency to avoid failure is determined by three factors combined in a multiplicative way. They are the motive to avoid failure, the expectancy about failure, and the incentive value of failure.

The motive to avoid failure (M_{af}) is also a relatively stable personality factor. It relates to one's desire to avoid negatively affective situations, such as failure situations, that cause shame. It is generally measured by tests of anxiety. The probability of failure (P_f) is one's expectations about failure and is equal to $(1 - P_s)$. In other words, it is assumed that the probability of success and the probability of failure sum to 1.0.

Finally, the incentive value of failure (I_f) reflects the value a person places on avoiding failure in achieving the particular goal being sought. It is a negative value, because it is assumed to be aversive. The emotions of shame and embarrassment accompany failure, and it is assumed that the easier the task (i.e., the lower P_f), the greater the shame and the greater the incentive to avoid failure. Hence, with easy tasks the incentive value of failure will be strongly negative. This all implies that the incentive value of failure (I_f) $= -(1 - P_f)$.

The tendency to avoid failure (T_{af}) becomes: $T_{af} = M_{af} \times P_f \times I_f$, and, as we said earlier, it will be a negative number. Thus, the tendency to avoid failure is a negative tendency to approach, in other words, a tendency not to perform the activity in order to avoid failing at it.

The resultant tendency to approach or avoid an achievement situation (T_a) is equal to the tendency to approach success plus the tendency to avoid failure (the latter being a negative number):

$$T_a = (M_s \times P_s \times I_s) + (M_{af} \times P_f \times I_f)$$

If T_s is greater than $-T_{af}$, the person will tend to approach the situation (i.e., engage in the behavior), but if $-T_{af}$ is greater than T_s he or she will tend to avoid the situation.

It can be shown, through algebraic manipulations, that the resultant tendency to approach or avoid is equivalent to

$$T_a = [M_s - M_{af}] \; [P_s \times (1 - P_s)]$$

In other words, a person's tendency to achieve depends on the two independent personality factors of motive to succeed and motive to avoid failure, on the one hand, and the more immediate and unstable factor of the probability of success, on the other hand. Probability of success, of course, relates to a person's ability and the difficulty of the task, so Atkinson's model has considered factors related to the person and to the environment, which is one of Lewin's basic postulates.

Atkinson's model, although based on the general motivational notions of Lewin and Tolman, is specific to achievement behaviors. The components of the model are the more stable, achievement-related motives and the less stable, achievement-related incentives. In other words, this model predicts achievement behavior based on achievement motivational concepts. All of the emphasis is on the satisfaction of achieving, and that satisfaction accrues from the value of immediate success.

Raynor (1974) pointed out that the value of success derives not only from the satisfaction of immediate achievement but also from the fact that current achievement sometimes opens doors for future achievement. He suggested the importance of including this future orientation in the model by having the tendency to approach success and the tendency to avoid failure contain an instrumental component. When future orientation is irrelevant, the model takes the form proposed by Atkinson, but when future orientation is relevant, the model includes not only the incentive value of immediate success but also the incentive value of the current achievement activity for the possibility of achieving in the future.

Further, it is also the case that many achievement-oriented behaviors are motivated at least in part by extrinsic rewards. A complete theory of achievement behavior needs to include the extrinsic incentives as well. Feather (1961) pointed out that the tendency to approach or avoid an achievement situation must include the tendency to do a task for extrinsic reasons (T_{ext}), which leads Atkinson's model to be formulated as follows: $T_a = T_s + T_{af} + T_{ext}$. The extrinsic component of the model has received virtually no attention, yet it does include the possibility for a more complete description of achievement motivation.

In a still further elaboration of the theory, Atkinson and Birch (1974) stated that behavior is ongoing, so the initiation of behavior is really a process of changing from one behavior to another rather than beginning a behavior. One changes to a particular achievement behavior when the resultant tendency to achieve is the strongest tendency that exists for a person at that time. Not only is the tendency determined by the formulation that includes the future orientation and extrinsic extensions, but the tendency can be affected by the immediately preceding activity through the processes of displacement and substitution. If a preceding activity is closely related to the activity being analyzed, the motives for the target activity may be partially satisfied by the prior activity and thereby lessen the tendency to approach. Satisfaction of one motive substitutes for another. Analogously, the instigation of one activity may under certain circumstances increase the likelihood of the instigation of the target activity. If one is starting a new business and watches a movie about entrepreneurs, one may begin to feel an even stronger tendency to succeed at the new venture.

The issue of achievement motivation as it relates to intrinsic versus extrinsic motivation is an interesting one. As originally defined, achievement motivation referred to the motivation to match an internal standard of excellence. As such, it sounds rather like intrinsic motivation, and in fact Deci (1975) referred to it as a special type of intrinsic motivation. In practice it is not necessarily intrinsic, for an internal standard can be either intrinsic or internalized, and an internalized standard can be either introjected or integrated. A person who is obsessed with achieving is probably not intrinsically motivated, and his or her behavior is probably not even self-determined. If the behavior is regulated by internal controls and pressures, it is not self-determined. Recent work by Helmreich (1983) has shown, in fact, that there are both intrinsic and extrinsic components to achievement motivation.

The Issue of Task Difficulty

Both Atkinson and Vroom proposed expectancy models that are represented as a set of algebraic relationships and are relevant to the prediction of action in the general domain of achievement. Atkinson's was specifically formulated to explain achievement behavior, whereas Vroom's was formulated to explain behavior in the workplace, which is, of course, achievement related. Still, the theories are very different, and this can be seen largely with respect to the way they assign valence to outcomes and the implications of that for task difficulty.

For Atkinson, the valence of a goal has to do with the value of achievement *per se*, whereas for Vroom it has to do with the consequences of attaining the goal. In Atkinson's theory, valence derives directly from expectancy, yielding the greatest motivation for moderately difficult tasks (where $P_s = .5$). In Vroom's theory, however, valence does not accrue from the difficulty of the task; motivation is enhanced when the task is easy (i.e., when the expectancy is high) so that the product of expectancy times valence will be maximized.

As Shapira (1976) pointed out, the two theories seem to be contradictory with respect to the relationship of task difficulty to the strength of one's motivation. However, Shapira reasoned that because Atkinson's model tends to be more intrinsically oriented, whereas Vroom's is more extrinsically oriented, the predictions from Atkinson's model are more likely to hold when the conditions are free from extrinsic incentives, and those from Vroom's model should hold in conditions of extrinsic incentives.

Intrinsically motivated behavior, based in the need for competence and self-determination, involves undertaking optimal challenges. And although achievement motivation is not exclusively intrinsic motivation, the incentives for achievement behavior are still the feelings of accomplishment that result from succeeding. Challenges that are too difficult, however, may involve undue risk of failure and therefore be less attractive, so a moderately difficult task might well be preferred, as Atkinson asserted. By contrast, in extrinsic situations, if one is seeking a particular reward and the reward depends on completing a task, one seems likely to choose the easiest task that will yield the reward. When extrinsically motivated, people tend to take the shortest path to the desired extrinsic reward.

To test his reasoning, Shapira (1976) did an experiment in which half the subjects chose their preferred difficulty levels under extrinsic reward conditions and half chose under no-reward conditions. Subjects were told they would be working on a spatial-relations puzzle for which they would use 3-dimensional pieces to reproduce a drawn figure. There were seven drawings from which they would choose one. Some of the drawings looked quite complicated, others, less so. Each drawing had printed under it the percentage of past subjects who had correctly solved the puzzle. These percentages, which represented difficulty level, ranged from 3% probability of success (very difficult) to 97% (very easy) and included 51% (moderately difficult). Half the subjects were told that if they solved their selected puzzle within 15 minutes, they would receive $2.50 from the box of cash that was in plain view on the table. For the others there were no payments and no money cues.

Results of the Shapira study revealed that the modal difficulty level selected by the extrinsically motivated subjects was .82, the second easiest puzzle. It was selected by 45% of the group, whereas 10% selected the easiest and 20% selected the third easiest. For the no-reward group, the results were a virtual mirror image: 45% selected the second most difficult, 20% selected the hardest, and 15% selected the third hardest.

There are several interesting points in these results. First, as Shapira predicted, people's selection of difficulty level depends on whether they are being extrinsically motivated or intrinsically motivated. This finding was also reported by Gorn and Goldberg (1977). Extrinsically motivated subjects tend to select quite easy tasks to increase their expectancies of getting the desired extrinsic reward, whereas intrinsically motivated subjects tend to select more difficult tasks to increase the amount of challenge and hence the magnitude of intrinsic rewards for succeeding. Nonetheless, for the extrinsic group, only 10% of the subjects chose the easiest task. Apparently there was some motivational force other than the desire for the money that was influencing their choices; perhaps they wanted some amount of challenge even if it slightly decreased their chances of obtaining the desired reward. For the intrinsic group, 80% of the subjects selected the three most difficult tasks, with the average being at 18% probability of success, which is far more difficult than the 50% predicted by Atkinson's theory. This was a situation where future orientation was irrelevant, and where there were no clear cut extrinsic rewards for performance (except perhaps the desire to choose a hard puzzle to look good to the experimenter). Thus, it appears that when people are intrinsically motivated, their preferred challenge on achievement-related tasks has a difficulty level greater than 50:50.

Bandura's Theory

Bandura's (1977a) theory, which is central to what is called cognitive behaviorism, is also based on the notion that people behave in an attempt to achieve desired reinforcements. As a social learning theorist, Bandura, like Rotter (1954, 1966) is concerned primarily with people's expectations about whether reinforcements are contingent on their behavior. However, Bandura made the important observation that expectations about the behavior-reinforcement link are not sufficient to promote behavior and behavioral change; people must also believe that they are effective at the required behavior. In other words, people will not typically engage in a behavior that they expect to yield desired reinforcements if they do not expect that there is a good chance of their succeeding at the behavior (i.e., of their being efficacious). In making this point, Bandura was advocating dividing expectancy into two factors rather than treating it as one, the way Vroom and Atkinson had done.

Bandura's (1977b) theory was presented as a theory of behavioral change and is most often applied to behavior modification in clinical settings. Practically, the separation of expectancies into two factors is useful for developing an intervention strategy. Because expectations of behavior-reinforcement independence produce what Abramson *et al.* (1980) referred to as universal helplessness, whereas expectations of behavior-reinforcement dependence but low efficacy expectations lead to what they called personal helplessness, the separation of expectancies is relevant for the treatment plan.

Theoretically, Bandura's concept of efficacy is an instrumental or extrinsic concept. He asserted that efficacy expectations are important, not because there are any intrinsic rewards associated with efficacy, but because efficacy is instrumental for the attainment of reinforcements. In our view, not recognizing the intrinsic satisfaction of efficacy is a major problem for Bandura's theory and makes his position very different from ours.

In a more recent statement (Bandura & Schunk, 1981), Bandura has discussed the idea of self-motivation, although it was still not related to intrinsic needs. People are said to hold internal standards against which they judge their performance. Matching their standards leads to satisfaction, and failing to match the standards leads to dissatisfaction, both of which provide incentives for continued action. Bandura and Schunk hypothesized that setting goals that spanned a relatively short period of time would serve more effectively as the standard for self-motivation than those that spanned a relatively long period. An interesting experiment in which children learned arithmetic with either proximal or distal goals provided support for their hypothesis. We agree that the proximal goals would be more effective in situations such as the one in their experiment, where children who had done poorly in arithmetic were engaged in a self-directed process of learning arithmetic, because proximal goals represent the optimal challenge for these children. However, the same would not be true in situations where people who have a strong sense of competence and self-determination are engaged in some challenging activity. Indeed, the Manderlink and Harackiewicz (1984) study reported in Chapter 3 showed that proximal goals were detrimental to intrinsic motivation, relative to distal goals.

A second problem with Bandura's theory, in addition to its failure to recognize intrinsic motivation, can be seen clearly in this recent Bandura and Schunk presentation. It is that the theory does not address the nature of the internal standards that are said to be the basis of self-motivation. There is no distinction made between what we call internally informational standards and internally controlling standards. As Ryan (1982) has clearly shown, the effects of the two kinds of standards are very different. Although an internally controlling standard may sustain behavior until the standard is met, it reduces subsequent intrinsic motivation and has the added disadvantage of inducing anxiety and tension. Internally informational standards, on the other hand, maintain intrinsic motivation and minimize tension.

Just as expectations of external reinforcements will motivate behavior, self-motivation of a controlling sort will motivate behavior; but neither represents self-determination and both tend to undermine intrinsic motivation and induce anxiety. In the Bandura and Schunk (1981) experiment this did not occur, presumably because the standards happened to be informational—the experimenter "suggested that they might consider" setting more proximal goals (p. 589). However, by disavowing intrinsic motivation and failing to recognize the crucial difference between internally informational and internally controlling regulation, Bandura's theory could as easily lead to applications that undermine intrinsic motivation and induce anxiety as to ones that enhance intrinsic motivation and reduce anxiety.

Hunt's Theory

Hunt (1965), as we discussed in Chapter 2, conceptualized intrinsically motivated behavior in terms of the organism's pursuing optimal incongruity in its interactions with the environment. He then outlined a theory of intrinsically motivated behavior, which, as we will see, is more a theory of regulating one's behavior in accord with goals or plans than it is one of selecting goals or plans. Whereas Vroom's and Atkinson's theories were developed to predict what goals one will select, Hunt's theory describes how one behaves in accord with the goals that one has. Hunt (1965) presented his theory by raising and offering his answers to the critical motivational questions of instigation, energization, direction, and termination. We consider them in turn.

The first question was the instigation question, What initiates behavior? Hunt answered the question within the framework of the feedback loop as conceptualized by Miller, Galanter, and Pribram (1960). Their model is called the TOTE (Test, Operate, Test, Exit) unit. Within the TOTE unit there is a mechanism that compares stimulus inputs to some standard such as an adaptation level or an expectation. When there is an incongruity between a stimulus input and the standard of comparison, the organism will be motivated to behave, that is, it will operate to reduce the incongruity. As it operates, there will be continual testing of the stimulus and standard, and the operating will continue so long as the incongruity exists. When there is congruity between the stimulus and standard, the operation will terminate (i.e., exit).

In short, behavior is said to be instigated when a test reveals a discrepancy between a stimulus input and an internal standard. For example, if a young man were playing the violin, he might listen to the sounds. The auditory inputs would be compared to a standard in his memory, and if there were incongruity he would practice the discordant part until it matched the standard. The practicing therefore could be seen as being instigated by the incongruity. Once congruity was achieved, the young man would go on to something else, that is, he would exit from that sequence.

The next question Hunt dealt with was, What is it that provides the energy for an organism to engage in an intrinsically motivated activity? Here, Hunt suggested that incongruity energizes as well as instigates. Where there exists an incongruity between a stimulus input and an internal standard, the organism will be energized to behave. Hunt explained that an incongruity between a circumstance (i.e., a stimulus input) and a plan (i.e., an internal standard) constitutes either an uncompleted task or a frustration. Both have been shown to be motivating. For example, an abundance of evidence has indicated that people are motivated to finish uncompleted tasks (Rickers-Ovsiankina, 1928) and to remember uncompleted tasks more often than completed ones (Zeigarnik, 1927). Clearly, then, an unfinished plan would constitute an incongruity and provide the energy for behavior. In another vein, Hunt pointed out that an incongruity between a plan and one's current state could cause frustration and motivate the organism to reduce the frustration by completing the plan. Additionally, if the plan were aimed at the reduction of a drive, the incongruity implies that the drive has not been reduced, so the drive could also provide energy for the action. Finally, Hunt suggested that any incongruous input, one that does not match a standard, is arousing and can provide the energy for behavior. He cited the James (1890) example of orienting to a clock only when its ticking ceases, and he pointed out that this incongruity establishes energy.

Hunt, like other cognitive theorists, specifically rejected the use of the concept of needs as a way of addressing the issue of energization. In so doing, however, he has failed to give a satisfactory explanation of the process of energization. We agree that interrupted tasks tend to be resumed, because there is a tendency or need in the organism to complete gestalts or bring closure to a behavioral sequence. However, whereas it is true that the interruption of a task is arousing and motivating, the fact of an interruption implies that behavior was already underway, so it fails to address the more fundamental issue of how intrinsically motivated behavior was initially energized. This, then, highlights why Hunt's theory is more a theory of regulating one's already planned behavior than it is a theory of selecting plans or standards.

Hunt also considered the direction-hedonic question: Toward what, and away from what, will an organism move? In answering this question, Hunt proposed the central hypothesis of his theoretical position: namely, that organisms approach situations that provide an optimal amount of incongruity. When there is insufficient incongruity, they approach situations that provide more (up to the optimum) and avoid situations that provide less. Further, if people are overstimulated by incongruity, they approach situations with less and avoid situations with more.

The final motivational question that Hunt considered was about termination: What causes an organism to terminate an intrinsically motivated behavior such as manipulation or exploration? His answer was based in work on the orienting reflex (cf. Sokolov, 1960), and fitted neatly into the information-processing approach to motivation. The essence of the answer is that organisms habituate to novel stimuli on repeated presentation, so the stimuli lose their incongruity. This notion is also central to Helson's adaptation level theory (1964). An organism's adaptation level changes in the direction of the stimulus it encounters. Soon, the stimulus and adaptation level are the same and there is no discrepancy.

To summarize, there are two central notions in Hunt's theory. First, he asserted that organisms are motivated to encounter an optimal amount of psychological incongruity. Second, he said that intrinsically motivated behavior is instigated by incongruity and terminated by congruity.

It seems to us that these two aspects of the theory are logically inconsistent as stated. If organisms have optimal incongruity as their goal, then it is inconsistent for their behavior to be initiated by incongruity and terminated by congruity, for that implies that the goal of their behavior is achieving congruity rather than optimal incongruity. To be coherent, the theory needs the provision of ongoing cycles in which the organism seeks incongruity and then works to reduce the incongruity, only to begin again seeking new incongruity. But this runs into trouble because of the stimulus-bound idea that behaviors are initiated by incongruities between stimuli and standards. By replacing the stimulus-bound energization concept with an explication of a need for novelty or challenge that could motivate the cyclical process of the organism's seeking optimal incongruity and then working to reduce it, the theory would be more adequate for explaining intrinsically motivated behavior. In fact, as we said in Chapter 2, Hunt (1975a) later recognized that a concept such as novelty or challenge would work better than incongruity as a central concept for intrinsic motivation.

Inadequacies of the Cognitive Theories

Throughout this chapter we have mentioned inadequacies of the cognitive theories with respect to the issue of energization. The theories of Vroom and Bandura do not address the issue directly, focusing instead on the valence or functional value of outcomes. Atkinson postulated needs in the domain of achievement behavior but failed to deal with needs in the more general sense. And Hunt, who addressed energization in terms of the arousal created by incompleted plans failed to consider where the plans came from. In general, cognitive theories begin their analysis with what Kagan (1972) called a motive, which is a cognitive representation of some future desired state. What is missing, of course, is a consideration of the conditions of the organism that make these future states desired. Concomitant with the failure to give the needs of the organism an initial role in the analytic sequence is the tendency to perpetuate the behavioral traditions of making behavior stimulus bound, that is, of beginning the behavioral sequence with a stimulus. Although the cognitive theories have made the extremely important contribution of giving cognitive activity an interpretative role vis-à-vis the stimuli, they still have accepted the view that environmental stimuli impinge on the organism rather than that needs of the organism energize it to seek out environmental affordances that will be useful in satisfying those needs.

Our second general criticism of cognitive theories is that they portray all behavior as being chosen in the sense that it is regulated by goal selection. As such, they make no qualitative distinction between what we have referred to as self-determined versus control-determined behaviors. In other words, when environmental circumstances and/or the strength of one's causality orientations lead one to be non-self-determined, to be controlled by environmental forces or internally controlling events, the cognitive models treat the behavior in the same way as when the environment and the person's orientations permit genuine choice. In Chapter 6 we discussed this issue with respect to the meaning of choice, and we can now see its implications for an information processing theory. As a behavior is determined more by controls and less by choice, the processes involved in the behavioral sequence need to be represented differently.

SELF-DETERMINATION THEORY:
AN INFORMATION-PROCESSING REPRESENTATION

Deci (1980) and Deci and Ryan (1980b) utilized an information-processing framework to show how the various aspects of a sequence of motivated behavior could be represented analytically. In those discussions, which will be elaborated and extended here, they suggested that it is possible to incorporate the important contributions of the cognitive theories into a more complete motivational theory. When used to describe the elements in a sequence of behavior, our organismic theory is represented in the form of a flow chart. This framework serves as an integrating structure to explicate the relationships among various aspects of motivation, but it also has the liabilities associated with representing an organismic process in a serial fashion.

The framework, which is set up to describe a sequence of motivated behavior, includes two paths, one for self-determined behavior and one for non-self-determined behavior.

Inputs of Information

A sequence begins with information inputs from the organism's need structure and from the environment. Parenthetically, the term *information input* does not mean that the input is necessarily informational in the cognitive evaluation theory sense of the term; an information input may be informational, controlling, or amotivating in its functional significance. Throughout a sequence of motivated behavior information is being continually processed in a way that allows self-correction. Information can be processed in either of the two ways that Arnold (1960) called *intruitive appraisal* and *reflective judgment*. When a stimulus is perceived, there may be immediate apprehension of its meaning and initiation of a response. For example, when one starts to fall, one is instantaneously reaching for something to grab or preparing to fall easily. Information is processed instantaneously; the evaluation and interpretation of stimuli is immediate. On the other hand, information is sometimes processed with deliberation and reflection. In choosing between two pieces of antique furniture, one may size them up, weigh the pros and cons of each, and make judgments quite deliberately.

Information that is relevant to what the organism needs and how it can get those needs met may become available in a variety of ways. It may impinge on the organism from the environment or it may be sought by the organism from the environment. It may appear spontaneously from memory or the organism may search its memory for the

information, and it may come from other internal sources, whether physiological (e.g., non-central-nervous-system tissue deficits) or psychological (e.g., one's attitudes). The organism works with a cognitive
representation of its internal and external environment, and various
elements of this representation may have affective loadings: for example,
an image of one's best friend may be associated with joy and an image
of a place where one had an accident, with fear. All of this is information
that is involved in the initiation and regulation of behavior.

Information inputs from the environment may be expected or unexpected, planned or unplanned, and they may prompt additional inputs
from memory. For example, if one sees a photograph of Big Ben or the
Golden Gate Bridge, one might remember a set of events and feelings
that occurred when one last visited London or San Francisco. These
memories can be inputs to the initiation of behavior. Memories may also
occur spontaneously; however, as is the case with unfinished activities
that tend to be remembered spontaneously (Rickers-Ovsiankina, 1928),
and with spontaneous memories that occur when one's mind wanders
idly, spontaneous memories are more likely to occur when there are no
pressing needs or stimuli.

Finally, information is provided by one's need structure, and it is
this information that is the primary energizer of behavior. Need-structure
information comes from non-nervous-system physiology related to the
basic drives—for example one's blood sugar level and glandular activity—and from nervous-system physiology related to intrinsic motivation. The concept of an intrinsic need for competence and self-
determination, which provides energizing inputs, is the element that
makes this theory a truly active-organism theory, for it not only describes
the energization of intrinsically motivated behavior but also the energization of the psychological processes involved in self-determined
behavior.

We have not attempted to describe the need structure *per se*. Instead,
we have suggested simply that there are organismic needs, including
primary drives and intrinsic needs; derivative needs that result from
differentiation processes or integrated internalizations (see Chapter 5);
or substitute needs that result from the thwarting of organismic needs
(see Deci, 1980). There may be great variability among people's need
structures, for the development of derivative and substitute needs can
be very different from person to person.

Maslow (1943, 1955, 1970) has presented the most extensive theory
dealing with the structure of needs. His theory includes five categories
of human needs: physiological needs (for oxygen, food, sex, etc.); safety
needs (to be free from pain, discomfort, and danger); love needs (for
various types of interpersonal relatedness); esteem needs (from others

and from oneself); and the need for self-actualization (becoming all that one is capable of, thus realizing one's full potential). In addition, he postulated a growth motivation that helps move the organism through these classes of needs, which are said to be arranged hierarchically, toward self-actualization. The theory has been researched relatively extensively (see Wahba & Bridwell, 1976) with mixed results. We have mentioned the theory here as an illustration of the possibilities for explicating a human need structure.

Causality Orientations

In our own work we have suggested that people develop causality orientations that influence their interpretation of information and that represent an aspect of their personality. We characterize people as having certain levels of autonomy, control, and impersonal orientations. People with different patterns of causality orientations tend to process information differently, to attend differently to the environment, to experience emotions differently, and to be differentially motivated. They have different internal structures that can affect all aspects of their behavior.

With different orientations the energy from one's needs would lead one to be more or less active in satisfying the needs and to differentially interpret—as informational, controlling, or amotivating—the inputs relevant to satisfying the needs. The interpretation of inputs can be influenced by causality orientations, so one's orientation can lead to different interpretations. Further, the pattern of one's causality orientations, in interaction with the information inputs, determines whether the resulting behavior will be self-determined or non-self-determined. Self-determined behavior is based in awareness of one's organismic needs and involves choosing behaviors that are intended to satisfy one's needs. Non-self-determined behaviors, however, do not involve genuine choice and can thus be said to be automatic. They are controlled by an interaction of external stimuli and nonintegrated internal factors, such as substitute needs, introjected regulations, or drives and emotions that overwhelm one's structures. Because the self-determined and non-self-determined behaviors function differently, there is a divergence in the model subsequent to the point where inputs from one's need structure and the environment have interacted with one's pattern of causality orientations.

Self-Determined Behavior

The self-determined sequence begins with a motive, which is an awareness of a need of the organism. We sometimes refer to it as an "awareness of potential satisfaction," for the teleological component of a human need is the desired satisfaction toward which one directs one's behavior. Motives can emerge from drives or their derivatives, intrinsic needs, or emotions. Negative affect, such as fear, can motivate behavior that is aimed at the reduction of fear, whereas positive affect, such as esthetic pleasure, can motivate behavior that is aimed at the maintenance or enhancement of that experience.

Drives. The first important source of information for establishing motives and energizing behavior is the set of primary drives. Drives may emerge as motives to initiate self-determined behavior, or they may be the initiator of automatic behavior. A young baby cries automatically in response to the discomfort of a drive. Gradually, the organismic need for effective, self-determined interactions with one's world leads the child to introject or integrate the regulation of these drives, thereby allowing mediation either by self-controlling or by more self-determined, integrated structures.

One feature of all of the drives (except for the avoidance of pain) that distinguishes them from the other primary sources of motivational energy—intrinsic motivation and emotions—is that they operate cyclically. When a drive is satisfied, the organism is said to be in equilibrium in relation to that drive. Gradually, with the passage of time, the organism moves into disequilibrium, and at some point the information about this condition breaks into awareness as a motive. This leads to behavior that restores the equilibrium, and the cyclical process continues.

Intrinsic Motivation. The second important source of information for the formation of motives is the innate need for competence and self-determination. This basic, ongoing motivational propensity is present to energize and direct behavior unless it is interrupted by a homeostatic disequilibrium, a controlling input, or a strong emotion. Instrinsic motivation may lead people to undertake challenges, to create order from chaos, to regulate their drives, or to become involved in interesting activities.

With drives there is typically an external event that can be identified as a reward. Food is the reward for eating, for example, and praise, water, and touch are also rewards. But with intrinsically motivated activities there are no rewards separate from the internal, spontaneous states that accompany or immediately follow the behavior. The "reward" is a feeling or a set of feelings. As Irwin (1971) suggested, states of the organism can be treated as objects of preference just as external rewards can, so intrinsically motivated and affectively motivated behavior can be understood in the same purposive framework as drive-motivated behavior. Indeed, within our framework the actual end state that is desired for all behavior is the affective experience associated with motive satisfaction.

Stimulus inputs associated with the primary drives can break into the ongoing flow of intrinsically motivated activity if they are sufficiently salient to take attention away from the activity and the spontaneous satisfaction that is associated with it. However, when people are highly interested in the activity they may forego eating or postpone normal sleeping until the task is completed.

Affect. Emotions, like drives and intrinsic needs, provide information that may lead to the formation of motives and to subsequent purposive behavior. Anger, for example, might lead to the formation of a motive to change the aspect of one's environment at which one is angry. Emotions play a role in the motivational process as antecedents and as consequences of behavior. In self-determination theory emotional reactions are sources of information that precede and energize behavior, and they are the results of successful behavior in the form of experienced satisfaction or of unsuccessful behavior in the form of frustration.

In our theory, emotions can energize either self-determined or non-self-determined behavior. Self-determined behavior is energized by the motive that emerges from the emotion, the desire for a future satisfying state, whereas non-self-determined, emotional behavior is energized directly by an unintegrated emotion and appears as an automatic, expressive reaction. For example, if a man felt very anxious the first time he drove on a freeway, an anticipation of satisfaction that would accrue from conquering the challenge of driving on the freeway without fear could motivate self-determined behavior such as practicing freeway driving. Alternatively, the fear could motivate the non-self-determined behavior of yelling obscenities at someone who drove up beside him unexpectedly.

The anticipation of a future satisfying state could lead people to engage in self-determined, emotion-based behaviors that they expect, over the short run, to be unpleasant. For example, people sometimes choose to explore dark rooms even if they know they will be in near panic because of their fear of darkness. This self-determined regulation of emotions results from the people's having integrated the regulaton of the emotion in a way that was explicated by organismic integration theory. This process, one will recall, is intrinsically motivated, so the self-regulation of emotions can have the secondary gain of intrinsic satisfaction. Going into the room will be aversive, but doing it is intended to help overcome a fear—in other words to conquer this challenge—so there will be the anticipated intrinsic reward of feeling competent and self-determining for overcoming the fear.

The assertion that emotions can be motivators of behavior is also a tenet of the affective arousal theories (e.g., McClelland *et al.*, 1953), yet our position differs somewhat from theirs. McClelland (1965) defined motives as affectively toned, associative networks that determine behavior. Cues redintegrate affective experiences and the responses associated with those experiences are initiated.

Our point of disagreement is with the idea that associations always lead automatically to behavior. We suggest that when cues redintegrate affective experiences, the current affective experience is information that could lead to the formation of a motive and in turn to behavior. The behavior can be mediated by information processing and choice. This is in fact the critical point in self-determined versus non-self-determined, affectively motivated behavior. If the behavior follows directly from an emotion, because of associative bonds for example, the behavior is not self-determined.

Intrinsic Needs, Drives, Emotions. Intrinsic motivation is ever present as a motivator unless it is blocked or interrupted by some other process. People's early experiences lead to the development of causality orientations that affect the extent to which they are self-determined and intrinsically motivated; however, leaving aside these individual differences, being intrinsically motivated is the natural ongoing state of the organism unless it is interrupted. Behavior motivated by primary drives will, when there is a homeostatic urgency, interrupt intrinsically motivated activity and direct attention toward the satisfaction of the primary drive. Further, strong emotions may break into either intrinsically motivated or drive motivated behaviors.

Simon (1967) submitted that emotions work like interrupt mechanisms to break into behavior and substitute new goals for the ones being pursued. He emphasized that he meant "interrupt" rather than "disrupt," thereby agreeing with the notion that emotional behavior is usually organized, motivated behavior that is adaptive for the organism. It does not usually disrupt and disorganize; it merely shifts attention and energy to a more salient concern.

Simon pointed out that a person will respond to real time needs in an ever-changing and unpredictable environment. An unpredicted event, such as a car pulling out in front of you, represents a real time need, which interrupts the goal-directed behavior that is in progress at the time, whether the behavior is intrinsically motivated or motivated by a primary drive. However, not all emotions call for interruption in the way that real time needs do. Behavior motivated by less intense emotions, such as esthetic pleasure, may be deferred to a later time when other motives are less salient.

Multiple Motives. At any given time, a person may have many different salient motives. These motives, awarenesses of potential satisfaction, provide the basis for goal selection and behavior. Often behaviors are selected in an attempt to satisfy several motives at once. Going to dinner at a fine restaurant with a companion could simultaneously satisfy motives related to hunger, thirst, esthetic pleasure, novelty, and affiliation. Frequently, however, one cannot satisfy all one's salient motives with one behavioral sequence. In such cases the most salient motives are typically the ones attended to, unless internally controlling or internally informational regulations function to hold them in abeyance.

Goal Selection. When a motive or motives are salient, people are in a position to select goals on the basis of their expectations about the satisfaction of those motives. Goals, which are intended effects that follow the completion of a set of behaviors, are chosen by processing information relevant to behavior–outcome relationships, one's perceived competence vis-à-vis attaining the possible goals, and other factors such as the costs of attaining certain goals relative to the satisfaction that is expected to accrue from them. To be hungry is to be aware of potential satisfaction from the ingestion of nutriments, and when one experiences this awareness one may decide how to achieve the desired satisfaction. Having a drink might be expected to yield minimal satisfaction; eating a piece of candy, moderate satisfaction; and eating a full, balanced meal, maximal satisfaction. Thus, it is probable that the person would eat the full meal, but doing so might take time away from some other interesting activity, or the person might have a particular taste for sweet things. All such factors may be considered in the selection of goals, that is, in the decision about what to do. The expectancy theories presented earlier specifically address the issue of goal selection.

Awareness of potential satisfaction is a psychological state that is independent of particular behaviors and goals. One does not have a motive to eat in a Greek restaurant; the motive would be to satisfy one's hunger. Eating in a Greek restaurant would be a goal that could satisfy the motive. Motives do not involve specific behaviors or outcomes, but they are the basis for evaluating behavior and outcomes. The most preferred outcomes are the ones that give the greatest amount of motive satisfaction at the least psychological cost. They are the ones with the greatest valence.

Goal-Directed Behavior. Once people have selected goals, they engage in self-determined behavior that is self-correcting and is aimed toward goal attainment. In behaving, people will need to be attending to the goal and to whether the path is leading them closer to the goal. The mechanism through which this occurs is the TOTE feedback loop (Miller et al., 1960) that we discussed when presenting Hunt's (1965) theory. Recall that people begin with an internal standard, in this case their goal. They test their current state against the standard: if there is not congruity they operate (behave) and then test again; if there is congruity they exit; in other words, they terminate the behavior, having achieved their goal. Whether or not the goal attainment produces the desired motive satisfaction that terminates the whole sequence is, however, a different question that will be addressed later.

Quality of Performance. The types of goals that people set for themselves vary greatly. They can be easy or difficult, vague or specific, extrinsic or intrinsic. Considerable research has shown that the nature of the goals affects people's goal-directed behavior. Locke (1968) reported that when people accept specific goals (for example, to complete eight puzzles in 20 minutes) they perform better than when they accept vague goals (for example, to complete as many puzzles as they can in 20 minutes). He also found that people performed better with difficult goals than with easier goals. This last point is related to our earlier discussion about preferred difficulty levels, although it is a somewhat different issue. Vroom's and Atkinson's theories addressed the question of what goals people prefer, and Shapira's experiment confirmed that they prefer relatively easy goals under conditions of contingent, extrinsic rewards and relatively difficult goals under conditions of intrinsic motivation. It appears from the combined work of Shapira and Locke that when people are intrinsically motivated, they prefer relatively difficult goals and they perform better when they have selected more difficult goals than when they have selected easy ones. It should also be remembered, however, that the imposition of goals by others was shown to decrease intrinsic motivation (Manderlink & Harackiewicz, 1984; Mossholder, 1980).

In recent years, a number of investigators have explored the differences in performance when the goal involves an extrinsic reward and when it does not. It has long been believed that rewards enhance performance; pay a man for each widget he produces and he will produce more widgets. Research shows that this is so if the task is a simple, routinized, or overlearned task. With jobs like producing widgets, or moving piles of bricks, task-contingent rewards tend to enhance performance, but with more difficult tasks, ones that require ingenuity or creativity, the story is different (Amabile, 1983; McGraw, 1978). Research on learning and problem solving has shown that the introduction of a reward increased the number of errors and slowed the rate of learning (Miller & Estes, 1961; Spence, 1970). In a study by McGraw and McCullers (1979), that was described in Chapter 3, subjects were given a series of 10 problems to solve. The solutions to the first 9 were the same, whereas in the 10th problem, the solution was different and easier. In the study, half the subjects were rewarded and half were not. The results revealed that rewarded subjects were significantly slower in finding the correct solution than those who had not been rewarded. In a similar vein, Grolnick and Ryan (1985) found that children's conceptual learning was worse when they learned the material to get a good grade.

It appears that when people's goals involve obtaining an extrinsic reward, part of their attention is focused on the reward, so if the activity is one that requires meaningful attention, the rewards will be distracting and will hinder performance.

Satisfaction and Termination. In our theory, people engage in self-determined behavior because they have an awareness of potential satisfaction. Their behavior, then, is directed toward the ultimate experience of that satisfaction, mediated of course by the attainment of a goal that is expected to yield the satisfaction. If all goes well and the goal does yield the expected satisfaction, the behavior will terminate. If not, the person would need to select a different goal, which with the additional information may have a higher probability of yielding the satisfaction.

Termination through motive satisfaction is governed by the operation of a second TOTE mechanism: the motive is the standard and the sequence will exit when the standard has been matched. This means that the theoretical structure involves the operation of one TOTE unit (that related to the goal) wholly within another (that related to the motive). When a person experiences a motive, it becomes a standard that will persist until it has been matched (or until it is interrupted). Once a motive has become salient, the person selects goals that he or she expects, when completed, will yield the satisfaction. The goal selection begins the operation of the inner TOTE unit, which is terminated when the goal is achieved. This may or may not, in turn, terminate the outer TOTE unit. If the person was accurate in his or her expectations, satisfaction will follow; if not, satisfaction will not follow. In this latter case, the person may go back to the goal selection phase and select a new goal that is aimed at the desired satisfaction. Presumably with the added information obtained from the first try, the new goal will have a higher probability of resulting in the desired motive satisfaction.

One can see from the preceding discussion that the matter of termination involves two separate, though related issues. The first involves the termination of goal-directed behavior *per se*, and the second involves the termination of what we call a sequence of motivated behavior. The termination of the former operates in relation to the goal; the termination of the latter operates in relation to the motive(s).

Consider the termination of a particular behavior or set of behaviors that is goal-directed. As we saw, one way that behavior will terminate is when the goal has been achieved. A second way is when the person discovers that persistence at the behavior either will not lead to the goal or that goal attainment will not yield the desired satisfaction. This may occur through frustration; the path to the goal has been blocked and the person sees no way around the barricade. In such cases the person may respond emotionally, with anger and upset, or the person may simply go back and set a new goal that is aimed at the same motive satisfaction. Two related occurrences suggested by Simon (1967) involve impatience or discouragement. When one becomes impatient, for example when the goal is very difficult, one may simply take an easy way out and terminate behavior. Or if one tries and fails, one may simply give up discouraged. In any of these three cases, the person may or may not select a new goal and try again. Whether he or she does depends on the issue of motive salience at that time.

The third way in which goal-directed behavior may be terminated is through what Simon (1967) referred to as "satisficing"; the person stops even though the goal has not been fully achieved, because it has been achieved well enough under the circumstances. In a complex world, people cannot always persist at a goal until it is obtained. For example, when hunting for a new house, a couple may have the goal of getting just the right house. They look for a while and see houses that they like, but not the right one. The search takes time and it costs money, so eventually they will stop. They will accept a house that is good enough under the circumstances; they will "satisfice" rather than optimize.

So far, we have considered ways that a goal-directed behavior is terminated. We now consider the closely related question of the termination of the whole sequence. The standard governing this, of course, is the motive, and one way that a sequence will terminate is when the motive is satisfied. Generally, the satisfaction comes about when intrinsic goal completion results in the spontaneous feelings of competence and self-determination or when extrinsic goal completion results in the rewards that satisfy the original motives. However, the satisfaction may at times result from a process of dissonance reduction.

Deci, Reis, Johnston, and Smith (1977) found that when people's outcomes are inequitably low they may either experience dissatisfaction and be motivated to get more, or they may convince themselves through cognitive dissonance reduction that they are actually satisfied. When there was ambiguity about whether the outcomes were adequate, people tended to accept them and to become satisfied by reducing dissonance. But when it was made clear by salient norms that the outcomes were inequitable, they were dissatisfied and thus presumably motivated to get more.

Whenever someone forms an intention, in other words experiences a motive, this sets up a tension that presses for completion (Heider, 1960; Lewin, 1951b). This tension, that results from the organism's tendency to complete gestalts (Zeigarnik, 1927), and from the broader tendency toward organismic integration (Chapter 5), provides some impetus to carry through with a sequence. We can assume that a sequence will be terminated whenever the salience of a new motive or set of motives is greater than the sum of the force of the currently active motive(s) plus the tension created by the need to complete ongoing business. For example, we said earlier that homeostatic urgencies, such as the need to sleep or to eat, will often break into a sequence of intrinsically motivated behavior. And real time needs (strong emotional reactions) can break into any type of behavior. In short, a sequence of motivated behavior will be terminated when a new motive(s) becomes sufficiently more salient than the motive that is governing the ongoing behavior.

In sum, a sequence of motivated behavior will terminate when the energizing motive is satisfied, when it is partially satisfied and therefore becomes weaker than another motive(s), or when another motive becomes strong enough to break into the sequence. If a sequence is terminated before the motive is satisfied, there is a tendency for it to reemerge at a later time, to try once again for satisfaction (Lewin, 1951b; Zeigarnik, 1927). Whether this occurs will depend on the relative salience of motives at that subsequent time.

Non-Self-Determined Behavior

The sequence of behavior just outlined, which appears as the top pathway in Figure 4, is a sequence of self-determined behavior. Out of an awareness of an organismic need (hence, of potential satisfaction) the person chooses how to behave. Much behavior, however, is not self-determined. It is determined either by controls in oneself or the environment or by uncontrollable forces in oneself or the environment. The former, of course, is control-determined behavior and the latter is amotivated behavior. Deci (1980) has referred to them as automatic behaviors, for they are determined by processes other than choice, processes that seem to function automatically. In the case of non-self-determined behavior, the sequence is different from that outlined in the self-determined sequence.

Non-self-determined behaviors all involve some nonintegrated (often nonconscious) motive that plays a role in the motivational process. In the case of control-determined behavior, this frequently involves the need for approval or love, which may be nonconscious and underlies the compliance. Guilt and shame, for example, which serve as punishments for internally controlled behavior, were derived originally from these needs. But there may be other nonintegrated needs as well, needs that were never adequately gratified and led to the introjection of controls and/or the development of substitute needs. Substitute needs develop when some organismic need is thwarted. For example, when a child does not receive adequate love, he or she may develop a need

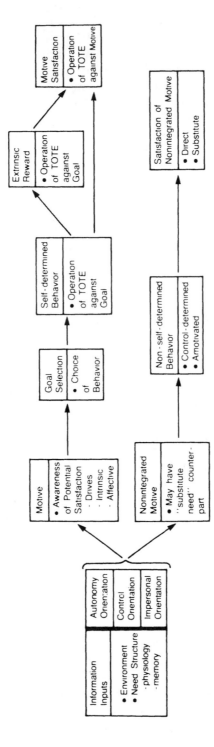

FIGURE 4. Schematic representation of self-determination theory's explanation of sequences for self-determined and non-self-determined behavior.

for food, one that is over and above the organismic hunger need. This then motivates automatic eating behaviors. The substitute need for food would be conscious, but the original need for love would be nonconscious and would be the real motivator of the behavior.

Finally, with amotivated behaviors, ones in which the persons are buffeted about by forces beyond their control, the forces may also include nonconscious motives associated with drives or emotions that were not integrated, or they may be forces in the environment that interact with nonconscious needs in the person. An example of the latter would be behavior-outcome noncontingencies in the environment interacting with a nonconscious need to fail. In either case there are nonintegrated motives that are often nonconscious; people feel helpless with respect to these forces and are unable to control their behavior.

It is interesting to note the difference in these two broad classes of non-self-determined behaviors. With control-determined behavior, people experience some sense of intentionality with respect to the behavior. They are consciously satisfying a substitute need or complying with a demand, so "part of the person" wants to do the behavior even though it is controlled rather than truly chosen. With amotivated behavior, however, the people have no sense of intentionality, so goals are not even set let alone carried out. With non-self-determined behaviors, then, the sequence is: a nonintegrated motive; the behavior; and some form of direct or substitute satisfaction of the nonintegrated motive. This appears as the bottom pathway in Figure 4.

Control-determined behaviors are complex in that they are non-self-determined (i.e., not genuinely choiceful), and yet the person may be making actual decisions to engage in them. For example, in the case mentioned above of the substitute need for food, the person may decide between pizza and hamburgers. Thus, it appears that the behavior is chosen. But it is not truly chosen, for it is the fact of eating (rather than what is eaten) that is not chosen. It is the fact of eating that is automatic. In a sense, then, control-determined behavior may appear, on the surface, to follow the self-determined pathway, for there is intentionality, but the true, underlying, motivational process follows the non-self-determined pathway.

This fact is, of course, complex and difficult to study empirically, and yet it is this very issue that is involved in the research reported in much of this book. Perhaps the most important empirical contribution made by all of our research is that control-determined behavior is not self-determined; it denies autonomy and undermines intrinsic motivation. The motivational dynamics involved with such behaviors are frequently different than they appear.

Summary

In this chapter we have reviewed information-processing theories of motivated behavior. These included Vroom's expectancy theory of extrinsically motivated behavior, Atkinson's expectancy theory of achievement behavior, Hunt's theory of intrinsically motivated behavior, and Bandura's expectancy theory of behavior change. We concluded that these cognitive theories made important contributions, but they shared two prominent shortcomings. First, they failed to deal adequately with the issue of how behavior is energized, focusing instead on how it is directed. And second, they made no distinction between chosen (self-determined) and automatic (non-self-determined) behaviors, instead treating all behaviors as if they were chosen.

We then outlined the organismic theory of motivated behavior, using the schematic flow-chart-style representation initially used by Deci (1980). Self-determined behavior begins with information from the environment and the person's need structure, which interacts with the person's pattern of causality orientations. This leads to the formation of a motive(s)—an awareness of future satisfaction—which is the basis for goal selection and goal directed behavior. When a goal is achieved, that is, when the behavior is completed and in some cases an extrinsic reward is received, the entire sequence will terminate if the goal attainment leads to the motive satisfaction that was expected. If, however, the person's expectations were inaccurate so that satisfaction does not follow, the person may go back and select a new goal that is aimed at the same satisfaction. The entire sequence of self-determined behavior will terminate when the energizing motive(s) has been satisfied or when another motive(s) becomes sufficiently more salient to interrupt the sequence.

Automatic, non-self-determined behaviors, which can be either control-determined or amotivated, work differently. They all involve nonintegrated (often nonconscious) motives that interact with control structures or impersonal, unmasterable forces to yield behaviors that are not genuinely chosen. These may be intentional, as in the case of control-determined behaviors, or they may result from a person's being overwhelmed by forces that counteract their intentions. In either case they are terminated by some form of direct or substitute satisfaction of the nonintegrated motive.

IV

APPLICATIONS AND IMPLICATIONS

9

Education

Curiosity is a basic propensity in human functioning. The desire to explore, discover, understand, and know is intrinsic to people's nature and is a potentially central motivator of the educational process. Yet all too frequently, educators, parents, and policymakers have ignored intrinsic motivation and viewed education as an extrinsic process, one that must be pushed and prodded from without. Recent reviews of motivation in education (e.g., Dweck & Elliott, 1983; Harter & Connell, 1984; Ryan *et al.*, 1985; Thomas, 1980) have increasingly recognized the importance of intrinsic motivation and have emphasized the role of both intrinsic and extrinsic motivational processes in the promotion of children's learning and achievement. With the recognition of the importance of intrinsic motivation has come a new perspective on extrinsic motivation that is more congruent with the active, growth-oriented nature of the child.

Intrinsic motivation is in evidence whenever students' natural curiosity and interest energize their learning. When the educational environment provides optimal challenges, rich sources of stimulation, and a context of autonomy, this motivational wellspring of learning is likely to flourish. On the other hand, there are numerous learning and behavioral goals which our culture requires children to master in school but which are not, in themselves, intrinsically interesting or engaging. For most children there are significant portions of the academic curriculum that are not spontaneously compelling or inherently interesting, and most children do not appear to be intrinsically motivated for the socially sanctioned activities and behavioral regulations that are expected of them by the schools. Most children are simply not intrinsically motivated to sit still and remain quiet, do routinized homework assignments, or eat their lunch in a relatively orderly fashion. Many aspects of both the acculturation and achievement of children require the employment of extrinsic supports and structures.

The applied issues raised by education can be viewed as falling into two broad categories. Accordingly, we will first address the issue of how to facilitate and channel the intrinsic motivation of children toward the promotion of learning, discovery, and achievement. Following that we will turn to the issue of implementing extrinsic structures effectively. The central problem is how to utilize extrinsic structures in such a way as to encourage self-regulation and not alienate the children from the process of learning or stifle their intrinsic motivation for related topics and concerns. In exploring these issues we will apply the principles of cognitive evaluation theory that have guided much of our own field research on education, and we will also draw on organismic integration theory, which is pertinent to the internalization of learning and behavioral regulations.

Growing evidence in the education literature strongly suggests that such issues have significant implications that extend well beyond learning and achievement. Children's experiences in school affect not just the development of their mental talents, but also their emotional adjustment and psychological well-being. The school, both because it is the context for the primary activities of childhood and is the primary non-familial socializing agent, shapes the self-esteem, coping capacities, social development, and personal values of the children. Consequently, motivational strategies need to be assessed not only for their success at producing performance and achievement, but also for their impact in these broader and perhaps more important areas of development. A theory of motivation in education needs to address the whole child.

INTRINSIC MOTIVATION IN THE CLASSROOM

From the perspective of cognitive evaluation theory, the central question in the classroom is how to maintain or enhance children's intrinsic motivation for learning. Prior to recent research and formulation of the theory, several psychologists and educational specialists considered this same question.

Bruner (1962), for example, suggested that one of the most important ways to help children think and learn is to free them from the control of rewards and punishments. Rewards and punishments, he said, all too easily establish patterns of doing what is believed to yield rewards and forestall punishments. Those patterns, he added, typically result in impoverished learning. By learning what to do to get rewards and by doing just what the teacher wants, children can become overachievers, but they will fail to develop the capacity to transform their learning into flexible, useful cognitive structures. They may memorize well, but they will not develop their capacity to think creatively. Bruner stated, "To the degree that one is able to approach learning as a task of discovering something rather than learning 'about' it . . . there will be a tendency for the child to work with the autonomy of self-reward or, more properly, be rewarded by discovery itself" (1962, p. 88). He added that when children are learning intrinsically, they tend to interpret their successes and failures as information rather than as rewards and punishments.

Neill (1960), founder of the well-known Summerhill School in England, echoed the point about using successes and failures constructively by advocating trial-and-error learning in which children learn what they need or want to learn and do so by experimenting with the relevant materials. They are permitted failures and are encouraged to learn from the failures rather than use them as a basis for critical self-evaluation. Neill advised against the use of rewards and punishments to motivate learning, suggesting that although punishments are worse than rewards, "to offer a prize for doing a deed is tantamount to declaring that the deed is not worth doing for its own sake" (Neill, 1960, p. 162). Effective learning occurs, Neill asserted, when the primary reward is one's intrinsic satisfaction with one's accomplishments.

Holt (1964), an outspoken critic of American education, and Montessori (1967), a pioneer in the development of progressive education, have also cautioned against reliance on rewards for motivating children to learn. Montessori suggested that rewards are not necessary and are potentially harmful, whereas Holt (1964) was even more condemning of their use:

> We destroy the . . . love of learning . . . in children by encouraging and compelling them to work for petty and contemptible rewards—gold stars, or papers marked 100 and tacked to the wall, or A's on report cards, or honor rolls, or dean's lists, or Phi Beta Kappa keys. (p. 168)

Much of Montessori's contribution to education came through her development of stimulating and interesting materials for use in teaching basic skills. Through the use of such materials, she suggested, children are more likely to learn out of curiosity and wonder and their learning will be enhanced over the learning that results from external control. Rogers (1969) made many similar points. His concern was with children's having the opportunity for exploration and discovery, for growth and development. This, he suggested, can occur only when children are allowed to be active in the learning process, to follow their own interests and direct their own learning. One of the most important elements for promoting this active, intrinsically motivated learning is the attitudes of the teacher. Teachers who are trusting and empathic seem to be most successful in promoting the type of learning that leads not only to flexible cognitive structures but also to greater self-esteem in the learner.

There is considerable consistency in the messages of these various educational theorists, and many of their assertions, directly derivable from cognitive evaluation theory, have been supported by an abundance of research. One theme that runs through the various writings is that the reliance on rewards for the motivation of learning is ill advised. From the perspective of our theory, we would suggest that whenever rewards are experienced as controlling—and, we suspect, children's modal experience of grades and other classroom rewards is of their being controlling—they will adversely affect children's intrinsic motivation for learning. Further, as Covington and Beery (1976) pointed out, classroom reward structures tend to implicate children's self-worth in their achievement, and this too has been shown to be detrimental to intrinsic motivation (Ryan, 1982). Because research has shown that intrinsically motivated learning is superior to extrinsically motivated learning, the way one uses grades and other rewards needs to be carefully considered.

The writings sampled earlier also stressed the importance of stimulating learning materials and constructive feedback. In the language of cognitive evaluation theory this means several things. First, it highlights the importance of interesting, optimally challenging activities for maintaining or enhancing intrinsic motivation. In a recent paper, Malone (1981) suggested the use of fantasy as one way of making many activities more interesting than they might otherwise be. By giving children the opportunity to experiment in their minds without the immediate demands of the external world, children may develop creative solutions that can then be applied to real problems. Further, the call for stimulating, informational environments underscores the importance of task involvement and internally informational regulation. When children are involved with the interesting elements of the task rather than being concerned with interpersonal or intrapsychic controls, their intrinsic motivation will remain high, and they will be more likely to experience competence feedback informationally. According to the theory and the previously reported research, even negative feedback can maintain intrinsic motivation if the person is task-involved and the negative feedback helps him or her understand how to do better the next time.

Finally, the writings, particularly those of Rogers (1969), emphasize the importance of a trusting, supportive interpersonal context. In our theory, we address this in terms of the interpersonal environments' being informational—supporting autonomy, providing effectance-enhancing information, and acknowledging conflicting feelings—and although the issue of trust is not specifically mentioned, we believe it is both an underlying condition for and a result of an informational context. One must trust in order to experience an interpersonal environment as informational, and one's trust will be strengthened when the elements of an informational environment are present.

Although much of the research reported in Chapters 3 and 4 is directly relevant to the educational milieu, most of those studies were not done in the classroom. Numerous other studies, however, have been done in educational settings, so we shall now review those studies that are most relevant to the direct application of cognitive evaluation theory to education.

DeCharms (1976) described a measure of classroom climate that assesses the degree to which the children perceive the classroom climate and teacher's behavior as supportive of self-determination—the environments that we refer to as informational rather than controlling or amotivating. In a study of 35 classrooms, Deci, Nezlek and Sheinman (1981) administered the questionnaire to 610 children. In addition, the children completed a questionnaire that was designed by Harter (1981b) to assess children's intrinsic motivation in the classroom. The scale has three motivational subscales—preference for challenge, curiosity, and independent mastery attempts—that are theorized to represent aspects of intrinsic motivation and are often combined into a general mastery motivation factor.

Children's descriptions of their classrooms were then correlated with the children's intrinsic motivation, their perceived competence, and their self-esteem. Results indicated significant correlations between the degree to which the classroom was perceived by the children as supportive of self-determination and the children's intrinsic motivation. Further, the classroom climate was found to be related to perceived competence and self-esteem, thereby confirming our assertion that informational environments are important for children's sense of self and general well-being as well as for their intrinsic motivation. Ryan and Grolnick (1984) replicated these results and found that children who experienced their classrooms as more controlling also projected compliant, pawn-like behavior onto children in stories that they were then asked to write.

It seems clear that children's intrinsic motivation and sense of self will benefit from a classroom climate that is informational, in other words, that offers the opportunity for self-determination. Several studies have helped to clarify the conditions that create such a climate and support intrinsic motivation. These studies have considered two kinds of variables, those related to classroom structures and those related to the teacher's orientations.

Classroom Structure

Several proponents of intrinsic education have experimented with making school environments more open. The specifics of an open classroom vary considerably, but they relate to the physical structure of the classroom and the structure of time during school. Open classrooms tend to be structured more loosely: frequently they do not have four walls so they open into other classes or a central lounge area; they often have seats arranged in a circle or some other nontraditional pattern; and they generally have learning materials clustered into interest centers—with math materials in one area, art in another, and so on. This way children can go to the appropriate area when they choose to work with certain materials. Unlike traditional classes, different children can work on different things at the same time, and children tend to have greater choice about when to do what.

Harter (1981b) measured the intrinsic motivation of children in open classrooms and contrasted it with matched children from traditional classrooms. She reported that on each subscale, children in the open classroom were more intrinsically motivated. Of course, the assignment to conditions had not been random, so one cannot draw a causal conclusion, but one can conclude that there is some type of positive relationship between open education and intrinsic motivation.

Solomon and Kendall (1976) compared children from open versus traditional classrooms within the same school system and reported that open classes tended to produce more creativity, involvement, and cooperation than traditional classes, though the traditional classes tended to produce more traditionally academic, on-task behavior. Ramey and Piper (1974) also reported greater creativity in open classes than in traditional classes. These various results do suggest that a more open setting enhances children's intrinsic motivation and creativity.

Grades. There has not been a great deal of research exploring the impact of grades on students' intrinsic motivation, although a study by Grolnick and Ryan (1985) that will be reviewed later in the chapter showed that grades had a negative effect on children's conceptual learning. Presumably, grades, like other types of rewards and feedback, can be administered either informationally or controllingly, and their impact would depend on how they are interpreted. It seems probable that in this culture, where so much pressure is focused around grades, there would be a general tendency for grades, like money, to be interpreted as controlling. Thus, it requires special attention by the teacher to de-emphasize the controlling nature of grades. Numerous studies (e.g., Lepper *et al.*, 1973) have shown that even symbolic rewards such as good-player awards, rewards with which far less pressure is associated, can undermine intrinsic motivation, which emphasizes how important it is to give careful consideration to one's grading practices if one is interested in maintaining children's intrinsic motivation for learning.

Recent research reported by Eison and Milton (1981) found that students who were oriented primarily toward grades (extrinsic) rather than learning (intrinsic) were more anxious and less self-confident. It seems probable, then, that although grades motivate students to prepare for tests, they also have unintended negative consequences for the student's attitudes, intrinsic motivation, and self-esteem. In fact, several writers have broadened this conclusion to rewards in general. As Bates (1979) submitted, following an extensive review of research, teachers would be well advised to look beyond rewards to find means of motivating learning. Levine and Fasnacht (1974) made a similar point when they stated that "token rewards may lead to token learning" (p. 816).

Limit Setting. We have emphasized that because children are curious and intrinsically motivated to learn, providing them the opportunity for self-determination is important for their learning and development. That does not mean, however, that children should be left fully to their own devices, nor that they should be allowed to do whatever they want. Allowing self-determination does not mean being permissive, as we explained in Chapter 4. Self-determination involves initiating and being active, but it also involves accommodating to unyielding elements of the environment and functioning harmoniously within certain structures. How, then, can this be facilitated in a way that will maintain intrinsic motivation?

The Koestner *et al.* (1984) study reviewed in Chapter 4 addressed this question directly. These researchers argued that limits, like rewards and other communications, can be either controlling or informational. Controlling limits pressure people toward specific behaviors, whereas informational limits provide informative structures around which people tend to experience greater choice. Koestner *et al.* argued that the same limits could be communicated controllingly or informationally and that whereas the former would be likely to undermine intrinsic motivation, the latter would maintain or enhance it.

In this study, first- and second-grade children were involved with a painting activity and limits were set with respect to their neatness. For the controlling group, this was done in what might be thought of as a typical way. Children were told that they should keep themselves and the materials neat, so they would have to wear a smock, keep the paints neat, and not spill them. The informational group was given the same limits, but there were two subtle differences. First, the phrases "should" and "have to" were not used—they were simply asked to comply with the three limits. And, second, it was acknowledged that they might not feel like doing these things, but they were asked to do them nonetheless. Thus, for example, the experimenter said, "I know that sometimes it's fun to slop the paint around, but for now, please keep it on the small center sheet."

The point here is an important one that is emphasized by organismic integration theory as well as cognitive evaluation theory. Setting limits typically involves asking children to do something that conflicts with one of their needs or feelings. By acknowledging the potential conflict, perhaps providing an alternative outlet for satisfaction of the need or expression of the feeling, but at least affirming the legitimacy of the need or feeling, one can generally avoid the kind of power struggle (whether interpersonal or intrapersonal for the child) that undermines the child's self-determination and intrinsic motivation. The child can accept the limit and still maintain self-esteem.

Results of the Koestner *et al.* experiment revealed that children who had been given controlling limits evidenced significantly less intrinsic motivation than those who had been given informational limits, whereas the intrinsic motivation of this latter group did not differ from that of a no-limits comparison group. Clearly, then, it seems possible to limit children's behavior without undermining their intrinsic motivation if care is taken to allow as much choice as possible (i.e., making the limits as wide as possible), to provide competence feedback, and to acknowledge conflicting feelings.

In Chapter 4 we saw that feedback can be either informational or controlling (Ryan, 1982), which is a very important point for education. It is quite common for children in schools to get feedback; it is almost continual. The crucial point demonstrated by Ryan was that when the feedback has implicit reference to how children should be doing, the feedback, even when positive, can undermine intrinsic motivation.

Schools are keenly involved in evaluating children's performance, and they pressure the children toward good performance in a variety of subtle and not-so-subtle ways. It is as if there were no motivation in the children to do well, so school personnel take it upon themselves to pressure the children toward it. In turn, this pressure robs children of self-determination and saps their intrinsic motivation. It seems likely that children would perform better if they were not pressured so much. Paradoxically, allowing them to fail may increase the likelihood of their succeeding.

The Interpersonal Context: Teachers' Orientations

In schools, the climate of the classrooms is determined to a large extent by the teachers' behavior. Whether they let children work autonomously, how they handle problems, what they do about grading, are all elements that contribute to the climate of the classroom. Teachers' use of rewards and communications can be primarily informational or primarily controlling, and the classroom climate is largely a derivative of these teacher behaviors. Because, Le Compte (1978) reported, more than half of the statements made by late-elementary school teachers are intended to regulate behavior, whether they do this informationally or controllingly would seem to be particularly important.

There are a number of situational factors that influence teachers' behaviors vis-à-vis their being informational or controlling; however, one main factor that influences their behavior and has been shown to impact children's intrinsic motivation and self-esteem is the teachers' orientations. Enduring characteristics of the teachers affect how they relate to children and what impact they have on the children.

Deci, Nezlek, and Sheinman (1981) reasoned that adults tend to have a general orientation toward dealing with children that can be viewed as ranging from supporting the children's autonomy to controlling the children's behavior. Autonomy-oriented teachers tend to reward and communicate informationally, thereby providing structures that are useful for the children in making their own decisions and getting competence feedback. Control-oriented teachers tend to reward and communicate controllingly, thereby pressuring the children to behave in specific ways. They may even, whether overtly or subtly, control not only the children's behavior but also the children's feelings and thoughts. "You should not feel angry," one might say, attempting to get the child to block awareness of a feeling and believe he or she does not feel it.

Deci, Schwartz, Sheinman, and Ryan (1981) developed a scale to assess adults' orientations toward controlling children versus supporting their autonomy. The scale includes eight short vignettes, each describing a common problem that occurs in classrooms—things like a child's being listless and not completing assignments or stealing small objects from other children's desks. Each vignette is followed by descriptions of four ways of dealing with the situation. One way is highly controlling: it involves the teacher's deciding what the child or children must do and using sanctions to be sure that solution is carried out. A second way is moderately controlling: the teacher decides on a solution and emphasizes that the child *should* do it. The third is somewhat more autonomy oriented: the teacher encourages the child to compare his or her behavior to others, and to use that information in figuring out what to do. Finally, the fourth option is highly autonomous: the teacher supports the child to consider the problem and to arrive at a solution that seems right for him or her. Teachers (and other adults) read each vignette, then consider each option and rate the degree to which they think it is appropriate. By weighing and combining the 32 responses, one arrives at an index that is said to reflect the teacher's orientation toward controlling versus supporting autonomy.

Deci, Schwartz, Sheinman, and Ryan (1981) reported various data that confirmed the internal consistency and temporal stability of the scale. The scale was then given to 35 teachers in the fourth- through sixth-grade of a suburban, middle-class school system (Deci, Nezlek, & Sheinman, 1981). In addition, all of the children in those classes were given Harter's (1981b) measure of intrinsic versus extrinsic motivation in the classroom and a perceived competence scale that was also developed by Harter (1982).

As mentioned earlier, the motivation scale had three intrinsic motivation subscales: curiosity, preference for challenge, and independent mastery attempts. In addition, it had two evaluative subscales: independent judgment versus reliance on teacher's judgment; and internal versus external criteria for success and failure. The perceived competence scale has four subscales: cognitive competence; social competence; physical competence; and self-worth.

In the Deci et al. (1981) study, children in the 35 classrooms completed the scale twice, once in late October and once the following May. The classroom was treated as the unit of analysis, so the data for all the children within a classroom were averaged. They were then correlated with the teacher's orientation scores. The results revealed a significant correlation between the teacher's orientation and all three of the children's intrinsic motivation subscales, for the October administration. In other words, within the first 2 months of school a significant relationship had developed between the teacher's orientations and the children's intrinsic motivation; the teachers who were oriented toward supporting autonomy had children who were more intrinsically motivated. Correlations between the teacher measure and the children's intrinsic motivation subscale scores from the administration done 7 months later were also significant and of approximately the same magnitude. Thus, the relationship that apparently developed in the first 2 months remained constant over the remainder of the school year.

On the other hand, the teacher's orientation was completely unrelated to the two evaluative variables on the Harter intrinsic-extrinsic scale. Harter (1981b) reported that people's evaluation and judgment become increasingly internal over the span of time ranging from third to ninth grade. It appears, therefore, that whereas the teacher's orientation has a major impact on children's intrinsic motivation, their basis for making independent judgments and internal evaluations of success is largely affected by maturation and the development of cognitive structures that allow for internal criteria for self-evaluation.

It was also the case that the teachers' orientations toward controlling versus supporting autonomy were significantly related to children's feelings of self-worth and their perceived cognitive competence. There was a marginally significant relationship of the teacher measure to the children's perceptions of their social competence, but no relationship to physical competence. This pattern of relationships existed in late October and was essentially the same the following May.

The results make good sense. The teachers had the greatest impact on children's beliefs about how good they were at their school work and how good they felt about themselves in general. Teachers had less impact on the specific perceptions of how well children got along with other children; presumably much of their social activity goes on outside the classroom, so it would be expected to be less strongly affected by the teacher. And the teachers had no impact on the children's perceptions of their physical competence; presumably this is largely a function of physical characteristics and of play activity that goes on outside the classroom.

In sum, then, the teachers' orientations were strongly related to the children's intrinsic motivation, self-esteem, and beliefs about their intellectual competence. Teachers oriented toward supporting autonomy seemed to promote intrinsic motivation and self-esteem; teachers oriented toward controlling behavior seemed to undermine it. Further, teachers appear to have had a significant impact on the children within 2 months.

In actuality, of course, because the analyses were correlational, these conclusions must be treated as speculation. Consequently, Deci, Schwartz, Sheinman, and Ryan (1981) did a follow-up study to explore the nature of the causal relationship. In it, they preselected three teachers who were oriented more toward supporting autonomy and three who were oriented more toward controlling behavior. The selection was made simply by determining whether their scores were above or below the mean. Then on the second day of a new school year, the children's intrinsic motivation and perceived competence were assessed. This was done for the three intrinsic motivation subscales, the perceived cognitive competence subscale, and the general self-worth subscale. Because the two independent evaluation subscales as well as the social and physical competence subscales had not been clearly related to the teachers' orientations, they were not included in this study. Then, in late October, the children completed the questionnaire a second time. Change scores were computed, and those for the children in the autonomy-oriented classes were compared with those for the children in the control-oriented classes.

Analyses yielded significant differences on two of the five subscales and marginally significant differences on two others. Only one subscale (independent mastery attempts) did not show a difference. These results, although somewhat weaker than the first set, were in clear agreement with the earlier results. The weaker results were presumably due to the much smaller sample (6 classes rather than 35). The important thing about this study was that it mapped the changes from the beginning of the school year to the end of the first 2 months of school, and was done in such a way that it lends credence to a causal interpretation.

Finally, another study using the teacher orientation scale found complementary results in a South African primary school. In that study Green (1983) used a behavioral measure of intrinsic motivation and found greater intrinsic motivation in the children with an autonomy-supporting teacher than in those with a controlling teacher. The use of a different measure and different culture adds further strength to the finding of teacher effects.

Intrinsically Motivated Learning

Several different lines of research have now been conducted that point toward the conclusions that being intrinsically motivated to learn improves the quality of learning and that those conditions that are autonomy supporting and informational will promote more effective learning as well as enhanced intrinsic motivation and self-esteem.

Some correlational studies, for example, have related motivational variables to learning and achievement. In one such study, Gottfried (1981) used an intrinsic motivation inventory that she had developed to assess children's intrinsic motivation for the specific subject areas of reading, math, social studies, and science. The same children who completed the intrinsic motivation measure also took standardized achievement tests in each of the four content areas. Their intrinsic motivation scores were then correlated with their achievement scores. The analyses revealed significant correlations between intrinsic motivation and achievement, particularly within the four content areas. In addition, Gottfried (1982) reported negative correlations between intrinsic motivation and anxiety, a finding that is complementary with Ryan's (1982; Ryan et at., 1983) experimental findings of a positive correlation between controlling conditions and expressed tension.

Sadowski and Woodward (1981) explored the relationship between children's perceptions of the classroom climate and their performance and found positive correlation between perceptions of the classroom climate as autonomy oriented and grades. Connell and Ryan (1985) found a negative correlation between children's reports that they do school work for extrinsic reasons (e.g., to avoid disapproval) and their scores on the Stanford Achievement Test. It seems clear, then, that intrinsic motivation is related to academic performance, and various experimental studies have confirmed this.

In several studies, learning has been compared under two or more conditions that have been shown in other research to have differential effects on intrinsic motivation. These include conditions such as rewards, choice, evaluation, and so on. Because these conditions have been shown to affect intrinsic motivation, and if they are also shown to affect learning similarly, one can reasonably conclude that intrinsic motivation is associated with improved learning.

Several investigators have employed paradigms taken from verbal-learning research to explore the effects of extrinsic rewards and the effects of choice on learning. In the studies of reward effects, we interpret the reward conditions as promoting less intrinsically motivated learning, and the no-reward conditions as promoting more intrinsically motivated learning. In the studies of choice effects, we interpret the choice conditions as more intrinsically motivating and the no-choice conditions as less intrinsically motivating, because choice has been shown to enhance intrinsic motivation (Zuckerman et al., 1978).

McGraw (1978) reviewed several studies, with children and adults, in which subjects were either rewarded or not rewarded for some type of learning activity. In most instances, rewards impaired learning. Providing extrinsic rewards, such as money, for learning words or for forming concepts seems to have distracted subjects from the learning task and increased the time necessary for learning or problem solving. When extrinsic rewards are introduced into a learning situation, some of the learner's attention appears to shift from the learning task to the reward. The learners, to some extent, become pawns to the rewards, and as Condry and Koslowski (1979) stated, the learners lose control of the situation. With rewards come standards and evaluations by others, and the whole nature of the experience seems to change.

A study by Inagaki and Hatano (1984), in fact, showed that the mere expectation of evaluations impaired students' comprehension of material that they were translating from English into Japanese. Thus, it appears that any external condition that decreases intrinsic motivation will also impair performance on conceptual activities.

Perlmuter and Monty (1977) reviewed a series of studies that explored the effects of choice on learning. Using several variants on a paired-associates, verbal-learning paradigm, they found repeatedly that when subjects were given choices about what they learned, their learning improved. Even a modest opportunity to be self-determining in relation to one's learning appears to enhance intrinsic motivation and facilitate learning.

Several researchers have explored the effects of cooperation versus competition on learning. Because competition has been shown to decrease intrinsic motivation (Deci, Betley, Kahle, Abrams, & Porac, 1981) and dampen creativity (Amabile, 1982a), competitive learning settings are interpreted as less intrinsically motivating and cooperative learning settings as more intrinsically motivating. A review of research by Johnson and Johnson (1974) corroborated that the cooperative setting promotes intrinsic motivation in that it leads to less anxiety, greater task involvement, and a more positive emotional tone (all characteristics of intrinsically motivated behavior) than does competition (e.g., Haines & McKeachie, 1967; Phillips & D'Amico, 1956). Several studies have shown that problem solving tends to be more effective and achievement tends to be greater under cooperative than under competitive conditions (e.g., Laughlin & McGlynn, 1967; O'Connell, 1965; Wodarski, Hamblin, Buckholdt, & Ferritor, 1973). Further, cooperative conditions seem to improve social adjustment and general cognitive development (e.g., Flavell, 1968; Johnson, 1975; Rothenberg, 1970). Only routine learning tasks seem to be facilitated by competition (Julian & Perry, 1967), a finding which parallels the conclusion drawn by McGraw (1978) that performance on a routine task may be improved by rewards, whereas performance on problem-solving and conceptual-learning tasks is impaired.

Aronson, Blaney, Stephan, Sikes and Snapp (1978) also explored cooperative learning with their jigsaw procedure. This procedure involves structuring classroom learning in such a way that small groups of children, of five or six, become interdependent by teaching each other. Each member of a group learns a portion of the material, and then each teaches his or her portion to the others. This shifts the focus from beating the others to helping the others; the personal rewards come for working together. Each child represents a part of the jigsaw puzzle, and the picture emerges when the pieces are put together.

Experimental evaluations of the jigsaw procedure yielded a number of interesting results. First, children showed increases in self-esteem when compared to children in traditional classrooms. In addition, interpersonal relations tended to improve, even in classrooms that had recently been racially desegregated and where considerable tension existed. Finally, the jigsaw procedure led to overall increases in academic performance relative to that of the traditional classes. When given conventional tests on the material covered over week-long periods, jigsaw children excelled. A more detailed look at the results indicated that it was the low-achievement children who improved most. The children who were typically high achievers did equally well in both types of classes, but the typically low achievers did much better in the jigsaw classes (Lucker, Rosenfield, Sikes, & Aronson, 1977).

In another set of experiments, the role of intrinsic motivation in learning was studied more directly. Benware and Deci (1984) reported an experiment in which they compared conditions that they hypothesized would induce more intrinsically oriented versus less intrinsically oriented learning. They reasoned that if people learned material with the expectation of putting it to effective use, they would be more intrinsically motivated than if they learned it merely to be examined on it. The researchers had college students read and learn an article on neurophysiology. Each student spent about 3 hours learning the material using whatever study methods he or she preferred. Half the subjects had been told they would be examined on the material when they returned to the lab about 2 weeks later, and the other half had been told that they would teach the material to another student when they returned.

When the subjects returned to the lab, they all completed a questionnaire assessing their attitudes about their learning experience and the material they learned. Then all subjects were given a written examination on the material. Half the subjects still expected to be teaching the material, but they were told that a few of the subject teachers had been selected randomly to take this unexpected written exam so the researchers could compare the comprehension of the teachers with that of the students whom the teachers would be teaching. The exam, it was said, was the same one that all the students would eventually take.

Subjects who learned the material with the expectation of teaching it reported finding the material more interesting, enjoying the learning experience more, being more active in the learning process, and being more willing to do a similar experiment in the future, than did the subjects who learned with the expectation of being tested. All these results indicate that, in fact, the subjects who learned with the expectation of putting their learning to active use were more intrinsically motivated than the subjects who learned with the expectation of being tested. Thus, the manipulation was successful in creating the desired motivational orientations.

The examination had two types of questions, some that assessed rote memorization and others that assessed conceptual learning. Results revealed that those subjects who were in the condition that promoted more intrinsically oriented learning scored significantly better on the conceptual learning than did subjects in the condition that promoted more extrinsically oriented learning. On the other hand, the two groups did equally well on the rote-memorization phase of the exam.

The results of this study tend to confirm the assertions of Bruner (1962), Rogers (1969), and other theorists who had speculated that whereas extrinsic controls lead people to memorize well, they fail to promote the type of engagement with the task that results in conceptual learning and creative thinking.

Grolnick and Ryan (1985) did an experiment in which fifth-grade children read an age-appropriate social studies passage under one of three conditions. Children in one group were told that they would be tested on the material and would receive a grade. This was referred to as the extrinsic condition. Children in a second group received an intrinsic set: they were asked to read the passage to see what they could learn from it. And the final group of children represented a spontaneous learning condition: they were merely asked to read the passage with no prompts for learning the material.

Results of a test that was given to all children just after they read the passage revealed that the children who had been given an intentional learning set, whether intrinsic or extrinsic, evidenced higher rote recall than those with the spontaneous set. However, the extrinsic children were inferior to either of the other groups on conceptual learning. Thus, although extrinsic pressure did not interfere with the memorization of facts, it did interfere with their grasping the meaning of the passage.

In spontaneous learning, children do not necessarily learn facts, but they seem to gain a conceptual understanding of material that interests them. In one study, Ryan, Connell, Plant, Robinson, and Evans (1984) gave college students a passage to read and rate on various attitudinal dimensions. Subsequently, they tested the subjects' recall of the material and found positive correlations between recall and interest, and negative correlations between recall and experienced pressure and tension. When free to learn what they wanted, their learning was organized and guided by their interests.

DeCharms (1976) has also done research that is directly relevant to the issue of intrinsic versus extrinsic learning effects. DeCharms and his colleagues carried out a large-scale research and training project in an inner-city school system. The aim of the project was to create more intrinsically oriented education for the children in these schools. The project involved training the teachers in more intrinsically oriented procedures, developing instructional materials that emphasize self-determination and promote self-esteem, and consulting with the trained teachers throughout the school year.

Concomitant with the training and consultation aspects of the project was an evaluation–research aspect. Classrooms that had trained teachers and employed the instructional materials were compared with classes that did not. The primary dependent measure for our current purposes was learning performance as measured by a standardized achievement test. Children in classes of trained teachers improved markedly in their performance on the standardized test relative to the children of untrained teachers. The facts that the children from the trained classrooms were also more intrinsically motivated and that there was a correlation between intrinsic motivation and achievement in the untrained classes strongly suggest that the children's intrinsic motivation mediated the improvements in the classrooms of the trained teachers.

The weight of all this evidence is rather clear. When conditions are created that facilitate intrinsic motivation, students' learning, particularly conceptual learning and creative thinking, increases dramatically relative to that of students in settings that foster extrinsically oriented learning. Furthermore, as Harter and Connell (1984) have shown, it is likely that improved learning will have the additional effect of further enhancing intrinsic motivation, thereby creating a kind of positively synergistic effect.

EXTRINSIC MOTIVATION IN THE CLASSROOM

The process of learning, of elaborating one's internal structures, is intrinsically motivated, and if supported to do so children would be continually learning without any need for demands or reinforcements. The problem, however, for parents and teachers is that intrinsically motivated children would learn what interests them and avoid what does not. This is a problem, of course, because society prescribes a set of learnings—academic and behavioral—that is considered essential and in many cases consists of things that hold little or no spontaneous interest for the developing child. Memorizing lists of spelling words has minimal appeal for most fourth-graders, and walking to the auditorium quietly in a single line is by no means their locomotion of choice. Still, whether right or wrong, these things have been widely agreed to be useful and necessary, so they represent primary agendas for elementary teachers.

From a motivational perspective, such agendas require the use of extrinsic principles, and it is here that we find superficial similarity but underlying divergence between the behavioral perspective and our motivational perspective. From the point of view of behavioral psychology, this like all other learning is a matter of conditioning. For us, however, although it differs from intrinsic learning in that it requires the use of extrinsic incentives, it is not a matter of conditioning behavior. Instead, it is a matter of prompting integrated self-regulation, an issue that is addressed by organismic integration theory (Connell & Ryan, 1984).

Reinforcement Programs

For the conditioning theorist, the most important thing children must learn is to understand reinforcement contingencies and to look toward future outcomes. Believing that people's behavior is governed by reinforcements, theorists of the conditioning persuasion advocate the control of children's learning through the use of rewards and punishments and the specification of the behaviors that are instrumental to the attainment of rewards and the avoidance of punishments. Several recent developments in education are consistent with the behavioral-control approach. Competency testing, which involves the use of standardized tests to asses and ensure the quality of student's achievement, has been gaining prominence and the standardized curricula that are coordinated with the competence tests have been increasingly imposed on teachers and students, leaving little room for self-determination by either party.

The paradigmatic case of the conditioning approach is the token economy procedure. This procedure developed out of the operant framework and involves the identification of desired, learning-related behaviors and the administration of tokens for instances of those identified behaviors. The tokens can be exchanged by the children for rewards such as candy, awards, or free-play time. When token programs are introduced, they are explained in detail so the children will understand what behaviors will be reinforced and what rules will apply to the exchange of tokens for rewards. The token itself is typically a neutral object, such as a poker chip. These and other methods for the establishment of token economies are discussed in detail by Kazdin and Bootzin (1972).

Token reinforcement programs have been shown to be quite effective for achieving certain goals in the classroom. O'Leary and Drabman (1971) reviewed several studies that demonstrated that while token programs were in effect in classrooms, children were more orderly, displayed more on-task behavior, and in some instances improved their performance on memory-type tests. The most impressive results (e.g., Kuypers, Becker, & O'Leary, 1968; Martin, Burkholder, Rosenthal, Tharp, & Thorne, 1968; Meichenbaum, Bowers, & Ross, 1968; O'Leary & Becker, 1967; O'Leary, Becker, Evans, & Saudargas, 1969) have been found when token systems have been used with emotionally disturbed or disorderly children. The clearest conclusion from the data is that token programs improve the social conduct and on-task behavior of disturbed or disorderly children while the programs are in operation. Improvements in learning are less frequent and when evident tend to be of the rote-memorization type. These improvements are important in that the disruptive classroom behavior of some children is costly for others, and appropriate social behavior may be a useful goal for seriously disturbed children. However, promoting orderly social behavior, although important, is not typically the most important goal for most classrooms. More meaningful goals are promoting conceptual learning and flexible thinking and nurturing children's curiosity and self-directed exploration. Furthermore, even in the realm of appropriate social conduct, the more desirable goal is flexible self-regulation of such conduct rather than the conduct itself. These goals can all be seen to be related to self-determination: they both reflect the attainment of self-determined regulation and are more likely to be achieved when the children's mastery attempts are self-determined. Thus, even when behaviors require the use of extrinsic supports, it is important that they be informationally, rather than controllingly, administered. Because token reinforcement programs tend to be quite controlling, they are likely to forestall rather than promote self-determination. Consequently, if they are used at all, great care must be taken to make them more informational.

Greene *et al.* (1976) reported a study that was designed to explore whether behaviors that had been regulated by a token-reinforcement program would persist once the reinforcements had been terminated. Such persistence would imply that the behaviors were either intrinsically motivated or regulated by more integrated internalizations. These researchers created a token economy in a public junior high school to explore its effects on children's postprogram interest in and persistence at math activities. There were four different activities available to the subjects, and the time they spent on each was recorded during three different phases. First, there was a baseline period in which there were no tokens; all children were free to spend as much time as they liked on any of the four activities. Then there was a reinforcement period in which some children (the experimentals) received tokens, whereas the other children did not. Finally, there was a withdrawal period in which, once again, there were no reinforcements.

There were three experimental groups: one group was reinforced for working with the two activities they had spent most time on during baseline; one group was reinforced by working with the two activities they had spent least time on during baseline; and one group was reinforced for working with the two activities for which they chose to be reinforced. The fourth group received no token reinforcements and therefore served as the control group. The same people served as controls for each of the three experimental groups; their times spent on the target activity were used for comparison with the three different experimental groups. Their times at the two activities that they themselves spent most time on during baseline were used as control times for the group that was reinforced for their high-interest activities; the times for the two activities that the control subjects spent least time on during baseline were used for comparison with the group that was reinforced for their low-interest activities; and the times that provided comparisons for the choice group were the ones for the two activities that represented the same relative preference during baseline as those chosen by the choice subjects.

Results indicated that the time spent at the rewarded activity increased dramatically for all three reinforcement groups while the token program was in effect. This, of course, is to be expected, because people are typically willing to do the things that get them rewards. However, following removal of the token program, all three experimental groups evidenced a decline in persistence at the reinforced activities, relative to the comparable control-group persistence, although only the choice group and high-interest group showed statistically significant declines.

The declines in postreward persistence for the high-interest and choice groups are as relevant for cognitive evaluation theory as for organismic integration theory, for there may have been some initial intrinsic motivation for the target activity in those children. If so, it represents a straightforward, though clearly applied, replication of many previous studies. For the low-interest group, however, we have clear relevance for organismic integration theory. Token-reinforcement programs, one can be sure, are typically experienced as controlling, and as the Greene *et al.* data showed, they did not promote internalization and self-regulation; indeed, if anything, they may have decreased it.

In one recent study, Bry and Witte (1982) argued that token economy programs can be set up in a way that is primarily informational rather than controlling. They created such a program with middle-school children who had been identified as having adjustment problems and reported increases in perceived competence and a more internal perceived locus of causality. Thus, it appears that although token economies are typically quite controlling, they may be structured in a way that facilitates self-determination.

There are many procedures used in classrooms that involve the controlling use of extrinsic rewards, although they are typically less systematic than token economies. Grades, gold stars, praise from teachers, and related procedures all involve rewarding children for doing the behaviors the teacher wants. And one could raise the same questions about them as about token economies. It is probable that they are somewhat effective in producing the behaviors that are desired by the teachers and school systems, but it is also probable that the rewarded behaviors will not become self-determined.

Organismic Integration

Organismic integration theory, as presented in Chapter 5, details the movement from extrinsic regulation toward integrated self-determined regulation of activities that are not themselves intrinsically interesting. We have asserted that each step from extrinsic toward integrated self-regulation will be accompanied by improvements in the quality of learning. Recent data collected by Grolnick and Ryan (1985) have confirmed this. They used Connell and Ryan's (1985) measure of self-regulatory styles to measure fifth-grade children for the degree to which their regulation of school-related activities was extrinsic, introjected, identified, and intrinsic. The first three, of course, represent phases in the internalization process and are relevant here. The children read a passage and were tested on it upon completion. Ten days later, without expecting it, they were retested for retention of the material from the passage. Both tests were scored for conceptual and rote learning, and their regulatory styles were related to learning and retention.

Results revealed that extrinsic regulatory styles were negatively related to conceptual learning as assessed immediately. This individual-difference result, of course, parallels several previously reported findings related to the effects of extrinsic experimental conditions on learning. In the 10-day, unexpected follow-up, extrinsic regulation continued to be negatively associated with conceptual learning and with rote learning as well. In fact, the extrinsic style was strongly predictive of the amount of loss in the memorized facts from the first to the second testing sessions. The more extrinsic the children in their regulatory style, the more they evidenced forgetting of the once known material.

It appears, then, that until children are able to internalize the regulation that must of necessity be initially extrinsic, the regulation will have a negative impact on the very outcomes that are desired by enlightened educators. Extrinsic controls, and the individual difference of an extrinsic regulatory style, can produce immediate rote learning, but they impair conceptual learning and they lead to greater loss of the rote learning. Furthermore, they are associated with lower levels of self-esteem and higher levels of anxiety.

The conditions that promote internalization of regulations and thus enhanced learning of material that is not itself intrinsically interesting are the ones that we have labeled informational. Similarly, the internalization of behavioral regulations are theorized to be promoted by informational structures and limits of the sort described in the Koestner et al. (1984) study. Children must, for example, learn to manage their drives and emotions effectively and responsibly. To allow a child to hit others at will is irresponsible for the adult and fosters irresponsibility in the child. The child can feel and accept his or her anger and desire to hit, but the child must learn to accommodate other people's rights as well. This accommodation, in other words the integrated internalization of regulations, occurs in environments that provide informational, rather than controlling, structures.

Factors Affecting the Teacher

As we have described the research related to intrinsic motivation and internalization in the classroom, the burden of responsibility has fallen repeatedly on the teacher to provide the atmosphere that allows self-determination and encourages intrinsically motivated learning. Unfortunately, it is not so easy for the teachers to do this; they too are dealing with the types of pressures that make it difficult for them to maintain their own enthusiasm and interest in classroom affairs. In our interviews with teachers we have heard over and over how they are feeling increasing pressures and how their own self-determination in the classroom is being undermined by institutional procedures.

In this section we will review research that has used teachers' behavior, namely, whether teachers tend to control behavior or support autonomy, as the dependent measure. Teachers tend to have an orientation toward controlling behavior versus supporting autonomy that can be thought of as a relatively enduring personality characteristic, but situational factors also influence the degree to which they will control behavior versus support autonomy in that situation.

Pressure from Above

Teachers work within a system. They report to a principal and to a central administration. The people who occupy those roles, and the policies of the system, all have an impact on the teachers. When the administrators are oriented toward control, when they are demanding and unreasonable, they may negatively affect the motivation and self-esteem of the teachers just as controlling teachers negatively affect their children. When administrators impose restrictions and allow little space for self-determination, they are likely to undermine the teachers' intrinsic motivation just as the teachers' imposing restrictions undermines the children's intrinsic motivation. When teachers are pressured by administrators, when their own autonomy in the classroom is not supported, it is hypothesized that they will become more controlling with the children.

To test this hypothesis, Deci, Spiegel, Ryan, Koestner, and Kauffman (1982) did a laboratory experiment with college student subjects. In each experimental session there were actually two subjects; one served as teacher and the other as student. The teacher was given the task of teaching the student how to work with a spatial relations puzzle, and they were allowed 20 minutes for the teaching activity. The teacher and student were in separate rooms, though the teacher observed the student through a one-way window, and the two communicated through an intercom system. The teacher entered the laboratory earlier to have a chance to become familiar with the puzzles, to review a set of hints, and to learn the solutions to the six puzzles that would be used in the teaching.

There were two conditions in the experiment; they were referred to as a performance-standards condition and as a no-standards condition. The idea in the former case was to impress on the teachers that it was their responsibility to make sure that their students performed up to standards. A strong emphasis on performance standards is quite common in schools and is something that we (Deci & Ryan, 1982a) have asserted is typically experienced as controlling by teachers. In the other experimental condition, teachers were told that there were no specific performance requirements, that their job was to help the students learn to solve this type of puzzle.

Of interest was the effect on the teachers' behavior of emphasizing the standards, in other words, of treating them in ways that they are likely to experience as pressure. To assess this effect, the researchers tape recorded the teachers' vocalizations during the 20-minute teaching session. At a later time, the tapes were rated by a set of judges who were unfamiliar with the nature of the experiment. First, each utterance was coded into categories. These included "directives," "requests for clarification," etc. Subsequently, other raters listened to the tapes and made subjective judgments about the teachers' styles.

Results of these analyses revealed that teachers in the performance-standards condition made twice as many utterances, spent twice as much time talking, and allowed students to work alone much less than did the no-standards teachers. They also gave three times as many directives, made three times as many should-type statements, and asked twice as many controlling questions as did the no-standards teachers. Further, the performance-standards teachers were rated as being more demanding and controlling, as giving students less choice and less time to work alone, and as being less effective in promoting conceptual learning, than the no-standards teachers. Finally, the raters indicated that they would prefer to be taught by the no-standards teachers.

The typical pattern in the performance-standards condition was that the teachers would read the solutions to the students as the students assembled the puzzles. Thus, the students of the performance-standards teachers assembled an average of 13 puzzles (each of the 6 puzzles more than twice), whereas the no-standards students assembled an average of only 6. However, the no-standards students solved 2.1 of the puzzles alone, whereas the performance-standards students solved only 0.4 alone.

These performance data are very interesting; they give one an idea of the difference in the kind of teaching and learning that goes on in the classrooms that we call controlling (non-self-determined) versus informational (self-determined). In the former, the teacher seems to instruct, telling the students what to do, when to do it, and how to do it. The students seem to comply and to cover a lot of material. But they get little opportunity for exploration and self-determination, and as other studies have demonstrated, they do not do nearly as well at conceptual learning.

We do not, of course, interpret the Deci *et al.* (1982) study as indicating that performing up to standards is not important. But placing a strong emphasis on performing up to standards seems to interfere with rather than facilitate attainment of that goal. The likelihood of children's performing well seems to be increased when their intrinsic motivation is nurtured rather than when they are pressured. Teachers are generally very interested in having their children learn effectively and perform well; they do not need to be pressured toward that. What they need is to be supported to do what they would do intrinsically and what would make them feel effective (Deci & Ryan, 1982b).

Maehr (1976) suggested that the facilitation of intrinsic learning is in part a cultural matter. In essence, this suggestion extends what we have said about school administrators and school policies to the culture as a whole. Schools exist within the larger society. As public institutions they are affected directly by public policy, and they are also affected indirectly by the cultural milieu. Insofar as the culture is oriented toward pressuring people to achieve—which ours certainly is—it is difficult for school administrators and teachers to maintain the kind of orientation that supports self-determination in the children. Children cannot be pressured into self-determination; they can be pressured into compliance, reactance, ego-involvement, and helplessness. To achieve self-determination, one must provide informational structures, ones that provide choice and competence feedback in the absence of pressure for specific performance. And the teachers need this as much as the children do.

Pressure from Below

Not only are teachers subjected to pressure from administrators, parents, and society at large, they are also subjected to various pressures from the children. Teachers frequently make statements like, "It would be fine if I had 8 pupils who were interested and well-behaved; then I could support autonomy more easily. But with 32 children, some of whom are learning-impaired and others of whom are always causing trouble, I have my hands full just trying to keep order so the interested ones can have a chance to learn something."

The point is that the behavior of the children in a classroom has a big impact on the way teachers behave with respect to controlling the children versus supporting their autonomy. Bell (1968) argued cogently that research on socialization (the same could have been said for education) has focused on the effects adults have on children without giving adequate attention to the effects children have on adults. Their behavior has an important influence on the way the adults relate to them, which in turn may have a further effect on them. It stands to reason that if children are cooperative, for example, the teachers are more likely to support their self-determined learning and problem solving than if they are not. As the children become more difficult, as they try the teacher's patience, the teacher is more likely to feel stressed and to be controlling, which in turn is likely to make the children even less cooperative.

Jelsma (1982) did a study to test this reasoning. She gave mothers the task of teaching anagrams to children (9 to 11 years of age) whom they had never met. Each mother taught one child. The experimental manipulation involved training the children, who were actually experimental accomplices, to behave in different ways. For half the subjects the children were cooperative and interested, for the other half they were a bit unruly and less interested.

The teaching session was tape recorded and subsequently the tapes were coded and rated in a fashion very similar to that used in the Deci *et al.* (1982) study. The results supported the predictions. Adults were much more controlling with children who seemed less interested. It appears that teachers become more controlling either when they are pressured from above by controlling administrators and demanding parents or from below by unruly or uninterested children. Remaining oriented toward supporting self-directed learning is no easy feat.

The problem is a difficult one facing the educational community. Most educators agree that having children gain conceptual understanding, having them learn to learn, having them take responsibility for their own learning, are preferred goals for education. Yet the educators' task of achieving these goals is not easy, for they too are under pressure from the government and from parents and they live and work in a society that is accustomed to controlling and pressuring people toward performing up to standards and conforming to societal norms.

Administrators pressure teachers who in turn pressure children, and all this pressure works against the goals of exploration, creative problem solving, and self-determined learning. The solution seems to lie in understanding. By understanding the impact the various forces can have, one can begin to free oneself from those forces. It is encouraging, for example, to note that when deCharms and his colleagues (1976) undertook a major teacher-training program in an inner-city school system, they had a remarkable effect. Teachers became more autonomy oriented, the classroom climate felt better to the children, who themselves became more intrinsically motivated and performed better. Perhaps more concerted efforts of this sort with administrators and teachers (as well as with politicians and parents) could help achieve the educational goals that we have outlined and that make the school systems more pleasant and productive for the staff and children alike.

Summary

In this chapter we considered the application of cognitive evaluation theory and organismic integration theory to the area of education. Several psychologists and educators have called for stimulating learning environments—free from the pressures of grades, rewards, and controls—emphasizing that intrinsically motivated learning is preferable. Much of the research reported in this book is congruent with that point of view, and in this chapter we reviewed other confirmatory research that has been done in educational settings. The research highlighted the importance of teachers' orientations for creating informational contexts within which children can explore, discover, and learn. When the environments become more controlling, children lose intrinsic motivation and self-esteem.

Several lines of research also converged on the conclusion that intrinsically motivated learning is superior to extrinsically motivated learning, particularly with respect to conceptual understanding. Experiments indicated that learning material in order to put it to use increased students' intrinsic motivation to learn and improved the quality of their conceptual learning. On the other hand, learning in order to get grades impaired conceptual learning.

Although intrinsically motivated learning is preferable, there are many instances in which the subject matter or the behaviors that children are required to learn are not inherently interesting. In those cases extrinsic regulation is necessary. However, we reviewed research suggesting that when the regulations are internalized and integrated, the quality of learning is improved. Thus, we suggested the use of informational environments to facilitate the organismic integration of self-regulation and to maintain intrinsic motivation.

Finally, we addressed the issue of why teachers tend to be controlling, and in that vein reviewed research showing that when teachers are pressured, whether from above by administrators or from below by pupils, they tend to become more controlling. Given the current problems in the educational system, it seems important that more attention be devoted to the creation of informational, autonomy-supporting environments for teachers as well as students.

10

Psychotherapy

The application of motivation theory is nowhere more complex and multifaceted than in the domain of psychotherapy and behavior change. The wide array of goals, styles, methods, and approaches bears witness to the fact of there being differing motivational assumptions and the absence of an accepted set of unifying principles for practice. Perhaps the one common denominator among mental health practitioners is that all are concerned with some type of human change. Strupp (1978), for example, argued that all approaches to therapy are concerned with bringing about changes in the behavior or personality of the patient seeking help, but the various approaches disagree regarding what is to be changed and how the changes can best be achieved.

Current research on psychotherapy suggests that practitioners, regardless of their approach or the aims they hold for change, have been moderately successful in their efforts to bring about positive therapeutic outcomes. Bergin and Lampert (1978), for example, reported that across approaches there is an estimated 65% improvement rate for patients receiving psychological or behavioral treatments, compared to an estimated 43% spontaneous recovery rate for those not receiving treatment.

Perhaps the more penetrating question, however, is not just whether therapists can facilitate positive change in the therapeutic context (which, it appears, they can) but whether the change will persist following the termination of treatment. There has been a growing focus within the psychotherapy-outcome literature on the degree of persistance and stability of treatment change, whether psychological or behavioral, following the termination of treatment. This concern has been highlighted by reviews that suggest that the average duration of behavior change following therapy may be quite short (e.g., Franks & Wilson, 1975; Goldstein, Lopez, & Greenleaf, 1979; Stokes & Baer, 1977). The difficulty in bringing about meaningful change that endures over time has, in the words of Kanfer (1979), led to increased concern with variables that promote "the development of the patient's *motivation* to strive for and maintain new behaviors and life patterns" (p. 197). We are in agreement with this point. Indeed, we argue that self-determination, with its motivational basis and motivational ramifications, is an important organizing concept for understanding the effectiveness of treatment and the persistence of treatment change. Thus, it is these motivational factors, which we hypothesize to underlie both positive change and its stability over time and circumstance, that are the foci of this chapter.

The Therapeutic Process as Development

Frank (1961), in his classic comparative study of therapy and healing, characterized psychotherapy as relying "primarily on the healer's ability to mobilize healing forces in the sufferer by psychological means" (p. 1). Embedded in this definition is the key motivational point that has always distinguished psychotherapy from both behavioral and medical treatments, namely the belief that the sufferer has inherent healing forces within him or herself which must be activated for meaningful change to occur. Implicit in this belief, of course, is the assumption of an active organism. And from our perspective, the healing forces are the intrinsic tendency toward development and the organismic integration process through which development occurs. In other words, we suggest that the inherent tendency toward health and well-being implicit in Frank's characterization of psychotherapy, is in fact the inherent tendency toward development that we discussed in Chapter 5. People, we suggested, are intrinsically motivated to be effective in their interactions with the environment, or in other words, to develop increasingly elaborated and unified internal structures that reflect their continuing experiences and represent the basis for effective functioning. When the developmental process gets sidetracked, for example by nonresponsive amotivating environments, the organism fails to develop the competencies that allow successful interactions with the inanimate and interpersonal environments. Nonetheless, the organism still maintains some motivation, in however weakened a form, to repair the damage and get back on the developmental track. Viewed in this way, psychotherapy can be understood as a process that supports the human being, as an active organism striving for competence and self-determination, to work toward the integration of internal and external forces into a more consistent, less conflictful, and more adequate internal structure.

In Chapter 5 we mentioned Nunberg's (1931) assertion that the yardstick of psychological health is the degree to which the ego has achieved unity or synthesis in its elements. Conceptually, we, too, view the issue of psychological well-being in terms of the development of elaborated, unified structures. It is our contention, therefore, that many, if not most, clinical problems can be characterized as a forestalling of the organismic integration process with respect to certain issues or regulations. In other words, insofar as something interferes with the continued development of adequate structures for managing the internal forces of drives and emotions and the external forces of the demanding and often inconsistent environment, we would expect maladaptive functioning.

From our perspective, then, integration of thoughts, feelings, and behaviors is central to the process of therapy, and the lack of integration is the dynamic that underlies many psychological problems. The integration continuum of organismic integration theory (see Figure 1, p. 139), therefore can be seen as a schematic framework for understanding these issues.

In the more extreme cases of maladaptation, we would expect to find what we have called *nonregulation*, in which the person has failed to achieve even rudimentary self-control with respect to various external or internal forces. Here we might find severe despondence, resulting from extreme incompetence, as well as inadequate control of one's drives and emotions. The inadequate structures will be overwhelmed by the forces facing the person. More often, and in the less extreme cases, one is likely to find problems stemming from the conflict and tension inherent in *external* and *introjected* regulation. Here, the integration process has been arrested, and the external and introjected forms of regulation, which are developmentally appropriate at certain points when not accompanied by undue anxiety and fear, remain unintegrated and function sternly to interrupt organismic processes and adaptations.

In either case, there is an absence of unified, flexible functioning. Drives and emotions either run rampant to overpower structures, or they are contained by such rigid structures that they produce considerable pressure and anxiety. Similarly, the regulatory processes that manage the internal and external forces have either not been learned or have been taken on in a rigid, punitive form.

When clinical problems are viewed in this way, their amelioration could then be conceptualized in terms of the organismic integration process. Here, the focus is structural development, rather than mere accretive change, and movement toward a more coherent, unified sense of self is the organizing end state. This, of course, is a function of the differentiation of one's experience and the integration of those differentiated elements into a motivationally meaningful organization. The organismic approach to psychotherapy, then, involves the aim of mobilizing the intrinsically motivated integrative process. Regardless of how dis-integrated the client may be with respect to a particular regulation, therapy involves working toward greater integration of the regulation and the accompanying affects and cognitions.

External and introjected regulation, as we have seen, are inherently conflictive, so the process of integration necessarily involves the client's bringing these implicit conflicts into awareness and working toward an integrative resolution. In cases where the client's behavior would be characterized by nonregulation, the person is lacking in the structures for even rudimentary self-regulation and in the intrinsic motivation that would energize the integrative developmental process. Consequently, the necessary change is more difficult and involves acquiring regulatory structures and unbinding or regenerating the intrinsic energy necessary for intentionality.

Considered in terms of causality orientations theory, the goal of therapy can be said to be a strengthening of one's autonomy orientation. Because the control orientation is characterized by one's being controlled either by external factors or by internally controlling events, the therapeutic process for someone unduly high on the control orientation would involve the integrative resolution of the conflicts inherent in these controls. The determination of one's behavior would shift from the controls to one's choice processes by bringing the conflicts into awareness and working toward transforming the controls into sources of information rather than rigid structures. This transformation (i.e., this integration) will result in the weakening of one's control orientation and in the strengthening of one's autonomy orientation. In cases where the client has a very strong impersonal orientation, we find nonregulation and nonintentionality with respect to behavior. In such cases, any intentional regulation represents an improvement, so the goal might be to strengthen his or her control orientation by developing some external and introjected regulation of behaviors and emotions, though this would, we suggest, be most effectively accomplished when it is viewed as part of the integrative process rather than the conditioning of behavior.

From this organismic view of psychotherapy, one can see that the most meaningful and enduring therapeutic change would be predicted to occur when the perceived locus of causality for change is internal rather than external, because internal causality facilitates the integrative process. This means that environmental factors are best viewed in terms of nurturing or thwarting the natural process rather than in terms of causing the therapeutic change. Different therapeutic approaches place greater or lesser emphasis on the natural integrative process and to a greater or lesser extent see the client (as opposed to the environment) as the locus of change. Compare for example the common action words of psychologically based therapies—facilitating, supporting, accepting, promoting, interpreting, or mirroring—with those of the more behaviorally based therapies—training, changing, programming, shaping, conditioning, or managing. The two sets of words reflect basic differences in the orientation of practice, at least as theoretically represented. We predict that when therapists understand their role in a way that is more consistent with the former sets of words than with the latter, there will be more meaningful long-term therapeutic change for the clients.

This prediction can be formally stated in terms of cognitive evaluation theory, because informational environments, environments that promote perceived internal causality, perceived competence, and minimal tension and conflict, are best described with the former set of words, whereas controlling environments, those that pressure people toward specified outcomes, are best described with the latter set.

Maintenance and Transfer of Treatment Gains

The bulk of the research that has explored the relationship of treatment methods to therapeutic outcomes has been done in the behavioral and cognitive-behavioral tradition. We will therefore look at the issue of the endurance of change from that perspective and then review the outcome research as it relates to cognitive evaluation theory.

Numerous authors have attempted to define stability operationally under the rubrics of either the "maintenance and transfer" or the "generalization" of treatment gains. For example, Goldstein *et al.* (1979) stated:

> A behavior learned in treatment is said to have been maintained when it (the *same* behavior) is used by the (ex-) patient in the absence of any immediate or planned reward for performing it. (p. 2)

And Stokes and Baer (1977) suggested that

> generalization will be considered to be the occurrence of relevant behavior under different, non-training conditions (i.e. across subjects, settings, people, behaviors, and/or time) without the scheduling of the same event in those conditions as has been scheduled in the training conditions. (p. 350)

Maintenance is thus said to occur when a behavior change continues in the absence of any external supports, reinforcements, or controls that originally brought it about. Generalization is a somewhat more encompassing term, which includes not only the maintenance of change, but also its transfer to new circumstances and situations.

The emphasis in these definitions, which are representative of a number of others within the therapy outcome literature, is on behavior change. However, because the focus of psychotherapeutic interventions is often not on behavior change *per se*, but rather changes in attitudes, self-evaluations, affects, and personality dynamics, these definitions could be broadened to cover those foci, as well. Thus, generalization of change, whether in behavior or personality, is in evidence when the change persists following the withdrawal of therapeutic interventions, supports, reinforcements, or controls; and when those changes can be flexibly applied or performed in a variety of relevant contexts and conditions.

From this, one can see clearly that generalization of therapeutic change would be expected to occur when there is a transfer of regulation from external factors to internal factors. In other words, generalization is really an issue of whether the regulation for behavioral or personality change has been internalized, and ultimately integrated. As we said earlier, we would expect this to occur when there is perceived competence and an internal perceived locus of causality for the change. Let us therefore consider the therapy outcome literature in terms of these variables. Because no studies have been conducted using precisely our concepts, we must resort to making inferences about the relationships.

Perceived Competence. According to our theory, there are three important factors relating to perceived competence. First, the task at hand must be optimally challenging; second, there must be either immediate spontaneous feedback from the task or interpersonal feedback from a significant other; and third, the action and feedback must be experienced as informational rather than controlling. The third of these issues, which according to our theory is essential for integrated internalization, has not been explicitly addressed in the outcome studies and therefore makes it difficult even to explore evidence regarding the first two. Nonetheless, there are a number of procedures and studies that have employed concepts related to perceived competence.

Shelton (1979) emphasized the importance of setting realistic goals in therapy, an issue related to optimal challenge. Only when the goals are realistic, given the client's current capacities for change, would we expect the person to maintain the motivation for change. In the same vein, systematic desensitization utilizes tasks and goals that are hierarchically structured to provide the client with increased perceptions of competence and lowered levels of anxiety (Franks & Wilson, 1979b), and Bandura (1977a) has stressed that the clients' efficacy expectations are the key to successful behavior change.

The procedure of positive self-monitoring (e.g., McFall, 1970) in which the client's attention is focused on positive rather than negative outcomes is intended to enhance perceived competence. In this regard Mischel, Ebbesen, and Zeiss (1973) and Kirschenbaum and Karoly (1977) have reported that focusing on positive outcomes resulted in clients having more positive self-evaluations and self-attitudes in general, than focusing on negative outcomes. Positive outcomes emphasize the development of competence, which as Kanfer (1979) suggested, may generalize beyond the monitored behavior to help clients cope effectively with life's problems.

In general, then, increasing numbers of behaviorally oriented therapists seem to be recognizing the importance of perceived competence for the persistence of therapeutic treatment gains, and we would assert that when this is accompanied by the perception of internal causality, the likelihood of effective persistent change is enhanced.

Perceived Causality. The perceived-causality prediction with respect to therapeutic outcomes has received increasing empirical attention and can be easily illustrated with a study involving the use of rewards. As previously noted, rewards tend to facilitate an external perceived locus of causality for a given behavior, and thus if used to promote behavior change, should result in poor maintenance. The study of a weight reduction program by Dienstbier and Leak (1976) tested this directly. Briefly, subjects (i.e., clients) in their program were instructed in self-monitoring and stimulus-control techniques for weight loss. Half the subjects were assigned to a payment condition where they received monetary rewards contingent on successful weight loss, whereas the other half received no payments and were not aware of the payment condition. Results showed that subjects who were rewarded for losing weight lost more weight in the treatment period than control subjects; however, during a 5-month maintenance period following the termination of payments, experimental subjects showed an average weight gain, whereas no-payment controls continued to lose weight. Presumably, the paid subject became dependent on the rewards for losing weight, so when the rewards stopped, the behavior change stopped as well.

In a similar study (Bogart, Loeb, & Rutman, 1969), patients in a psychiatric rehabilitation center were paid for attending vocational workshops. Subjects were assigned either to a low-reward group, receiving $.25 per week for daily attendance, or a high-reward group, receiving $2.00 per week. After 4 weeks, rewards were terminated, and a 4-week follow-up period ensued. Results from this period showed that low-payment subjects became significantly more positive in their attitudes as measured from pre- to posttreatment periods, whereas high-payment subjects became slightly more negative. Further, following the removal of rewards, attendance of low-reward subjects remained constant, whereas high-reward subjects showed a marked increase in absences, resulting in significant differences between the two groups.

These studies illustrate how reward procedures that control an activity may initially motivate clients to perform the activity, but they may also undermine continued performance following the termination of rewards. Such procedures facilitate a perceived external locus of causality for behavior, and thus are expectably deleterious to the development of more internalized or self-determined regulation, and correspondingly to generalization.

A number of studies employing an attributional framework have explored the proposition that internal versus external attributions of causality for change are related to maintained therapeutic outcomes. Davison and his colleagues performed some of the earliest studies concerned with perceived causality and subsequent behavior change. In studies of shock tolerance (Davison & Valins, 1969), smoking reduction (Davison & Rosen, 1972), and insomnia (Davison, Tsujimoto, & Glaros, 1973), they attempted to facilitate perceived external causality for behavior change by leading subjects to attribute changes to various drug compounds. Comparisons between subjects who were led to attribute their treatment change to drugs and those who received no drugs or who were told that they had received a placebo confirmed that the external attributions were negatively related to maintained behavior changes following treatment. Related findings were obtained in a more recent report by Liberman (1978). Psychiatric patients who were told that their improvements in treatment were helped by or due to their medication (actually a placebo) were shown at a 3-month follow-up to evidence significantly lower maintenance of treatment gains than a group of patients who received no "medication."

Another investigation of attributional effects in therapeutic maintenance was conducted by Nentwig (1978), in a study of smoking reduction. Participants were assigned to one of four separate attributional treatments, internal, neutral, external, and very external. The internal group received information emphasizing their own role in behavior change; the externals were informed that the most essential elements in the change were the therapeutic procedures; and the very external group received a placebo smoking-deterrent drug. Although the most impressive short-term gains in smoking reduction during treatment were obtained by the very external attribution group, 6-month follow-up results showed a significant superiority of the internal-attribution group in the maintenance and continued reduction of smoking behavior.

In these studies the facilitation of perceived external causality for change was brought about by leading subjects to believe in the effectiveness of pharmacological agents or specific therapeutic procedures. One might expect that factors that lead patients to believe that specific settings or therapists, rather than the patient's own activity or effort, are responsible for change would also result in poor generalization. This viewpoint has been supported by a number of studies that have been extensively reviewed by Winett (1970) and Kopel and Arkowitz (1975).

Less amenable to these types of investigations are the more subtle facilitators of perceived external causality that may be implicit in the interpersonal style of the therapist. Nonetheless, we maintain that the more evaluative, directive, or controlling the therapist, the less likely it is that therapeutic change will be maintained and transfered following treatment. Therapists who are less oriented toward controlling change should, we suggest, be more successful in facilitating maintenance and transfer of the change that does occur.

In the discussion thus far, we have focused on studies where the presence of a strong external influence was compared to a situation where that factor was absent. The complementary strategy for exploring the general relationship between perceived causality and generalizations begins with providing the client with the opportunity for self-determination concerning aspects of the treatment. Laboratory experiments have shown that choice of activity (Zuckerman *et al.*, 1978), choice of performance level (Fisher, 1978), and choice of rewards (Margolis & Mynatt, 1979) have enhanced or been less detrimental to subjects' internal motivation for target behaviors than comparable conditions not involving choice. Thus, we suggest, the more a client experiences active participation, responsibility, and self-determination over the course and outcomes of therapy, the greater would be the predicted degree of generalization.

The positive impact of self-determination or choice has been supported in several studies related to behavior change. Kanfer and Grimm (1978), for example, showed that college students given choice over training procedures in a reading improvement program showed significantly more improvement than students not given that opportunity. A study by Liem (1975) showed that choice over classroom setting resulted in greater satisfaction and better academic performance in college students.

Bandura and his colleagues have also provided evidence for the utlity of self-determined versus therapist-determined performance in a clinically relevant area. Bandura, Jeffery, and Gajdos (1975) reported that snake-phobic subjects given self-directed mastery experiences with the feared object displayed more generalized and greater fear reduction than subjects whose mastery experiences were directed by the therapist. A subsequent study (Bandura, Adams, & Beyer, 1977) found that subjects given the opportunity for self-directed interaction with phobia stimuli prior to termination evidenced greater generalization of fear reduction than subjects not given this opportunity. The authors pointed out that the self-mastery treatment was intended to lead the subjects to attribute their successes to personal efficacy rather than external factors.

For obvious reasons, the study of maintenance and transfer of treatment gains has most frequently been done with respect to relatively easily targeted behaviors, such as weight loss, smoking reduction, and overcoming phobias. Although the persistence and transfer of behavior change has been difficult to achieve, it appears from these studies that it may be more likely to occur following interventions that enhance the client's experience of self-determination—interventions that lead to an internal perceived locus of causality—than following ones that do not. Although we have reviewed only a few such studies, the combination of their results with the evidence reviewed throughout this book underscores the importance of incorporating the concepts of self-determination and perceived locus of causality into the understanding and practice of personality and behavior change.

In interpreting the findings and arguing for consideration of the concept of self-determination in therapeutic treatment planning, we would emphasize that the attribution of internal causes is a necessary though not sufficient condition for self-determination and thus for predicted generalization of treatment effects. Consequently, we would not always expect attributional manipulations to be successful in producing generalization, and in fact there have been several reported studies in which manipulations that were aimed at producing attributions of internal causes were not successful in achieving the predicted positive effects (e.g., Miller & Arkowitz, 1977; Singerman, Borkovec, & Baron, 1976).

The fact that the attribution of internal causes does not necessarily imply self-determination revolves around two key points that have been raised at earlier points in this book. The first is the difference between cognitions and motivations as the organizing antecedents of behavior; and the second is the difference in the meaning of *internal* in the attribution and motivation literatures.

We suggest that any treatment that merely alters cognitive responses or attributions without actually influencing the underlying motivational processes, will not have a lasting impact on behavior. Superficial attributions of internal causes, attributions that do not entail conflict resolution, integration, or experience of freedom and competence, are unlikely to be resilient to the stresses of the real world and are therefore unlikely to result in the generalization of intervention effects.

Our second point of concern relates to the fact that for many researchers the term *internal causality* pertains to any type of regulation that is not attributed to external causes. The internal-external boundary is defined by the skin of the actor, and the nature or quality of the internal regulation of behavior is not addressed. We, however, believe it is important to distinguish between various types of internalized regulation, which can range from rigid and constricted self-control to more flexible and integrated self-regulation.

A similar point can be made with respect to the behavioral criteria of maintenance and transfer, which distinguish only between changes that continue to be under the control of external or environmental factors and those for which the regulation is inside the person's skin. From this behavioral perspective, no distinctions are made between the important gradations of internalized regulatory processes that we believe have great relevance to therapeutic outcomes. Internalized regulations that involve pressured self-coersion and self-reward, or that hinge one's self-esteem and self-worth on one's behavior, represent less than ideal regulatory processes. Indeed, they may bear greater resemblance to control by external forces than to regulation by integrated processes. Our clinical observations have indicated that the internally controlling styles of regulation have, in fact, been associated with relatively unstable and conflicted outcomes. For example, extreme internally controlling styles of regulation are evident in eating disorders, where failure to live up to relatively rigid and inflexible, but internal standards, is often accompanied by self-disparagement, depression, and at times total loss of behavioral control, as in binge-eating episodes. But the issue of pressured self-control is more general in its application, and can be involved in other problems as diverse as aggression, addictive disorders, study deficits, and obsessive-compulsive disorders, to name just a few. The dynamics of such rigid self-control styles have been aptly described by Perls, Hefferline, and Goodman (1951), in whose theory "self-control" was viewed as an "epidemic disease" of the culture:

> What happens within [one's] own behavior is similar to what occurs in a shop or office where the boss is a slave driver; the "slaves," by slowdowns, errors, sickness, and the myriad other techniques of sabotage, wreck his best efforts to coerce them. (p. 155)

We too believe that the more controlling types of self-regulation create polarities of tension within the person and result in an interplay between compliance and rebellion with respect to the "self"-enforced regulation.

On the other hand, internalized regulation of behavior can be actualized through more flexible, self-determined processes. When a change in behavior or personality regulation is characterized by an integration of the opposing tendencies, and when an identification with and valuing of the emerging synthetic formation is evident, then stable and healthy generalization can be expected to follow. Integrated self-regulation therefore involves not just the introjection or taking in of extrinsic regulations, but also their integration into a flexible, transferable set of values and capacities that would have a true internal perceived locus of causality. The acquired regulation would be experienced as self-determined.

Because of these motivational distinctions, it is important to supplement behavioral criteria of maintenance and transfer with psychological criteria. Psychologically, maintenance and transfer mean more than simply the persistence of a behavior or regulation in the absence of ongoing supports. They mean that one generalizes a pattern of change because that pattern is congruent with one's beliefs, attitudes, and affects, and because one understands the pattern to be the most fitting and integrated solution to the circumstances met. One can flexibly alter the pattern to fit new situations because it is not rigidly tied to particular cues or dependent on particular controls. It persists because it has been fully internalized and integrated into one's self, such that when that pattern is emitted it is experienced as one's own choice. In short, it persists because it is experienced as self-determined. It is not a mere change; it is a development.

The goal of psychotherapy when psychologically rather than behaviorally defined suggests clearly that behavioral criteria do not always distinguish between different motivational states, between conflict and harmony, or between self-coersion and self-determination. When one defines the psychotherapeutic process in psychological terms, the goals and mechanisms of therapy will change accordingly. We thus suggest that the outcome of behavioral or personality change that is initiated or catalyzed within the context of therapy can be evaluated most appropriately through the assessment of the nature and quality of the motivational or regulatory processes that maintain, or fail to maintain, behavioral or personality change.

APPROACHES TO THERAPY

Because our understanding of psychotherapy is organized with respect to the organismic integration process, we will briefly consider three broad therapeutic approaches with respect to their theoretical treatment of the issue of the facilitation or mobilization of internal organismic processes and capacities toward the end of psychological well-being. Of course each approach is portrayed differently by different writers and practiced differently by different therapists, so we will focus our remarks on what we understand to be the general theoretical thrust of the approach.

Behavior Therapies

Classic behavior therapy emerged out of the conditioning (especially the operant) perspective (Wolpe, 1969) and shunned all consideration of organismic processes in favor of a focus on the external environmental factors that can produce changes in observable behaviors. Historically, this involved the use of treatment plans that called for reinforcing desired behaviors and extinguishing undesired ones. These procedures have been reasonably successful in eliciting the desired behaviors while the reinforcements are in effect, but they have been predictably unsuccessful in achieving generalization. As we explained in Chapter 7, with the aid of the response-rate curve (Figure 2, p. 180), there is no theoretical reason to expect maintenance of change following the removal of reinforcements, because maintenance would be represented by nonbaseline responding in the extinction phase (phase IV on the curve). The theory is very clear in its prediction that the effects of reinforcement would extinguish and the response rate would return to baseline.

In an attempt to promote maintenance (i.e., posttreatment responding that is higher than baseline), several techniques have been suggested. These can all be understood as attempts to prolong the reinforcement phase or to delay the onset of extinction. Some researchers (Ashby & Wilson, 1977; Kingsley & Wilson, 1977) have suggested the use of booster sessions in which there is occasional therapist–client contact following the termination of regular treatment. Although some people have reported success with this method, the results have generally been discouraging (e.g., Relinger, Bornstein, Bugge, Carmody, and Zohn, 1977).

Another recently suggested procedure for maintenance involves instituting operant controls in the natural environment (e.g., Bootzin, 1975). Although this procedure may prove successful in eliciting the desired behavior, it is often quite problematic from a practical standpoint because therapists do not typically have access to the natural environment. Furthermore, it does not address the issue of freeing the desired behaviors from therapist-instituted reinforcement contingencies.

Stokes and Baer (1977) have advocated concealing reinforcements so the client will not recognize their presence and thus will not realize that they have been terminated. Similarly, they suggested the use of increasingly intermittent reinforcement as termination approaches, because intermittent reinforcements have been shown to slow the return to baseline. Both procedures, even if they were to prolong desired responding, must be recognized as merely delaying the onset of extinction and thus, at best, to be temporary solutions.

The real problem with these procedures, from our perspective, is not so much that they tend not to facilitate generalization of behavior change, but rather that they conceptualize the clients' problems in terms of behaviors rather than in terms of psychological processes. In many cases behaviors are merely symptoms of deeper problems that will not disappear when the behavior stops. A child, for example, who is in desperate need of attention and is disruptive in class to get it would not be helped by having his disruptive behavior controlled. Further, in other cases, people are displaying appropriate behaviors but are feeling tremendous conflict and anxiety about it. The issue is not in the behavior; it is the underlying psychological processes. A focus only on behavior change could in some situations actually lead to greater internal tension or to less integration of internal structures. From our perspective, that would be counterproductive. Eliciting desired behaviors is not the only, indeed, not even necessarily the most important outcome of psychotherapy.

The more recent behavior therapies have been based on a cognitive-behavioral (e.g., Bandura, 1977a; Franks & Wilson, 1979a; Kanfer, 1977), rather than an orthodox, operant framework. This approach focuses on the mediating role of cognitions in the alteration of behavior, suggesting that it is one's expectations about reinforcements that determine behavior. The shift to cognitions as the focus of treatment has lead to the introduction of procedures for self-administering reinforcements. With these important changes, the newer behavior therapies have been somewhat more successful than the operant-based therapies in maintaining behavior change. Indeed, most of the studies reviewed earlier showing that attributions of internal causes can enhance the prospects for generalization were done within this cognitive-behavioral framework. The problem with this approach, as Carver and Scheier (1981) pointed out, is that their sequence of behavior change always ends with reinforcements, whether self- or other-administered. Thus, they still view behavior as reinforcement determined and have therefore been unable to capture the meaning of self-determination. As such, the therapies have tended not to work toward the motivational integration of cognitions, affects, and behaviors, and have not recognized the difference between internally controlling and internally informational self-regulation.

Psychoanalytic Therapies

Although the theory underlying psychoanalytic therapies is quite diverse, an organismic perspective similar to our own is particularly evident in the theories labelled psychoanalytic ego psychology. Freud (1923), pioneered ego psychology and laid the groundwork for an organismic therapy with the construct of synthetic function. As Freud described it, "The ego is an organization characterized by a very remarkable trend towards . . . synthesis" (1969, p. 20).

Synthesis or unity within the psyche is, from the psychoanalytic perspective, a hallmark of psychological health, whereas its absence is the basis of ill-being. Neurosis, for example, is often characterized by the repression, isolation, or nonintegration of psychic elements, that then remain out of one's awareness and alien to the ego. These elements pose a threat to the ego, in such a way that the ego is "impaired or inhibited in its synthesis" (Freud, 1969, p. 30). In the course of therapy, the therapist provides support for the threatened ego so that the threatening elements can be released from repression and subsequently integrated. In other words, Freud's characterization of therapy in terms of, "Where id was there ego shall be" (Freud, 1964, p. 80), refers to enlarging the ego's organization through the synthesis of repressed or nonintegrated elements of the psyche. This point was echoed by Nunberg (1931) who stated that the "cure" for neurosis involves the assimilation or synthesis into the ego of those psychic elements that previously had been rendered alien.

From this, one can see that psychoanalytic theory conceptualizes many psychological difficulties as resulting from excessive conflict between an impulse and an external or introjected prescription that has been temporarily resolved either through repression of the impulse or through rebellious defiance of the prescription. In both cases, the victory of one side of the conflict and the renunciation of the other serves to minimize immediate anxiety and distress but represents a loss of ego control and an interruption of the synthetic process. Under conditions of less pressure and conflict, the integrative process could have fashioned a compromise in which neither side would win but both would be acknowledged. The aim of therapy, of course, would be the integrated compromise, and the process, according to French (1958) involves remobilizing the conflict, so that both poles of the conflict will come into awareness and the synthetic capacities of the ego can operate. The natural developmental process of synthesis will be resumed.

It is important to note that the agent of change in this therapeutic process is not so much the therapist as it is the active, integrative tendencies in the clients themselves. Alexander and French (1946), in their discussion of psychoanalytic therapy, explicitly argued against the notion that the treatment process results from any therapeutic acts of the therapist on the patient. Rather, psychoanalytic treatment relies on the general processes involved in ego development, facilitated by the therapeutic context.

Similarly, Dewald (1969), in his explication of the processes involved in psychodynamic therapy, emphasized that the therapist does not actively intervene or advise clients regarding the solutions to problems. Instead, the therapist remains neutral with regard to specific solutions and encourges clients toward the formation of their own active resolutions, based on insight and increased awareness. Dewald specifically stated that reliance on reinforcements, external authority, or therapist controls is antithetical to the most basic goal of therapy, namely "the development of independent judgment and motivation" (p. 109). This point was developed in a more recent monograph by Meissner (1981), in which he argued that analysts should increasingly minimize even their interpretive functions as analysis proceeds, in order to maximize and support the clients' tendencies toward growth and autonomous functioning. However, both authors seemed to suggest that to the degree that a client is not currently able to formulate or exhibit autonomous solutions, the therapist may appropriately provide some "ego-surrogate" functions. Dewald labelled such interventions supportive psychotherapy. Ideally such methods would gradually give way to more insight-oriented methods as therapy progresses and the patient is increasingly able to assume responsibility for the process and outcome of treatment. This notion of a continuum of strategies from supportive to insight-oriented, suggests that the degree of what we call self-determination in the therapeutic context must be tailored to the developmental and regulatory capacities evident in the client. In other words, the task for the client must be optimally challenging.

Our brief discussion of psychoanalytic therapy has highlighted two aspects of their formulation that parallel our motivational analysis. First, the individual has within him- or herself tendencies toward growth and development that can be mobilized in treatment. In psychoanalytic theory this is referred to as the synthetic function of the ego, whereas in our theory it is labelled the organismic integration process. Second, both approaches suggest that under appropriate circumstances the synthetic process will operate in the direction of autonomy (Shapiro, 1981), self-motivation (Dewald, 1969), regulation through identificatory processes (Meissner, 1981), or in our terminology, self-determination. The role of the therapist in facilitating such change is to remain neutral with respect to specific outcomes, while providing sufficient support for the person to address and resolve his or her own conflicts through increased awareness and ego synthesis.

Humanistic Therapies

A general approach to psychotherapy that relies heavily on forces within the client to generate psychological health and well-being is humanistic psychotherapy, as exemplified by Rogers' (1951) client-centered therapy and Perls *et al.*'s (1951) Gestalt therapy. In Rogers' view there is but one motive that has significance: the actualizing tendency. This construct describes the inherent propensity of organisms toward maintenance and enhancement. Actualization is a directional tendency, implying movement toward increased differentiation and integration in functioning, movement away from heteronomy and toward autonomy. In the theory of client-centered therapy, change and development are seen to be a function of the actualizing tendency. Persons go to a therapist because they have not been able to experience, assimilate, or resolve aspects of their life situation. Most typically, there are organismic needs that have not been fulfilled, perhaps not even adequately symbolized in consciousness, because they are contradictory to the client's introjected "conditions of worth." Drives and emotions have not been acknowledged because doing so would be in conflict with internalized values that the client believes define him or her as worthy of love. This dependent self-evaluation, or rigidity in self-structure, results in the distortion or denial of significant experiences or tendencies, which in turn are the basis of maladaptive functioning.

The thrust of client-centered therapy is to aid the individual in bringing about adequate symbolization or expression of disowned or problematic aspects of the phenomenal field. By articulating and reflecting the client's experiences the therapist provides an opportunity for the client to differentiate aspects of his life situation, and assimilate or integrate these into experience. This results in a wider scope of consciousness and a greater opportunity for self-regulation.

In discussing therapy, Rogers raised the central question of what is necessary in the therapeutic setting for the client's actualizing tendencies to be mobilized toward growth and positive change. His answer was that the central element is an interpersonal atmosphere in which the client experiences freedom from any controlling pressure (including that inherent in praise) emanating from the therapist. Suggesting that any nonneutrality on the part of the therapist conveys conditional regard to the client, Rogers explained that the therapist must show an acceptance and valuing of all aspects of the person, including his or her doubts, hopes, fears, perceptions, and resistances, rather than appearing to accept only some aspects. Under such conditions, a client can begin, albeit cautiously, to move out, explore, and assimilate previously unacceptable or threatening aspects of the perceptual field. Empathy, which is implicit in unconditional acceptance, facilitates this process, because when the client's world is clear to the therapist, movement and communication within it occur more freely (Rogers, 1957).

Under such conditions the client can come to differentiate, experience, and reevaluate threatening aspects of the world, so as to emerge with his or her own creative solutions. This is often not a smooth process, however. One typically uncovers complex, contradictory experiences that are in conflict with existing self-structures. The therapeutic process may involve the disorganization of some structures so that reorganization and integration can occur. One's self, as Rogers views it, becomes revised in its organization. Insofar as this occurs without the experience of pressures, evaluations, or prods from the therapist, the new values, behaviors and attitudes that emerge will be experienced as one's own. Considerable research summarized by Truax and Carkhuff (1967) has supported the validity of this Rogerian perspective.

Using our own terminology, we suggest that the therapeutic milieu advocated by Rogers is an informational one. The therapist does not join either side of the client's conflicts, nor does he or she pressure or prod toward particular outcomes. Instead, the therapist offers support for autonomy and provides feedback in the form of reflections of the client's phenomenal world. Insofar as the client experiences the atmosphere as informational, the conditions are ripe for the intrinsically motivated processes of differentiation and integration to occur. This is the basis of constructive personality change, change that Rogers describes as movement in the direction of increased potentialities and self-direction and that we label self-determination and competence.

Perls *et al.* (1951) likened the therapist's function to what in chemistry is called a catalyst. It percipitates a reaction, but it neither prescribes the form of the reaction or enters into the compound that is formed by the reaction. In Gestalt theory, awareness—a relaxed and interested attending to aspects of oneself—is a necessary condition for assimilation (i.e., for the organismic integration process). Because awareness is a process that is fuller than mere cognitive understanding (fuller in the sense of involving the emotion of interest and the quality of psychological flexibility), it cannot be accomplished by the therapist's directing the client, it can occur only when the therapist catalyzes an interest in the client.

Awareness is not only the basis for growth (i.e., assimilation), but also for self-regulation. When one is self-regulating, organismic needs will emerge spontaneously to organize perception and behavior toward their satisfaction. This suggests that there are inherent mechanisms for active self-regulation, if these can be freed up to play their natural role.

In terms of our theory, self-regulation through awareness of one's needs and feelings is the paradigmatic description of an autonomy orientation, and is an outcome of organismic integration. As such, we could characterize the goal of Gestalt therapy as being the strengthening of autonomous self-regulation, through natural, intrinsically motivated, organismic processes.

General Principles

Although our discussion has been brief and highly selective, it was intended to highlight the extent to which different approaches to therapy are built around the ideas of organismic functioning. From the discussion we can derive what appear to be the central ingredients of effective psychotherapy. The first is the assumption that there are inherent tendencies in the sufferer toward further development and well-being and that such forces must be mobilized for effective changes to occur. In our theory this is the intrinsically motivated, organismic integration process. The second is a focus on consciousness or awareness as a prerequisite for the differentiation and integration to occur. It is through awareness of conflict, disowned elements, and inadequate regulatory processes that one moves toward resolution and integration. In our theory, awareness was addressed most explicitly in our discussion of the autonomy orientation. It was more implicit in our discussion of the organismic integration process, and thus in our application of organismic integration to psychotherapy, though we consider it centrally important. The final element is the therapist's serving as catalyzer of change, rather than a director, controller, or external motivator. The therapeutic environment must be informational, it must encourage independent, autonomous change in the context of supportive, effectance-enhancing feedback. It is these elements that we believe to be essential for integrated change, for accretions to become developments and for therapeutic outcomes to be generalized.

Summary

In this foray into the motivational aspects of psychotherapy we portrayed psychotherapeutic change as a special case of human development, one that is necessary when the intrinsically motivated, organismic integration process has been thwarted or sidetracked. We suggested that psychological ill-being results from conflict and disintegration, and that the process of therapy involves mobilizing the integrative process in the service of a more unified, autonomous self. The contextual conditions that facilitate this mobilization are the ones that in cognitive evaluation theory we called informational. The therapist's role is to support autonomy, provide nonevaluative feedback, and accept conflicting aspects of the person. In terms of causality orientations theory, we described the goal of therapy to be a strengthening of one's autonomy orientation, that is, one's capacity to be self-determining.

After this introduction, we raised the question of what factors are associated with persisting therapeutic effects following the termination of therapy. Operational definitions of persistent change or generalization of treatment effects suggested that changes must be internalized to meet the criterion of generalization. Because cognitive evaluation theory describes the conditions that facilitate integrated internalization, we reviewed outcome studies that tended to support the view that methods that facilitate perceived internal causality and perceived competence increase the likelihood of generalization.

Finally, we briefly discussed three broad approaches to therapy—behavioral, psychoanalytic, and humanistic—in terms of the extent to which their underlying theory is congruent with the organismic-integration conception that meaningful therapeutic change involves integrated development.

11

Work

Most adults organize their lives around work. It structures their days and restricts their mobility, determines their living standards and affects their friendship patterns. Work goes beyond just influencing their behavior, however; it plays a major role in their sense of self. Work stresses people and provides them satisfaction. It affects their self-esteem and impacts their health. To a large extent, people define themselves in terms of their work.

The nature and conditions of work vary considerably—from dirty factories to posh offices, from back-breaking labor to strategic planning, from swing shifts to flexible hours. But there are notable similarities that crosscut these differences. People depend on work for money. They have to maintain a minimum level of effectiveness; they have to follow schedules and meet deadlines; and in most cases they have to answer directly to a boss. The word *work*, in fact, carries the connotation of "having to" and is often used to describe difficult or stressful activities.

In a recently popular book, Turkel (1972) presented interviews with an array of working people, ranging from receptionists to baseball players, from garbage collectors to stock brokers. The diversity of jobs and the difference in status were great, but there was remarkable similarity in the issues expressed by all these working Americans. As Turkel summarized it, a book about modern work life is a book about violence to one's body and spirit. It is a book about the coping strategies and tension outlets that people devise for dealing with the stresses of their jobs.

A large survey reported by Quinn and Staines (1979) suggests that things may even be getting worse. Their data indicate greater dissatisfaction among workers in 1977 than in 1973. Add to that the uncertain economy subsequent to 1977, the dramatic rise in unemployment in the early 1980s, and other job stresses, such as the rapid introduction of computers to many people's work lives, and one is left to presume that the downward trend in worker satisfaction is continuing.

Within this world of work, motivation is an important concern. For organizations to thrive, indeed in many cases even to survive, members of the organization must be motivated to perform well. Few things are more important or more troubling for managers in their efforts to promote organizational effectiveness than the motivation of their subordinates. To have committed, involved, responsible, and self-directed subordinates is a goal of most managers, and yet providing the conditions that facilitate these qualities is by no means easy. Managers must work to alleviate the stresses of their subordinates, but this is made difficult by the fact that the managers themselves are coping with the same kinds of stresses.

Traditionally, the effectiveness of organizations has been measured solely on the basis of profits. Of course profits are necessary for organizational survival; however, writers such as Lawler (1982) have been increasingly arguing that the quality of work life should be valued, along with profits, in the assessment of organizational effectiveness. Lawler went so far as to suggest that improving the quality of work life should become an important national priority. In light of the clearly established link between work stress and health (e.g., Kahn, 1981; Selye, 1975) and, as we will see, the positive relationship between quality of work life and worker motivation, it seems increasingly important that the quality of work life be used as a criterion against which policies and decisions are judged.

Self-Determination in Organizations

The application of our motivation theory to work organizations suggests that working toward maximal self-determination for each organizational member should be a central organizing principle. Increasing quantities of research indicate that the qualities associated with self-determined functioning—qualities such as creativity, self-regulation, and flexibility—are qualities that most workers value in their subordinates, peers, and supervisors and that enhance organizational effectiveness. Furthermore, the conditions that support self-determined functioning, conditions of personal autonomy and meaningful feedback, for example, are important aspects of a high quality of work life. A focus on self-determination in organizations, it would seem, might very well work toward the dual goals of organizational profits and high quality work life.

In the compilation of interviews by Turkel (1972), a few factors stood out as profoundly stressful aspects of nearly all jobs. Over and over people complained about how closely they were being watched and evaluated—"spied on" is how they often put it. And they reported not having received recognition for their efforts. Their accomplishments and competencies have typically gone unacknowledged, and the feedback they have gotten has tended to be critical and demoralizing. These intriguing, if anecdotal, accounts indicate that people feel like pawns who fill organizational roles when the roles need to be filled and are let go when they do not. The things they report missing are the very things that have been shown to promote self-determination.

In this chapter we will discuss the application of the concept of self-determination to organizations. This will include reviews of relevant management theories and of research on intrinsic motivation and self-determination in organizational settings.

Theories Y and Z

In 1960 McGregor analyzed traditional management practices in terms of the implicit assumptions they make about the nature of people. Referring to this management approach as Theory X management, McGregor contended that it portrays workers as lazy, indolent, and resistant to change. Proponents of Theory X advocate that, at any level of the organization, supervisors should make the decisions and subordinates should carry out those decisions; Theory X therefore entails the use of controlling procedures, such as stringent deadlines and close supervision, to ensure that decisions will be implemented as planned. Piece-rate payments (i.e., controlling task-contingent rewards without positive feedback) are used at the level of production workers and competitively contingent rewards are used at the level of management. By pitting individuals or teams against each other, the reasoning goes, everyone will try hard to win and overall performance will be maximized.

McGregor (1960) argued that these practices have a deleterious effect on people who are subjected to them, and that they tend to become self-fulfilling prophesies. Treat people with controlling procedures, as if they were lazy, indolent, and resistant to change, and they will tend to become lazy, indolent, and resistant to change. In other words, said McGregor, people are not that way by nature, so if one observes them acting that way it is because of the way they have been treated.

The alternative that McGregor offered was what he called the Theory Y approach. This approach is based on the assumption that people are intrinsically motivated to perform effectively and that the satisfaction inherent in doing a job well is an important reward. With this assumption comes the prescription for greater personal autonomy because it is necessary for maintaining people's intrinsic motivation. But the added benefit of the prescription is that it relieves managers from having to maintain close surveillance over all their subordinates. In fact, the intrinsic approach to management involves a redefinition of the management process. No longer is it the managers' job to control subordinates' behavior; instead, managers are charged with the responsibility of creating the conditions within which subordinates will motivate themselves. In such a system rewards are used more as a source of feedback than as a controller of behavior.

Theory Y management, which has been widely advocated by researchers such as Argyris (1964), Likert (1967), and Myers (1970), has come to be called participative management (Marrow, Bowers, & Seashore, 1967), and descriptions of this approach, written for managers, have become recent best sellers (e.g., Peters & Waterman, 1982). In essence, participative management calls for greater integration of deciding and doing. Those who are expected to carry out decisions have greater particiption in making them.

During the past 25 years there has been considerable research on participative methods of management. This has included laboratory simulations, observational studies, and evaluations of major experimental changes in ongoing organizations. Marrow *et al.* (1967), for example, reported marked improvements in organizational effectiveness when participative changes were introduced in a clothing manufacturing company. Likert (1967) discussed several organizational-change studies in which participative methods proved superior.

Lawler and Hackman (1969) designed an experiment specifically to explore the effects of participation in the design and implementation of a bonus plan aimed at the improvement of attendance rates. Some groups of workers designed their own plans, some had plans imposed that were essentially the same as those designed by the participtive groups, and some got no bonus plan, thus serving as control groups. Following the implementation of the plans, the participative groups showed marked improvement in attendance, whereas neither the groups that got the same bonus plans without having participated in their design nor the no-bonus-plan groups showed any change.

By the time of a 1-year follow-up (Scheflen, Lawler, & Hackman, 1971), some of the plans had been discontinued whereas others remained. For the participative groups whose plans were intact, attendance remained at the high level, whereas for those participative groups whose plans had been discontinued, attendance had dropped significantly to a level below initial baseline. The plans for the imposed groups remained intact, and results showed that attendance did improve over the year that the plan was in effect, but it did not approach the high level that the participative groups had attained. The control groups showed no change. In sum, then, the data show that the participation in the design of change has a significantly positive effect on the implementation and results of the change.

An extensive review (Lowin, 1968) of research studies on participation indicated that participative methods are generally preferred by workers and are effective for improving motivation, although as Lowin pointed out, the issues involved with participation are so complex that one cannot simply prove or disprove its utility.

Participative management emphasizes supporting autonomy and allowing participation, but this does not mean that structures, goals, and performance appraisals should be abandoned, nor that subordinates should be allowed to participate in all decisions. Participative management, if properly implemented, would employ all of the elements that we have come to understand as being important for maintaining intrinsic motivation. Managers would encourage their subordinates to set optimally challenging goals and then give them considerable lattitude to work out how to achieve those goals. Managers would then encourage subordinates to be active in assessing their own performance, though managers would also provide the type of constructive feedback that facilitates competence. In short, all structures, including limit setting, would be designed to be informational rather than controlling, and managers would work to create an informational rather than controlling interpersonal context for implementing them.

Vroom and Yetton (1973) have pointed out that although the spirit of participation is important, there are a number of considerations that determine when participation is appropriately used in decison making. They suggested that participative decision making is appropriate when the problem is wholly within the manager's discretion, when time permits group discussion, when the particular discussion is not likely to generate irreparable conflict, and when the subordinates have information that is relevant to the decision being made.

In styles of decision making, as in any structural event, the interpersonal climate is as important as the event itself. Regardless of the style of decision making used for a particular problem, whether it is democratic or autocratic, for example, an informational, supportive climate is necessary to ensure effective implementation of the decision. Subordinates do not need to, or even want to, participate in making all decisions; what they need is a supportive work climate that allows some autonomy in making and carrying out decisions but which provides them with appropriate explanations and other relevant information when decisions are made by their superiors.

Theory Z. The efficiency of Japanese companies during the last decade has made them a major competitor in the marketplace and has hurt many American producers. This has increasingly led American managers to wonder about the Japanese "secrets." Ouchi (1981), in a recently popular book, described the Japanese approach to management as it applies to industry in America where customs and values are different. Referring to the approach as Theory Z, Ouchi emphasized that a focus on people is the key to enhanced productivity. In fact, he said, the central issue for increased productivity in American industry is trust. When greater trust is built, when managers come to know their subordinates as people so they can build more cohesive and openly communicating teams, productivity will rise accordingly. Along with trust and team work, of course, goes autonomy. Trusted and trusting subordinates are given greater autonomy, because they are often in the best position to make effective decisions and because when they are given greater autonomy they also display more intrinsic motivation and less resentment. Theory Z is much like Theory Y; the two theories overlap considerably. Perhaps the main difference is that the organizing concept for Theory Y tends to be autonomy (i.e., participation in decision making), whereas the organizing concept for Theory Z tends to be trust. In practice, trust and autonomy go hand in hand. The autonomy of Theory Y requires a trusting environment to be effective, and Theory Z advocates participative decision making as a fundamental aspect of a trusting relationship between supervisors and subordinates.

In summation, the trend in management theory over the past quarter century, and to a small extent in management practice just recently, has been toward methods that tend to facilitate intrinsic motivation and self-determination. This presumably has resulted from the fact that these methods are being found to be profitable, though it has the important consequence of improving the quality of work life. With all the stress-inducing factors that are operating in modern business, a serious attempt to implement a more participative approach to management may be the one possibility for stemming the tide of growing dissatisfaction.

Whether one defines the quality of work life in terms of the conditions of work or in terms of the degree to which human needs are satisfied (Davis & Cherns, 1975), one can conclude that a higher quality of work life is associated with the opportunities to be autonomous and to develop competencies in a safe environment. To a great degree, the call for an improved quality of work life has to do with a commitment to the management practices that facilitate intrinsic motivation.

REWARD STRUCTURES

The research reported in Chapters 3 and 4 is directly relevant to work organizations. One general conclusion was that reward structures that tend to be experienced as controlling also tend to induce pressure and tension and undermine intrinsic motivation, relative to structures that tend to be experienced as informational. It is, of course, not always easy to predict when a particular structure will be experienced as controlling, because part of the variance in how it is experienced is a function of the perceiver and part of the variance is a function of the rewarder (i.e., the interpersonal context); however, the research has consistently shown that any contingent payment system tends to undermine intrinsic motivation. The use of rewards to motivate behavior can in general be said to be deleterious to intrinsic motivation (Notz, 1975).

Several writers have argued against this point of view, suggesting that their research does not support cognitive evaluation theory (Boal & Cummings, 1981), and that there is no evidence of its applicability to industry (Guzzo, 1979). In the Boal and Cummings research, the authors did find an undermining of intrinsic motivation, but they claimed there was no evidence for the mediating processes of perceived causality and perceived competence. Their measures of these variables were, however, inadequate. First, their questions were worded as if they were assessing traits rather than states (e.g., "Doing my job well increases my sense of self-esteem"). Further, some questions were unrelated to perceived self-determination or perceived causality (e.g., "I always work as hard as I can"). And finally, some questions could as easily have been reflecting internally controlling as internally informational regulation (e.g., "I feel bad when I do my job poorly"). Thus, their study is irrelevant as a test of our theorized mediating processes, but it did support our assertion that contingent rewards run a substantial risk of undermining the intrinsic motivation of workers.

As for the assertion that there is no empirical evidence of the applicability of the research to industry, we agree that relatively little of the research has been done in existing organizations. Certainly that is unfortunate, though the experimental findings from the laboratory and other applied settings are so clear and so persuasive that their applicability seems well assured. Some of the reasons that the effects of rewards on the undermining process have not been studied in organizations are that it is difficult to do controlled experimental manipulations of pay structures and it is hard to get a clear measure of intrinsic motivation. Typically it is measured with a questionnaire, but whenever satisfaction or attitudes are measured it is difficult to be sure that one is getting a measure of intrinsic satisfaction rather than extrinsic satisfaction.

In a quasi-field study, Caldwell, O'Reilly, and Morris (1983) did find that M.B.A. students who were in graduate school primarily because of their interest in learning and who got most of their costs reimbursed by their employers expressed less subsequent intrinsic interest in school work than comparable, initially interested students whose costs were not highly reimbursed. The financial rewards seemed to decrease students' intrinsic interest in business subjects.

The important point is that rewards, like feedback, when used to convey to people a sense of appreciation for work well done, will tend to be experienced informationally and will maintain or enhance intrinsic motivation, but when they are used to motivate people, they will surely be experienced controllingly and will undermine intrinsic motivation. A study by Lopez (1981) in a large telephone company indicated that a bonus program may enhance intrinsic motivation, although there was no control group in the study, so the results are at best tentative. In her study, workers voted for one of their peers to receive a monthly bonus. This is a structure that could either facilitate motivation or could backfire and be quite deleterious. There are elements of competition in it, and there are rewards. The reward, which each worker would seldom, perhaps never, receive, was hardly enough to motivate someone to perform and would possibly leave people feeling like failures were they not to receive it. So the elements of the structure are generally counter to promoting intrinsic motivation and productivity. If, in fact, the bonus had a positive effect on intrinsic motivation, as the author claimed, it would have been because of the interpersonal context. It is possible that a system such as this could be implemented in a way that would be fun and would boost spirits. Undoubtedly the bonus would be passed around to a different worker each month, and people may have been excited by the process. But it is very risky. Each month, all but one person in a group would be a loser. And as the months passed, people would be losers several times and may never be winners. The message to them would be either that they were not well liked or were believed to be among the worst performers. Both messages can be quite devastating.

Consistently, from our interviews in organizations, we have heard evidence of employees not liking competitively-contingent recognition programs. Often the winners report feeling guilty and the losers report feeling bad. In one such example, teams competed to see which one could be most improved for a 3-month period. Two out of eight teams showed great improvement whereas the rest lagged far behind. One of those two teams just barely beat out the other and thus received the recognition and the prize. Because of the structure of the program, the other much improved team received nothing. In a team meeting a few days later, the manager of the "losing" team was asked by the members to explain why they had not been recognized. He felt on the spot and ended up pointing to the areas they had performed least well. The team had done extremely well, and yet what happened is that the manager ended up emphasizing their bad points. The result was demoralizing.

The alternative to these systems is one in which everyone or every team would get recognized for what they had done well. Everyone can be acknowledged for some unique contribution. If bonuses are to be used, everyone could get something, even if it is just points that accumulate toward some eventual prize or bonus. That way there are no losers. Because all the research on the effects of rewards and competition has shown that even when people get rewards and when they win they tend to lose intrinsic motivation, imagine the effects of working for a reward and not getting it or of competing and losing!

Performance-contingent rewards, if administered informationally (Ryan *et al.*, 1983), have been shown to be the most beneficial rewards for those who receive them and receive positive competence information from them. However, Meyer (1975) has argued that there are some additional dangers in such a merit payment system. First, to determine the level of rewards that subordinates will receive may require closer supervision than would otherwise be necessary, thereby leaving the subordinates feeling closely scrutinized. Further, the judgments of supervisors can be strongly influenced by a range of biases. Finally, Meyer argued, evidence indicates that people tend to overrate their own performance relative to others, so most people expect and think they deserve a higher rating than they actually receive. When rewards are tied directly to rated performance, most people get less than they think they deserve, and thus feel like losers.

In short, when rewards are used to motivate, they tend to be experienced as controlling and they frequently convey a sense of incompetence. It is obviously necessary that people be paid and it is clearly important that they be paid equitably. Furthermore, people need and want recognition for a job well done. But the use of rewards to motivate and the use of competitively contingent recognition are likely to have deleterious effects.

RESEARCH ON SELF-DETERMINATION IN ORGANIZATIONS

Repeatedly throughout the book we have reported evidence that the interpersonal context within which rewards and communications occur is an important determinative factor in their effects on the motivationally relevant variables of the recipients. Recently Deci, Connell, and Ryan (1985) tested this and other hypotheses in field studies and experiments in a large corporation.

The setting for the research was a set of five branch centers in the service division of an office machines corporation. Each branch was composed of slightly more than 100 employees, with three levels in the hierarchy. There was a branch manager, 6 to 8 first-line field managers reporting to the branch manager, and 12 to 18 field technicians reporting to each field manager. In addition, there was a team of dispatchers with its own manager, who also reported to the branch manager. Different phases of the research were conducted in different of these five locations and involved different personnel.

The Interpersonal Context

The first phase of the research was a correlational study that explored the relationship between the interpersonal context and a set of motivationally relevant variables in field technicians. Of interest in terms of the interpersonal context was a dimension describing managers' orientations ranging from supporting the autonomy of their subordinates to controlling the behavior of their subordinates. The orientations of the field managers were correlated with the motivation of the technicians on their teams.

The managers' orientations toward supporting autonomy versus controlling behavior were assessed with the Problems at Work Questionnaire. This was patterned after the Problems in School Questionnaire that we used to assess teachers' orientations in the research described in Chapter 9, though the problems and strategies for handling them were ones that managers typically encounter with subordinates rather than ones teachers encounter with pupils. Each problem vignette was followed by four responses that varied in their degree of controllingness, and these were algebraically combined to give an overall score on the supporting-autonomy-to-controlling-behavior dimension.

Motivatonally relevant variables of the field technicians were assessed with a work climate survey that was developed for this research. The survey, some of which was patterned after the Hackman and Oldham (1975) Job Diagnostic Survey and some of which was original to the current questionnaire, involved three kinds of responses. The first was the workers' perceptions and feelings about their jobs and the work climate; the second was the ranked importance of certain job characteristics; and the third was their rated satisfaction with each of those characteristics and their general satisfaction with their jobs. The perceptual and feeling factors related to autonomy, trust, quality of supervision, and the experience of pressure and tension. The importance and satisfaction items included these as well as security, pay and benefits, and other extrinsically relevant items.

Data from 176 technicians on 22 teams revealed a strong correlation, $r = .53$, between managers' orientations and technicians' trust in the corporation's top management. In addition, managers' orientations also correlated with subordinates' satisfaction with their level of trust in the corporation (r = .46), satisfaction with pay and benefits (r = .37), and satisfaction with security (r = .35). When first-line managers were more supporting of autonomy, subordinates felt more secure, were satisfied with their pay, and had more trust in the organization. When managers were more controlling, subordinates tended to fear for their jobs, were less satisfied with their pay, and had less trust in the organization. The managers' orientations did not however correlate with the factors or items related to the quality of the supervision or the climate created by the managers.

Deci *et al.* (1985) interpreted the data in terms of a displacement effect. When subordinates are dissatisfied with the quality of supervision from their immediate manager, the researchers suggested, they seem to displace the satisfaction onto top management rather than experience a potentially quite threatening situation. In interviews and group meetings, the same thing seemed to happen. Virtually all of the strong negative emotions that were expressed were stated in terms of the corporation or the top management. Workers would make many of their negative comments in forms such as, "This is the type of corporation that. . . ."

This observed displacement may be prompted by the way immediate managers implement decisions made by top management. In this corporation, for example, a pay freeze had been in effect for several months prior to our assessments, and subordinates' satisfaction with pay was correlated with their immediate supervisors' management style. Apparently, then, the way the pay freeze had been explained and implemented by the immediate manager affected the subordinates' satisfaction with pay. And more generally, the way all top management decisions are communicated or implemented by immediate managers may affect their subordinates' level of trust in top management. Perhaps the controlling managers actually blame top management for policies and, in essence, for their own managerial behavior. When they controllingly impose a policy, they may do so by saying they have no choice, that top management is responsible for the policy and is making them implement it. Autonomy-supporting managers, on the other hand, may implement such policies in a way that parallels the process of setting limits informationally, which as Koestner *et al.* (1984) showed, does not negatively impact intrinsic motivation. This involves being clear in stating the policy, providing the reasons for it, acknowledging conflicting feelings or dissatisfactions, and allowing as much flexibility as possible in carrying it out.

In general, then, this study indicates that managers' orientations toward supporting autonomy versus controlling behavior affect the interpersonal context of subordinates' work and have an effect on motivationally relevant variables. This, of course, complements the teachers' orientations study reported in Chapter 9 and the laboratory studies reported in Chapter 4, as the motivation variables were slightly different in each.

In other organizational research, Kobasa and Puccetti (1983) reported significant negative correlations between the extent to which subordinates found their bosses supportive and the amount of illness they experienced in the face of stress. It appears, therefore, that the nature of the interpersonal context, as determined by the orientation of the manager, not only affects people's motivations and emotions, but can also impact on their physical health.

Individual Differences

The Deci *et al.* study just described involved examining whether factors in the workers' environment, specifically their managers' orientations, would affect their motivation. The second project, conducted in two other service branches, explored whether individual differences in the workers themselves would relate to the motivation variables of interest. The individual-differences variables of greatest relevance and concern for our hypotheses, of course, are the causality orientations. Thus, we explored whether workers with different levels of the three causality orientations perceive their jobs to be different, place different importance on various job characteristics, and express different levels of satisfaction with those characteristics.

To do this research we developed a new causality orientations scale for the work domain. This new scale has exactly the same format as the general scale described in Chapter 6, and in fact used six of the same vignettes, with their 18 items. We created six new vignettes, with 18 new items, to replace the vignettes from the general scale that tapped the interpersonal rather than work domain. This causality orientations at work scale was administered to 201 field technicians and dispatchers, along with the work climate survey, and the relevant scores from the two scales were correlated.

Results of the analyses revealed that the autonomy orientation correlated significantly and positively with worker's perceptions of the amount of personal autonomy that their jobs provide and the quality of the supervision they receive from their managers. It was marginally positively related to their level of trust in the top management of the corporation. In addition the autonomy orientation was significantly positively related to workers' satisfacton with their opportunities to make inputs, their trust in the supervisor, their job security, and their trust in the corporation. It was also marginally related to their satisfaction with the level of personal autonomy on the job.

The control orientation was significantly positively related to the importance the workers place on pay and benefits; security on the job; and potential for advancement. In addition, it was significantly negatively related to their expressed satisfaction with their job security. Finally, the impersonal orientation was positively related to employees' experiencing the work environment as stressful and their feeling pressured and tense in it. It was negatively related to their satisfaction with job security and with trust in the corporation.

Clearly, we can see that individuals' causality orientations are importantly related to motivationally relevant variables at work. Although the correlations were fairly low, with a median correlation in the high teens, the pattern was consistent and theoretically meaningful. No correlation appeared that was counter to the theory. Of the three orientations, autonomy was related to the greatest number of motivation variables. In Chapter 6 we saw that the autonomy orientation was related to several self-constructs: self-actualization, self-esteem, and self-development. Here we see that out of a stronger sense of self, people relate to their work differently. It is interesting to speculate that the autonomy orientation not only affects the workers' perceptions of their supervisors and work environment, but also affects the supervisor and environment in an interactive way. That is, if workers are more autonomy oriented, supervisors may sense this and allow them greater autonomy, which would give the workers the experience of both greater autonomy and higher quality supervision.

The control orientation was here found to be related to the importance workers place on extrinsic, control-related job characteristics. This supplements the findings from the general scale showing that this orientation is negatively related to performance on heuristic or conceptual activities. The stronger one's control orientation, the more one's attention is focused on context factors such as pay and the less it is focused on the activity itself within that context.

The impersonal orientation was related to workers' feeling stressed and tense. This corroborates previous findings of high impersonality being associated with the so-called negative emotions. It was also correlated with satisfaction with the level of trust and security they experienced at work.

Satisfaction with security is the only variable that correlated significantly with all three causality orientations—positively with autonomy and negatively with control and impersonal. Satisfaction with trust in the organization correlated with two—positively with autonomy and negatively with impersonal. These findings give credence to our earlier assertion that there is a descriptive dimension of self-determination that cuts across the causality orientations: a high level of autonomy can be described as representing high self-determination; a high level of control orientation can be described as representing less self-determination; and a high level of impersonal orientation can be described as representing the least self-determination. It seems that security and trust are implicated in self-determination; one's sense of security and trust seems to parallel, perhaps even be integral to, one's self-determination.

Other investigators have also explored the relationship between other individual-difference variables relevant to causality orientations and people's motivation at work. Helmreich (1983), for example, distinguished between intrinsic and extrinsic aspects of achievement motivation, which are measured by the Helmreich and Spence (1978) Work and Family Orientations Questionnaire. Helmreich reported research with airline pilots, professional psychologists, and business school graduates that indicated that performance on the various jobs was positively correlated with the intrinsic factors of mastery and work orientations but negatively related with competitiveness and the orientation toward extrinsic factors, such as salary. These data, of course, are very much in line with our findings related to causality orientations, and they parallel the experimental findings reported in Chapters 3 and 4.

A great deal of research has been conducted on the relationship between locus-of-control and work variables. Recall, as we saw in Chapter 6, that an external locus of control is highly correlated with the impersonal causality orientation, so evidence on the relationship of the external locus-of-control to work variables is suggestive of relationships of the impersonal causality orientation to those variables. Spector (1982) reviewed considerable evidence indicating that an external locus of control is correlated with lowered work motivation, poorer performance, and less job satisfaction. Feeling unable to control one's outcomes seems quite detrimental to motivational variables in the workplace.

Experimental Change

The final segment of the organization project followed from the fact that there was a relationship between managers' orientations and subordinates' motivation. It involved two questions: Is it possible to train managers to be more supportive of autonomy? And, if that is possible, Would the change radiate to the level of the subordinates? These questions required the design of an experimental intervention based on the principles that had been isolated in all of our previous research.

The Intervention. The primary focus of the intervention was the management team in each branch—including the branch manager and the field managers who reported to the branch manager—although each person in the branch was involved in the program. The abstract goal of the program was to facilitate the experience of self-determination, with its various concomitants and manifestations, among the organization's members. We expected this to be reflected in the perceptions and satisfactions of the members. The behavioral goal was for organizational members to become more involved in identifying and working toward solutions for the problems they face in their work lives. This means less shirking of responsibility and blaming of others, and giving more serious consideration to what the real problems are and to whether or how they could be solved. Thus, for example, we expected to see less blaming of the corporation and its top management, a more honest assessment of the problems in the immediate situation, and a more active stance toward dealing with those problems.

The intervention itself involved a change agent's working in each branch for a total of 13 days. One day was used for meetings between the consultant and branch manager, 5 days were devoted to meetings between the consultant and the management team, and 7 involved the consultant's working with one or more managers along with a group of field technicians. Most of these latter meetings were with existing work groups rather than ad hoc groups, and most technicians had contact with the change agent two or three times.

The objective in the meetings with the branch manager was to build trust so the manager would be comfortable with the change agent and eager to participate in the program. The objectives in the meetings with the management team were to facilitate a climate of mutual trust and support among the team members, to begin a process of identifying and solving management-team problems, and to emphasize the principles that would allow managers to create a more informational, autonomy-supporting climate with their subordinates. The objectives in the meetings with technicians were to emphasize their working more actively with their managers and fellow group members to identify and solve their problems. And the objectives in work group meetings that involved field managers and their subordinates were for the consultant to observe the process and to give feedback to the team and to the manager that might stimulate change toward greater commitment and involvement.

There are three principles that constituted the theme of the intervention: minimally sufficient control; informational feedback; and acknowledging conflicting feelings. All three of these, one will recognize, came directly from the experimental work reviewed throughout the book. Each principle had a short, roughly one-half day, training component for the management team. These were composed of a brief lecture and discussions led by the consultant, and a practical aspect in which the managers practiced putting the principles into operation. The work relating to the principle of minimal control involved managers reflecting on ways that they are controlling with subordinates—through reward structures, rules, deadlines, and close supervision, for example—and considering alternative behaviors. In particular, one alternative that was the focus of discussion and practice was the use of subordinates' participation in decision making. This, of course, is central to Theory Y management and allows subordinates the experience of greater involvement and autonomy.

Discussions on the principle of informational feedback involved three points. The first was that there is a relative paucity of positive feedback in most organizations. Interview and questionnaire data show repeatedly that people feel like they get very little recognition and positive feedback. And much of the recognition that they do get is based on winning a competition, such as having the lowest parts budget or the highest supplies revenues, for example. As a result of one discussion, a management team decided to change its recognition policy such that, at its recognition meetings, each work group would be recognized for the things they did best rather than just having the best group on each of the criteria be recognized. This both ensured positive feedback for everyone and freed the feedback from the competition-dependent structure that had been employed. That structure, one will recall, was shown to be the most detrimental to intrinsic motivation. The second main point emphasized in the feedback discussions was that negative feedback that signifies incompetence tends to be amotivating whereas negative feedback that is given in such a way that it encourages subordinates to solve problems and view improvement as a challenge will be less detrimental and can be quite motivating. The third point with respect to informational feedback is that, although people function best with a minimum of control, they need informative structure. To support autonomy does not mean to neglect; it means to provide the structures that allow people to assess their own competence. Meetings with subordinates in which they set their own goals and then monitor their own performance is one such means of implementing informative structures.

The principle of acknowledging feelings necessitates an understanding of the difference between automatic emotional behavior and chosen rational behavior, the former being expressive of feelings and the latter being purposive and goal oriented. The ability to recognize emotional behavior allows one to reflect and acknowledge the feelings being expressed rather than getting caught in an argument over the apparent content. As such, it provides the setting whereby subordinates can accept limits and integrate necessary changes.

As was the case with the first two principles, managers were encouraged to consider how their own behavior may be contributing to the problems of the subordinates. Thus, for example, as they become better able to recognize automatic emotional behavior, they are encouraged to consider when they become emotional themselves and whether their own automatic emotional behavior might be counterproductive.

Finally, the role of the consultant throughout the entire program was to model the processes through which one supports autonomy. Occasionally, for example, a participant would become uneasy or irritated with the minimally controlling agenda—participants were not told what they should do or when they should do it, for example. The consultant's response was to accept and acknowledge their feelings and to encourage them to take greater initiative in figuring out what they wanted to get out of the meeting and how they might go about getting it. In other words, the consultant encouraged them to treat their feelings as indicators of a problem to be solved and to become active in solving it.

The most frequent set of problems that emerged was related to communications among members of the management team. They gradually identified that they were not relating as well to each other as they would like, that they were not getting the support they needed from the branch manager and from each other, and that they were not working together well as a team. In each case they would be encouraged to talk about these concerns with each other, to open the channels of communication that had gotten closed, and to work out ways of getting the support they need from each other.

The effects of the intervention on the field managers was assessed by administering the problems at work questionnaire following the intervention. A set of managers from two other branches served as a control group by also completing the questionnaire at the same two times as the experimental managers. Results revealed a significant change, such that managers who had been involved in the intervention displayed a greater orientation toward supporting autonomy, whereas those who had not yet gone through the intervention showed no change.

The effects on field technicians of the intervention, and more particularly of the change in their managers toward greater support for autonomy, were assessed in two ways. First, they completed the work climate survey about 5 months after the intervention, and those data were compared with their preintervention data. Unfortunately, during this 5-month period, the two control-group branches received the intervention, so they could not serve as the control group for this portion of the program evaluation. Because this phase was intended to assess whether the effects of the change in manager's orientations radiated to the level of subordinates, we compared the technicians' preintervention scores with their postintervention scores on those variables that had been found to be related to managers' orientations. Of those four variables—trust in top management, satisfaction with trust in the corporation, satisfaction with pay and benefits, and satisfaction with security—one variable, the degree of trust in the corporation and its top management, increased most (and significantly) over the experimental period. This variable, one will recall, was most highly correlated with the managers' orientations, so it would be expected to increase given the positive shift in managers' orientations.

The second way in which the effects of the intervention on the technicians was assessed was that two branches where the intervention had taken place participated in a work-attitudes survey conducted within the organization by the personnel research department of the corporation about 3 months prior to the intervention and again 5 months after the intervention. These surveys are standard procedure in the corporation and had nothing to do with the intervention. Two other branches in the country that were on the same survey schedule served as a control group for the two experimental branches. This internal corporate survey is summarized into a work-climate index that describes the field technicians' general attitudes and feelings about their jobs. Results of this survey indicated that the work-climate index increased over the intervention period for the two experimental branches but decreased for the two nonexperimental branches. It appears, then, that the intervention was generally effective in terms of improvements in motivationally relevant variables.

SUMMARY

In this chapter we have considered the application of the concepts of intrinsic motivation and self-determination to the working world. We began by noting that recent theories of management, variously referred to as participtive management, Theory Y management, and Theory Z management, have inherent in them the concept of promoting personal autonomy and thereby facilitating intrinsic motivation.

The research on reward structures reviewed throughout several earlier chapters was seen to be directly relevant to work. Whenever rewards are used to motivate people—in other words, to control them—it is probable that they will have a negative effect on the people's intrinsic motivation. Competitively-contingent rewards were said to be the most detrimental. However, rewards that are appropriately linked to performance, representing positive feedback in an informational context, ought not to be detrimental. The cost to the system, however, in signifying good performance through the use of performance-contingent rewards is that many people end up receiving the message that they are not doing very well, and this is likely to be amotivating.

Finally, we described research showing that managers' orientations toward supporting the autonomy versus controlling the behavior of their subordinates had a direct relationship to motivationally relevant variables in subordinates. Motivational variables of the subordinates were also found to be affected by their own causality-orientations scores. And finally we described an experimental intervention that focused on creating an informational climate in the workplace by minimizing control, using structures that allow people to assess their own competence, administering feedback informationally, and accepting subordinates' conflicting feelings. Research indicated that the intervention enhanced the managers' orientation toward supporting autonomy and appears to have radiated positively to the motivation of their subordinates.

12

Sports

Sports are the focus of a tremendous amount of energy and resources among the people of industrialized nations. Twenty million American youngsters between the ages of 6 and 16, for example, participate in organized sports programs (Magill, Ash, & Smoll, 1978), and numerous sporting events draw the attention of tens of millions of television viewers. Although the history of organized sport dates back to ancient times, most social commentators agree that the magnitude of involvement, both in terms of numbers and time, has never been greater and is continuing to rise.

Socioeconomic factors have undoubtedly played a role in this trend. The technology of industrial economies, for example, has allowed children to begin working later and adults to work fewer hours, resulting in a sharp rise in the amount of leisure time. This dramatic increase in leisure time is certainly a necessary condition for the widespread involvement in sports, but it is not sufficient to explain why so much of people's leisure-time energy is devoted to athletics and sports. Psychological factors need to be taken into account for a more complete explanation of this phenomenon.

When one brings the needs and dynamics discussed in this book to bear on the interaction of work and leisure activity, an interesting explanatory framework begins to emerge. It may well be that the psychological needs that are left unsatisfied in the work place have a strong influence on the selection of leisure activities. In particular, we suggest that the nature of modern work entails an increased subordination of self-determination to economic and technological forces and a decreased identification with the products of one's labors. Even though working conditions have improved in the past century, experienced pressure and alienation seem to have increased. These factors, we hypothesize, have led people to seek leisure activities that they believe will allow self-determination and creative expression within the context of social interaction. Sports provide an excellent opportunity to be self-determining, to get competence feedback, and to have social involvements. They are generally engaged in freely, and they afford one the chance to stretch capacities and build skills. Simply stated, sports provide an opportunity to play; they are an arena for one's intrinsic motivation; and they represent a possibility for recovering the self-esteem that is lost in the work lives of many individuals.

But sports are more than simply play. Although they have many play elements, with their intrinsic satisfactions, sports have additional elements that are not present in some forms of play. Alderman (1974) reviewed the definitional distinctions that have been made between play, games, and sports. He argued that *play* is best considered a general category for activities done solely for fun or enjoyment. *Games* represent play that is structured: they are play activities with rules concerning acceptable behavior. Finally, *sports* are structured play activities that have been institutionalized. They have an enduring pattern or form that organizes behavior and has wide social acceptance. Sports are social phenomena that have a history and a significance within a cultural group.

Interestingly, as we move along the structural dimension from play, to games, to sports, the complexity of the motivational dynamics increases as well. On the one hand, the added structure and form represent challenge. They provide the opportunity for the comparison of one's skills and competencies against a standard, so they enhance the likelihood of meaningful feedback, thereby supporting intrinsic motivation. On the other hand, the structure and form also represent pressures to conform, and the widespread social acceptance of sports has made them fertile ground for the introduction of a wide range of extrinsic factors.

The few surveys that have explored the reasons why people engage in sports suggest that for the average amateur, intrinsic factors are dominant in their motivation. Wankel and his colleagues (Wankel & Kreisel, 1982; Wankel & Pabich, 1982) found evidence from youths in amateur sports that the most important factors influencing their sports enjoyment and participation were improvement of skills, sense of personal accomplishment, and excitement derived from the activity. Consistently less important were the more extrinsic factors such as rewards, uniforms, and social approval. Similarly, Alderman and Wood (1976) found that the primary motivators for young hockey players were the desires for competence, challenge, and affiliation. At least in the minds of the young participants, the satisfactions and purposes of sports seem to be intrinsic.

However, technological advances in the mass media have increasingly lead sports to be as much an activity for spectators as for players. "Monday Night Football" is so widely watched that it represents common ground for social conversation among business associates and politicians, as well as social acquaintances and friends. This increased interest has led to an ever stronger focus on winning (which is itself an extrinsic pressure), and winning has been backed by further extrinsic motivators such as social approval, prizes, and monetary rewards. In these situations, the preservation of one's self-esteem tends to be hinged on one's athletic performance, and with the social investment in outcomes, the very societal pressures prevalent in other behavioral domains have to some degree become involved in sports.

In sum, then, it appears that although people have sought out sports for fun and for the opportunity to be free of extrinsic pressures, those same pressures have increasingly been brought into the world of sports. As such, the interaction between intrinsic motivation and extrinsic controls that has been explicated by cognitive evaluation theory is directly relevant to the field of sports (Ryan, Vallerand, & Deci, 1984).

COGNITIVE EVALUATION THEORY AND SPORTS

The understanding that the major motivators for amateur athletes are intrinsic has significant ramifications for programs that aim toward increasing people's involvement in and persistence at physical activity. If, as Wankel (1980) suggested, the factor that most influences persistence in fitness programs is participant enjoyment, the question of what factors are likely to undermine versus enhance intrinsic motivation for sport activities becomes central. A closely related question asks how extrinsic motivators, such as those that are present in public competitions and professional athletics, affect various qualitative aspects of task engagement. Several studies, which will now be reviewed, have addressed these questions within the context of sports psychology.

Self-Determination and Perceived Locus of Causality

Participation in sporting activities appears, initially at least, to be largely self-determined; the perceived locus of causality is internal. For most of us there is little pressure to get onto the ball field or the slopes; we choose these activities when the pressures to do less desirable things subside or when we can escape the controls that pervade so much of our lives. All too frequently, however, rewards, and other extrinsic factors begin to come into play. We are pressured to improve and rewarded when we do. According to cognitive evaluation theory, these factors are likely to result in a more external perceived locus of causality and a decrease in intrinsic motivation for the activity.

Orlick and Mosher (1978) tested the impact of rewards on intrinsic motivation for a motor activity. Using the standard free-choice measure, they pretested children ranging in age from 9 to 11 years to assess their intrinsic motivation for the stabilometer task, an activity that involves motor balancing. Subsequently, the children returned for more of this activity under either reward or no-reward conditions. Subjects in the reward conditions received a trophy for engaging in the activity, whereas subjects in the no-reward conditions did not. Four days later subjects returned for a posttest assessment of intrinsic motivation, once again measured by a free-choice period. Subjects in the reward conditions exhibited a decrease in free-choice time spent on the target task from the presession to the postsession, whereas subjects in the no-reward conditions showed an increase. As summarized by Orlick and Mosher, the data suggest that a child's motivation for this interesting activity can be undermined through the introduction of extrinsic rewards. Thomas and Tennant (1978) reported results that are congruent with those of Orlick and Mosher, and Halliwell (1979) reported that observers who are more than 7 or 8 years old tend to attribute less intrinsic motivation to rewarded athletes than to unrewarded ones.

E. Ryan (1977, 1980) has explored this issue in the real-life circumstances of intercollegiate sports. He used Deci's (1975) statement of cognitive evaluation theory as a guide to investigate the impact of athletic scholarships on male and female undergraduate athletes. In the first study, Ryan (1977) used a questionnaire survey of athletes at two institutions to assess intrinsic motivation. He compared male athletes on scholarships to those not on scholarships, expecting that those receiving money for playing sports would be less intrinsically motivated for their sport than their nonscholarship counterparts. Scholarship athletes listed more extrinsic reasons for participation and reported less enjoyment of the activity than nonscholarship athletes.

In a second, more extensive study, E. Ryan (1980) used the information–control distinction of cognitive evaluation theory to predict an interaction between athletic scholarship and sex of athlete on intrinsic motivation. He reasoned that the male athlete receiving a scholarship would see himself as performing the sport for money and would thus enjoy the sport less than nonscholarship males; the reward would be controlling. On the other hand, the female athlete receiving a scholarship, which at the time was new and relatively infrequent in women's sports, would experience it as information regarding her individual competence; the reward would be more informational. Ryan sampled athletes from 12 institutions, 424 males and 188 females. Males were either wrestlers or football players, whereas females, because they were less prevalent, were drawn from seven different sports. The data indicated that females reacted as predicted; scholarships did not undermine their intrinsic motivation for the sports. Males displayed differences in their reaction to scholarships depending on the sport. Football players reacted as predicted by Ryan, with "pay for play" undermining their intrinsic motivation. Wrestlers, however, were more like females in that scholarships did not decrease their intrinsic motivation. Ryan suggested that scholarships may be more controlling for football players because the use of scholarships to attract such athletes is a common practice. For wrestlers, however, the scholarships may be experienced more in terms of competence affirmation because they are less commonly used. To support this post hoc interpretation, Ryan drew on data suggesting that wrestlers expected a lower percentage of their cohorts to be on scholarship than did football players.

As with all real-world studies, Ryan's data are multifaceted and suggest that pay for play is a complex issue with respect to intrinsic motivation. However, they provide support for the notion that the extrinsic incentives for sports, which are relatively common in the college and especially the professional milieu, *can* decrease one's enjoyment and intrinsic motivation for those activities. This suggests that the perceived locus of causality is an important dimension to be considered in programs designed to enhance motivation for sports. However, as with other domains, it is not the fact of the reward *per se* that determines its impact on intrinsic motivation; instead, it is whether the reward is controllingly or informationally salient for the recipient. For example, an award that signifies competence and is not overly controlling may not undermine intrinsic motivation.

Intrinsically motivated activities are freely chosen by the participant, and choice implies self-determination. The feeling or perception that the performance of an activity is by one's own choice, rather than externally imposed should, therefore, have a positive effect on one's intrinsic motivation (Zuckerman *et al.*, 1978). The perceived locus of causality would be more internal. Thompson and Wankel (1980) recently tested this proposition in a field study where they examined the impact of perceived choice of activities on participation in an adult women's fitness program. Registrants in a commercial fitness program were randomly assigned to either an experimental or control condition. Subjects in the control (no-choice) condition were led to believe that a program of exercise had been assigned to them without consideration of their preferences. Subjects in the experimental (choice) group were informed that their activity choices had been considered in their program design. Actually, the exercise programs for both groups had been designed so that the degree of activity preference was equal for both; hence, only their perception of choice differed. Examination of subsequent attendance records over a 6-week period revealed that the perceived-choice group had significantly higher program attendance. This is consistent with the point of view that perceived freedom (Iso-Ahola, 1980) or self-determination is basic to persistence in the absence of extrinsic rewards for sporting activities.

Optimal Challenge and Perceived Competence

Proposition II of cognitive evaluation theory suggests that intrinsic motivation will be related to felt competency at an optimally challenging activity. Feedback that signifies or promotes competence within a context of self-determination will enhance intrinsic motivation, particularly when the activity is optimally challenging. However, feedback that leads to perceptions and feelings of incompetence, will diminish intrinsic motivation and perhaps lead to amotivation for that activity.

Studies exploring the effects of feedback on intrinsic motivation have ensured optimal challenge in a variety of ways. Some have balanced the feedback in a slightly positive direction; some have used subjects' stated expectations of being moderately competent at the task; and some have used tasks that pilot subjects had reported to be challenging. Except for a study by Danner and Lonky (1981), intrinsic motivation studies have generally not tailored the task to the individual subject's skill level. Although these various means of ensuring optimal challenge have been adequate for experimental purposes, the sports psychologist working with individual athletes would need to attend more carefully to the athlete's psychological experience of optimal challenge.

Csikszentmihalyi (1975) has provided perhaps the fullest psychological definition of optimal challenge, one which is especially applicable in the domain of sports. He argued that when people exercise their skills optimally, in other words, when the opportunities for action are in balance with their skills, they will experience flow. When a person perceives that the opportunities for action are too demanding for his or her capabilities, anxiety or worry will be the person's experience; alternatively, when the opportunities for action are perceived to be too easy, given the person's skills, boredom will result. This provides sport psychologists with a handle for understanding, and therefore defining, optimal challenge. They can examine the athlete's experience with regard to the activity, and the degree to which flow is evident suggests the degree to which the athlete is optimally engaged in the activity.

Several investigators have been examining the utility of the perceived competence proposition in its application to sport motivation. Of particular importance is a series of studies carried out by Vallerand and his associates on the impact of positive and negative performance feedback on perceived competence and intrinsic motivation.

Vallerand and Reid (1984) demonstrated that positive verbal feedback about performance can increase intrinsic motivation, whereas negative verbal feedback tends to have a detrimental effect. Subjects performing a stabilometer task were presented with either positive verbal feedback or negative verbal feedback after every fourth trial. The results revealed a main effect for feedback, in which positive verbal feedback increased, and negative verbal feedback decreased, intrinsic motivation for the task.

Vallerand (1983) also investigated whether the amount of positive feedback would determine its impact on subsequent intrinsic motivation. Subjects were 50 hockey players between 13 and 16 years of age who performed an interesting task involving decision making in simulated hockey situations. There were 24 experimental trials, and subjects received 0, 6, 12, 18, or 24 positive verbal statements regarding their performance. The results revealed that subjects who received some positive feedback were more intrinsically motivated than no-feedback subjects, although there was no effect for the amount of feedback. Furthermore, in accord with cognitive evaluation theory, the changes in intrinsic motivation paralleled those of perceived competence. Vallerand interpreted the results as indicating that the objective amount of feedback is not the critical factor in determining the effects of feedback on intrinsic motivation, rather it is the subjective experience. If subjects perceive themselves to be competent following a modest amount of positive feedback, additional feedback appears not to be necessary.

Vallerand, Gauvin, and Halliwell (1982) provided further support for the effects of feedback on feelings of competence. In this investigation they made an award contingent on performance. Then, in one condition, subjects were told they had won the award and in another condition subjects were told they had not. The performance-contingent nature of the award was intended to be informationally salient. Results revealed that subjects who did not receive the reward felt less competent and less intrinsically motivated than those who won the award.

In the Vallerand and Reid (1984) study, the investigators explored the specific proposition suggested by Deci and Ryan (1980a) that changes in intrinsic motivation following feedback would entail changes in perceived competence. They identified 84 subjects who had at least moderate interest in the stabilometer task and assigned these subjects to positive, negative, or no verbal feedback conditions. As reported previously, positive feedback increased whereas negative feedback decreased perceived competence and intrinsic motivation relative to no verbal feedback. The researchers then performed a path analysis with feedback, competence ratings, and intrinsic motivation and found that perceived competence mediated the changes in intrinsic motivation.

Weinberg and Jackson (1979) provided further support for the proposed effects of feedback on intrinsic motivation and obtained data concerning the attributions that accompany success and failure. They asked subjects to perform the stabilometer task under conditions of either monetary rewards or no rewards, and they provided the subjects with either success feedback (better than 82nd percentile) or failure feedback (better than 18th percentile), supposedly based on normative information. Following the experiment, task interest, enjoyment, and excitement were assessed as measures of intrinsic motivation. As expected, there was a main effect for feedback, with success related to higher intrinsic motivation. There was no reward effect, which Weinberg and Jackson attributed to the overshadowing effect of feedback. Corollary attributional data pertaining to the relation of outcomes to ability, effort, luck, and task difficulty indicated that success outcomes were attributed to high ability, high effort, and good luck, whereas failure outcomes were attributed to low ability, low effort, and bad luck.

Together these results support the utility of proposition II for understanding the effects of feedback and the related feelings and perceptions of competence on intrinsic motivation. It seems clear that positive feedback increases and negative feedback decreases perceived competence and intrinsic motivation. There is also evidence that the feelings and perceptions of competence mediate the motivational effects (e.g., Vallerand & Reid, 1984). Practically, this would turn out to be somewhat distressing if, as Curtis, Smith, and Smoll (1979) reported, coaches are often very negative in their interactions with young athletes.

Most of the empirical validation of proposition II has taken the form of feedback studies, in which the experimenter provided the feedback that affected feelings and perceptions of competency. The efficacy of such procedures for the laboratory is obvious, but it may obscure a more basic manner through which feedback is often obtained, namely through self-evaluations. Most sports activities have sources of performance feedback built into them. The difficulty of the slope that one can negotiate in skiing or the degree to which one can coordinate dribbling a basketball with one's nondominant hand are sources of direct feedback; one can observe one's own competencies. Whether one is satisfied with the progress one makes and experiences the intrinsic joy of competency building depends most of all on the standards one employs and the absence of detrimental pressure to meet those standards.

Another means by which feedback is, so to speak, naturally obtained is through comparison with others. The Weinberg and Jackson (1979) study that used normative information as a source of feedback was a formalization of this type of input, but generally it is much more informal. People watch their friends, cohorts, or older siblings and compare their own performance to that of the model. Social comparison is an important means through which people obtain effectance-relevant information. By comparing their skiing to that of others, for example, people can see how to use their poles more effectively or how to shift their weight in a more satisfactory manner. Such comparisons, which aim toward gaining inputs relevant to one's own improvement, should generally facilitate intrinsic motivation, especially when the focus is on subskills that are optimally challenging and therefore within one's potential to master.

A particularly salient and motivationally compelling form of social comparison in sports and games is competition. So significant is competition in our culture, and so motivationally complex, that it deserves consideration in its own right.

COMPETITION AND INTRINSIC MOTIVATION

Competition is a component of many sport activities (Martens, 1975) and seems quite intertwined with intrinsic motivation. Csikszentmihalyi (1975), for example, stated that competition is one of the basic components of autotelic or intrinsically motivated activities, and McClelland *et al.* (1953) argued that achievement motivation (itself a complex of intrinsic and extrinsic motivation) involves competition against a standard of excellence. However, many definitions of competition seem antithetical to intrinsic motivation. For example, Deutsch (1969) defined competition in terms of two or more people or groups having directly opposing goals. This is common in sporting activities where one person wins and the other must lose. Similarly, Kelley and Thibaut (1969) used the term *perfect competition* to refer to so-called zero-sum situations where there is a perfect negative relationship between the wins of one side and the losses of the other. They reported that perfect competition tends to foster mutual distrust and deceit, and some research (e.g., Berkowitz, 1962; Deutsch, 1969) has suggested that competition can impair performance and facilitate aggression. It is unfortunate, therefore, to note that Luschen (1970) defined sport as zero-sum competition.

It appears from the preceding that competition has different meanings to different investigators, and this contributes to the difficulty in examining its motivational underpinnings. One useful distinction was offered by Ross and Van den Haag (1957), who suggested classifying competition as either indirect or direct. In *indirect* competition the individual or group struggles to perform well against an impersonal standard such as one's best previous performance or the performance norms for one's ability level. The concept of indirect competition thereby allows us to include as competitive such activities as mountain climbing, skiing, canoeing, exercising, and individual running. Indeed, all athletic activities have components of indirect competition. *Direct* competition, however, involves people struggling against one another, with each attempting to maximize one's own successes and to minimize the successes of the opponent. Playing a game of tennis (as opposed to volleying with a tennis ball) is an example, as are most organized team sports. In the same vein, Csikszentmihalyi (1975) distinguished between "measuring self against ideal" and "measuring self against others." These definitions suggest that there are real differences between competition that involves meeting or not meeting a standard and competition that involves winning or losing with respect to other persons. We typically use the term competition to refer solely to direct competition in our own analyses of the motivational effects of such factors (e.g., Deci, Betley, Kahle, Abrams, & Porac, 1981; Ryan *et al.*, 1983), though we shall review research related to both types of competition.

Indirect Competition

Indirect competition may be a freely chosen activity that helps people improve their competence, in which case it would be expected to maintain or enhance intrinsic motivation. In such situations, winning would be expected to result in higher levels of intrinsic motivation than would losing, because winning represents positive competence feedback. Only when one's performance in indirect competition becomes pressured, from outside sources or from ego-involvements, would it be expected to decrease intrinsic motivation.

In a study by Weinberg and Ragan (1979), subjects in an indirect competition situation reported enjoying the task more and finding it more like a leisure-time activity than noncompetition subjects. In another study of indirect competition done by Vallerand, Gauvin, and Halliwell (1982), however, subjects were pressured to try to beat the scores of other participants, even though face-to-face (i.e., direct) competition was not involved. Subjects in the no-competition control group were told to perform as they pleased, with self-determination of performance being emphasized. Using cognitive evaluation theory, the researchers predicted that the competition subjects, who were pressured by the instruction to beat the standard, would be subsequently less intrinsically motivated for the stabilometer task than self-determined subjects. That prediction was supported by the results. The self-determined performance subjects engaged the task significantly longer during a subsequent free-choice period than did the competition subjects. In sum, then, indirect competition can lead to either increased or decreased intrinsic motivation depending on whether people experience the indirect competition as an opportunity to gain competence feedback (informational indirect competition) or as pressure to beat a standard (controlling indirect competition).

Weinberg and Jackson (1979) explored the impact of winning versus losing at an indirect competition on ratings of intrinsic motivation for the stabilometer task. Results revealed, as expected, a main effect for success/failure (i.e., win/loss), with success leading to more intrinsic motivation and failure to less. We interpret this as straightforward support for proposition II of our theory, because winning versus losing at a noncontrolling indirect competition amounts to positive versus negative feedback.

Direct Competition

Deci, Betley, Kahle, Abrams, & Porac (1981) reported the first experiment that investigated the effects of direct competition on intrinsic motivation. They reasoned that (direct) competition is an extrinsic factor because attempting to win *per se* is extrinsic to mastering an activity for its own sake. Thus, they predicted that the competitive element of trying to beat another person would decrease subjects' intrinsic motivation for the activity. To examine this hypothesis, Deci *et al.* used a variant of the typical Soma puzzle paradigm discussed in Chapter 3. Half the subjects were instructed to compete (i.e. to try to solve the puzzles faster than the other person with whom they were paired), whereas half were simply instructed to work as quickly as they could so as to finish in the allotted time. Actually, in each pair of subjects, one of the people was an experimental accomplice, posing as a subject. This person was instructed to allow the actual subject to win on each of the puzzles and was familiar enough with the configurations to make the performance differences appear close. As predicted, the results revealed that competition decreased subjects' intrinsic motivation for the Soma activity, an effect that was particularly strong for females. Thus, even though the subjects were allowed in every instance to beat the confederate, the competition undermined their intrinsic motivation for the task.

Let us now clarify the nature of the competitive element in games and sport. Many games have competition built into them as an integral element; it is endogenous to the games. Nonetheless, although competition is built into games such as basketball, it is exogenous to dribbling well, making skilled passes and assists, shooting baskets, and mastering other components of the game. Although direct competition may be part of a game's structure, we assert that it is by nature an extrinsic element, just as it is in activities like puzzle solving where competition is clearly exogenous. The competitive aspect of games is the focus on winning rather than engaging with the activity itself. Insofar as one plays in order to win, rather than to play well, an extrinsic orientation dominates over an intrinsic one.

To the degree that one is competitively oriented, one is involved in a particularly keen form of extrinsic relating, and there is likely to be the type of strong social investment that promotes face-saving behaviors, performance disruption, and emotionality. As an example, note the finding of increased aggression reported by Berkowitz (1962) in competitive settings.

Results complementary to those of Deci, Betley, Kahle, Abrams, & Porac (1981) have been reported by several investigators who have explored the effects of competitively-contingent rewards. Recall, for example, from the review in Chapter 3, that when Pritchard *et al.* (1977) offered a $5 reward for doing better at an activity than the other people in one's group, the rewards decreased intrinsic motivation relative to a no-payment condition. Recall also Amabile's (1982a) finding that competitively-contingent prizes decreased subjects' creativity on artistic tasks. Although her study was not a study of sports, it may indicate that a strong competitive orientation will make people more rigid and less creative on the ball field as well.

One study, reported by Weinberg and Ragan (1979), of subjects' motivation for the pursuit rotor has been interpreted as contradictory to our viewpoint. These investigators looked at the effects of direct, face-to-face competition on intrinsic motivation as assessed by a question asking how much time subjects would be willing to volunteer for a future experiment of the same type. The results indicated that male subjects in direct competition expressed greater willingness to return to do more of the same activity than males who did not compete. Thus, males were said to have greater intrinsic motivation following competition.

In interpreting these results, it is important to note the conceptual difference between the dependent measure employed by these researchers and the one employed by Deci, Betley, Kahle, Abrams, & Porac (1981). In the Deci *et al.* study, the dependent measure for the competition and no-competition groups was subsequent involvement with the activity in the *absence* of competition. But in the Weinberg and Ragan study, the dependent measure for the competition group was willingness to return to the task in the *presence* of competition, whereas for the no-competition group, it was willingness to return to the task in the *absence* of competition. Thus, the two studies assessed different things. In the competition group of the Weinberg and Ragan study, the dependent measure assessed motivation to compete rather than intrinsic motivation for the task. This paradigm would be comparable, in a study of the effects of rewards, to contrasting the rewarded subjects' willingness to continue doing the activity for rewards with the nonrewarded subjects' willingness to continue doing the activity for no rewards. It is, in fact, closer to a measure of extrinsic motivation in the competition condition than to a measure of intrinsic motivation. Of course direct competition is motivating (extrinsically motivating), but it appears to have the unintended consequence of undermining intrinsic motivation for the activity itself.

A second aspect of the Weinberg and Ragan study explored the effects of success (i.e., winning) versus failure (i.e., losing) at the activity. As one would expect, success led to greater willingness for future participation than failure.

The Weinberg and Ragan study has highlighted two important points. First, to argue that competition undermines intrinsic motivation for an activity does not mean that competition is not motivating. It motivates in much the same way that other extrinsic factors motivate. This leads to the second important point, namely that when one is involved in direct competition, one needs the reward of winning in order to persist at the competitive activity. In the absence of the reward of winning, subsequent persistence will show a marked decline, as evidenced by the Weinberg and Ragan finding that subjects who received negative feedback were less willing to return than subjects who received positive feedback.

We believe that the competitive situation, like all extrinsic structures, can have both controlling and informational aspects. The controlling aspect of competition comes into play when one focuses on the activity as something that one must win. When this is of central importance then the extrinsic nature of competition will be most apparent. However, competition also has informational elements. It allows participants to obtain information about their competence or effectiveness, especially when there is optimal challenge and ongoing feedback, as, for example, in a close-scoring game. When there is less focus on winning or losing and more focus on playing well in a competitive situation, there will be less detrimental effects of competition on intrinsic motivation. When someone loses an extremely difficult, well-played game by one point, the information inherent in the loss is really very positive. If the informational aspect were actually salient for the person, the person would feel good (though perhaps disappointed) and maintain intrinsic motivation. However, if the controlling aspect were salient, the person would feel bad and lose intrinsic motivation. We know of no study that has attempted to separate the informational and controlling aspects of competition, though isolating these factors would seem to be an important next step.

Competition and Ego-Involvement

The concept of competition is, in many ways, similar to the concept of ego-involvement. Ryan (1982) has argued that ego-involvement represents an internally controlling state in which one's self-esteem is contingent on certain outcomes. He suggested that this can be very motivating—very extrinsically motivating—but it is likely to undermine intrinsic motivation. It may be that the reason competition is so often experienced as controlling (and therefore undermines intrinsic motivation) is that people very easily become ego-involved in the competition. Rather than remaining task-involved with the activity, people tend to hinge their self-esteem on the outcome of the competition. This of course would not be surprising as there is such a strong emphasis on competition in most modern societies—in some situations, one must win even to survive.

When people become ego-involved in competition, they need to win to maintain self-esteem. When they win, they have achieved their goal and are ready to compete again, but, seeing the activity as an instrument for winning, they are less likely to persist at the activity in the absence of competition. If, on the other hand, they lose a competition, they will be less willing to compete again, but they may persist at the activity in the absence of competition to improve their skills and to prove to themselves that they can do well (i.e., to recover their lost self-esteem).

In sum, we would argue that a competitive focus on winning and the state of ego-involvement can be very motivating, though neither is intrinsically motivating. Because self-esteem is hinged on winning or achieving some other specific outcome, both competition and ego-involvement represent stable, persistent forms of motivation only for those people who consistently win or meet the expected standards. The participants who are losers are likely to suffer the motivational consequences associated with negative self-esteem. Over the short run, this may involve persistence at the activity in the absence of competition, but continued negative feedback and the perceived incompetence that accompanies it would eventually lead to amotivation.

Sex Differences in Competitive Settings

The Deci, Betley, Kahle, Abrams, & Porac (1981) investigation of the effects of competition on intrinsic motivation revealed a marginal interaction between competition and the sex of the subject. The intrinsic motivation of women was somewhat more undermined than was the intrinsic motivation of men. This preliminary finding may be interpreted using the work of Deaux (1977), who suggested that competition is more congruent with a male orientation than with a female orientation. Consequently, competition may be experienced as somewhat more aversive by females than by males, who may find it more enjoyable and more congruent with their expectations of themselves as males. They may also, however, become more ego-involved in it.

Three additional studies of sex differences in direct competition have indicated that the interaction of gender and competition is even more complex than the previously cited Deci *et al.* data had suggested. In the study by Weinberg and Ragan (1979) mentioned earlier, there was face-to-face competition between same-sex pairs working with the pursuit rotor. In their study the major dependent variable was the degree to which competition subjects would volunteer to return for more competitive activity and no-competition subjects would volunteer to return for more noncompetitive activity. Males volunteered for a significantly larger amount of time in competitive conditions than did males in no-competition conditions, whereas there were no significant differences for females. Males, it seems, prefer competition over no competition, though females do not. Furthermore, the results suggested that males who had won accounted for most of this willingness to continue to compete. Taken together, these results support the point of view that males are more oriented toward competition: they prefer it to no competition, and their desire to engage in future competitions is more dependent on current competitive outcomes than is the case for females. Males, relative to females, seem to view many activities as instruments for winning some competition.

In a recent study of direct competition (Driver, Ryan, & Deci, 1985), another interesting interaction appeared between gender and competitive outcome. The task in this experiment was a kind of hand hockey game in which pucks were slid along a board into areas that yielded different numbers of points. Point differentials could also be affected by knocking the opponent's pucks out of high-scoring areas. Males and females competed against same-sex or opposite-sex opponents. Intrinsic motivation was assessed during a subsequent free-choice period when each subject was alone in the room with the target activity. Results revealed that losing decreased the intrinsic motivation and perceived competence of females, thereby straightforwardly following the predictions of proposition II of cognitive evaluation theory. For males, however, the story was different. Winning decreased their subsequent intrinsic motivation for the activity itself, relative to losing. This suggests that the activity was experienced as an instrument to winning. When they won, they were no longer interested in the activity (they had gotten their reward), but when they lost, they persisted during the free-choice period, presumably to recover their self-esteem by proving to themselves they could do it. In the future, of course, they may want to compete more with the activity, but they seem to have lost interest in the activity itself.

This study suggests that males take a more instrumental orientation toward competitive activities than do females. They experience such activities as instruments for winning rather than as interesting activities. They may even see them as instruments for preserving their self-worth. In such situations winning leads to less subsequent persistence than losing, as was the case for males. Methodologically, this represents a problem for our frequently used free-choice measure of intrinsic motivation, because free-choice-period persistence that is aimed at restoring self-esteem is not really intrinsic motivation; it is internally controlling persistence. Sorting out these issues and problems is a task for future research.

A final study of sex differences and intrinsic motivation following competition was performed by Reeve, Olson, and Cole (1984). These investigators reported that females who won a competition displayed more subsequent intrinsic motivation than females who lost, thus replicating the Driver et al. (1985) results for females. For males, however, free-choice activity was high following both winning and losing. Thus, although they did not replicate the males' low level of persistence following winning, their results do suggest that competition affects males and females differently.

It is of course difficult to know why Reeve et al. found results for males that were different from those found by Driver et al. It may be due to the different tasks. Reeve et al. used a noninteractive puzzle-solving task, whereas Driver et al. used a competitively interactive game. Because puzzle solving is not really an activity that involves competitive interacting (each person does his or her own task without interacting directly with the other person), the male subjects may not have gotten so ego-involved in winning at this noninteractive activity as they did with the competitively interactive hand-hockey game. If this were so, the winning may have been experienced more informationally, and this could account for the winners not showing a low level of subsequent persistence.

To summarize, there has been relatively little work that has explored sex differences in competition. That which has been done suggests that there are interesting sex differences, although many important questions remain unanswered. From the studies that have been done we can draw the following tentative conclusions. Males seem to find competition more compelling and involving, whereas females seem to find it more aversive. Thus, competition seems to undermine the intrinsic motivation of females more than of males. Further, competitive outcome seems to affect males and females differently. When males win at a competition they are more eager to compete again than when they lose, whereas the fact of winning versus losing has less impact on females' desire to compete again. Further, competitive outcome affects the intrinsic motivation of males and females differently. When females win at a competition, their subsequent intrinsic motivation for the target task is higher than when they lose. However, when males compete, although winning (relative to losing) increases their desire to compete again, it may actually decrease their subsequent intrinsic motivation for the task more than losing does. This, we suggested, results from their being more ego-involved in winning.

Goals and Values

Turning now to the applied issues involved in this research, we can ask: To what extent should extrinsic pressures, evaluative feedback, or rewards be used in sports programs, and to what degree should competition be emphasized in sporting activities? We suggest that the answer is very much dependent on one's goals and values.

If, for example, one is a professional coach or a team owner, then perhaps one's sole goal is winning. In this context an exclusively extrinsic focus tends to exist and may be appropriate. Recall the popularly quoted statement from one of America's most famous coaches, Vince Lombardi: "Winning isn't everything; it's the *only* thing." In his milieu, where not winning could entail financial loss and possible unemployment, this focus is entirely understandable. Furthermore, in professional-sport contexts, as in any other highly pressured business, concern with the intrinsic motivation of the players is unlikely to be salient because coaches, like corporate managers, tend to believe that intrinsic motivation does not have a direct and immediate effect on performance, and that without pressure people will not perform up to standards. Thus, where the emphasis is simply on maximizing performance or output, irrespective of psychological ramifications, many people believe that the more pressure the better.

In a recent essay, Mahoney (1979), whose cognitive-behavioral approach is focused entirely on improved performance, went so far as to advocate coaches' giving false performance feedback to athletes, although he did caution that it be used in small doses lest its effectiveness be undermined by "generalized distrust" (p. 429). This underscores the concept that where *only* performance matters, a controlling psychology is often advocated, although the data are not all in on whether controls help or hinder performance. Similarly, one might suggest that if a program director or team coach cares only about winning, hooking the players' self-esteem on the game's outcome, providing salient rewards or pressures for winning, or using other extrinsic procedures might indeed have a motivating impact. But it is certainly not an intrinsically motivating impact, and we believe that such techniques may impair performance and produce reactance.

Leaving professional athletics aside, we suggest that winning is not the appropriate focus for physical education programs and amateur sports. Rather, the goals of importance would seem to be the promotion of the kind of interest and participation in physical activity that extends beyond the program, perhaps to a lifelong involvement with physical fitness and constructive athletics. Physical education could serve to enhance appreciation of sport and physical skills, while fulfilling the psychological needs of all participants (not just the winners). It could serve to facilitate self-esteem by providing an outlet and structure for self-determined, competent engagement within a social context. Such goals could be achieved, we believe, when the factors that facilitate intrinsic motivation for sports are operative. Where the desire is to promote an intrinsic motivation to participate in sports, then external pressure, competitive emphasis, and evaluative feedback are contradictory to the goal. Perhaps we could even define good sportsmanship accordingly. The good sportsman does not just perform well, but also allows others to enjoy the sport context by focusing on how the game is played rather than on who wins it.

MOTIVATION AND THE EXPERIENCE OF SPORTS

In recent years there has been increasing attention paid to the inner experience of athletes and the relationships of this experience to performance and motivation. Our own work, although not done in the context of sports, has led to the explication of three inner states or regulatory processes that would seem to be directly relevant to the realm of sports activities. These processes are intrinsically motivated, internally informational, and internally controlling.

We have argued that the experience associated with intrinsic motivation has qualities such as spontaneity, flexibility, direct experience of one's engagement with the environment, and an absence of self-consciousness. The other two types of self-regulation represent differing degrees of self-determination and integration of the motivation for action. Internally informational states involve considerable self-determination, though they also involve a certain degree of self-consciousness or self-focus. They entail truly chosen accommodation to external realities and regulating oneself to do something that is not itself fun. In sports, this is most apparent in practicing, where one works in an interested and nonpressured way to match an internalized standard. Finally, there are internally controlling processes in which there is a self-imposed pressure to achieve particular outcomes. This involves feelings of pressure, tension, and conflict; and cognitively, there is an increase in self-evaluation, with accompanying self-criticism and self-praise. Here, there is the least self-determination, for one is working with introjected regulations or standards that have never been fully accepted as one's own. Internally informational regulations are functioning when there is nonpressured self-monitoring or self-instruction, whereas internally controlling regulations are functioning when there is a pressured ego-involvement.

The study of internal states has always been difficult, and this has led many psychologists to ignore the significance of experience, and to focus instead on performance or behavior. In the realm of sports, however, a more experiential approach has been taken by some writers. And where this has been done, we have found a correspondence with and an enrichment of the point of view we have expressed concerning intrinsic and extrinsic motivation, and internally informational and internally controlling regulation. In the domain of sports the major distinctions have been between states of task involvement (which corresponds to informational regulation) and ego-involvement (which corresponds to controlling regulation).

One such set of distinctions has emerged in the popular literature on the inner experience of sports (Gallwey, 1974, 1981; Gallwey & Kriegel, 1977). These authors have distinguished two experiential states within the athlete, designated Self 1 and Self 2. Self 1 involves the experience of an inner voice that is evaluative in nature. Self 1 tells the athlete what is right and wrong, how to do this or that, how good or how bad the athlete is, and so on. Gallwey and his associates have argued that this internal chatter not only does not help performance, it actually impedes it. They assert that performance is best when thinking is least. Their description of Self 1 corresponds nicely to our theoretical notions of internally controlling regulation and ego-involvement. The non-self-conscious, spontaneous experience associated with Self 2, on the other hand, is of complete task involvement and direct awareness. There is no trying, no pressure, no instructor or coach within the head. Instead, there is a quieting of the mind and a trusting engagement of the body's full capabilities. This accurately describes the state of intrinsic motivation, which is devoid of pressures toward particular outcomes and is focused on the activity for its own sake. Correspondingly, we expect that external demands and pressures or excessive involvement of self-esteem in outcomes will break up this spontaneous, direct inner experience, as our research has tended to indicate. It can also be seen that

Self 2 as a predominant mode of functioning corresponds to the autonomy orientation, and Self 1, to the control orientation, each of which
were discussed in Chapter 6.

Similarly, research by Csikszentmihalyi (1975, 1978) has addressed
the experiential aspects of sports, and more generally of intrinsic motivation, by documenting the inner experience of flow, in which action
merges with awareness. One is totally involved in what one is doing;
there is an absence of self-consciousness; concentration is complete and
direct. There is a loss of ego and an experience of oneness with the
activity. There is also an absence of evaluative feedback, because the
direction of activity is in a sense natural and autotelic. Csikszentmihalyi's
(1975) interviews with athletes and players who had experienced flow
show a striking correspondence with the inner games descriptions of
Self 2 now popularized by Gallwey.

Csikszentmihalyi (1975, 1978) has argued that the flow state emerges
when the opportunities for action are in balance with one's capabilities,
as we described earlier in this chapter. Whereas we are in agreement
with this, we would like to emphasize the related, and implicit, conditions that we believe to be necessary for flow, namely the experience
of self-determination and the absence of pressure toward particular
outcomes.

Thus, in the realm of sports we have often questioned whether the
behavioristic emphasis that is uniquely on performance and that involves
the introduction of rewards, pressures, and self-statements accurately
reflects the experiential underpinnings of excellent performance in sports.
Although it is useful to employ internally informational regulation (i.e.,
self-monitoring) for improving one's skills, the strong emphasis on
improvement or performance seems likely to be disruptive and to facilitate internally controlling regulations. In sports as in other applied
domains where motivational psychology is relevant, it appears that
attending to experience may be the road to the best performance and
to the fullest understanding of the phenomena. Indeed, it may also be
the road to the most interesting and useful psychology.

SUMMARY

In this chapter we have argued that the field of sports is one of the
places where intrinsic motivation is most germane because people engage
in sports to play—to have fun and feel free. We suggested that people
are strongly attracted to sports in our modern culture in part because
most work settings provide relatively little opportunity for intrinsic
enjoyment and the experience of self-determination. However, even

though people seek sports activities to gratify intrinsic needs, extrinsic pressures have increasingly come into play in sports settings, so we considered the interaction of intrinsic and extrinsic motivation in sports.

Several studies in physical activity settings have shown that a range of rewards, such as trophies and prizes, tended to decrease intrinsic motivation, as cognitive evaluation theory would predict. Additional research showed the predicted increases and decreases in intrinsic motivation following positive and negative feedback, respectively. Competition was seen to decrease subjects' intrinsic motivation for the target task, but to increase their desire to compete again, particularly following a win. Males appeared to be more interested in competition than females, and competition was more likely to undermine the intrinsic motivation of females than males. Gender also interacted with performance outcomes to affect subsequent intrinsic motivation. Losing (relative to winning) decreased the subsequent intrinsic motivation of females when they did compete, but winning (relative to losing) decreased the subsequent intrinsic motivation of males who competed. It seems that males saw the task as an instrument for winning. When they won, they lost interest in the activity itself, but when they lost, they persisted at the activity, perhaps attempting to regain self-esteem.

Finally, we discussed the inner experience of sports. Truly intrinsically motivated activity may produce the experience of flow, the total, non-self-conscious involvement with the activity that yields the fullest experience and most refined performance. Further, the study of inner experience, particularly with respect to self-determination, may yield the fullest understanding of motivation for sports. Indeed, we suggested, the study of inner experience is necessary for a full understanding of human motivation, and perhaps for the most interesting and useful psychology.

References

Abramson, L. Y., Seligman, M. E. P., & Teasdale, J. D. Learned helplessness in humans: Critique and reformulation. *Journal of Abnormal Psychology*, 1978, *87*, 49–74.

Abramson, L. Y., Garber, J., & Seligman, M. E. P. Learned helpless in humans: An attributional analysis. In J. Garber & M. E. P. Seligman (Eds.), *Human helplessness*. New York: Academic Press, 1980.

Ainsworth, M. D. S., Blehar, M. C., Waters, E., & Wall, S. *Patterns of attachment*. Hillsdale, NJ: Erlbaum, 1978.

Alderman, R. B. *Psychological behavior in sport*. Philadelphia: Saunders, 1974.

Alderman, R. B., & Wood, N. L. An analysis of incentive motivation in young Canadian athletes. *Canadian Journal of Applied Sports Sciences*, 1976, *1*, 169–176.

Alegre, C., & Murray, E. J. Locus of control, behavioral intention, and verbal conditioning. *Journal of Personality*, 1974, *42*, 668–681.

Alexander, F., & French, T. M. *Psychoanalytic therapy: Principles and application*. New York: Ronald, 1946.

Allport, G. W. *Personality: A psychological interpretation*. New York: Holt, 1937.

Amabile, T. M. Effects of external evaluations on artistic creativity. *Journal of Personality and Social Psychology*, 1979, *37*, 221–233.

Amabile, T. M. Children's artistic creativity: Detrimental effects of competition in a field setting. *Personality and Social Psychology Bulletin*, 1982, *8*, 573–578. (a)

Amabile, T. M. Social psychology of creativity: A consensual assessment technique. *Journal of Personality and Social Psychology*, 1982, *43*, 997 1013. (b)

Amabile, T. M. *The social psychology of creativity*. New York: Springer-Verlag, 1983.

Amabile, T. M., DeJong, W., & Lepper, M. R. Effects of externally imposed deadlines on subsequent intrinsic motivation. *Journal of Personality and Social Psychology*, 1976, *34*, 92–98.

Anderson, R., Manoogian, S. T., & Reznick, J. S. The undermining and enhancing of intrinsic motivation in preschool children. *Journal of Personality and Social Psychology*, 1976, *34*, 915–922.

Angyal, A. *Foundations for a science of personality*. New York: Commonwealth Fund, 1941.

Argyris, C. *Integrating the individual and the organization*. New York: Wiley, 1964.

Arnold, H.J. Effects of performance feedback and extrinsic reward upon high intrinsic motivation. *Organizational Behavior and Human Performance*, 1976, *17*, 275–288.

Arnold, M.B. *Emotion and personality, Vol. 1: Psychological aspects*. New York: Columbia University Press, 1960.

Aronson, E., Blaney, N., Stephan, C., Sikes, J., & Snapp, M. *The jigsaw classroom.* Beverly Hills, Calif.: Sage, 1978.

Ashby, W. A., & Wilson, G. T. Behavior therapy for obesity: Booster sessions and long-term maintenance of weight loss. *Behaviour Research and Therapy,* 1977, *15,* 451–464.

Atkinson, J. W. Motivational determinants of risk-taking behavior. *Psychological Review,* 1957, *64,* 359–372.

Atkinson, J. W. *Motives in fantasy, action and society.* Princeton, NJ: Van Nostrand, 1958.

Atkinson, J. W. *An introduction to motivation.* Princeton, NJ: Van Nostrand, 1964.

Atkinson, J. W. The mainspring of achievement oriented activity. In J. W. Atkinson & J. O. Raynor (Eds.), *Motivation and achievement.* Washington, D.C.: Winston, 1974.

Atkinson, J. W., & Birch, D. The dynamics of achievement-oriented activity. In J W. Atkinson and J. O. Raynor (Eds.), *Motivation and achievement.* Washington, D.C.: Winston, 1974.

Atkinson, J. W., & Feather, N. T. (Eds.), *A theory of achievement motivation.* New York: Wiley, 1966.

Ausubel, N. (Ed.). *A treasury of Jewish folklore.* New York: Crown, 1948.

Averill, J. R. Personal control over aversive stimuli and its relationship to stress. *Psychological Bulletin,* 1973, *80,* 286–303.

Bandura, A. Self-efficacy: Toward a unifying theory of behavioral change. *Psychological Review,* 1977, *84,* 191–215. (a)

Bandura, A. *Social learning theory.* Englewood Cliffs, N.J.: Prentice-Hall, 1977. (b)

Bandura, A., & Schunk, D. H. Cultivating competence, self-efficacy, and intrinsic interest through proximal self-motivation. *Journal of Personality and Social Psychology,* 1981, *41,* 586–598.

Bandura, A., Jeffrey, R. W., & Gajdos, E. Generalizing change through participant modeling with self-directed mastery. *Behaviour Research and Therapy,* 1975, *13,* 141–152.

Bandura, A., Adams, N. E., & Beyer, J. Cognitive processes mediating behavioral change. *Journal of Personality and Social Psychology,* 1977, *35,* 125–139.

Baron, R. M., & Ganz, R. L. Effects of locus of control and type of feedback on the task performance of lower-class, black children. *Journal of Personality and Social Psychology,* 1972, *21,* 124–130.

Bates, J. A. Extrinsic reward and intrinsic motivation: A review with implications for the classroom. *Review of Educational Research,* 1979, *49,* 557–576.

Baumrind, D. Current patterns of parental authority. *Developmental Psychology Monographs,* 1971, *4* (No. 1, Part 2).

Beck, A. T., & Beamesderfer, A. Assessment of depression: The depression inventory. *Modern Problems of Pharmacopsychiatry,* 1974, *7,* 151–169.

Bell, R. Q. A reinterpretation of the direction of effects in studies of socialization. *Psychological Review,* 1968, *75,* 81–95.

Bem, D. J. Self-perception: An alternative interpretation of cognitive dissonance phenomena. *Psychological Review,* 1967, *74,* 183–200.

Bem, D. J. Self-perception theory. In L. Berkowitz (Ed.), *Advances in experimental social psychology* (Vol. 6). New York: Academic Press, 1972.

Benware, C., & Deci, E. L. Attitude change as a function of the inducement for espousing a pro-attitudinal communication. *Journal of Experimental Social Psychology,* 1975, *11,* 271–278.

Benware, C., & Deci, E. L. Quality of learning with an active versus passive motivational set. *American Educational Research Journal,* 1984, *21,* 755–765.

Bergin, A. E., & Lampert, M. J. The evaluation of therapeutic outcomes. In S. L. Garfield & A. E. Bergin (Eds.), *Handbook of psychotherapy and behavior change* (2nd ed.). New York: Wiley, 1978.

Berkowitz, L. *Aggression: A social psychological analysis*. New York: McGraw-Hill, 1962.

Berlyne, D. E. Novelty and curiosity as determinants of exploratory behavior. *British Journal of Psychology*, 1950, *41*, 68–80.

Berlyne, D. E. The arousal and satiation of perceptual curiosity in the rat. *Journal of Comparative and Physiological Psychology*, 1955, *48*, 238–246.

Berlyne, D. E. *Conflict, arousal and curiosity*. New York: McGraw-Hill, 1960.

Berlyne, D. E. Motivational problems raised by exploratory and epistemic behavior. In S. Koch (Ed.), *Psychology: A study of a science* (Vol. 5). New York: McGraw-Hill, 1963.

Berlyne, D. E. Exploration and curiosity. *Science*, 1966, *153*, 25–33.

Berlyne, D. E. Arousal and reinforcement. In D. Levine (Ed.), *Nebraska symposium on motivation* (Vol. 15). Lincoln: University of Nebraska Press, 1967.

Berlyne, D. E. The reward value of different stimulation. In J. T. Trapp (Ed.), *Reinforcement and behavior*. New York: Academic Press, 1969.

Berlyne, D. E. What next? Concluding summary. In H. I. Day, D. E. Berlyne, & D. E. Hunt (Eds.), *Intrinsic motivation: A new direction in education*. Toronto: Holt, Rinehart & Winston of Canada, 1971. (a)

Berlyne, D. E. *Aesthetics and psychobiology*. New York: Appleton-Century-Crofts, 1971. (b)

Berlyne, D. E. The vicissitudes of aplopathematic and thelematoscopic pneumatology (or the hydrography of hedonism). In D. E. Berlyne & K. B. Madsen (Eds.), *Pleasure, reward, preference*. New York: Academic Press, 1973.

Bertalanffy, L. von. *General systems theory*. New York: G. Braziller, 1968.

Bexton, W.H., Heron, W., & Scott, T. H. Effects of decreased variation in the sensory environment. *Canadian Journal of Psychology*, 1954, *8*, 70–76.

Bialer, I. Conceptualization of success and failure in mentally retarded and normal children. *Journal of Personality*, 1961, *29*, 303–320.

Blanck, P. D., Reis, H. T., & Jackson, L. The effects of verbal reinforcements on intrinsic motivation for sex-linked tasks. *Sex Roles*, 1984, *10*, 369–387.

Blasi, A. Concept of development in personality theory. In J. Loevinger, *Ego development*. San Francisco: Jossey-Bass, 1976.

Boal, K. B., & Cummings, L. L. Cognitive evaluation theory: An experimental test of processes and outcomes. *Organizational Behavior and Human Performance*, 1981, *28*, 289–310.

Bogart, K., Loeb, A., & Rutman, I. D. *A dissonance approach to behavior modification*. Paper presented at the meeting of the Eastern Psychological Association, Philadelphia, Penn., 1969.

Boggiano, A. K., & Barrett, M. *Performance and motivational deficits of helplessness: The role of motivational orientations*. Unpublished manuscript, University of Colorado, 1984.

Boggiano, A. K., & Ruble, D. N. Competence and the overjustification effect: A developmental study. *Journal of Personality and Social Psychology*, 1979, *37*, 1462–1468.

Bootzin, R. R. *Behavior modification and therapy: An introduction*. Cambridge, Mass.: Winthrop, 1975.

Brehm, J. W. *A theory of psychological reactance*. New York: Academic Press, 1966.

Brehm, J. W., & Sensenig, J. Social influence as a function of attempted and implied usurpation of choice. *Journal of Personality and Social Psychology*, 1966, *4*, 703–707.

Brehm, S., & Brehm, J. W. *Psychological reactance: A theory of freedom and control*. New York: Academic Press, 1981.

Brennan, T. P., & Glover, J. A. An examination of the effect of extrinsic reinforcers on intrinsically motivated behavior: Experimental and theoretical. *Social Behavior and Personality*, 1980, *8*, 27–32.

Bridges, L., Frodi, A., Grolnick, W., & Spiegel, N. H. *Mothers' styles and mother-infant attachment patterns*. Unpublished manuscript, University of Rochester, 1983.

Bridgman, P. W. *The way things are*. Cambridge, Mass.: Harvard University Press, 1959.

Brockner, J., & Vasta, R. Do causal attributions mediate the effects of extrinsic rewards on intrinsic interest? *Journal of Research in Personality*, 1981, *15*, 201–209.

Brown, I., & Inouye, D. K. Learned helplessness through modeling: The role of perceived similarity in competence. *Journal of Personality and Social Psychology*, 1978, *36*, 900–908.

Bruner, J. S. *On knowing: Essays for the left hand*. Cambridge, Mass.: Harvard University Press, 1962.

Bry, B. H., & Witte, G. *Effect of a token economy on perceived competence and locus of causality and their relationship with outcomes*. Unpublished manuscipt, Rutgers University, 1982.

Buhrmester, D. *The children's concern inventory*. Unpublished manuscript, University of Denver, 1980.

Butler, R. A. Discrimination learning by rhesus monkeys to visual exploration motivation. *Journal of Comparative and Physiological Psychology*, 1953, *46*, 95–98.

Butler, R. A. The effect of deprivation of visual incentives on visual exploration motivation in monkeys. *Journal of Comparative and Physiological Psychology*, 1957, *50*, 177–179.

Butler, R. A. The differential effect of visual and auditory incentives on the performance of monkeys. *American Journal of Psychology*, 1958, *71*, 591–593.

Butler, R. A., & Harlow, H. F. Discrimination learning and learning sets to visual exploration incentives. *Journal of General Psychology*, 1957, *57*, 257–264.

Calder, B. J., & Staw, B. M. The interaction of intrinsic and extrinsic motivation: Some methodological notes. *Journal of Personality and Social Psychology*, 1975, *31*, 76–80. (a)

Calder, B. J., & Staw, B .M. Self-perception of intrinsic and extrinsic motivation. *Journal of Personality and Social Psychology*, 1975, *31*, 599–605. (b)

Caldwell, D. F., O'Reilly, C. A., & Morris, J. H. Responses to an organizational reward: A field test of the sufficiency of justification hypothesis. *Journal of Personality and Social Psychology*, 1983, *44*, 506–514.

Carone, D. P. *The effects of positive verbal feedback on females' intrinsic motivation*. Unpublished master's thesis, University of Bridgeport, 1975.

Carver, C. S., & Scheier, M. F. *Attention and self-regulation: A control theory approach to human behavior*. New York: Springer-Verlag, 1981.

Chandler, C. *The effects of parenting techniques on the development of motivational orientations in children*. Unpublished doctoral dissertation, University of Denver, 1981.

Chandler, C. L., & Connell, J. P. *Children's intrinsic, extrinsic, and internalized motivation: A developmental study of behavioral regulation*. Unpublished manuscript, University of Rochester, 1984.

Collins, B. E. *Internalization: Towards a micro-social psychology of socialization or enduring behavior control*. Unpublished manuscript, University of California, Los Angeles, 1977.

Condry, J. Enemies of exploration: Self-initiated versus other-initiated learning. *Journal of Personality and Social Psychology*, 1977, *35*, 459–477.

Condry, J., & Koslowski, B. Can education be made "intrinsically interesting" to children? In L. Katz (Ed.), *Current topics in early childhood education*, (Vol. II). Norwood, N.J.: Ablex, 1979.

Connell, J. P. A new multidimensional measure of children's perceptions of control. *Child Development*, 1985, *6*, 281–293.

Connell, J. P., & Ryan, R. M. A developmental theory of motivation in the classroom. *Teacher Education Quarterly*, 1984, *11(4)*, 64–77.

Connell, J. P., & Ryan, R. M. *A theory and assessment of children's self-regulation within the academic domain*. Unpublished manuscript, University of Rochester, 1985.

Coopersmith, S. *The antecedents of self-esteem*. San Francisco: Freeman, 1967.

Covington, M. V., & Beery, R. G. *Self-worth and school learning*. New York: Holt, Rinehart, & Winston, 1976.

Crowne, D. P., & Marlowe, D. *The approval motive.* New York: Wiley, 1964.

Crutchfield, R. Conformity and creative thinking. In H. Gruber, C. Terrell, & M. Wertheimer (Eds.), *Contemporary approaches to creative thinking.* New York: Atherton, 1962.

Csikszentmihalyi, M. *Beyond boredom and anxiety.* San Francisco: Jossey-Bass, 1975.

Csikszentmihalyi, M. Intrinsic rewards and emergent motivation. In M. R. Lepper & D. Greene (Eds.), *The hidden costs of reward.* Hillsdale, N.J.: Erlbaum, 1978.

Curtis, B., Smith, R. E., & Smoll, F. L. Scrutinizing the skipper: A study of leadership behavior in the dugout. *Journal of Applied Psychology*, 1979, *64*, 391–400.

Daniel, T. L., & Esser, J. K. Intrinsic motivation as influenced by rewards, task interest, and task structure. *Journal of Applied Psychology*, 1980, *65*, 566–573.

Danner, F. W., & Lonky, E. A cognitive-developmental approach to the effects of rewards on intrinsic motivation. *Child Development*, 1981, *52*, 1043–1052.

Dashiell, J. F. A quantitative demonstration of animal drive. *Journal of Comparative Psychology*, 1925, *5*, 205–208.

Davis, L. E., & Cherns, A. B. (Eds.), *The quality of working life* (Vol. 1.). New York: Free Press, 1975.

Davis, R. T., Settlage, P. H., & Harlow, H. F. Performance of normal and brain-operated monkeys on mechanical puzzles with and without food incentive. *Journal of Genetic Psychology*, 1950, *77*, 305–311.

Davison, G. C., & Rosen, R. C. Lobeline and reduction of cigarette smoking. *Psychological Reports*, 1972, *31*, 443–456.

Davison, G. C., & Valins, S. Maintenance of self-attributed and drug attributed behavior change. *Journal of Personality and Social Psychology*, 1969, *11*, 25–33.

Davison, G. C., Tsujimoto, R. N., & Glaros, A. G. Attribution and the maintenance of behavior change in falling asleep. *Journal of Abnormal Psychology*, 1973, *82*, 124–133.

Deaux, K. Sex differences in social behavior. In T. Blass (Ed.), *Personality variables in social behavior.* Hillsdale, N.J.: Erlbaum, 1977.

deCharms, R. *Personal causation: The internal affective determinants of behavior.* New York: Academic Press, 1968.

deCharms, R. *Enhancing motivation: Change in the classroom.* New York: Irvington, 1976.

Deci, E. L. Effects of externally mediated rewards on intrinsic motivation. *Journal of Personality and Social Psychology*, 1971, *18*, 105–115.

Deci, E. L. Effects of contingent and non-contingent rewards and controls on intrinsic motivation. *Organizational Behavior and Human Performance*, 1972, *8*, 217–229. (a)

Deci, E. L. Intrinsic motivation, extrinsic reinforcement, and inequity. *Journal of Personality and Social Psychology*, 1972, *22*, 113–120. (b)

Deci, E. L. *Intrinsic motivation.* New York: Plenum Press, 1975.

Deci, E. L. *The psychology of self-determination.* Lexington, Mass.: D.C. Heath (Lexington Books), 1980.

Deci, E. L., & Cascio, W. F. *Changes in intrinsic motivation as a function of negative feedback and threats.* Paper presented at the meeting of the Eastern Psychological Association, Boston, April, 1972.

Deci, E. L., & Ryan, R. M. The empirical exploration of intrinsic motivational processes. In L. Berkowitz (Ed.), *Advances in experimental social psychology* (Vol. 13). New York: Academic Press, 1980. (a)

Deci, E. L., & Ryan, R. M. Self-determination theory: When mind mediates behavior. *Journal of Mind and Behavior*, 1980, *1*, 33–43. (b)

Deci, E. L., & Ryan, R. M. Curiosity and self-directed learning. In L. Katz (Ed.), *Current topics in early childhood education* (Vol. 4). Norwood, N.J.: Ablex, 1982. (a)

Deci, E. L., & Ryan, R. M. Intrinsic motivation to teach: Possibility and obstacles in our colleges and universities. In J. Bess (Ed.), *New directions in teaching and learning*. San Francisco: Jossey-Bass, 1982. (b)

Deci, E. L., & Ryan, R. M. The general causality orientations scale: Self-determination in personality. *Journal of Research in Personality*, 1985, *19*, 109–134.

Deci, E. L., Cascio, W. F., & Krusell, J. *Sex differences, verbal reinforcement, and intrinsic motivation*. Paper presented at the meeting of the Eastern Psychological Association, Washington, D.C., May, 1973.

Deci, E. L., Benware, C., & Landy, D. A. The attribution of motivation as a function of output and rewards. *Journal of Personality*, 1974, *42*, 652–667.

Deci, E. L., Cascio, W. F., & Krusell, J. Cognitive evaluation theory and some comments on the Calder and Staw critique. *Journal of Personality and Social Psychology*, 1975, *31*, 81–85.

Deci, E. L., Reis, H. T., Johnston, E. J., & Smith, R. Toward reconciling equity theory and insufficient justification. *Personality and Social Psychology Bulletin*. 1977, *3*, 224–227.

Deci, E. L., Porac, J. F., & Shapira, Z. *Effects of rewards on interest and intrinsic motivation for an extrinsic activity*. Unpublished manuscript, University of Rochester, 1978.

Deci, E. L., Betley, G., Kahle, J., Abrams, L., & Porac, J. When trying to win: Competition and intrinsic motivation. *Personality and Social Psychology Bulletin*, 1981, *7*, 79–83.

Deci, E. L., Nezlek, J., & Sheinman, L. Characteristics of the rewarder and intrinsic motivation of the rewardee. *Journal of Personality and Social Psychology*, 1981, *40*, 1–10.

Deci, E. L., Schwartz, A. J., Sheinman, L., & Ryan, R. M. An instrument to assess adults' orientations toward control versus autonomy with children: Reflections on intrinsic motivation and perceived competence. *Journal of Educational Psychology*, 1981, *73*, 642–650.

Deci, E. L., Spiegel, N. H., Ryan, R. M., Koestner, R., & Kauffman, M. The effects of performance standards on teaching styles: The behavior of controlling teachers. *Journal of Educational Psychology*, 1982, *74*, 852–859.

Deci, E. L., Connell, J. P., & Ryan, R. M. *Self-determination in a work organization*. Unpublished manuscript, University of Rochester, 1985.

DeLamarter, W. A., & Krepps, P. E. *Intrinsic motivation and self-reinforcement: The role of task interest*. Unpublished manuscript, Allegheny College, 1982.

Dember, W. N., & Earl, R. W. Analysis of exploratory, manipulatory, and curiosity behaviors. *Psychological Review*, 1957, *64*, 91–96.

Deutsch, M. Socially relevant science: Reflections on some studies of interpersonal conflict. *American Psychologist*, 1969, *24*, 1076–1092.

DeVellis, R. F., DeVellis, B. M., & McCauley, C. Vicarious acquisition of learned helplessness. *Journal of Personality and Social Psychology*, 1978, *36*, 894–899.

Dewald, P. A. *Psychotherapy: A dynamic approach* (2nd ed.). New York: Basic Books, 1969.

Dienstbier, R. A., & Leak, G. K. *Effects of monetary reward on maintenance of weight loss: An extension of the overjustification effect*. Paper presented at the American Psychological Association Convention, Washington, D.C., 1976.

Di Vitto, B., & McArthur, L. Z. Developmental differences in the use of distinctiveness, consensus, and consistency information for making causal attributions. *Developmental Psychology*, 1978, *14*, 474–482.

Dollinger, S. J., & Thelen, M. H. Overjustification and children's intrinsic motivation: Comparative effects of four rewards. *Journal of Personality and Social Psychology*, 1978, *36*, 1259–1269.

Driver, R. E., Ryan, R. M., & Deci, E. L. *Males' and females' responses to winning and losing a competition*. Unpublished manuscript, University of Rochester, 1985.

Dunham, P. The nature of reinforcing stimuli. In W. K. Honig & J. Staddon (Eds.), *Handbook of operant behavior*. Englewood Cliffs, N.J.: Prentice Hall, 1977.

Duval, S., & Wicklund, R. A. *A theory of objective self-awareness*. New York: Academic Press, 1972.

Dweck, C. S., & Elliot, E. S. Achievement motivation. In P. H. Mussen (Ed.), *Handbook of child psychology* (Vol. 4) (4th ed.). New York: Wiley, 1983.

Earn, B. M. Intrinsic motivation as a function of extrinsic financial rewards and subjects' locus of control. *Journal of Personality*, 1982, *50*, 360–373.

Eden, D. Intrinsic and extrinsic rewards and motives: Replication and extension with Kibbutz workers. *Journal of Applied Social Psychology*, 1975, *5*, 348–361.

Eisenberger, R. Explanation of rewards that do not reduce tissue needs. *Psychological Bulletin*, 1972, *77*, 319–339.

Eison, J. A., & Milton, O. *Assessing student attitudes toward grades and learning*. Unpublished manuscript, Roane State Community College, 1981.

Elkind, D. Cognitive growth cycles in mental development. In J. K. Cole (Ed.), *Nebraska symposium on motivation* (Vol. 19). Lincoln: University of Nebraska Press, 1971.

Engle, J.S. *Analytic interest psychology and synthetic philosophy*. Baltimore, Md.: King Brothers, 1904.

English, H., & English, A. C. *A comprehensive dictionary of psychological and psychoanalytic terms*. New York: David McKay, 1958.

Enzle, M. E., & Look, S. C. *Self versus other reward administration and the overjustification effect*. Paper presented at the meeting of the American Psychological Association, New York, September, 1979.

Enzle, M. E., & Ross, J. M. Increasing and decreasing intrinsic interest with contingent rewards: A test of cognitive evaluation theory. *Journal of Experimental Social Psychology*, 1978, *14*, 588–597.

Enzle, M. E., Hansen, R. D., & Lowe, C. A. Causal attributions in the mixed motive game: Effects of facilitory and inhibitory environmental forces. *Journal of Personality and Social Psychology*, 1975, *31*, 50–54.

Erikson, E. H. *Childhood and society*. New York: Norton, 1950.

Farr, J. L. Task characteristics, reward contingency, and intrinsic motivation. *Organizational Behavior and Human Performance*, 1976, *16*, 294–307.

Farr, J. L., Vance, R. J., & McIntyre, R. M. Further examination of the relationship between reward contingency and intrinsic motivation. *Organizational Behavior and Human Performance*, 1977, *20*, 31–53.

Fazio, R. H. On the self-perception explanation of the overjustification effect: The role of the salience of initial attitude. *Journal of Experimental Social Psychology*, 1981, *17*, 417–426.

Feather, N. T. The relationship between persistence at a task to expectations of success and achievement related motives. *Journal of Abnormal and Social Psychology*, 1961, *63*, 552–561.

Fegley, B. J. *The effects of contingent versus noncontingent instruction on children's responses to selected radiologic procedures*. Unpublished doctoral dissertation, University of Rochester, 1984.

Feingold, B. D., & Mahoney, M. J. Reinforcement effects on intrinsic interest: Undermining the overjusification hypothesis. *Behavior Therapy*, 1975, *6*, 367–377.

Fenichel, O. *The psychoanalytic theory of neurosis*. New York: Norton, 1945.

Fenigstein, A., Scheier, M. F., & Buss, A. H. Public and private self-consciousness: Assessment and theory. *Journal of Consulting and Clinical Psychology*, 1975, *43*, 522–527.

Festinger, L. *A theory of cognitive dissonance*. Evanston, Ill.: Row, Peterson, 1957.

Fisher, C. D. The effects of personal control, competence, and extrinsic reward systems on intrinsic motivation. *Organizational Behavior and Human Performance*, 1978, *21*, 273–288.

Fiske, D. W., & Maddi, S. R. *Functions of varied experience*. Homewood, Ill.: Dorsey, 1961.

Flavell, J. *The developmental psychology of Jean Piaget.* Princeton: Van Nostrand, 1963.

Flavell, J. *The development of role-taking and communication skills in children.* New York: Wiley, 1968.

Flavell, J. *Cognitive development.* Englewood Cliffs, N.J.: Prentice-Hall, 1977.

Flavell, J. H., & Wohlwill, J. F. Formal and functional aspects of cognitive development. In D. Elkind & J. H. Flavell (Eds.), *Studies in cognitive development: Essays in honor of Jean Piaget.* New York: Oxford University Press, 1969.

Fowler, H. *Curiosity and exploratory behavior.* New York: Macmillan, 1965.

Fowler, H. Satiation and curiosity. In K. W. Spence & J. T. Spence (Eds.), *Psychology of learning and motivation* (Vol. 1). New York: Academic Press, 1967.

Frank, J. D. Recent studies of the level of aspiration. *Psychological Bulletin,* 1941, *38,* 218–226.

Frank, J. D. *Persuasion and healing: A comparative study of psychotherapy.* Baltimore: Johns Hopkins Press, 1961.

Franks, C. M., & Wilson, G. T. (Eds.), *Annual review of behavior therapy: Theory and practice* (Vol. III). New York: Brunner/Mazel, 1975.

Franks, C. M., & Wilson, G. T. Behavior therapy: An overview. In C. M. Franks & G. T. Wilson (Eds.), *Annual review of behavior therapy: Theory and practice* (Vol. VII). New York: Brunner/Mazel, 1979. (a)

Franks, C. M., & Wilson, G. T. Progressive relaxation-training, systematic desensitization, flooding, and modeling. In C. M. Franks & G. T. Wilson (Eds.) *Annual review of behavior therapy: Theory and practice* (Vol. VII). New York: Brunner/Mazel, 1979. (b)

French, T. M. *The integration of behavior.* Chicago: University of Chicago Press, 1958.

Freud, S. Instincts and their vicissitudes. In *Collected Papers* (Vol. 4). London: Hogarth, 1925 (Originally published, 1915).

Freud, S. *A general introduction to psycho-analysis.* New York: Perma Giants, 1949. (Originally published, 1917.)

Freud, S. On narcissism. In *The standard edition of the complete works of Sigmund Freud* (Vol. 14). London: Hogarth Press, 1957. (Originally published, 1914.)

Freud, S. *The ego and the id.* New York: Norton, 1962. (Originally published, 1923.)

Freud, S. *New introductory lectures on psychoanalysis.* New York: Norton, 1964. (Originally published, 1933.)

Freud, S. *The question of lay analysis.* New York: Norton, 1969. (Originally published, 1926.)

Galbraith, J., & Cummings, L.L. An empirical investigation of the motivational determinants of task performance. *Organizational Behavior and Human Performance,* 1967, *2,* 237–257.

Gallwey, W. T. *The inner game of tennis.* New York: Random House, 1974.

Gallwey, W. T. *The inner game of golf.* New York: Random House, 1981.

Gallwey, W. T., & Kriegel, R. *Inner skiing.* New York: Random House, 1977.

Garbarino, J. The impact of anticipated reward upon cross-aged tutoring. *Journal of Personality and Social Psychology,* 1975, *32,* 421–428.

Garber, J., & Seligman, M. E. P. (Eds.), *Human Helplessness.* New York: Academic Press, 1980.

Garvey, C. *Play.* Cambridge, Mass.: Harvard University Press, 1977.

Gately, M. J. *Manipulation drive in experimentally naive rhesus monkeys.* Unpublished master's thesis, University of Wisconsin—Madison, 1950.

Gibson, J. J. *The ecological approach to visual perception.* Boston: Houghton-Mifflin, 1979.

Ginott, H. *Group psychotherapy with children: The theory and practice of play-therapy.* New York: McGraw-Hill, 1961.

Glanzer, M. Stimulus satiation: An explanation of spontaneous alternation and related phenomena. *Psychological Review,* 1953, *60,* 257–268.

Glanzer, M. Curiosity, exploratory drive, and stimulus satiation. *Psychological Bulletin*, 1958, *55*, 302–315.

Glass, D. C., & Singer, J. E. *Urban stress: Experiments on noise and social stressors.* New York: Academic Press, 1972.

Goldstein, A. P., Lopez, M., & Greenleaf, D. O. Introduction. In A. P. Goldstein & F. H. Kanfer (Eds.), *Maximizing treatment gains: Transfer enhancement in psychotherapy.* New York: Academic Press, 1979.

Goldstein, K. *The organism.* New York: American Book Co., 1939.

Gorn, G. J., & Goldberg, M. E. The effects of intrinsic and extrinsic rewards in a risk-taking situation. *Journal of Experimental Social Psychology*, 1977, *13*, 333–339.

Gottfried, A. E. *Measuring children's academic intrinsic motivation: A psychometric approach.* Paper presented at the Meeting of the American Psychological Association, Los Angeles, August, 1981.

Gottfried, A. E. Relationships between academic intrinsic motivation and anxiety in children and young adolescents. *Journal of School Psychology*, 1982, *20*, 205–215.

Green, L. C. *Intrinsic motivation in primary school children: The effects of gender, developmental level and teacher orientation toward autonomy versus control.* Unpublished master's thesis, University of Cape Town, South Africa, 1983.

Greene, D., & Lepper, M. R. Effects of extrinsic rewards on children's subsequent intrinsic interest. *Child Development*, 1974, *45*, 1141–1145.

Greene, D., Sternberg, B., & Lepper, M. R. Overjustification in a token economy. *Journal of Personality and Social Psychology*, 1976, *34*, 1219–1234.

Greenspan, S. I. *Intelligence and adaptation.* New York: International Universities Press, 1979.

Grolnick, W. S., & Ryan, R. M. *Self-regulation and motivation in children's learning: An experimental investigation.* Unpublished manuscript, University of Rochester, 1985.

Grolnick, W., Frodi, A., & Bridges, L. Maternal control styles and the mastery motivation of one-year-olds. *Infant Mental Health Journal*, 1984, *5*, 72–82.

Guzzo, R. A. Types of rewards, cognitions, and work motivation. *Academy of Management Review*, 1979, *4*, 75–86.

Haber, R. N. Discrepancy from adaptation level as a source of affect. *Journal of Experimental Psychology*, 1958, *56*, 370–375.

Hackman, J. R., & Oldham, G. R. Development of the Job Diagnostic Survey. *Journal of Applied Psychology*, 1975, *60*, 159–170.

Haddad, Y. S. *The effect of informational versus controlling verbal feedback on self-determination and preference for challenge.* Unpublished doctoral dissertation, University of Rochester, 1982.

Haines, D. B., & McKeachie, W. J. Cooperation versus competitive discussion methods in teaching introductory psychology. *Journal of Educational Psychology*, 1967, *58*, 386–390.

Halliwell, W. The effect of cognitive development on children's perceptions of intrinsically and extrinsically motivated behavior. In D. Landers & R. Christina (Eds.) *Psychology of motor behavior and sport—1978.* Champaign, Ill.: Human Kinetics Press, 1979.

Hamner, W. C., & Foster, L. W. Are intrinsic and extrinsic rewards additive: A test of Deci's cognitive evaluation theory of task motivation. *Organizational Behavior and Human Performance*, 1975, *14*, 398–415.

Harackiewicz, J. The effects of reward contingency and performance feedback on intrinsic motivation. *Journal of Personality and Social Psychology*, 1979, *37*, 1352–1363.

Harackiewicz, J., Manderlink, G., & Sansone, C. Rewarding pinball wizardry: The effects of evaluation on intrinsic interest. *Journal of Personality and Social Psychology*, 1984, *47*, 287–300.

Harlow, H. F. Learning and satiation of response in intrinsically motivated complex puzzle performance by monkeys. *Journal of Comparative and Physiological Psychology*, 1950, *43*, 289–294.

Harlow, H. F. Motivation as a factor in the acquisition of new responses. In *Current theory and research on motivation*. Lincoln: University of Nebraska Press, 1953. (a)

Harlow, H. F. Mice, monkeys, men, and motives. *Psychological Review*, 1953, *60*, 23–32. (b)

Harlow, H. F., Harlow, M. K., & Meyer, D. R. Learning motivated by a manipulation drive. *Journal of Experimental Psychology*, 1950, *40*, 228–234.

Harter, S. Pleasure derived by children from cognitive challenge and mastery. *Child Development*, 1974, *45*, 661–669.

Harter, S. Effectance motivation reconsidered: Toward a developmental model. *Human Development*, 1978, *1*, 34–64. (a)

Harter, S. Pleasure derived from optimal challenge and the effects of extrinsic rewards on children's difficulty level choices. *Child Development*, 1978, *49*, 788–799. (b)

Harter, S. A model of intrinsic mastery motivation in children: Individual differences and developmental changes. *Minnesota Symposium on Child Psychology* (Vol. 14). Hillsdale, N.J.: Erlbaum, 1981. (a)

Harter, S. A new self-report scale of intrinsic versus extrinsic orientation in the classroom: Motivational and informational components. *Developmental Psychology*, 1981, *17*, 300–312. (b)

Harter, S. The perceived competence scale for children. *Child Development*, 1982, *53*, 87–97.

Harter, S., & Connell, J. P. A comparison of alternative models of the relationships between academic achievement and children's perceptions of competence, control, and motivational orientation. In J. Nicholls (Ed.), *The development of achievement-related cognitions and behaviors*. Greenwich, Conn.: JAI Press, 1984.

Hartmann, H. *Ego psychology and the problem of adaptation*. New York: International Universities Press, 1958. (Originally published, 1939.)

Hartmann, H., & Loewenstein, R. M. Notes on the superego. *The Psychoanalytic Study of the Child*, 1962, *17*, 42–81.

Hebb, D. O. Drives and the c.n.s. (conceptual nervous system). *Psychological Review*, 1955, *62*, 243–254.

Heider, F. *The psychology of interpersonal relations*. New York: Wiley, 1958.

Heider, F. The Gestalt theory of motivation. In M. R. Jones (Ed.), *Nebraska symposium on motivation* (Vol. 8). Lincoln: University of Nebraska Press, 1960.

Helmreich, R. L. *The three faces of n-Ach*. Paper presented at the meeting of the Society for Experimental Social Psychology, Pittsburgh, October, 1983.

Helmreich, R. L., & Spence, J. T. The Work and Family Orientation Questionnaire: An objective instrument to assess components of achievement motivation and attitudes toward family and career. *JSAS Catalog of Selected Documents in Psychology*, 1978, *8*, 35.

Helson, H. *Adaptation-level theory*. New York: Harper & Row, 1964.

Hendrick, I. Instinct and the ego during infancy. *Psychoanalytic Quarterly*, 1942, *11*, 33–58.

Hennessey, B. *Effects of reward and task label on children's creativity in three domains*. Unpublished manuscript, Brandeis University, 1982.

Heron, W., Doane, B. K., & Scott, T. H. Visual disturbances after prolonged isolation. *Canadian Journal of Psychology*, 1956, *10*, 13–18.

Hiroto, D. S. Locus of control and learned helplessness. *Journal of Experimental Psychology*, 1974, *102*, 187–193.

Hiroto, D. S., & Seligman, M. E. P. Generality of learned helplessness in man. *Journal of Personality and Social Psychology*, 1975, *31*, 311–327.

Holt, J. *How children fail*. New York: Dell, 1964.

Hom, H. L., & Maxwell, F. R. *Duration of detrimental effects of task perception in children*. Paper presented at the Meeting of the Society for Research in Child Development, San Francisco, April, 1979.

Hull, C. L. *Principles of behavior: An introduction to behavior theory*. New York: Appleton-Century-Crofts, 1943.

Hunt, J. McV. Motivation inherent in information processing and action. In O. J. Harvey (Ed.), *Motivation and social interaction*. New York: Ronald, 1963.

Hunt, J. McV. Intrinsic motivation and its role in psychological development. In D. Levine (Ed.), *Nebraska symposium on motivation* (Vol. 13). Lincoln, NB: University of Nebraska Press, 1965.

Hunt, J. McV. The epigenesis of intrinsic motivation and early cognitive learning. In R. N. Haber (Ed.), *Current research in motivation*. New York: Holt, Rinehart & Winston, 1966.

Hunt, J. McV. Intrinsic motivation: Information and circumstances. In H. M. Schroeder & P. Suedfeld (Eds.), *Personality theory and information processing*. New York: Ronald, 1971. (a)

Hunt, J. McV. Toward a history of intrinsic motivation. In H. I. Day, D. E. Berlyne, & D. E. Hunt (Eds.), *Intrinsic motivation: A new direction in education*. Toronto: Holt, Rinehart & Winston of Canada, 1971. (b)

Hunt, J. McV. *Sequential order and plasticity in early psychological development*. Paper presented at the meeting of the Jean Piaget Society, Philadelphia, May, 1972.

Hunt, J. McV. Implications of sequential order and hierarchy in early psychological development. In B. Z. Friedlander, G. M. Sterritt, & G. E. Kirk (Eds.), *Exceptional infant* (Vol. 3). New York: Brunner/Mazel, 1975. (a)

Hunt, J. McV. Psychological assessment in education and social class. In B. Z. Friedlander, G. M. Sterritt, & G. E. Kirk (Eds.), *Exceptional infant* (Vol. 3). New York: Brunner/Mazel, 1975. (b)

Inagaki, K., & Hatano, G. *Effects of external evaluation on reading comprehension and intrinsic interest*. Paper presented at the meeting of the American Education Research Association, New Orleans, April, 1984.

Irwin, F. *Intentional behavior and motivation: A cognitive theory*. New York: Lippincott, 1971.

Isaac, W. Evidence for a sensory drive in monkeys. *Psychological Reports*, 1962, *11*, 175–181.

Iso-Ahola, A. *The social psychology of leisure and recreation*. Dubuque, Ia.: W. C. Brown, 1980.

Izard, C. *Human emotions*. New York: Plenum Press, 1977.

Izard, C. E., Dougherty, F. E., Bloxom, B. M., & Kotsch, W. E. *The differential emotions scale: A method of measuring the subjective experience of discrete emotions*. Unpublished manuscript, Vanderbilt University, 1974.

James, W. *The principles of psychology*. New York: Holt, 1890.

Janis, I. L., & Field, P. B. The Janis and Field personality questionnaire. In C. I. Hovland & I. L. Janis (Eds.), *Personality and persuasibility*. New Haven, Conn.: Yale University Press, 1959.

Jelsma, B. M. *Adult control behaviors: The interaction between orientation toward control in women and activity level of children*. Unpublished doctoral dissertation, University of Rochester, 1982.

Jenkins, C. D., Rosenman, R. H., & Friedman, M. Development of an objective psychological test for the determination of the coronary prone behavior pattern in employed men. *Journal of Chronic Diseases*, 1967, *20*, 371–379.

Johnson, D. W. Cooperativeness and social perspective taking. *Journal of Personality and Social Psychology*, 1975, *31*, 241–244.

Johnson, D.W., & Johnson, R. Instructional goal structure: Cooperative, competitive, or individualistic. *Review of Educational Research,* 1974, *44,* 213–240.

Jones, A. Supplementary report: Information deprivation and irrelevant drive as determiners of an instrumental response. *Journal of Experimental Psychology,* 1961, *62,* 310–311.

Jones, A., Wilkinson, H. J., & Braden, I. Information deprivation as a motivational variable. *Journal of Experimental Psychology,* 1961, *62,* 126–137.

Jones, E. E., & Berglass, S. Control of attributions about the self through self-handicapping strategies: The appeal of alcohol and the role of underachievement. *Personality and Social Psychology Bulletin.* 1978, *4,* 200–206.

Jones, E. E., & Davis, K. E. From acts to dispositions. In L. Berkowitz (Ed.), *Advances in experimental social psychology* (Vol. 2). New York: Academic Press, 1965.

Jones, E. E., & Nisbett, R. E. *The actor and the observer: Divergent perceptions of the causes of behavior.* New York: General Learning Press, 1971.

Julian, J. W., & Perry, F. A. Cooperation contrasted with intra-group and inter-group competition. *Sociometry,* 1967, *30,* 79–90.

Jung, C. G. *Contributions to analytic psychology.* New York: Harcourt, Brace & World, 1928.

Kagan, J. Motives and development. *Journal of Personality and Social Psychology,* 1972, *22,* 51–66.

Kahn, R. L.*Work and health.* New York: Wiley, 1981.

Kanfer, F. H. Self-management methods. In F.H. Kanfer & A.P. Goldstein (Eds.). *Helping people change: A textbook of methods.* New York: Pergamon, 1975.

Kanfer, F. H. The many faces of self-control, or behavior modification changes its focus. In R. B. Stuart (Ed.), *Behavioral self-management: Strategies, techniques, and outcomes.* New York: Brunner/Mazel, 1977.

Kanfer, F. H. Self-management: Strategies and tactics. In A. P. Goldstein & F. H. Kanfer (Eds.), *Maximizing treatment gains: Transfer enhancement in psychotherapy.* New York: Academic Press, 1979.

Kanfer, F. H., & Grimm, L. G. Freedom of choice and behavioral change. *Journal of Consulting and Clinical Psychology,* 1978, *46,* 873–878.

Kanfer, F. H., & Karoly, P. Self-control: A behavioristic excursion into the lion's den. *Behavior Therapy,* 1972, *3,* 398–416.

Kaplan, H. B., & Pokorny, A. D. Self-derogation and psychosocial adjustment. *Journal of Nervous and Mental Disease,* 1969, *149,* 421–434.

Karniol, R., & Ross, M. The development of causal attributions in social perception. *Journal of Personality and Social Psychology,* 1976, *34,* 455–464.

Karniol, R., & Ross, M. The effect of performance-relevant and performance-irrelevant rewards on children's intrinsic motivation. *Child Development,* 1977, *48,* 482–487.

Kast, A. D. *Sex differences in intrinsic motivation: A developmental analysis of the effects of social rewards.* Unpublished doctoral dissertation, Fordham University, 1983.

Kazdin, A. E., & Bootzin, R. T. The token economy: An evaluative review. *Journal of Applied Behavior Analysis,* (Monograph No. 1), 1972, *5*(3).

Keller, F. S. *Learning: Reinforcement theory* (2nd ed.). New York: Random House, 1969.

Kelley, H. H. Attribution theory in social psychology. In D. Levine (Ed.), *Nebraska symposium on motivation* (Vol. 15). Lincoln: University of Nebraska Press, 1967.

Kelley, H.H. *Attribution in social interaction.* New York: General Learning Press, 1971.

Kelley, H. H. *Causal schemata and the attribution process.* New York: General Learning Press Module, 1972.

Kelley, H. H., & Thibaut, J. W. Group problem solving. In G. Lindzey & E. Aronson (Eds.), *The handbook of social psychology* (Vol. 4). Reading, Mass.: Addison-Wesley, 1969.

Kelman, H. C. Processes of attitude change. *Public Opinion Quarterly,* 1961, *25,* 57–78.

Kernis, M. H. *Motivational orientations, anger, and aggression in males.* Unpublished doctoral dissertation, University of Rochester, 1982.

Kiesler, C. A., & Sakamura, J. A test of a model for commitment. *Journal of Personality and Social Psychology*, 1966, *11*, 321–327.

King, K. B. *Coping with cardiac surgery.* Unpublished doctoral dissertation, University of Rochester, 1984.

Kingsley, R.G., & Wilson, G.T. Behavior therapy for obesity: A comparative investigation for long-term efficacy. *Journal of Consulting and Clinical Psychology*, 1977, *45*, 288–298.

Kirschenbaum, D. S., & Karoly, P. When self-regulation fails: Tests of some preliminary hypotheses. *Journal of Consulting and Clinical Psychology*, 1977, *45*, 1116–1125.

Kite, W. R. *Attribution of causality as a function of the use of reward and punishment.* Unpublished doctoral dissertation, Stanford University, 1964.

Kobasa, S. C. O., & Puccetti, M. C. Personality and social resources in stress resistance. *Journal of Personality and Social Psychology*, 1983, *45*, 839–850.

Koch, S. Behavior as "intrinsically" regulated: Work notes toward a pre-theory of phenomena called "motivational." In M. R. Jones (Ed.). *Nebraska symposium on motivation* (Vol. 4). Lincoln: University of Nebraska Press, 1956.

Koestner, R., Ryan, R. M., Bernieri, F., & Holt, K. Setting limits on children's behavior: The differential effects of controlling versus informational styles on intrinsic motivation and creativity. *Journal of Personality*, 1984, *52*, 233–248.

Kohlberg, L. Stage and sequence: The cognitive-developmental approach to socialization. In D. A. Goslin (Ed.), *Handbook of socialization theory and research.* Chicago: Rand McNally, 1969.

Kopel, S., & Arkowitz, H. The role of attribution and self-perception in behavior change: Implications for behavior therapy. *Genetic Psychology Monographs*, 1975, *92*, 175–212.

Kruglanski, A. W. The endogenous-exogenous partition in attribution theory. *Psychological Review*, 1975, *82*, 387–406.

Kruglanski, A. W., Friedman, I., & Zeevi, G. The effects of extrinsic incentive on some qualitative aspects of task performance. *Journal of Personality*, 1971, *39*, 606–617.

Kruglanski, A., Alon, S., & Lewis, T. Retrospective misattribution and task enjoyment. *Journal of Experimental Social Psychology*, 1972, *8*, 493–501.

Kruglanski, A. W., Riter, A., Amitai, A., Margolin, B. , Shabtai, L. , & Zaksh, D. Can money enhance intrinsic motivation?: A test of the content-consequences hypothesis. *Journal of Personality and Social Psychology*, 1975, *31*, 744–750.

Kruglanski, A. W., Stein, C., & Riter, A. Contingencies of exogenous reward and task performance: On the "minimax" strategy in instrumental behavior. *Journal of Applied Social Psychology*, 1977, *7*, 141–148.

Kuhn, T. S. The essential tension: Tradition and innovation in scientific research. In F. Barron & C. W. Taylor (Eds.), *Scientific creativity: Its recognition and development.* New York: Wiley, 1963.

Kun, A. Development of the magnitude-covariation and compensation schemata in ability and effort attributions of performance. *Child Development*, 1977, *48*, 862–873.

Kuypers, D. S., Becker, W. C., & O'Leary, K. D. How to make a token system fail. *Exceptional Children*, 1968, *35*, 101–109.

Langer, E. J. The illusion of control. *Journal of Personality and Social Psychology*, 1975, *32*, 311–328.

Langer, E. J., & Rodin, J. The effects of choice and personal responsibility for the aged: A field experiment in an institutional setting. *Journal of Personality and Social Psychology*, 1976, *34*, 191–198.

Langer, E., & Saegert, S. Crowding and cognitive control. *Journal of Personality and Social Psychology*, 1977, *35*, 175–182.

Lanzetta, J. T. Information acquisition in decision making. In O. J. Harvey (Ed.), *Motivation and social interaction*. New York: Ronald, 1963.

Lanzetta, J. T. The motivational properties of uncertainty. In H. I. Day, D. E. Berlyne, & D. E. Hunt (Eds.), *Intrinsic motivation: A new direction in education*. Toronto: Holt, Rinehart & Winston of Canada, 1971.

Laughlin, P. R., & McGlynn, R. P. Cooperative versus competitive concept attainment as a function of sex and stimulus display. *Journal of Social Psychology*, 1967, 7, 498–501.

Lawler, E. E. Strategies for improving the quality of work life. *American Psychologist*, 1982, 37, 486–493.

Lawler, E. E., & Hackman, J. R. Impact of employee participation in the development of pay incentive plans: A field experiment. *Journal of Applied Psychology*, 1969, 53, 467–471.

Le Compte, M. Learning to work: The hidden curriculum of the classroom. *Anthropology and Education Quarterly*, 1978, 9, 22–37.

Lee, D. Y., Syrnyk, R., & Hallschmid, C. Self-perception of intrinsic and extrinsic motivation: Effects on institutionalized mentally retarded adolescents. *American Journal of Mental Deficiency*, 1977, 81, 331-337.

Lepper, M. R. Social-control processes and the internalization of social values: An attributional perspective. In E. T. Higgins, D. N. Ruble, & W. W. Hartup (Eds.), *Social cognition and social development*. New York: Cambridge University Press, 1983.

Lepper, M. R., & Greene, D. Turning play into work: Effects of adult surveillance and extrinsic rewards on children's intrinsic motivation. *Journal of Personality and Social Psychology*, 1975, 31, 479–486.

Lepper, M. R., & Greene, D. On understanding "overjustification": A reply to Reiss and Sushinsky. *Journal of Personality and Social Psychology*, 1976, 33, 25–35.

Lepper, M. R., Greene, D., & Nisbett, R.E. Undermining children's intrinsic interest with extrinsic rewards: A test of the "overjustification" hypothesis. *Journal of Personality and Social Psychology*, 1973, 28, 129–137.

Lepper, M. R., Sagotsky, G., Dafoe, J. L., & Greene, D. Consequences of superfluous social constraints: Effects on young children's social inferences and subsequent intrinsic interest. *Journal of Personality and Social Psychology*, 1982, 42, 51–65.

Leuba, C. Toward some integration of learning theories: The concept of optimal stimulation. *Psychological Reports*, 1955, 1, 27–33.

Levenson, H. *Distinctions within the concept of internal-external control expectancies in a reformatory population*. Paper presented at the meetings of the American Psychological Association, Honolulu, Hawaii, 1972.

Levenson, H. Multidimensional locus of control in psychiatric patients. *Journal of Consulting and Clinical Psychology*, 1973, 41, 397–404. (a)

Levenson, H. Perceived parental antecedents of internal, powerful others, and chance locus-of-control orientations. *Developmental Psychology*, 1973, 9, 260–265. (b)

Levine, F. M., & Fasnacht, G. Token rewards may lead to token learning. *American Psychologist*, 1974, 29, 816–820.

Lewin, K. *Principles of topological psychology*. New York: McGraw-Hill, 1936.

Lewin, K. *The conceptual representation and measurement of psychological forces*. Durham, N.C.: Duke University Press, 1938.

Lewin, K. *Field theory in social science*. New York: Harper, 1951. (a)

Lewin, K. Intention, will, and need. In D. Rapaport (Ed.), *Organization and pathology of thought*. New York: Columbia University Press, 1951. (b)

Lewis, M., & Goldberg, S. Perceptual-cognitive development in infancy: A generalized expectancy model as a function of the mother–infant interaction. *Merrill-Palmer Quarterly*, 1969, 15, 81–100.

Liberman, B. L. The role of mastery in psychotherapy: Maintenance of improvement and prescriptive change. In J. D. Frank, R. Hoehn-Saric, S. D. Imber, B. L. Liberman, & A. R. Stone (Eds.), *The effective ingredients of successful psychotherapy.* New York: Brunner/Mazel, 1978.

Liem, G. R. Performance and satisfaction as affected by personal control over salient decisions. *Journal of Personality and Social Psychology,* 1975, *31,* 232-240.

Likert, R. *The human organization.* New York: McGraw-Hill, 1967.

Locke, E. A. Toward a theory of task performance and incentives. *Organizational Behavior and Human Performance,* 1968, *3,* 157–189.

Loevinger, J. *Ego development.* San Francisco: Jossey-Bass, 1976. (a)

Loevinger, J. Origins of conscience. In M. M. Gill & P. S. Holzman (Eds.), *Psychology versus metapsychology: Psychoanalytic essays in memory of George S. Klein* (Psychological Issues Monograph No. 36). New York: International Universities Press, 1976. (b)

Loevinger, J. On the self and predicting behavior. In R. Zucker, J. Aronoff, & A. Rabin (Eds.), *Personality and the prediction of behavior.* New York: Academic Press, 1984.

Lonky, E., & Reihman, J. *Cognitive evaluation theory, locus of control, and positive verbal feedback.* Paper presented at the meeting of the American Psychological Association, Montreal, September, 1980.

Lopez, E. M. Increasing intrinsic motivation with performance-contingent reward. *Journal of Psychology,* 1981, *108,* 59–65.

Loveland, K. K., & Olley, J. G. The effect of external reward on interest and quality of task performance in children of high and low intrinsic motivation. *Child Development,* 1979, *50,* 1207–1210.

Lowin, A. Participative decision making: A model, literature critique, and prescriptions for research. *Organizational Behavior and Human Performance,* 1968, *3,* 68–106.

Luchins, A. S. Mechanization in problem solving: The effect of Einstellung. *Psychological Monographs,* 1942, *54* (6, Whole No. 248).

Lucker, G. W., Rosenfield, D., Sikes, J., & Aronson, E. Performance in the interdependent classroom: A field study. *American Educational Research Journal,* 1977, *13,* 115–123.

Luschen, G. Cooperation, association and contest. *Journal of Conflict Resolution,* 1970, *14,* 21–34.

Luyten, H., & Lens, W. The effect of earlier experience and reward contingencies on intrinsic motivation. *Motivation and Emotion,* 1981, *5,* 25–36.

Maehr, M. L. Continuing motivation: An analysis of a seldom considered educational outcome. *Review of Educational Research,* 1976, *46,* 443–462.

Magill, R. A., Ash, M. J., & Smoll, F. L. *Children in sport: A contemporary anthology.* Champaign, Ill.: Human Kinetics Press, 1978.

Mahoney, M. J. *Cognition and behavior modification.* Cambridge, Mass.: Ballinger, 1974.

Mahoney, M. J. Cognitive skills and athletic performance. In P. C. Kendall & S. D. Hollon (Eds.), *Cognitive behavioral interventions: Theory, research and procedures.* New York: Academic Press, 1979.

Malone, T. W. Toward a theory of intrinsically motivating instruction. *Cognitive Science,* 1981, *4,* 333–369.

Manderlink, G., & Harackiewicz, J. M. Proximal vs distal goal setting and intrinsic motivation. *Journal of Personality and Social Psychology,* 1984, *47,* 918–928.

Margolis, R. B., & Mynatt, C. R. *The effects of self and externally administered reward on high base rate behavior.* Unpublished manuscript, Bowling Green State University, 1979.

Marrow, A. J., Bowers, D. G., & Seashore, S. E. *Management by participation.* New York: Harper & Row, 1967.

Martens, R. *Social psychology and physical activity.* New York: Harper & Row, 1975.

Martin, J. A. Effects of positive and negative adult–child interactions on children's task performance and task preferences. *Journal of Experimental Child Psychology*, 1977, *23*, 493–502.

Martin, M., Burkholder, R., Rosenthal, R. L., Tharp, R. G., & Thorne, G. L. Programming behavior change and reintegration into school milieux of extreme adolescent deviates. *Behaviour Research and Therapy*, 1968, *6*, 371–383.

Maslow, A. H. A theory of human motivation. *Psychological Review*, 1943, *50*, 370–396.

Maslow, A. H. Deficiency motivation and growth motivation. In M.R. Jones (Ed.), *Nebraska symposium on motivation* (Vol. 3). Lincoln: University of Nebraska Press, 1955.

Maslow, A. H. *Motivation and personality* (2nd ed.). New York: Harper &Row, 1970.

Mawhinney, T. C. Intrinsic × extrinsic motivation: Perspectives from behaviorism. *Organizational Behavior and Human Performance*, 1979, *24*, 411–440.

McClelland, D. C. Risk taking in children with high and low need for achievement. In J. W. Atkinson (Ed.), *Motives in fantasy, action, and society*. Princeton, N.J.: van Nostrand, 1958.

McClelland, D. C. Toward a theory of motive acquisition. *American Psychologist*, 1965, *20*, 321–333.

McClelland, D. C., Atkinson, J. W., Clark, R. W., & Lowell, E. L. *The achievement motive*. New York: Appleton-Century-Crofts, 1953.

McDougall, W. *Social psychology*. New York: Luce & Co., 1908.

McFall, R. M. Effects of self-monitoring on normal smoking behavior. *Journal of Consulting and Clinical Psychology*, 1970, *35*, 135–142.

McGraw, K. O. The detrimental effects of reward on performance: A literature review and a prediction model. In M. R. Lepper & D. Greene (Eds.), *The hidden costs of reward*. Hillsdale, N.J.: Erlbaum, 1978.

McGraw, K. O., & Fiala, J. Undermining the Zeigarnik effect: Another hidden cost of reward. *Journal of Personality*, 1982, *50*, 58–66.

McGraw, K. O., & McCullers, J. C. Evidence of a detrimental effect of extrinsic incentives on breaking a mental set. *Journal of Experimental Social Psychology*, 1979, *15*, 285–294.

McGregor, D. *The human side of enterprise*. New York: McGraw-Hill, 1960.

McLoyd, V. C. The effects of extrinsic rewards of differential value on high- and low-intrinsic interest. *Child Development*, 1979, *50*, 1010–1019.

McMullin, D. J., & Steffen, J. J. Intrinsic motivation and performance standards. *Social Behavior and Personality*, 1982, *10*, 47–56.

Meichenbaum, D. H., Bowers, K. S., & Ross, R. R. Modification of classroom behavior of institutionalized female adolescent offenders. *Behaviour Research and Therapy*, 1968, *6*, 343–353.

Meissner, W. W. *Internalization in psychoanalysis*. New York: International Universities Press, 1981.

Meyer, H. H. The pay-for-performance dilemma. *Organizational Dynamics*, Winter 1975, 39–50.

Miller, G. A., Galanter, E., & Pribram, K. H. *Plans and the structure of behavior*. New York: Holt, 1960.

Miller, L. B., & Estes, B. W. Monetary reward and motivation in discrimination learning. *Journal of Experimental Psychology*, 1961, *61*, 501–504.

Miller, S. M. Why having control reduces stress: If I can stop the roller coaster, I don't want to get off. In J. Garber & M. E. P. Seligman (Eds.), *Human helplessness*. New York: Academic Press, 1980.

Miller, W. R., & Arkowitz, H. Anxiety and perceived causation in social success and failure experiences: Disconfirmation of an attribution hypothesis in two experiments. *Journal of Abnormal Psychology*, 1977, *86*, 665–668.

Mischel, W., Ebbesen, E., & Zeiss, A. R. Selective attention to the self: Situational and dispositional determinants. *Journal of Personality and Social Psychology*, 1973, *27*, 129–142.

Mitchell, T. R. Expectancy models of job satisfaction, occupational preference and effort: A theoretical, methodological, and empirical appraisal. *Psychological Bulletin*, 1974, *81* 1053–1077.

Montessori, M. *Spontaneous activity in education.* New York: Schocken, 1965.

Montessori, M. *The discovery of the child.* New York: Ballantine Books, 1967.

Montgomery, K. C. A test of two explanations of spontaneous alternation. *Journal of Comparative and Physiological Psychology*, 1952, *45*, 287–293.

Montgomery, K. C. Exploratory behavior as a function of "similarity" of stimulus situations. *Journal of Comparative and Physiological Psychology*, 1953, *46*, 129–133.

Montgomery, K. C. The role of exploratory drive in learning. *Journal of Comparative and Physiological Psychology*, 1954, *47*, 60–64.

Montgomery, K. C. The relation between fear induced by novel stimulation and exploratory behavior. *Journal of Comparative and Physiological Psychology*, 1955, *48*, 254–260.

Montgomery, K. C., & Segall, M. Discrimination learning based upon the exploratory drive. *Journal of Comparative and Physiological Psychology*, 1955, *48*, 225–228.

Morgan, G. A., Harmon, R. J., Gaiter, J. L., Jennings, K. D., Gist, N. F., & Yarrow, L. J. A method for assessing mastery motivation in one-year-old infants. JSAS *Catalog of Selected Documents in Psychology*, 1977, *7*, 68.

Morgan, M. The overjustification effect: A developmental test of self-perception interpretations. *Journal of Personality and Social Psychology*, 1981, *40*, 809–821.

Mossholder, K. W. Effects of externally mediated goal setting on intrinsic motivation: A laboratory experiment. *Journal of Applied Psychology*, 1980, *65*, 202–210.

Murray, H. A. *Thematic apperception test manual.* Cambridge, Mass.: Harvard University Press, 1943.

Myers, A. K., & Miller, N. E. Failure to find a learned drive based on hunger: Evidence for learning motivated by "exploration." *Journal of Comparative and Phsiological Psychology*, 1954, *47*, 428–436.

Myers, M. S. *Every employee a manager.* New York: McGraw-Hill, 1970.

Mynatt, C., Oakley, T., Arkkelin, D., Piccione, A., Margolis, R., & Arkkelin, J. An examination of overjustification under conditions of extended observation and multiple reinforcement: Overjustification or boredom? *Cognitive Therapy and Research*, 1978, *2*, 171–177.

Neill, A. S. *Summerhill: A radical approach to child rearing.* New York: Hart, 1960.

Nentwig, C. G. Attribution of cause and long-term effects of the modification of smoking behavior. *Behavior Analysis and Modification*, 1978, *2*, 285–295.

Nicholls, J. G. Conceptions of ability and achievement motivation. In R. Ames & C. Ames (Eds.), *Research on motivation in education* (Vol. 1). New York: Academic Press, 1984.

Nissen, H. W. A study of exploratory behavior in the white rat by means of the obstruction method. *Journal of Genetic Psychology*, 1930, *37*, 361–376.

Notz, W. W. Work motivation and the negative effects of extrinsic rewards. *American Psychologist*, 1975, *30*, 884–891.

Nunberg, H. The synthetic function of the ego. *International Journal of Psycho-Analysis*, 1931, *12*, 123–140.

O'Connell, E. J. Effect of cooperative and competitive set on the learning of imitation. *Journal of Experimental Social Psychology*, 1965, *1*, 172–183.

Okano, K. The effects of extrinsic reward on intrinsic motivation. *Journal of Child Development*, 1981, *17*, 11–23.

Olds, J., & Olds, M. Drives, rewards, and the brain. In T. Newcomb (Ed.), *New directions in psychology, II.* New York: Holt, Rinehart & Winston, 1965.

O'Leary, K. D., & Becker, W. C. Behavior modification of an adjustment class: A token reinforcement program. *Exceptional Children*, 1967, 9, 637–642.

O'Leary, K. D. & Drabman, R. Token reinforcement programs in the classroom: A review. *Psychological Bulletin*, 1971, 75, 379–398.

O'Leary, K. D., Becker, W. C., Evans, M. B., & Saudargas, R. A. A token reinforcement program in a public school: A replication and systematic analysis. *Journal of Applied Behavior Analysis*, 1969, 2, 3–13.

Orgel, A. R. Haim Ginott's approach to discipline. In D. Dorr, M. Zax, & J. Bonner (Eds.), *Comparative approaches to discipline for children and youth*. New York: International Universities Press, 1983.

Orlick, T. D., & Mosher, R. Extrinsic awards and participant motivation in a sport related task. *International Journal of Sport Psychology*, 1978, 9, 27–39.

Ouchi, W. G. *Theory Z*. Reading, Mass.: Addison-Wesley, 1981.

Pallak, S. R. Costomiris, S., Sroka, S., & Pittman, T.S. School experience, reward characteristics, and intrinsic motivation. *Child Development*, 1982, 53, 1382–1391.

Paulhus, D. Sphere-specific measures of perceived control. *Journal of Personality and Social Psychology*, 1983, 44, 1253–1265.

Pennebaker, J. W., Burnam, M. A., Schaeffer, M. A., & Harper, D. C. Lack of control as a determinant of perceived physical symptoms. *Journal of Personality and Social Psychology*, 1977, 35, 167–174.

Perlmutter, L. C. & Monty, R. A. The importance of perceived control: Fact or fantasy? *American Scientist*, 1977, 65, 759–765.

Perls, F. S. *The Gestalt approach and eyewitness to therapy*. Ben Lomond, Calif.: Science & Behavior Books, 1973.

Perls, F. S., Hefferline, R., & Goodman, P. *Gestalt therapy*. New York: Julian Press, 1951.

Peters, T. J., & Waterman, R. H. *In search of excellence*. New York: Harper &Row, 1982.

Phillips, B. W., & D'Amico, L. A. Effects of cooperation and competition on the cohesiveness of small face-to-face groups. *Journal of Educational Psychology*, 1956, 47, 65–70.

Phillips, J. S., & Lord, R. G. Determinants of intrinsic motivation: Locus of control and competence information as components of Deci's cognitive evaluation theory. *Journal of Applied Psychology*, 1980, 65, 211–218.

Piaget, J. *The origins of intelligence in children*. New York: International Universities Press, 1952.

Piaget, J. *Biology and knowledge*. Chicago: University of Chicago Press, 1971.

Piaget, J. Problems of equilibration. In M. H. Appel & L. S. Goldberg (Eds.), *Topics in cognitive development* (Vol. 1). New York: Plenum Press, 1977.

Piaget, J. *Intelligence and affectivity: Their relationship during child development*. Palo Alto, Calif.: Annual Reviews, 1981.

Pinder, C. C. Additivity versus non-additivity of intrinsic and extrinsic incentives: Implications for theory and practice. *Journal of Applied Psychology*, 1976, 61, 693–700.

Pittman, T. S., Cooper, E. E., & Smith, T. W. Attribution of causality and the overjustification effect. *Personality and Social Psychology Bulletin*, 1977, 3, 280–283.

Pittman, T. S., Davey, M. E., Alafat, K. A., Wetherill, K. V., & Kramer, N. A. Informational versus controlling verbal rewards. *Personality and Social Psychology Bulletin*, 1980, 6, 228–233.

Pittman, T. S., Emery, J., & Boggiano, A. K. Intrinsic and extrinsic motivational orientations: Reward-induced changes in preference for complexity. *Journal of Personality and Social Psychology*, 1982, 42, 789–797.

Plant, R., & Ryan, R. M. Self-consciousness, self-awareness, ego-involvement, and intrinsic motivation: An investigation of internally controlling styles. *Journal of Personality*, 1985, 53, 435–449.

Porac, J. F., & Meindl, J. Undermining overjustification: Inducing intrinsic and extrinsic task representations. *Organizational Behavior and Human Performance*, 1982, *29*, 208–226.

Premack, D. Toward empirical behavior laws: Part 1. Positive reinforcement. *Psychological Review*, 1959, *66*, 219–233.

Premack, D. Reversibility of the reinforcement relation. *Science*, 1962, *136*, 255–257.

Premack, D. Rate differential reinforcement in monkey manipulation. *Journal of the Experimental Analysis of Behavior*, 1963, *6*, 81–89.

Premack, D. Catching up with common sense or two sides of a generalization: Reinforcement and punishment. In R. Glaser (Ed.), *The nature of reinforcement*. New York: Academic Press, 1971.

Pritchard, R. D., Campbell, K. M., & Campbell, D. J. Effects of extrinsic financial rewards on intrinsic motivation. *Journal of Applied Psychology*, 1977, *62*, 9–15.

Quinn, R., & Staines, G. *The 1977 quality of employment survey*. Ann Arbor, Mich.: Institute for Social Research, 1979.

Ramey, C. T., & Piper, V. Creativity in open and traditional classrooms. *Child Development*, 1974, *45*, 557–560.

Ransen, D. L. The mediation of reward-induced motivation decrements in early and middle childhood: A template matching approach. *Journal of Personality and Social Psychology*, 1980, *39*, 1088–1100.

Rapaport, D. On the psychoanalytic theory of motivation. In M. R. Jones (Ed.), *Nebraska symposium on motivation* (Vol. 8). Lincoln: University of Nebraska Press, 1960.

Rapaport, D. Some metapsychological considerations concerning activity and passivity. In M. M. Gill (Ed.), *The collected papers of David Rapaport*. New York: Basic Books, 1967.

Raynor, J. O. Future orientation in the study of achievement motivation. In J. W. Atkinson, & J. O. Raynor (Eds.), *Motivation and achievement*. Washington, D.C.: Winston, 1974.

Reeve, J., Olson, B. C., & Cole, S. G. *Effects of competitive outcome and level of anxiety on intrinsic motivation*. Unpublished manuscript, Texas Christian University, 1984.

Reiss, S., & Sushinsky, L. W. Overjustification, competing responses, and the acquisition of intrinsic interest. *Journal of Personality and Social Psychology*, 1975, *31*, 1116–1125.

Relinger, H., Bornstein, P. H., Bugge, I. D., Carmody, T. P., & Zohn, D. J. Utilization of adverse rapid smoking in groups: Efficacy of treatment and maintenance procedures. *Journal of Consulting and Clinical Psychology*, 1977, *45*, 245–249.

Rickers-Ovsiankina, M. Die Wiederaufnahme unterbrochenen Handlungen. *Psychologische Forschung*, 1928, *11*, 302–375.

Rodin, J., & Langer, E. J. Long-term effects of a control-relevant intervention with the institutionalized aged. *Journal of Personality and Social Psychology*, 1977, *35*, 897–902.

Rodin J., Solomon, S. K., & Metcalf, J. The role of control in mediating perceptions of density. *Journal of Personality and Social Psychology*, 1978, *36*, 988–999.

Rogers, C. *Client centered therapy*. Boston: Houghton-Mifflin, 1951.

Rogers, C. The necessary and sufficient conditions of therapeutic personality change. *Journal of Consulting Psychology*, 1957, *21*, 95–103.

Rogers, C. The actualizing tendency in relation to "motives" and to consciousness. In M. R. Jones (Ed.), *Nebraska symposium on motivation* (Vol. 11). Lincoln: University of Nebraska Press, 1963.

Rogers, C. *Freedom to learn*. Columbus, Ohio: Merrill, 1969.

Rosenfield, D., Folger, R., & Adelman, H. When rewards reflect competence: A qualification of the overjustification effect. *Journal of Personality and Social Psychology*, 1980, *39*, 368–376.

Rosenthal, R. *Experimenter effects in behavior research*. New York: Appleton-Century-Crofts, 1966.

Ross, M. Salience of reward and intrinsic motivation. *Journal of Personality and Social Psychology*, 1975, *32*, 245–254.

Ross, M., Karniol, R., & Rothstein, M. Reward contingency and intrinsic motivation in children: A test of the delay of gratification hypothesis. *Journal of Personality and Social Psychology*, 1976, *32*, 245–254.

Ross, R. G., & Van den Haag, E. *The fabric of society*. New York: Harcourt, Brace, 1957.

Roth, S. A revised model of learned helplessness in humans. *Journal of Personality*, 1980, *48*, 103–133.

Rothenberg, B. B. Children's social sensitivity and the relationship to interpersonal competence, intrapersonal comfort, and intellectual level. *Developmental Psychology*, 1970, *2*, 335–350.

Rotter, J. B. *Social learning and clinical psychology*. Englewood Cliffs, N.J.: Prentice-Hall, 1954.

Rotter, J. B. Generalized expectancies for internal versus external control of reinforcement. *Psychological Monographs*, 1966, *80*(1, Whole No. 609).

Russell, J. C., Studstill, O. L., & Grant, R. M. *The effect of expectancies on intrinsic motivation*. Paper presented at the meeting of the American Psychological Association, New York, September, 1979.

Ryan, E. D. Attribution, intrinsic motivation, and athletics. In L. I. Gedvilas & M. E. Kneer (Eds.), *Proceedings of the National College Physical Education Association for Men/ National Association for Physical Education of College Women, National Conference*. Chicago: Office of Publications Services, University of Illinois at Chicago Circle, 1977.

Ryan, E. D. Attribution, intrinsic motivation, and athletics: A replication and extension. In C. H. Nadeau, W. R. Halliwell, K. M. Newell, & G. C. Roberts (Eds.), *Psychology of motor behavior and sport—1979*. Champaign, Ill.: Human Kinetics Press, 1980.

Ryan, R. M. Control and information in the intrapersonal sphere: An extension of cognitive evaluation theory. *Journal of Personality and Social Psychology*, 1982, *43*, 450–461.

Ryan, R. M. An appropriate, original look at appropriate originality. *Contemporary Psychology*, 1984, *29*, 533–535.

Ryan, R. M., & Grolnick, W. S. *Origins and pawns in the classroom: Self-report and projective assessments of individual differences in children's perceptions*. Unpublished manuscript, University of Rochester, 1984.

Ryan, R. M., Mims, V., & Koestner, R. Relation of reward contingency and interpersonal context to intrinsic motivation: A review and test using cognitive evaluation theory. *Journal of Personality and Social Psychology*, 1983, *45*, 736–750.

Ryan, R. M., Connell, J. P., Plant, R., Robinson, D., & Evans, S. *The influence of emotions on spontaneous learning*. Unpublished manuscript, University of Rochester, 1984.

Ryan, R. M., Vallerand, R. J., & Deci, E. L. Intrinsic motivation in sport: A cognitive evaluation theory interpretation. In W. F. Straub & J. M. Williams (Eds.), *Cognitive sport psychology*. Lansing, N.Y.: Sport Science Associates, 1984.

Ryan, R. M., Connell, J. P., & Deci, E. L. A motivational analysis of self-determination and self-regulation in education. In C. Ames & R. E. Ames (Eds.), *Research on motivation in education: The classroom milieu*. New York: Academic Press, 1985.

Ryan, R. M., Avery, R. R., & Grolnick, W. S. A Rorschach assessment of children's mutuality of autonomy: Relations with perceived control, interpersonal adjustment and school performance. *Journal of Personality Assessment*, 1985, *49*, 6–12.

Sadowski, C. J., & Woodward, H. R. Relationship between origin climate, perceived responsibility, and grades. *Perceptual and Motor Skills*, 1981, *53*, 259–261.

Sandelands, L. E., Ashford, S. J., & Dutton, J. E. Reconceptualizing of the overjustification effect: A template-matching approach. *Motivation and Emotion*, 1983, *7*, 229–255.

Schafer, R. *Aspects of internalization*. New York: International Universities Press, 1968.

Schafer, R. *A new language for psychoanalysis*. New Haven, Conn.: Yale University Press, 1976.

Scheflen, K. C., Lawler, E. E., & Hackman, J. B. Long-term impact of employee participation in the development of pay incentive plans: A field experiment. *Journal of Applied Psychology*, 1971, 55, 182–186.

Schorr, D., & Rodin, J. Motivation to control one's environment in individuals with obsessive-compulsive, depressive, and normal personality traits. *Journal of Personality and Social Psychology*, 1984, 46, 1148–1161.

Schulz, R. Effects of control and predictability on the physical and psychological wellbeing of the institutionalized aged. *Journal of Personality and Social Psychology*, 1976, 33, 563–573.

Schulz, R., & Hanusa, B. H. Long-term effects of control and predictability-enhancing interventions: Findings and ethical issues. *Journal of Personality and Social Psychology*, 1978, 36, 1194–1201.

Schultz, T. R., Butkowsky, I., Pearce, J. W., & Shanfield, H. Development of schemes for the attribution of multiple psychological causes. *Developmental Psychology*, 1975, 11, 502–510.

Schwartz, B., Schuldenfrei, R., & Lacey, H. Operant psychology as factory psychology. *Behaviorism*, 1978, 6, 229–254.

Scott, W. E., Jr. The effects of extrinsic rewards on "intrinsic motivation": A critique. *Organizational Behavior and Human Performance*, 1976, 15, 117–129.

Seligman, M. E. P. Chronic fear produced by unpredictable electric shock. *Journal of Comparative and Physiological Psychology*, 1968, 66, 402–411.

Seligman, M. E. P. *Helplessness: On depression, development, and death*. San Francisco: Freeman, 1975.

Selye, H. *The stress of life* (2nd ed.). New York: McGraw-Hill, 1975.

Shapira, Z. Expectancy determinants of intrinsically motivated behavior. *Journal of Personality and Social Psychology*, 1976, 34, 1235–1244.

Shapiro, D. *Autonomy and rigid character*. New York: Basic Books, 1981.

Shelton, J. L. Instigation therapy: Using therapeutic homework to promote treatment gains. In A. P. Goldstein & F. H. Kanfer (Eds.), *Maximizing treatment gains: Transfer enhancement in psychotherapy*. New York: Academic Press, 1979.

Shostrom, E. L. *Manual for the Personal Orientation Inventory*. San Diego, Calif.: Educational and Industrial Testing Service, 1966.

Sidman, M. *Tactics of scientific research*. New York: Basic Books, 1960.

Simon, H. A. Motivational and emotional controls of cognition. *Psychological Review*, 1967, 74, 29–39.

Simon, T., & McCarthy, B. *Choice and the enhancement of intrinsic motivation*. Unpublished manuscript, University of Sheffield, England, 1982.

Singerman, K. J., Borkovec, T. D., & Baron, R. S. Failure of a "misattribution therapy" manipulation with a clinically relevant target behavior. *BehaviorTherapy*, 1976, 7, 306–313.

Skinner, B. F. *The behavior of organisms: An experimental analysis*. New York: Appleton, 1938.

Skinner, B. F. *Science and human behavior*. New York: Macmillan, 1953.

Skinner, B. F. *Beyond freedom and dignity*. New York: Knopf, 1971.

Skinner, B. F. *About behaviorism*. New York: Knopf, 1974.

Smith, M. C. Children's use of the multiple sufficient cause schema in social perception. *Journal of Personality and Social Psyehology*, 1975, 32, 737–747.

Smith, T. W., & Pittman, T. S. Reward, distraction, and the overjustification effect. *Journal of Personality and Social Psychology*, 1978, 36, 565–572.

Smith, W. E. *The effects of social and monetary rewards on intrinsic motivation*. Unpublished doctoral dissertation, Cornell University, Ithaca, N.Y., 1974.

Sokolov, E. N. Neural models and the orienting reflex. In M.A.B. Brazier (Ed.), *The central nervous system and behavior.* New York: Josiah Macy, Jr. Foundation, 1960.

Solomon, D., & Kendall, A. J. Individual characteristics and children's performance in "open" and "traditional" classroom settings. *Journal of Educational Psychology,* 1976, *68,* 613–625.

Spector, P. E. Behavior in organizations as a function of employees' locus of control. *Psychological Bulletin,* 1982, *91,* 482–497.

Spence, J. T. The distracting effect of material reinforcers in the discrimination learning of lower- and middle-class chilidren. *Child Development,* 1970, *41,* 103–111.

Staw, B. M., Calder, B. J., Hess, R. K., & Sandelands, L. E. Intrinsic motivation and norms about payment. *Journal of Personality,* 1980, *48,* 1–14.

Stokes, T. F., & Baer, D. M. An implicit technology of generalization. *Journal of Applied Behavior Analysis,* 1977, *10,* 349–367.

Strupp, H. H. Psychotherapy research and practice: An overview. In S. L. Garfield & A. E. Bergin (Eds.), *Handbook of psychotherapy and behavior change* (2nd ed.). New York: Wiley, 1978.

Swann, W. B., & Pittman, T. S. Initiating play activity of children: The moderating influence of verbal cues on intrinsic motivation. *Child Development,* 1977, *48,* 1128–1132.

Tero, P. F., & Connell, J. P. *Children's academic coping inventory: A new self-report measure.* Paper presented at the meeting of the American Educational Research Association, Montreal, April, 1983.

Thomas, J. Agency and achievement: Self-management and self-regard. *Review of Educational Research,* 1980, *50,* 213–240.

Thomas, J. R., & Tennant, L. K. Effects of rewards on children's motivation for an athletic task. In F.L. Smoll & R.E. Smith, *Psychological perspectives in youth sports.* Washington, D.C.: Hemisphere Publishing, 1978.

Thompson, C. E., & Wankel, L. M. The effect of perceived activity choice upon frequency of exercise behavior. *Journal of Applied Social Psychology,* 1980, *10,* 436–443.

Thorndike, E. L. *The psychology of learning.* New York: Teacher's College, Columbia University, 1913.

Tolman, E. C. *Purposive behavior in animals and men.* New York: Century, 1932.

Tolman, E. C. Principles of purposive behavior. In S. Koch (Ed.), *Psychology: A study of a science* (Vol. 2). New York: McGraw-Hill, 1959.

Truax, C. B., & Carkhuff, R. R. *Toward effective counseling and psychotherapy: Training and practice.* Chicago: Aldine, 1967.

Turkel, S. *Working.* New York: Pantheon, 1972.

Vallerand, R. J. *Une analyse des déterminants de la motivation intrinsèque en contexte sportif.* Unpublished doctoral dissertation, University of Montreal, Quebec, 1981.

Vallerand, R. J. Effect of differential amounts of positive verbal feedback on the intrinsic motivation of male hockey players. *Journal of Sport Psychology,* 1983, *5,* 100–107.

Vallerand, R. J., & Reid, G. On the causal effects of perceived competence on intrinsic motivation: A test of cognitive evaluation theory. *Journal of Sport Psychology,* 1984, *6,* 94–102.

Vallerand, R. J., Gauvin, L. I., & Halliwell, W. R. *When you're not good enough: The effect of failing to win a performance-contingent reward on intrinsic motivation.* Unpublished manuscript, University of Montreal, Quebec, 1982.

Vaughn, B. E., Kopp, C. B., & Krakow, J. B. The emergence and consolidation of self-control from eighteen to thirty months of age: Normative trends and individual differences. *Child Development,* 1984, *55,* 990–1004.

Vroom, V. H. *Work and motivation.* New York: Wiley, 1964.

Vroom, V. H., & Yetton, P. W. *Leadership and decision making.* Pittsburgh: University of Pittsburgh Press, 1973.

Wahba, M. A., & Bridwell, L. G. Maslow reconsidered: A review of research on the need hierarchy theory. *Organizational Behavior and Human Performance*, 1976, *15*, 212–240.

Walker, E. L. Psychological complexity as a basis for a theory of motivation and choice. In D. Levine (Ed.), *Nebraska symposium on motivation* (Vol. 12). Lincoln: University of Nebraska Press, 1964.

Wankel, L. M. Involvement in vigorous physical activity: Considerations for enhancing self-motivation. In R. R. Danielson & K. F. Danielson (Eds.), *Fitness motivation*. Toronto: Orcol, 1980.

Wankel, L. M., & Kreisel, P. *An investigation of factors influencing sport enjoyment across sport and age groups*. Paper presented at the North American Society for the Psychology of Sport and Physical Activity conference, College Park, Md., May, 1982.

Wankel, L. M., & Pabich, P. *The minor sport experience: Factors contributing to or detracting from enjoyment*. Unpublished manuscript, University of Alberta, Edmonton, 1982.

Watson, J. B. Psychology as the behaviorist views it. *Psychological Review*, 1913, *20*, 158–177.

Watzlawick, P., Beavin, J. H., & Jackson, D. D. *Pragmatics of human communication*. New York: Norton, 1967.

Weinberg, R. S., & Jackson, A. Competition and extrinsic rewards: Effect on intrinsic motivation and attribution. *Research Quarterly*, 1979, *50*, 494–502.

Weinberg, R. S., & Ragan, J. Effects of competition, success/failure, and sex on intrinsic motivation. *Research Quarterly*, 1979, *50*, 503–510.

Weiner, B. *Theories of motivation: From mechanism to cognition*. Chicago: Markham, 1972.

Weiner, M. J., & Mander, A. M. The effects of reward and perception of competency upon intrinsic motivation. *Motivation and Emotion*, 1978, *2*, 67–73.

Welker, W. L. Some determinants of play and exploration in chimpanzees. *Journal of Comparative and Physiological Psychology*, 1956, *49*, 84–89. (a)

Welker, W. L. Effects of age and experience on play and exploration of young chimpanzees. *Journal of Comparative and Physiological Psychology*, 1956, *49*, 223–226 (b).

Werner, H. *Comparative psychology of mental development*. New York: International Universities Press, 1948.

Wheeler, B. L. *Awareness of internal and external cues as a function of the interaction between causality orientations and motivational subsystems*. Unpublished doctoral dissertation, Fordham University, 1984.

White, R. W. Motivation reconsidered: The concept of competence. *Psychological Review*, 1959, *66*, 297–333.

White, R. W. Competence and the psychosexual stages of development. In M. R. Jones (Ed.), *Nebraska symposium on motivation* (Vol. 8). Lincoln: University of Nebraska Press, 1960.

White, R. W. *Ego and reality in psychoanalytic theory* (Psychological Issues Series, Monograph No. 11). New York: International Universities Press, 1963.

Wicklund, R. A., & Brehm, J. W. *Perspectives on cognitive dissonance*. Hillsdale, N.J.: Erlbaum, 1976.

Williams, B. W. Reinforcement, behavior constraint, and the overjustification effect. *Journal of Personality and Social Psychology*, 1980, *39*, 599–614.

Wilson, T. D., Hull, J. G., & Johnson, J. Awareness and self-perception: Verbal reports on internal states. *Journal of Personality and Social Psychology*, 1981, *40*, 53–71.

Winett, R. A. Attribution of attitude and behavior change and its relevance to behavior therapy. *The Psychological Record*, 1970, *20*, 17–32.

Wodarski, J. S., Hamblin, R. L., Buckholdt, D., & Ferritor, D. Individual consequences versus different shared consequences contingent on the performance of low achieving group members. *Journal of Applied Social Psychology*, 1973, *3*, 276–290.

Wolpe, J. *The practice of behavior therapy*. New York: Pergamon, 1969.

Wolstein, B. The psychoanalytic theory of unconscious psychic experience. *Contemporary psychoanalysis*, 1982, *18*, 412–437.

Woodworth, R. S. *Dynamic psychology*. New York: Columbia University Press, 1918.

Woodworth, R. S. *Dynamics of behavior*. New York: Holt, 1958.

Wortman, C. B., & Brehm, J. W. Responses to uncontrollable outcomes: An integration of reactance theory and the learned helplessness model. In L. Berkowitz (Ed.), *Advances in experimental social psychology*, (Vol. 8). New York: Academic Press, 1975.

Wundt, W. *Grundzüge der physiologischen Psychologie* (5th ed.). (Vol. 3). Leipzig, E. Germany: W. Engelmann, 1903.

Yarrow, L. J., Klein, R. P., Lomonaco, S., & Morgan, G. A. Cognitive and motivational development in early childhood. In B. Z. Friedlander, G. M. Sterritt, & G. E. Kirk (Eds.), *Exceptional infant* (Vol. 3). New York: Brunner/Mazel, 1975.

Yarrow, L. J., Rubenstein, J. L., & Pederson, F. A. *Infant and environment: Early cognitive and motivational development*. New York: Wiley (Halsted), 1975.

Yoshimura, M. *The effects of verbal reinforcement and monetary reward on intrinsic motivation*. Unpublished manuscript, Kyoto University Psychology Laboratory, Kyoto, Japan, 1979.

Zajonc, R. B. Feeling and thinking: Preferences need no inferences. *American Psychologist*, 1980, *35*, 151–175.

Zeigarnik, B. Das Behalten erledigten und unerledigten Handlungen. *Psychologische Forschung*, 1927, *9*, 1–85.

Zimbardo, P. G., & Miller, N. E. Facilitation of exploration by hunger in rats. *Journal of Comparative and Physiological Psychology*, 1958, *51*, 43–46.

Zinser, O., Young, J. G., & King, P. E. The influence of verbal reward on intrinsic motivation in children. *Journal of General Psychology*, 1982, *106*, 85–91.

Zuckerman, M. Attribution of success and failure revisited, or: The motivational bias is alive and well in attribution theory. *Journal of Personality*, 1979, *47*, 245–287.

Zuckerman, M., Porac, J., Lathin, D., Smith, R., & Deci, E. L. On the importance of self-determination for intrinsically motivated behavior. *Personality and Social Psychology Bulletin*, 1978, *4*, 443–446.

Author Index

Subject Index